Scrivener®

ABSOLUTE BEGINNER'S GUIDE

Jennifer Kettell

800 East 96th Street,
Indianapolis, Indiana 46240

Scrivener Absolute Beginner's Guide

ISBN-13: 978-0-7897-5145-4
ISBN-10: 0-7897-5145-3

Library of Congress Control Number: 2013937699

Printed in the United States of America

Second Printing: December 2013

Trademarks

Warning and Disclaimer

Bulk Sales

Que Publishing offers excellent discounts on this book when ordered in quantity for bulk purchases or special sales. For more information, please contact

U.S. Corporate and Government Sales
1-800-382-3419
corpsales@pearsontechgroup.com

For sales outside the United States, please contact

International Sales
international@pearsoned.com

Editor-in-Chief
Greg Wiegand

Senior Acquisitions Editor
Laura Norman

Development Editor
Lora L. Baughey

Managing Editor
Sandra Schroeder

Project Editor
Seth Kerney

Indexer
Ken Johnson

Copy Editor
Karen Annett

Proofreader
Chuck Hutchinson

Technical Editor
Jennifer Hughes

Publishing Coordinator
Cindy Teeters

Book Designer
Anne Jones

Compositor
Mary Sudul

Contents at a Glance

Table of Contents

III Digging Deeper into Scrivener

About the Author

Jennifer Kettell switched from being a long-time Windows user to working on a Mac in 2006 for the primary purpose of being able to use Scrivener for her fiction writing. Since then, she's written several tutorials, given workshops, and helped many other writers adopt Scrivener as the keystone of their writer's toolkit.

Jenn is the author of *My Kindle Fire HD*, and has written or contributed to more than two dozen other books. When Jenn isn't writing about technology, she writes romantic fiction. She's a member of Romance Writers of America and recently served as president of her local chapter.

Jenn has lived all over the United States, but currently resides in upstate New York. She loves to read, debate current events, and do all manner of puzzles, but she spends the better part of every day thinking of ways to torture the fictional characters who live in her head.

Dedication

For Amanda and Zachary. Watching you grow up has been a privilege.

Acknowledgments

This book would not have been possible without my husband and children. They've always been supportive of my writing, even when it means cooking their own dinners and sorting through unfolded laundry. Greg, Zach, and Amanda, I love you!

Thank you to Jamie Hutchinson, my English professor at Bard College at Simon's Rock, for giving me the courage to write.

Thanks to the Romex sisterhood, especially Julie Hurwitz, Mary Strand, Judith Arnold, Carol Prescott, Katy Cooper, Beth Pattillo, Melissa McClone, Pam Baker, Teresa Hill, and Sharyn Cerniglia. You've inspired, supported, and prodded me, and I love you all for it. Thanks also goes to my CritGirls—Robin Thomas, Taryn Elliott, Karen Keyes, and Megan Ryder. I'd be lost without our collective snark and the excitement of discovering new office supplies together.

I want to thank Keith Blount and the entire Literature & Latte team for bringing Scrivener to life and sharing it with the writing world.

Finally, thank you to everyone who's had a hand in this book. Laura Norman saw the potential and fought for it. Jennifer Hughes has been an amazing tech editor and resource. Lora Baughey and Karen Annett caught my consistency and copy mistakes. Seth Kerney kept the project on track and offered guidance on formatting. I appreciate everything you do.

We Want to Hear from You!

As the reader of this book, *you* are our most important critic and commentator. We value your opinion and want to know what we're doing right, what we could do better, what areas you'd like to see us publish in, and any other words of wisdom you're willing to pass our way.

We welcome your comments. You can email or write to let us know what you did or didn't like about this book—as well as what we can do to make our books better.

Please note that we cannot help you with technical problems related to the topic of this book.

When you write, please be sure to include this book's title and author as well as your name and email address. We will carefully review your comments and share them with the author and editors who worked on the book.

Email: feedback@quepublishing.com

Mail: Que Publishing
ATTN: Reader Feedback
800 East 96th Street
Indianapolis, IN 46240 USA

Reader Services

Visit our website and register this book at quepublishing.com/title/9780789751454 for convenient access to any updates, downloads, or errata that might be available for this book.

INTRODUCTION

If you're reading this book, you've probably decided to write your own book. Congratulations and good luck! Maybe you've already written dozens of books and are looking for a new approach to your work. Congratulations and good luck to you, as well! No matter where you are in the writer's journey, your path is undoubtedly fraught with milestones and challenges. There will be all manner of dragons—in the form of sick children, reluctant heroes and heroines, inopportune empty printer cartridges, or poorly motivated villains—and it's your job to handle them all, be they real or in your fictional world, with aplomb.

What Is Scrivener?

The process of getting your words from your head onto the screen should not be one of those challenges. Thanks to Scrivener, it doesn't have to be. Unlike a word processor, which allows you to sequentially type your story, Scrivener acts as a complete writing project management system. Scrivener stores not only your manuscript, but also your research, target data, and synopsis and project notes. You can plot your book on virtual index cards or in an outline, and then use those elements to write scenes out of order or even move them around in the manuscript. When you've completed your manuscript, you can compile all of the scenes into one document. Scrivener can even compile your manuscript into ePub or Kindle format for self-publishing.

Perhaps the best part of Scrivener is that you can use it the way *you* choose. Plotters may want to dig deep into every feature of the application, plotting out their entire story in advance, attaching keywords to every scene, setting word count targets, and creating collections of scenes based on point-of-view characters. Pantsers may appreciate the ability to create a new scene on the fly, type as much or as little as they want, and then figure out where to place it later.

Although ideally suited to fiction writing, Scrivener is not limited to this use. Scrivener works well in an academic setting, with footnote features and the ability to collect research directly into the application or link to external sources. Screenwriters will appreciate the screenplay templates and formatting options, as well as the ability to export into Final Draft format. There are dozens of creative uses for Scrivener, as well. You can use it as a daily journal, creating a new entry every day and using keywords and collections to sort entries by topic. You can even use it to sort your recipe collection, creating folders for different courses or food groups and entering an image of the dish on the related index card.

Mac Versus Windows Versus Linux Versus iPad

Scrivener has been developed for multiple platforms. Scrivener for the Mac was first released in 2005 and is, therefore, the furthest along in development. Scrivener was released for the Windows platform in late 2011. Scrivener 1 for Windows did not initially contain all of the features of Scrivener 2 for Mac, although it is gaining features quickly. Scrivener for Windows 1.5 has recently been released, narrowing the gap between platforms. I will point out any differences between the versions throughout the book, along with workarounds where possible. Eventually, however, this point might well be moot, as the developers intend for the Mac and Windows platforms to reach parity.

Scrivener is also unofficially available for Linux as a free beta version. Development of the Linux version is on par with the Windows version. Thus, any differences between Mac and Windows platforms will be the same between Mac and Linux. Keep in mind, however, that there is no official support for the Linux version.

If you're an iPhone or iPad user, there's both good news and bad news. The good news is that an iOS version of Scrivener is in development. The bad news is that it most likely will not be released until late 2013, at the earliest. The other good news, however, is that in the meantime you can work on your Scrivener files in other iOS word processors using methods described in this book. Chapter 18, "Taking Scrivener Out and About," explains this process in detail.

How This Book Is Organized

This book is divided into six main parts, as follows:

- **Part I, "Getting Started in Scrivener,"** discusses the main components of Scrivener, how to customize your writing space, and how to begin writing your book in Scrivener.

- **Part II, "Organizing Your Writing Process,"** covers how to use the corkboard and outliner tools, how to use Scrivener to collect your research, and features to help you revise your manuscript.

- **Part III, "Digging Deeper into Scrivener,"** explains how to get the most out of the Inspector, keywords, and other meta-data. You also learn how to create your own template sheets and project templates to fully customize Scrivener to work with your writing process.

- **Part IV, "Managing Your Writing Projects,"** shows you how to track your progress with project and document targets. You learn how to search your project and create collections of related project elements. Finally, this section discusses how to back up your work and use Scrivener on multiple computers, share a project between Mac and Windows computers, or even work on a scene on your iPad and sync it back to your project.

- **Part V, "Generating a Completed Manuscript,"** covers the process of turning your scenes and chapters into a compiled manuscript or e-book to submit to an editor or agent or directly self-publish.

- **Part VI, "Using Scrivener in Other Scenarios,"** explains some of the other ways people use the application. If you're a screenwriter, lawyer, student, or translator, this section gives you ideas to help you integrate Scrivener into your workflow. If you purchased this book in hard copy format, please note that the chapters of Part VI are available online at quepublishing.com/title/9780789751454.

The chapters in this book are organized in a logical order, at least to my mind. If you're looking for an explanation of a particular Scrivener feature, however, feel free to skip around or use the index to hone in on exactly what you seek.

Conventions Used in This Book

This book uses standard conventions to explain menu commands and keyboard shortcuts. As with most computer-related topics, there is often more than one way to do things. In those cases, I've tried to present multiple options and leave it to you, the reader, to discover which method works best for you.

Menu and Toolbar Commands

When you need to access a command from the menu, you will see instructions such as "Select Project, New Text." This means you choose Project from the menu bar, and then click on New Text from that menu. When you need to access a command from the toolbar, you will see instructions such as "Click the Show Project Statistics icon." If there is any doubt as to where you can find a command, I specify to access the menu bar or click a button in the toolbar.

Although the Scrivener developers have attempted to put menu commands in the same locations across both platforms, there are some differences between Windows and Mac OS X, which occasionally hinder this effort. Table I.1 lists some of these differences.

TABLE I.1 Menu Differences Between Mac OS X and Windows

Menu Command	Mac OS X	Windows
Preferences	Scrivener, Preferences	Tools, Options
Scratch Pad	Window, Show Scratch Pad	Tools, Scratch Pad
Customize Toolbar	View, Customize Toolbar	Tools, Customize Toolbars
Special Characters	Edit, Special Characters	Edit, Character Map
Spelling	Edit, Spelling and Grammar	Tools, Spelling
Writing Tools	Edit, Writing Tools	Tools, Writing Tools
Exit	Scrivener, Quit Scrivener	File, Exit

Keyboard Shortcuts

Many commands can be accessed directly from the keyboard using a series of key combinations. For example, instead of going to the menu bar and clicking Project, New Text to create a new text file, you can use Cmd-N. To use this keyboard shortcut, press and hold the Cmd key while typing the letter N. If you're on a PC, you can use Ctrl+N to create a new text file—that is, press and hold the Ctrl key while typing the letter N.

I note keyboard shortcuts when introducing pertinent commands. You can also locate the keyboard shortcuts in the Scrivener menus themselves, which is a good way to learn the shortcuts for your most-accessed commands.

Scrivener for Mac follows the OS X convention of using characters to represent certain keys for keyboard shortcuts. Table I.2 explains the keyboard shortcut characters and the keys to which they correlate.

TABLE I.2   Keyboard Shortcut Characters

Character	Key
⌘	Cmd
⇧	Shift
^	Ctrl
⌥	Option/Alt
↻	Esc
⏎	Return
⌫	Delete

Context Menus

Context menus are pop-up menus that contain commands appropriate to the context of the position of the mouse pointer or cursor. Instead of moving the mouse to the menu bar and navigating a series of menus, you can often right-click to bring up a context menu and access the necessary command from there. As with keyboard shortcuts, I note where commands are available from a context menu.

Most Windows mice have two buttons, with the left button used to make a selection and the right button used to bring up context menus. If you are using a one-button Mac mouse or a Magic Mouse, you can press the Control key as you click to get the same result. If you're using a Mac trackpad, you can either Control-click or click with two fingers to bring up a context menu.

Special Elements

This book includes special elements that provide additional warnings or information about some features. These elements are designed to draw your attention to these points.

 TIP   A Tip is a piece of advice or a trick to help you use Scrivener more efficiently or effectively.

 NOTE   Notes are designed to provide additional information that may be useful but is not completely necessary to accomplish a task.

 CAUTION   A Caution warns you of quirks or problems when taking certain actions. Ignoring a caution may impede your work, so take special note of these!

Extra Sidebars

Scrivener Absolute Beginner's Guide also contains two extra sidebars specific to this book.

THE CREATIVE PROCESS

This element provides ideas for putting the tools and features of Scrivener to work for you. Beyond just the how-to, these sidebars explain *why* you may want to use certain features.

A WINDOWS VIEW

This element notes differences between the Mac and Windows/Linux versions of Scrivener. In some cases, I also provide workarounds, where available.

Assumptions About Computer Knowledge

Scrivener Absolute Beginner's Guide is an introductory-level book about Scrivener. It is not, however, an introductory-level book about computers in general. I assume that you know how and have already installed the Scrivener application and that you know how to perform basic computer tasks such as Cut and Paste.

If you need help with these basic computer topics, I suggest *OS X Mountain Lion Absolute Beginner's Guide* by Yvonne Johnson for Mac users and *Using Windows 8* by J. Peter Bruzzese or *My Microsoft Windows 7 PC* by Katherine Murray for Windows users. These books will get you up to speed.

Getting More Help

Scrivener is a complex application, and the demands your personal approach to writing make of it may not be fully covered in this book. Fortunately, help is always close at hand! The best source of support is the forum at the Literature & Latte website (http://www.literatureandlatte.com). On this site, you can join the thriving Scrivener user community and get help directly from the extremely helpful developer, Keith Blount, and his staff as well as other users. Come for the tech support—stay for the quirky conversations about writing and just about anything else under the sun.

The Help menu in Scrivener contains links to an interactive tutorial, the PDF Scrivener Manual, and online video tutorials. If you are a visual or kinetic learner, I highly recommend using the interactive and video tutorials along with this book.

You can also find information about Scrivener on my own website at http://www.jenniferkettell.com.

1

GETTING TO KNOW THE SCRIVENER INTERFACE

Scrivener might look like a word processor at first glance. There is a large empty space for you to type and a toolbar to change the font and paragraph styles. You can certainly use Scrivener much like a word processor, typing your entire manuscript in one long document—indeed, many users who adopt Scrivener in the middle of a manuscript do this before learning how to use the myriad of other features—but they miss out on the full power of the tool on their screen. As you begin to see in this chapter, Scrivener is a complete toolkit for writers, with tools to help you do everything from brainstorming to researching to helping you discover weaknesses in your story.

Understanding Projects

Scrivener uses projects to keep your manuscript and associated materials together. Think of a project as an accordion folder that expands to hold everything you accumulate when writing a book. When you write in Scrivener, you can create separate documents for each chapter or scene, each of which is stored in the project. You may have character or setting sheets you create related to your book, along with any other notes you take as you brainstorm or write. Your project may also contain photos, web pages, PDFs, and even audio/video files you've gathered for research.

On a Mac, a Scrivener project looks like a single file, but it is actually a package containing individual files for each item in the project. In Windows, a Scrivener project is a folder with subfolders and files for the various components of your project.

 CAUTION Do not edit or move the files in a Scrivener project outside the Scrivener application, as this may corrupt your project. Scrivener relies on the ability to locate the files within the project and track the current version of each component.

Creating a New Project

When you first launch Scrivener, the Project Templates window opens, as shown in Figure 1.1. This launchpad allows you to create and name a new project, as well as give the new work a basic structure. If you've previously created and closed a project in Scrivener, the Project Templates window enables you to reopen that project.

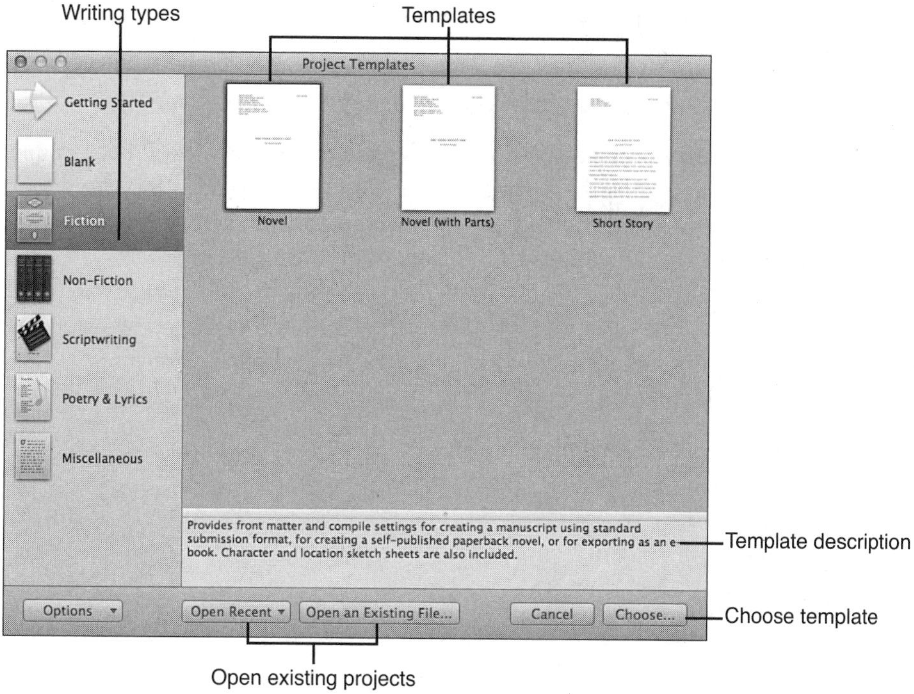

Writing types

Templates

Project Templates

Getting Started

Blank

Fiction

Novel Novel (with Parts) Short Story

Non-Fiction

Scriptwriting

Poetry & Lyrics

Miscellaneous

Provides front matter and compile settings for creating a manuscript using standard submission format, for creating a self-published paperback novel, or for exporting as an e-book. Character and location sketch sheets are also included. ——— Template description

Options ▾ Open Recent ▾ Open an Existing File... Cancel Choose... ——— Choose template

Open existing projects

FIGURE 1.1

The Project Templates window allows you to create a new project geared to a specific type of writing.

 NOTE On the Mac, if you don't close a project when you exit Scrivener, the project automatically reopens by default the next time you launch the application. This enables you to quickly access your current work in progress when you open Scrivener. The Project Templates window only appears when you launch Scrivener after having previously closed all open projects or when you choose File, New Project.

On Windows, the most recent project you opened automatically reopens the next time you launch Scrivener. If you want to automatically open the Project Templates window when you launch Scrivener, click on Tools, Options, and then deselect Open Recent Projects on Program Launch and select Show Start Panel When There Are No Projects Open.

To create a new project:

1. Choose the writing type appropriate to your new work from the left sidebar.

2. Choose a project template from the options on the right.

3. If you want to learn more about a template, read the description in the pane beneath the templates.

4. Click Choose to create a new project using the selected template.

5. Scrivener opens a Save As window, as shown in Figure 1.2. Provide a filename, which also becomes the project name. If you want to save the project into a different folder than the default, click the expansion button to the right of the Save As field and navigate to the folder you want.

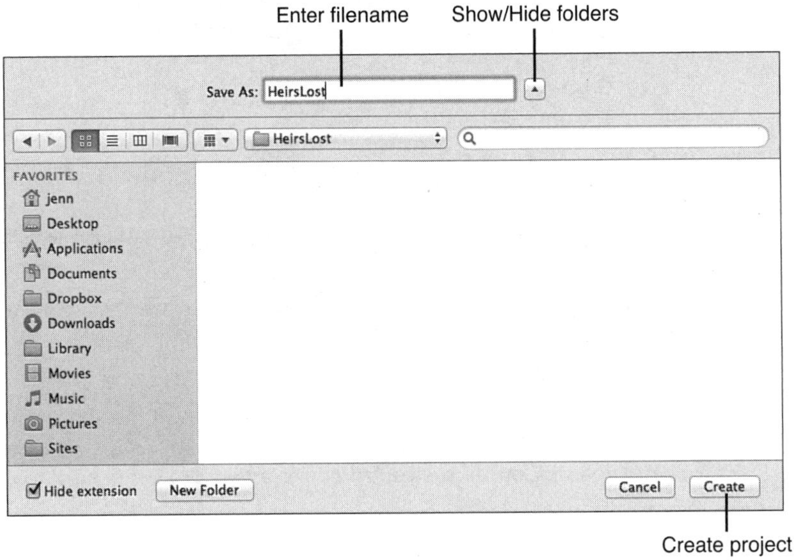

FIGURE 1.2

Name your new project in the Save As window.

6. Click Create.

After you've created a project, it opens in the main Scrivener window.

A WINDOWS VIEW: CREATING NEW PROJECTS

The New Project window, shown here, has minor differences from the Mac version. Enter a filename in the Save As field in the New Project window. Click the Browse button to choose a location for the project file. Then click Create.

NOTE   On the Mac, some templates automatically use the project name as the title of your manuscript and insert it into the title page and header when you compile the project into a completed manuscript. With this in mind, choose a filename carefully. Of course, you can always rename the project later or manually change the title page and header.

TIP   The Getting Started tab in the Project Templates window provides links to a hands-on tutorial and the Scrivener user manual. On the Mac, you can also access video tutorials from this window. Select the item and then click Open. The manual and video options open your default PDF reader and the YouTube website, respectively. The hands-on tutorial opens an introductory message and then a Save As dialog box for creating a sample project.

Both Mac and Windows users can access the PDF manual, hands-on tutorial, and video tutorial from the Help menu, as well.

Selecting a Project Template

Project templates provide a basic set of documents and formatting to help you start your new manuscript. The Blank project template provides only an empty folder for the draft of your manuscript and an empty folder for your research. The Novel project template, on the other hand, contains additional folders for characters and settings and front matter. If you are on a Mac, you will find a folder of page templates to generate multiple character and setting sheets. The template provides a guide on how to use it, including tips for compiling your manuscript. The Draft folder has even been renamed to Manuscript and contains an initial chapter folder with a scene document inside it to get you started.

Project templates also include Compile settings to work with the Binder structure established by the template. The Blank project uses the "Original" Compile preset by default, which compiles the manuscript exactly as it appears in the Editor. The Novel template uses the "Novel" Compile preset. The About document at the top of the Binder in the template explains how to use and modify the Compile settings when using that template.

If your goal right now is simply to get to work and begin writing, I suggest starting with the Blank template. You won't have to worry about figuring out what each additional folder or file is intended to do, so you can focus on getting words on the page. You can always drag folders or files from one of the other templates into your work in progress if you discover you need them later.

If, on the other hand, you want to take the time now to master Scrivener, by all means dive into one of the other templates.

 TIP   Don't feel locked in by project templates! A template is simply a starting point for a project, just extra documents and settings that were added to a blank project to make certain tasks easier. If you start a project in one template and want to add elements of another, you can open a project with the second template and drag and drop documents between them. You can also delete or ignore any elements you don't want to use.

If you obtained your copy of Scrivener during National Novel Writing Month (NaNoWriMo), you may see a NaNoWriMo Novel template in the Fiction tab. This template comes with preset project and daily writing targets to help you reach your NaNoWriMo goal of 50,000 words in one month.

As you become more familiar with Scrivener, you will almost certainly want to customize an existing template or create a brand-new one from scratch. You can also download additional project templates created by other Scrivener users. To learn more about project templates, see Chapter 14, "Creating and Using Project Templates."

THE CREATIVE PROCESS: SHORT-FORM WRITING

If you write short pieces—newspaper or magazine articles, poetry, short stories, or blog posts—you may want to create one master project to collect all these works. Doing so enables you to search the entire project to see common themes in your work, among other benefits. If one master project is too cumbersome a prospect, consider creating a monthly or yearly project for shorter works.

Saving Projects

After you create a project, you don't have to worry about saving it as you work. Scrivener automatically saves the project whenever you pause for more than 2 seconds. You can change this interval in the General preferences tab (Scrivener, Preferences on the Mac or Tools, Options in Windows), but I recommend leaving it as the default. Scrivener works quickly, so you won't experience any lag time with such frequent saves. You can also manually save the project at any time (File, Save, or Cmd-S for Mac, Ctrl+S for Windows), if you want.

 TIP Whenever you're tempted to manually save your project, consider using the Snapshot feature. A Snapshot saves the current version of your document, allowing you to roll back to a previous version if you don't like changes you make afterward. To take a Snapshot, choose Documents, Snapshots, Take Snapshot or press Cmd-5 (Ctrl+5 in Windows). Learn more about using Snapshots in Chapter 10, "Editing Your Manuscript."

Scrivener also automatically creates backups of your project. To learn more about backups, see Chapter 17, "Backing Up Your Work."

Introducing the Main Scrivener Components

After your project opens in the main Scrivener interface, you are presented with both the familiar and the new. As you can see in Figure 1.3, Scrivener has a large editing area, which may look comfortingly like a word processor. But there are also sidebars that may give you pause, and some of the toolbar buttons bring up floating panes with even more options. The rest of this chapter is devoted to introducing the key components of Scrivener, just to eliminate the fear factor. These are all explored in much more detail in the following chapters.

Toolbar   Menu bar   Group View Mode buttons

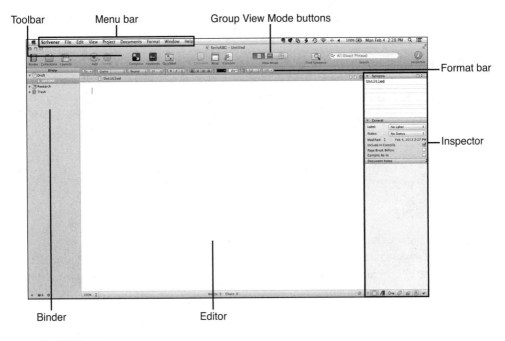

Format bar

Inspector

Binder   Editor

FIGURE 1.3

The Scrivener interface may be intimidating at first, but each component serves to help you work more efficiently once you understand them.

TIP If the Inspector doesn't appear in the Scrivener window when you first open your project, click the Inspector button in the toolbar (the blue circle with an *i* in it). You can also open the Inspector by choosing View, Layout, Show Inspector from the menu.

Examining the Editor

The largest area on the screen is the Editor, as shown in Figure 1.4. If you opened a project using the Blank template, the Editor opens to a blank screen. If you used a different template, the Editor opens an introduction page with details about the template and how to use any unique features.

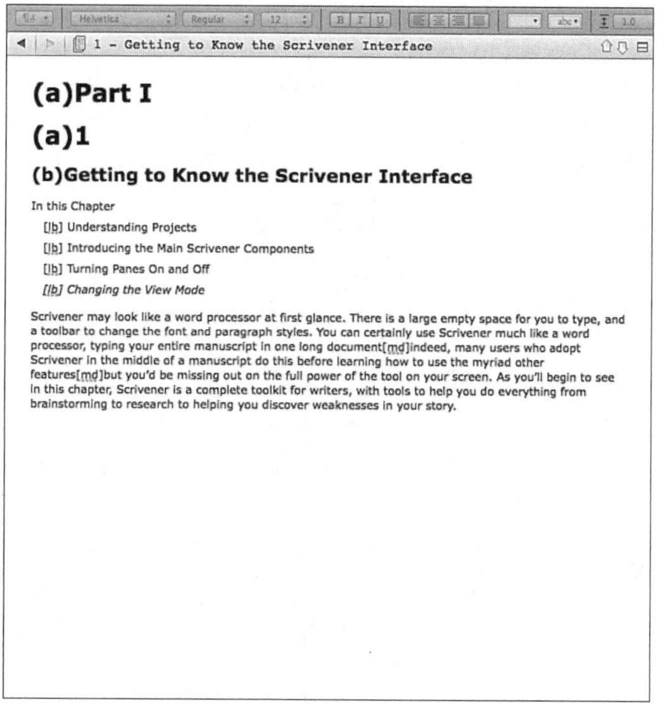
1 - Getting to Know the Scrivener Interface
(a)Part I
(a)1
(b)Getting to Know the Scrivener Interface
In this Chapter
[lb] Understanding Projects
[lb] Introducing the Main Scrivener Components
[lb] Turning Panes On and Off
[lb] Changing the View Mode
Scrivener may look like a word processor at first glance. There is a large empty space for you to type, and a toolbar to change the font and paragraph styles. You can certainly use Scrivener much like a word processor, typing your entire manuscript in one long document[md]indeed, many users who adopt Scrivener in the middle of a manuscript do this before learning how to use the myriad other features[md]but you'd be missing out on the full power of the tool on your screen. As you'll begin to see in this chapter, Scrivener is a complete toolkit for writers, with tools to help you do everything from brainstorming to research to helping you discover weaknesses in your story.

FIGURE 1.4

The Editor is where you type your manuscript.

TIP The Editor may open to the Corkboard or Outliner instead of the Document view, especially if you've opened Scrivener and played around with it in the past. If this is the case, you can switch to Document view by clicking on a single document in the Binder.

Use the Editor to type the body of your work. The format bar above the Editor can be used to control the font and style of your text. You can also insert images into your text. This isn't generally of much use to fiction writers, but may be necessary for writers of academic papers and other works of nonfiction.

To learn more about the Editor, see Chapter 4, "Writing in the Editor."

Using the Binder

The left sidebar, shown in Figure 1.5, is called the Binder. Use the Binder to organize your scenes, research, and notes into folders. The Binder allows you to quickly open one of these items in the Editor just by clicking on it. You can rearrange your scenes by dragging documents around the Binder or dropping them into different folders or subfolders. The buttons at the bottom of the Binder give you quick access to tools that help organize your project. Some of these functions include adding or duplicating items, grouping items together, and emptying the trash. These options are also available from the context menu if you right-click in the Binder.

FIGURE 1.5

The Binder is used to manage the files and folders in your project.

 NOTE Deleting a document or folder as you work doesn't mean all is lost. If you later realize you need a critical scene that was previously deleted, it can still be retrieved. When you delete an item, it moves to the Trash, which is accessible from the Binder. The item is not permanently deleted until you empty the Trash. If you're not certain if you may want to use a scene later, however, I recommend creating a folder for Scrap (or whatever you want to name it) and moving documents to that folder instead. Use the Trash for deleted blank documents and accidental duplicates.

Collections also appear in the Binder. A collection is a group of related files in your project. You can search for a character name, for example, and create a collection of all the scenes that contain that character. You can also create a collection manually, dropping in files that you consider relevant. You could create a collection of scenes that relate specifically to your protagonist's internal conflict to see if his or her growth follows a logical progression.

The Binder is open by default. If you want to close the Binder to focus on the Editor, choose View, Layout, Hide Binder from the menu. View, Layout, Show Binder restores the Binder. On Windows, this menu option is always titled Show Binder, with a check mark to indicate if it's toggled on or off. You can also click the Binder button in the toolbar or use Cmd-Option-B (or Ctrl+Shift+B in Windows) to toggle the Binder.

Discover more about the Binder in Chapter 3, "Organizing the Binder." To learn more about collections, see Chapter 16, "Searching Your Project."

Opening the Inspector

The right sidebar is the Inspector. This area displays information about the active file or folder. This information is known as meta-data. It's not the document itself, but all of the details about the document. To understand meta-data, think about a digital photograph. The image is the beautiful landscape or candid shot that evokes emotion. The meta-data is the information about where the shot was taken, the date of the event, the camera settings, and the filters you applied. This information is important to you as the photographer, but not to those who admire your work.

In the case of Scrivener, meta-data is divided into three areas in the Inspector, as shown in Figure 1.6. The Synopsis area at the top of the Inspector allows you to enter a brief summary of the scene or chapter. The General area in the middle displays the date the file was last modified, any labels or status you choose to tag, and information about how the file will be used when you compile your project into a completed manuscript. The Document Notes section at the bottom of the Inspector can be used to jot down notes about the document or project.

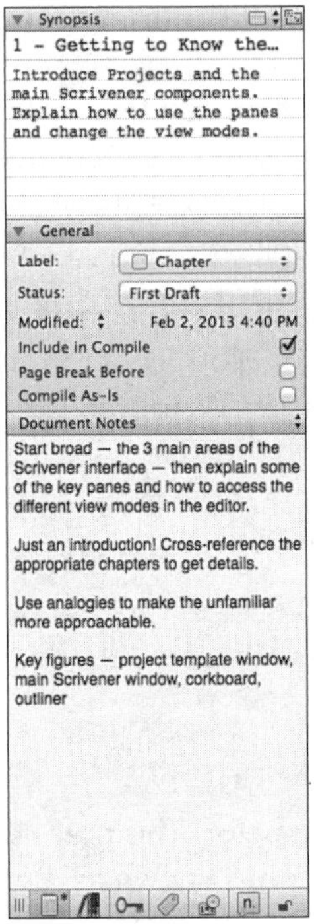

FIGURE 1.6

The Inspector displays meta-data about the current file.

The toolbar at the bottom of the Inspector provides access to additional meta-data, such as keywords, comments, and links to other information. When selected, these options appear in the Inspector sidebar. Some of these options fill the entire Inspector when selected.

Learn more about the Inspector and meta-data in Chapter 11, "Digging into the Inspector," and Chapter 12, "Putting Keywords and Meta-Data to Work."

Changing the Group View Mode

The Scrivenings, Corkboard, and Outliner modes are three other methods for viewing your work, each of which appears in the Editor when selected. The Corkboard, shown in Figure 1.7, looks just like its namesake—a blank board to which you can attach index cards. Each index card represents a file in your project and can contain a brief synopsis or an image. The Corkboard is good for viewing one level of documents at a time, such as all the scenes in a chapter. Folders and documents with subdocuments appear as a stack of index cards. To access the Corkboard, click the Corkboard icon in the toolbar (the second Group

View Mode button); choose View, Corkboard from the menu; or press Cmd-2 (Ctrl+2 in Windows).

Document with subdocuments

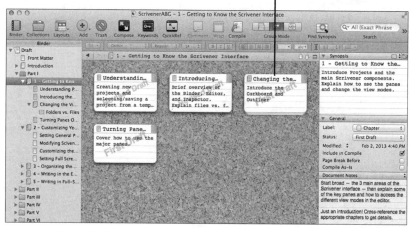

FIGURE 1.7

The Corkboard displays index cards to represent your documents.

 NOTE   The toolbar groups the Scrivenings, Corkboard, and Outliner icons together. If you have text displayed under your toolbar icons on the Mac, the label for this icon grouping changes from View Mode to Group Mode depending on whether you're viewing a single document or a group of documents in the active Editor window. Also, if you're viewing a single document, the Scrivenings icon switches to a single Document icon in the View Mode group on both Mac and Windows platforms.

The Outliner, shown in Figure 1.8, provides a hierarchical outline view of your project. Like the Corkboard, this is another way to get an overview of your project. You can view the synopsis and other meta-data in the Outliner, and can even add columns to display the word count, target word count, and progress bars to give you more control. One advantage of the Outliner over the Corkboard is that you can view the entire draft at once, rather than just one level (part, chapter, and so on). To access the Outliner, click the Outliner icon in the toolbar (the third icon in the Group View Mode grouping); choose View, Outline from the menu; or press Cmd-3 (Ctrl+3 in Windows).

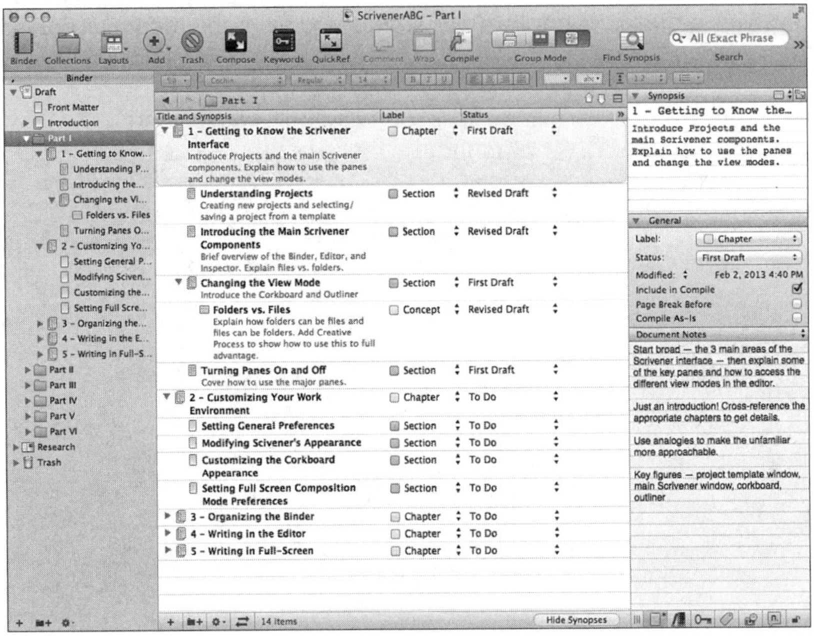

FIGURE 1.8

The Outliner displays a hierarchical outline view of your entire draft.

The Corkboard and Outliner are powerful plotting tools. If you are a plotter—someone who carefully preplans a book before writing—you may choose to create all your scene documents in advance, adding a brief synopsis in the Inspector for each document. You can then add, delete, and move the documents around in the Corkboard or Outliner until you're satisfied with the story and ready to write. This may take away the spontaneity of the story if you're a pantser—someone who likes to let his story unfold as he writes it. The Corkboard and Outliner are still useful tools for pantsers, however, because if you get an idea for a scene that will come later in the book, you can quickly generate a document and synopsis for it in either the Corkboard or Outliner, and then get back to writing. And as you're writing, you can use the Corkboard and Outliner along with judicious use of meta-data to see potential flaws in your story. In Chapter 6, "Storyboarding with the Corkboard," and Chapter 7, "Plotting in the Outliner," you discover more ways to put these tools to work, no matter how you approach your writing process.

The third Group mode is called Scrivenings. This mode is just like the standard text editor, but it displays all the selected documents on one screen. This mode is helpful when you write transitions from one scene or chapter to another. To access Scrivenings, select multiple documents or a folder in the Binder and then either click the Scrivenings icon in the toolbar (the first button in the Group View Mode grouping); choose View, Scrivenings from the menu; or press Cmd-1 (Ctrl+1 in Windows). Learn more about Scrivenings in Chapter 4.

Understanding Folders Versus Files

One key difference between Scrivener and other applications is the concept of files and folders. You may be accustomed to using folders strictly as a container for your files. In Scrivener, however, the folder itself can contain text, acting as both folder and document. Also, documents can contain subfiles and folders, acting as both document and folder. In other words, both files and folders serve the same purposes. Folders and files do, however, display different icons in the Binder depending on their content and whether they contain subdocuments.

 NOTE   You can see the different icons for folders and files in Figure 3.1 of Chapter 3.

Although this fluidity between files and folders may be confusing at first, you can use this flexibility to your advantage. For example, you can create a folder for each chapter, and put the chapter heading in the folder itself. Depending upon your Compile settings, this information may then be used to appear on the first page of the chapter when you compile your manuscript, as you discover in Chapter 19, "Compiling Your Completed Work." Another advantage is that you don't need to know when you begin writing if this will be just a scene or a complete chapter. You can easily convert files to folders and vice versa, or nest additional files and folders within a parent file or folder.

Accessing Other Panels

In addition to the main interface elements, Scrivener has additional panels accessible from the toolbar and menus. All of these are explained in the appropriate chapters of this book, but a couple are worth noting right out of the gate.

The QuickReference (QuickRef) panels allow you to open documents in a separate window rather than in the Editor. This is helpful when you want to refer to one or more documents while writing another. You can move the QuickRef panels around on the screen to keep them visible but out of your way. Access the QuickRef panel using one of these options:

- Select one or more documents in the Binder, Corkboard, or Outliner and then click the QuickReference button on the toolbar.

- Select one or more documents and drag them onto the QuickReference button on the toolbar.

- Select one or more documents and choose Documents, Open, As QuickReference.

- Select one or more documents and then right-click to open the context menu and select Documents, Open, As QuickReference.

- Choose View, QuickReference from the menu and then choose a document from the submenu.

- Select one or more documents and then press the spacebar.

A WINDOWS VIEW: LIVING WITHOUT QUICKREFERENCE PANELS

The QuickReference panel is only available on the Mac version. You can split the Editor window in both the Windows and Mac versions, however, so you can still view two documents at the same time. Chapter 4 explains how to split the Editor screen.

The Scratch Pad, as its name suggests, is a place for you to take notes. Yes, Scrivener already has a lot of other places for you to take notes—within a document, the Project and Document Notes in the Inspector, the Synopsis—but all of those are connected to a particular document or project. The Scratch Pad is separate from your projects, so you can take notes that don't necessarily apply to the open project. This makes the Scratch Pad a quick way to jot down other book ideas, your shopping list, or any other thoughts that come to mind while you're writing and then tuck them away so they don't clutter your head while you're trying to focus. You can also use the Scratch Pad to collect information from web pages or other applications and import those notes into your project later. Chapter 4 explains how to use the Scratch Pad and how to import notes from the Scratch Pad into a project. In the meantime, if you want to check it out, choose Window, Show Scratch Pad from the menu or press Shift-Cmd-Return. In Windows, choose Tools, Scratch Pad from the menu or press Ctrl+Alt+Shift+P.

 NOTE On the Mac, the keyboard shortcut can be changed in the General tab of the preferences window. In Windows, the keyboard shortcut can be changed in the Keyboard tab of the Options window.

THE CREATIVE PROCESS: JUMPING IN WHEN YOU'RE IN THE MIDDLE OF A BOOK

If you're in the middle of a book project when you decide to add Scrivener to your writing arsenal, you may be anxious to get back to work as quickly as possible. Although adding meta-data to each chapter and scene may seem enticing (or a fun procrastination method under the guise of work), and playing with the Corkboard and Outliner a great way to plot, you just don't have time right now. That's okay!

The most important features for you to master are how to import your current manuscript into Scrivener, how to split the manuscript into chapters and/or scenes, and how to use the Editor. You may also want to access the Full Screen or Composition modes to write in a distraction-free environment. Each of these is covered in Chapters 3–5. The rest can be learned in increments or can even wait until you're ready to compile your finished work (see Chapter 19) and take a breather before starting your next book.

THE ABSOLUTE MINIMUM

The most important takeaways from this chapter are as follows:

- Keep calm! Scrivener may appear intimidating at first, but you don't have to master all the features at once.

- Project templates provide an immediate structure for various types of writing. Templates are extremely flexible and customizable, however, so you aren't locked into any one way of organizing your manuscript.

- The three main components of the Scrivener window are the Binder, the Editor, and the Inspector. Each of these areas has multiple features, which are explained in this book.

2

CUSTOMIZING YOUR WORK ENVIRONMENT

Writing is an interesting enterprise. On the one hand, we can work just about anywhere. I once sketched out an entire scene on a bib in the dentist's chair. On the other hand, we can be incredibly picky about our work environment. This is especially true of our computers. If your workspace doesn't suit your personality, it's hard to get the words to flow.

Scrivener understands the need for writers to have control over their creative environment. Some writers need a lot of visual stimulation while others need a minimalist setup in order to focus. To that end, Scrivener's Preferences (Options in Windows) are numerous. To access the preferences window, choose Scrivener, Preferences (or press Cmd-,) on the Mac or Tools, Options (or press F12) in Windows.

A WINDOWS VIEW: DIFFERENCES IN OPTIONS AND TERMINOLOGY

The differences between the Mac and Windows versions of Scrivener are most obvious in the preferences that are available for each. These differences will diminish as Scrivener for Windows reaches feature parity with Scrivener for Mac, but the customization of some features inevitably continues to be determined by the constraints of each operating system. Even some of the terminology varies between versions, such as Preferences for Mac and Options for Windows.

This chapter focuses primarily on the preferences that control the visual aspects of your writing environment. When you enter the Preferences (or Options) window, you see several tabs that are not covered here, such as Navigation, Corrections, Import/Export, and Backup. Those options are covered in the appropriate chapters throughout the rest of the book.

Setting General Preferences

The General preferences determine how the Scrivener application will launch, save your data, and control the Scratch Pad. Figure 2.1 shows the General preferences window for the Mac version. Although not necessarily related to your visual workspace, these initial preferences are important to how you will work in Scrivener.

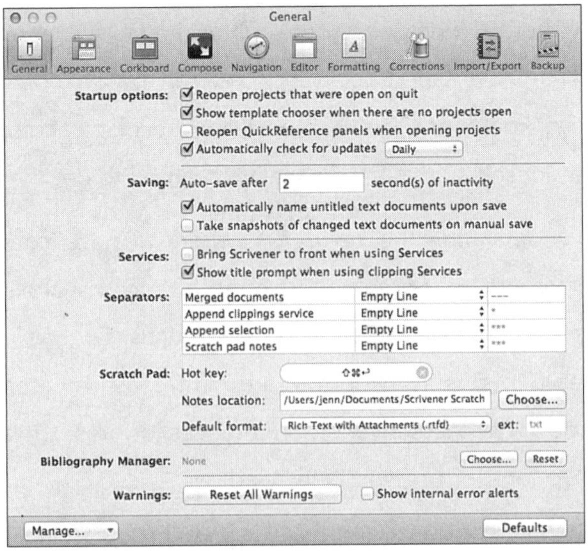

FIGURE 2.1

The General preferences window includes options for how Scrivener starts up and auto-saves.

Startup Options

After you create your first project in Scrivener, it automatically reopens any projects that you left open the last time you quit the program, rather than opening the Project Templates window. You can change this behavior with the Startup Options. If you want to manually open projects, deselect the Reopen Projects That Were Open on Quit check box. In Windows, this option is labeled Open Recent Projects on Program Launch.

Select or deselect the Show Template Chooser When There Are No Projects Open check box (Show Start Panel When There Are No Projects Open in Windows) to determine if the Project Templates window automatically displays when there are no open projects.

If you make use of QuickReference panels on the Mac, you may want to select the check box to Reopen QuickReference Panels When Opening Projects. This is convenient if you need to quit your work while you're in the middle of referring to multiple documents.

 TIP Reopen QuickReference Panels When Opening Projects is a good option to select even if you're not yet sure how frequently you want to use QuickReference panels. If you don't have any panels open, it doesn't do anything, so you've lost nothing. If you use panels, however, it ensures that they reopen in the same state you left them when you last exited Scrivener.

Scrivener is updated on a regular basis, with bug fixes and the addition of minor features to the program. To stay on top of these updates, select Automatically Check for Updates, and then choose an interval to perform the check.

Saving

Scrivener automatically saves your project whenever you pause in your work for 2 seconds. You can change this interval if you are on a slow machine or experience lag due to image-heavy documents, but it's generally best to leave it as the default to minimize the chance of any lost work.

If you are particularly worried about losing documents, you can set Scrivener to take Snapshots of any changed text documents whenever you perform a manual save (File, Save or Cmd-S). This is a Mac-only option, however.

If you have not titled a text document, Scrivener can name it when it saves the project. If the Automatically Name Untitled Text Documents Upon Save option is selected, Scrivener uses the first few words in the text as the document name. You can, of course, rename the document at any time.

Services (Mac Only)

Services are underutilized tools in Mac OS X. They are quick commands that allow you to perform an action in one app that relates to another app. The primary menu of an app (such as the Safari menu in Safari or the Word menu in Microsoft Word) has a Services submenu, which lists all available services for an action or selection. Scrivener has services that allow you to append a selection from a word processor, browser, or other application to a document or Scratch Pad note in Scrivener. You can also make a selection in one of these other apps and create a new clipping in Scrivener. Services can be very helpful when you utilize online research.

The Services preferences in Scrivener control how Scrivener behaves when you use one of its related services within another app. You can choose to bring Scrivener to the front after you use the services so you can immediately add your own notes or format the text, for example. You can also choose to be prompted to title a new clipping in Scrivener.

Separators (Mac Only)

When you merge two documents or append a selection or clipping to a document, the new text is separated from the existing text. The Separators preferences on the Mac allow you to set how that separation appears visually. There are four selections for which you can set automatic separators:

- **Merged Documents**: Controls how text is separated when you use the Documents, Merge command to combine multiple documents into one

- **Append Clippings Service**: Separates new text when you use the Append to Current Note or Append to Current Text services to clip a selection into Scrivener

- **Append Selection**: Separates selected text when you use the Edit, Append Selection to Document command

- **Scratch Pad Notes**: Controls the separation of text appended from the Scratch Pad into a text document

For each of the four types of selections, you can choose to separate the new text with a single return, an empty line, or custom characters.

TIP If you choose to separate text with custom characters, Scrivener provides some suggestions in the rightmost column of the Separators table. You can modify these suggestions. If you want to add one or more carriage returns to a custom setting, press Option-Return.

Scratch Pad

The Scratch Pad preferences allow you to set a keyboard shortcut to quickly access the Scratch Pad. You can also choose where Scratch Pad notes should be stored. Because these notes are not linked to a specific project, you should use a separate folder for them, such as the one created by default.

NOTE   The keyboard shortcut for the Scratch Pad is global, meaning that it will launch the Scratch Pad even if you are using another app. Therefore, be sure to choose a key combination that does not conflict with other shortcuts.

Scratch Pad notes are stored in Rich Text Format (`.rtf`) by default. Rich Text Format is compatible with a wide range of other applications, so it should suit your needs. If you prefer to save your notes in Plain Text Format (`.txt`), which is an option on the Mac, use the drop-down menu in the Default Format option to select it.

Bibliography Manager

If you are doing academic or nonfiction writing, you may have a need for a third-party Bibliography/Citations Manager. Scrivener is compatible with several bibliography managers, such as Sente and BookEnds for the Mac and EndNote for both Mac and Windows. Your chosen app must be installed on your computer before you can select it in the preferences. If you've previously selected an app and want to remove it, the Reset button clears the selection.

TIP If you don't need a citations manager, you can set this preference as a shortcut to launch a different type of app. If you use a timeline program, for example, you can select it here. Then you can press Cmd-Y (Ctrl+G, O in Windows) or go to Format, Bibliography/Citations in the menu whenever you need to access your timeline app.

A WINDOWS VIEW: GENERAL OPTIONS

Because the Windows version doesn't have the QuickReference panels feature, it obviously doesn't have an option to reopen those panels when opening projects. Scrivener for Windows does offer the option to display the full project path in the title bar. Windows does not have services—those are part of the Mac operating system—so you won't see options for them. You also won't see the Separators options in Windows. Because the Windows version already has a preset keyboard shortcut (Ctrl+Alt+Shift+P) for the Scratch Pad, you won't find that option in the Options window. You can also set a different interface language by selecting from the Language drop-down menu. If you change the interface language, you must restart Scrivener to see the change.

Customizing Scrivener's Appearance

For writers of a visual bent, the Appearance tab may be every bit as important as the rest. You can set Scrivener's colors to match your favorite desktop wallpaper, evoke the mood of your story, or simply provide as much or little distraction as you desire. You can also change the appearance of the Binder, Outliner, and other features. Figure 2.2 shows the Appearance tab.

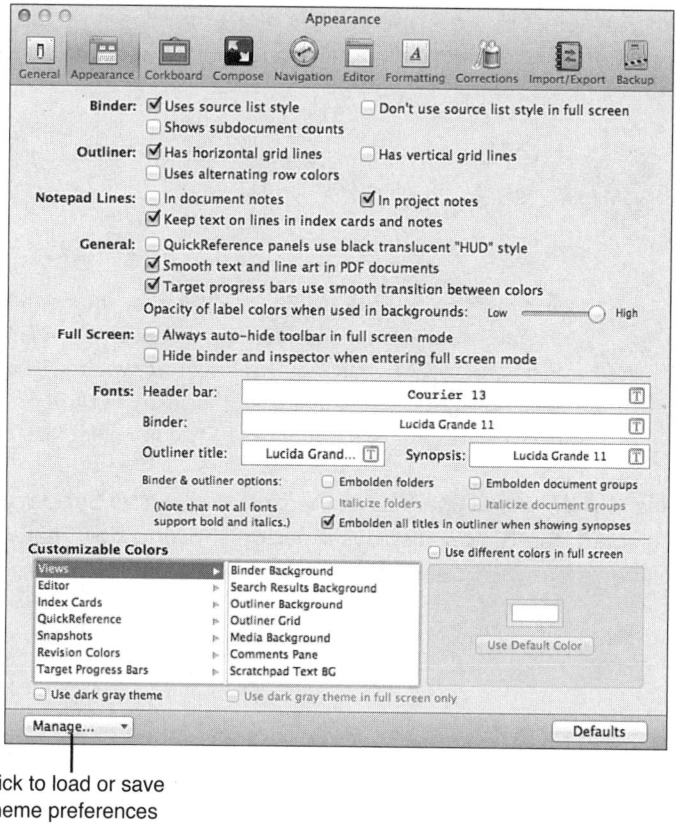

Click to load or save
theme preferences

FIGURE 2.2

The Appearance tab controls the color scheme and visual appearance of Scrivener.

 NOTE On the Mac, you can change the appearance of the Corkboard and Composition mode in other tabs, as described later in this chapter.

Binder

The preferences at the top of the Appearance tab affect how the Binder, Outliner, Notepad, and other screens appear. Most of these options are specific to Scrivener for Mac, although a couple are for both Mac and Windows.

The highlight color in the Binder is controlled by the Mac OS X System Preferences rather than by the Scrivener Preferences. When the Use Source List Style check box is selected, the active document in the Binder is highlighted by the color you select in the Appearance color of the General tab in the System Preferences. If you deselect this option, the Binder uses the Highlight Color instead.

 NOTE In Windows, the highlight color in the Binder is determined by the Windows theme.

 TIP If you're using OS X Lion or above, you can view Scrivener in Full Screen mode, which is covered in Chapter 5, "Writing in Full Screen." When in Full Screen mode, you may want to use the Highlight Color rather than the Source List Style. To do this, select the Don't Use Source List Style in Full Screen option.

Both Mac and Windows users have the option to Show Subdocument Counts. If this is selected, the Binder displays a badge showing how many subfolders and subdocuments are within each folder and document.

 NOTE The badge displays the number of folders/documents within that item as well as any subfolders/documents beneath those.

Outliner

The Outliner Appearance options control whether horizontal and vertical gridlines are displayed between rows and columns to make it easier to visually distinguish between items. This is a Mac-only feature. Personally, I use horizontal gridlines to separate items, but not the vertical gridlines to separate meta-data columns within an item.

You can also choose to alternate row colors on the Mac. This option applies two different shades of the Outliner Background color to alternate rows. In Windows, change the Outliner Background and Outliner Alternate Background colors in the General list.

Notepad Lines

The Notepad appears in the bottom pane of the Inspector. You can choose to display lines in the document or project notes if you want them to appear as they would in a ruled notebook. If these options are not selected, the Notepad appears as an unruled notebook. Select Keep Text on Lines in Index Cards and Notes if you want the lines to adjust to the font size of your notes.

General

The QuickReference panels appear as either a standard window or a translucent HUD-style display. HUD stands for heads-up-display and gives the impression of a floating screen rather than a distinct window. Your choice of how to display QuickRefs has little bearing on the functionality of these panels, so it's primarily a stylistic choice. The only functional difference is that the non-HUD style can display the format bar. This is not accessible from the HUD style.

If you have a slower Mac, you may want to disable Smooth Text and Line Art in PDF Documents in order to speed up the visual rendering of PDFs if you magnify them.

The Project Targets tools use gradients to display your progress toward your writing goals. If you prefer to see a more distinct transition as you reach your 50% and 100% goals, deselect the Target Progress Bars and use the Smooth Transition Between Colors option.

You can use the color associated with the Label tag of an item as a background color for that item in the Binder, Corkboard, and Outliner. Adjust the Opacity of Label Colors When Used in Backgrounds slider to set the vividness of the label color against the background color of the Corkboard.

 NOTE See Chapter 12, "Putting Keywords and Meta-Data to Work," to learn how to use the Label color as visual cues for your project.

Full Screen

If you use Mac OS X 10.7 or higher, you see settings for Full Screen in the Appearance tab. You can opt to Always Auto-Hide Toolbar in Full Screen to maximize your workspace even more. If you auto-hide the toolbar in this mode, you can access it along with the menu bar by moving your mouse to the top of the display. Similarly, you can hide the Binder and Inspector, turning your full screen into a large Editor.

 CAUTION Don't confuse Full Screen mode with Composition mode. Full Screen mode hides the Dock and menu bar and stretches the Scrivener application to make use of the full display screen. Composition mode is a distraction-free environment with a custom background and automatic scrolling that keeps your insertion point in the middle of the screen.

Full Screen mode in Scrivener for Windows is the same as Composition mode on the Mac. Despite the name, it is *not* the same as Full Screen mode on the Mac.

Fonts

The Fonts options control the appearance of the Scrivener interface items. You can change the default fonts for the Header Bar, Binder, Outliner Title, and Synopsis. To change a font, click the current font setting. This opens the Fonts dialog box, shown in Figure 2.3. Choose a font family, typeface, and size. Click the Close box to close the Fonts dialog box. Select the Embolden Folders and/or Italicize Folders options if you want to distinguish folders and document groups from individual documents. If the font you choose for the Binder or Outliner Title options does not have a bold or italic typeface, the associated Embolden Folders and Italicize Folders options are grayed out.

 TIP These options only control the interface elements. Set your writing fonts in the Formatting tab.

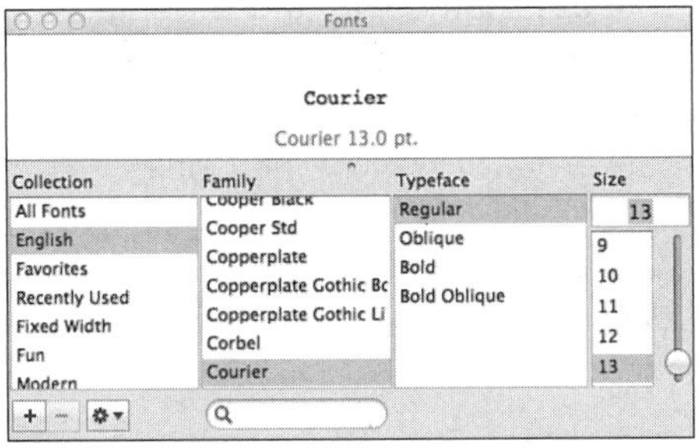

FIGURE 2.3

The Fonts dialog box is used to set fonts for various elements, such as the appearance of the Header bar in the Binder.

Modifying the Color Scheme

The meat of the Appearance tab is the Customizable Colors area. The plethora of options here allow you to change the color of almost every aspect of the Scrivener interface.

 NOTE Some elements, such as the color of the windows themselves, are controlled by the operating system. You cannot change the appearance of your windows to bright green on your Mac using the Scrivener Preferences, no matter how much the OS X graphite or aqua themes may interfere with your overall color scheme.

To change the color of an element in Scrivener:

1. Click a category in the left column, shown in Figure 2.4.

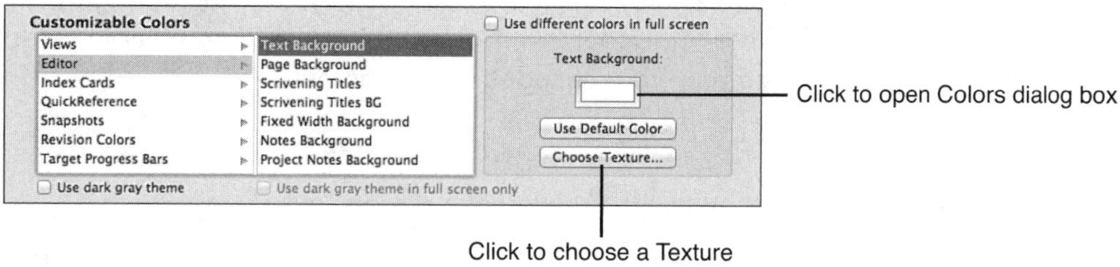

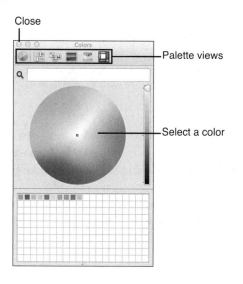

Click to open Colors dialog box

Click to choose a Texture

FIGURE 2.4

The Customizable Colors section of the Appearance preferences allows you to control almost every visual aspect of the interface.

2. Choose a specific option in the middle column.

3. Click the color well on the right to open the Colors dialog box, shown in Figure 2.5.

Close

Palette views

Select a color

FIGURE 2.5

Select a color from the Colors dialog box. You can view the available colors in different ways by switching palette views. You can download additional palettes from the Internet.

4. Select a color from the color wheel or one of the other color selectors.

5. Click the Close button to close the Colors dialog box.

The color change is immediately visible in the Scrivener interface, even while the preferences window is open. If you have a large display, you can arrange your windows to view the main Scrivener interface while customizing multiple color settings so you can see how your changes work together.

 NOTE In Windows, you must click Apply or OK to apply your color changes to the Scrivener interface.

Some options allow you to set a texture instead of a color. This allows you to use an image file as a background for the various Background or Paper options. Images that tile well work best here, and the smaller the file size, the better. To set a texture, click the Choose Texture button, and then navigate to the file you want to use. Double-click on the file or select the file and click Open to return to the Appearance tab.

There are too many customizable interface elements to list here. If you're in doubt about an option, try setting it to a particularly bright or dark color and then poke around the interface to see the changes. Once you know what's what, you can select the color that suits your needs.

 TIP For a complete table of Customizable Color options, visit my website at http://www.jenniferkettell.com.

If you use the Full Screen option on the Mac, you can choose to set different colors for the major features. To enable this feature, select the Use Different Colors in Full Screen check box above the right column. This adds another category for Full Screen. Personally, I don't prefer to use different colors for the same exact interface, but others might want to change the color of the Editor page to a less glaring color or mimic their Composition mode color settings.

A WINDOWS VIEW: APPEARANCE OPTIONS

The Appearance options window may not seem to contain as many options as the Mac version, but most of the "missing" options are unnecessary because of the operating system or are actually located on other Options tabs.

When you choose an element to customize color, the color well opens the Select Colors dialog box. Choose a color and then click OK. In Windows, you cannot automatically see your changes as you make them. Instead, click Apply to set your new choices while leaving the Options window open, or click OK to accept the changes and exit the window.

The same applies to changes in the Fonts panel. Select the element you want to change, and then click the Select Font button beneath the sample text. After choosing a font in the Select Font dialog box, click OK to return to the Options window, where you can then either click Apply or OK to accept the changes.

Unlike on the Mac, all of the interface-related color and font options (with the exception of the Corkboard Background) are listed in the Appearance tab, including those for the Corkboard and Full Screen. Windows users also have an advantage over Mac aficionados in how they control their entire workspace appearance. If you want your windows to complement your Scrivener color settings, access the Windows Control Panel to modify your display settings. You can also override the system font settings for Scrivener's windows and menus within the General fonts list.

Customizing the Corkboard Appearance

The Corkboard tab preferences, shown in Figure 2.6, control the appearance and function of the Corkboard. As you discover in Chapter 6, "Storyboarding with the Corkboard," this tool can be very helpful to both plotters and pantsers.

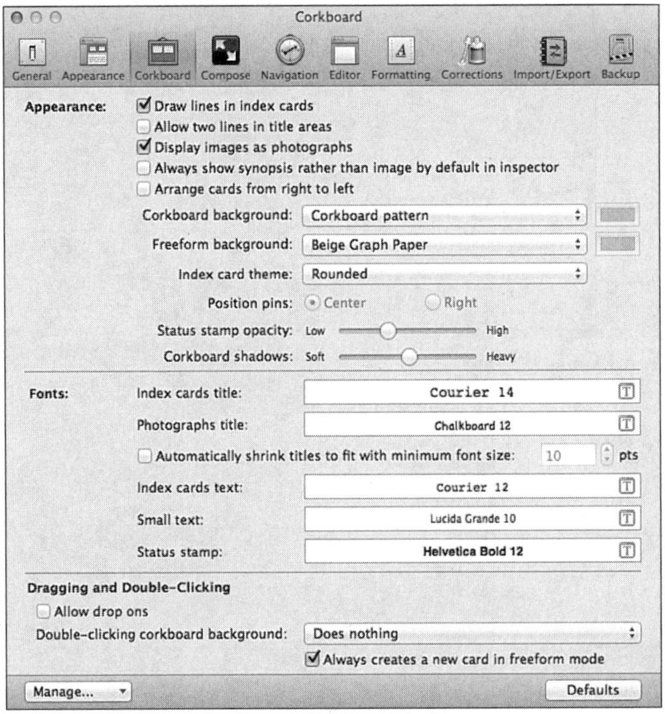

FIGURE 2.6

The Corkboard tab controls the appearance of the Corkboard and index cards as well as some of the basic functions of the Corkboard view.

NOTE In Scrivener for Mac, the default color of the index cards and the label color opacity are controlled in the Appearance tab. In Scrivener for Windows, all of the color and font settings for the Corkboard aside from the Corkboard Background are in the Appearance tab.

TIP In Windows, you can remove the lines on index cards with a Color Selector trick. In the Appearance tab, choose Index Card Lines from the Index Cards options in the Colors pane. Click on the color swatch to open the Select Color dialog box. Set the Alpha Channel option to zero (0), then click OK. You can apply the same trick to the Index Card Divider option.

Appearance

On the Mac, the Corkboard Appearance options have settings to control the arrangement and appearance of the Corkboard and index cards. In the Corkboard, each text document has an associated index card. The index card is drawn with lines by default to mimic a physical index card, but you can remove those lines. The top line contains the title of the document; this area is constrained to one line by default, but can be expanded on the Mac by selecting the Allow Two Lines in Title Areas check box.

Images attached to index cards appear as snapshots on the card in the Corkboard. If you deselect the Display Images as Photographs option, the Corkboard always displays the synopsis rather than the photograph. Similarly, you can toggle the Always Show Synopsis Rather Than Image by Default in Inspector check box to show either the synopsis or image in the Inspector.

> **TIP** If you use both a synopsis and an image on an index card, deselect both the Display Images as Photographs and the Always Show Synopsis Rather Than Image by Default in Inspector options. This allows you to view the photograph in the Inspector while seeing the synopsis in the Corkboard. Alternatively, select both check boxes to swap the view.

Index cards appear on the Corkboard from left to right by default, but if you use a right-to-left language, you may prefer to reverse the card order.

Scrivener for Mac has two types of Corkboards, as you discover in Chapter 6. To change the background for either the Corkboard or Freeform Corkboard, click the current setting and choose a different pattern. The drop-down menu also provides options to set a custom background or color. When choosing a custom background, choose an image that will tile well.

The index cards can be either square to mimic a physical card, or rounded. Mac users are limited in the appearance of the index cards, whereas Windows users can choose a card shape and then fully customize the colors of the divider and lines in the Appearance tab.

The pins on an index card assume the color of the Label assigned to that item in the Inspector. On the Mac, pins can be positioned in either the center or right side of the card if you use one of the two square index card options. If you opt to use rounded index cards, the pin is replaced by a square chip in the upper-right corner of the card. In Windows, use the Label Indicator option to select either a Corner Mark or a Pin.

The Status tag you apply to an item in the Inspector can be displayed as a watermark across the face of index cards. The watermark appears beneath any synopsis text you add to the card, so your synopsis always remains visible, but you can control the opacity using the Status Stamp Opacity slider. Figure 2.7 shows some of the configurations you can create using the different index card, pin, and status tab options.

Rounded cards, chips, status stamp

Square cards, pins right, status stamp

Square cards, pins center, no status stamp

FIGURE 2.7

The settings for index cards, pins, and the status stamp give you a range of options in how cards appear on the Corkboard.

TIP   You can toggle the display of pins on index cards with the View, Corkboard Options, Show Pins command in the menu. Toggle the display of stamps with the View, Corkboard Options, Show Stamps command.

You can alter the appearance of the shadow beneath each index card by adjusting the Corkboard Shadows slider. This option is referred to as Index Card Shadows in Windows.

Fonts

The Fonts options control the fonts that are used for Corkboard elements. As with the Fonts options in the Appearance tab, you can change these by clicking on the current font and choosing from the Fonts dialog box. You can set fonts for the following:

- **Index Cards Title**: The document title that appears at the top of the index card in both the Corkboard and the Inspector.

- **Photographs Title (Mac Only)**: The title of an image on an index card.

- **Index Cards Text**: The text of the synopsis on an index card.

- **Small Text**: An alternative font that can be used on index cards when the Use Small Font option is selected in the Corkboard Options.

 CAUTION   The Corkboard Options are different than the Corkboard Preferences and are covered in Chapter 6.

- **Status Stamp**: The stamp that appears on index cards to reflect the status you've set for an item. This text is automatically resized to fit the index cards, so you don't have to worry about the font size.

 NOTE   These font options are in the Appearance tab in Windows.

Dragging and Double-Clicking

The final options in the Corkboard tab control some of the behaviors of the Corkboard itself. If you select Allow Drop Ons, you can drop one index card onto another to move that item as a subdocument of that card.

 NOTE   These options appear at the bottom of the Mac Corkboard Preferences window but at the top of the Windows Corkboard Options window.

When you double-click on the Corkboard itself, you can set it to either open the parent of the current Corkboard (also known as the Enclosing Group) or create a new card. I suggest setting the double-click action to Creates a New Card when you're plotting and drafting your novel, as that's when you're most likely to be creating a lot of new index cards. You can change this preference to Opens the Parent Corkboard when you reach the editing phase of your work, as that's when you're more likely to be moving around the folders and file groups in your manuscript to get a broad overview of how the story flows. You can also set this option to Does Nothing.

TIP The keyboard shortcut to open the enclosing group is Control-Cmd-R (Alt+Shift+Up Arrow in Windows). The keyboard shortcut to create a new card is Cmd-N (Ctrl+N in Windows). So no matter which option you select for the double-click action in the Corkboard, you can quickly access the other.

On a Mac, if you select the Always Creates a New Card in Freeform Mode check box, double-clicking while in a Freeform Corkboard always creates a new index card where you clicked, no matter what option you choose for the standard Corkboard. Deselect this check box if you want the Freeform Corkboard's behavior to mirror that of the standard Corkboard.

Setting Full Screen Composition Mode Preferences

If you use Mac OS X 10.7 (Lion) or higher, Scrivener for Mac has two different "full-screen" options. Full Screen mode simply hides the Dock and menu bar so the Scrivener window can take advantage of the extra screen real estate. Composition mode is a full-screen writing environment that puts your manuscript front and center. You can learn more about these views in Chapter 5. Although the name of the Full Screen Composition Mode tab obfuscates which features it controls, these options relate to Composition mode. Figure 2.8 shows the Full Screen Composition Mode Preferences tab.

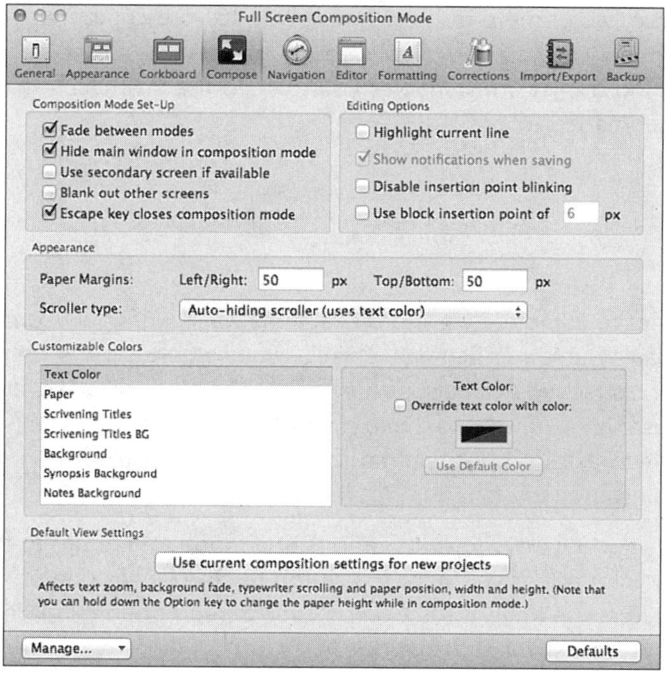

FIGURE 2.8

The colors and other options for Composition mode can vary greatly from those of the main Scrivener interface.

 NOTE Scrivener for Windows does not have an Options tab for Full Screen mode. Instead, all of the settings for this mode are in the Appearance tab.

Composition Mode Setup

On the Mac, the Fade Between Modes option fades the screen between the Composition mode and the full Scrivener mode when you switch modes. When you're in Composition mode, the background is translucent, so any open windows show through. The Hide Main Window in Composition Mode option hides the main Scrivener window while you're in this mode. This can speed up your typing because Scrivener doesn't have to update the screen in both Composition mode and the Editor at the same time. It's also less distracting.

In Windows, you might want to display the Binder, another document, or keep some other element visible. By arranging the Scrivener window and the Composition/Full Screen mode paper alignment, you can use the background fade slider on the control strip to view or hide the window.

If you have two or more displays hooked up to your computer, you can select the Use Secondary Screen If Available option to open the Composition window on your second display. This enables you to keep the main Scrivener interface open on your primary display.

 TIP Opening Composition mode on a second display is helpful if you want to keep your research open on your primary display while you write.

If you want to completely avoid distractions while writing in Composition mode, select Blank Out Other Screens. This fills your other displays with the background color. Of course, you can also just turn off your other displays, but this option can be useful if you want to avoid distractions while you're writing but also want the ability to exit Composition mode and have your other open applications immediately available on your desired displays.

There are several ways to exit Composition mode and return to the main Scrivener interface. If you want to use the Escape key as one of them on the Mac, select the Escape Key Closes Composition Screen option. In Windows, the Escape key always closes Full Screen mode.

Editing Options

In Composition mode, once you reach halfway down the screen while typing, Scrivener keeps the insertion point in the middle of the screen, scrolling like a typewriter. If you want to make it even easier to see the current line, use the Highlight Current Line option and then set a highlight color in the Customizable Colors panel. I personally find the highlighted line to be more of a distraction than a help, so I leave this option disabled.

The Show Notifications When Saving option is selected by default to provide a notice whenever you manually save your project. If you are using OS X 10.7 (Lion) or higher, this option uses the Notification Center. If you are using OS X 10.6 (Snow Leopard) or below, this feature requires the use of Growl, a third-party application that provides notices about other apps and activities on your Mac. If you don't have Growl installed, this option is grayed out.

The insertion point blinks by default. If you find this to be distracting, select Disable Insertion Point Blinking. You can also adjust the width of the insertion point. The default width is 1 pixel. If you choose to disable the blinking of the insertion point, I suggest increasing the width of the insertion point by a couple of pixels to make it easier to locate in a sea of text.

Composition Mode Appearance

The Composition mode screen looks like a sheet of endlessly scrolling paper. Increase or decrease the Left/Right Paper Margins to show more or less space between the edge of the paper and the text. It's generally not worth adjusting the Top/Bottom Paper Margins because those are only apparent when you reach the very top and bottom of a document.

There are five types of scrollbars available in Composition mode:

- **Regular Scroller**: Uses the default scroller from the operating system. If you're using OS X Lion or Mountain Lion, the scrollbar automatically hides unless you move your cursor to the edge of the paper.

- **Standard Full Screen Scroller**: Uses the default full-screen scrollbar from the operating system, which is always visible if there's more than one screen of text in the document.

- **Auto-Hiding Scroller (Uses Text Color)**: The scrollbar uses the same color as your text. Use this setting in conjunction with the Override Text Color with Color setting in the Customizable Colors panel. This scrollbar automatically hides unless the cursor is moved to the edge of the paper.

- **Minimalist Scroller (Uses Text Color)**: This setting is similar to the Auto-Hiding Scroller but uses a softer hue and is more rounded.

- **No Scroller**: If you don't want to see any scrollbar at all, use this option. You can still scroll through your document with your mouse, trackpad, or arrow keys.

 TIP   If you're very visually oriented and are customizing colors to suit a particular theme, choose either the Auto-Hiding or Minimalist Scroller, as they can assume the text color. This may be less intrusive to your theme than the default black.

Composition Mode Customizable Colors

As with the Customizable Colors in the Appearance tab, you can customize the colors of all of the major elements in Composition mode. You can use a texture or image for the Background instead of just a solid color. As with the other elements with texture options, choose an image that will tile well. Many writers choose an image that motivates their writing in general or the specific work they're writing.

On the Mac, you can also use a texture for the paper. In this case, you should choose an image that won't interfere with your text. If you search on the Internet for "paper textures," you can find dozens of options. Just remember that the image will tile, so images with borders won't work well.

Default View Settings

Aside from the Composition mode settings in the preferences window, you can control the opacity of your paper and background, the position of the paper, and how the text scrolls using the control strip at the bottom of the Composition mode. These options are covered in Chapter 5. Once you set up this view to your liking, you can click the button to Use Current Composition Settings for New Projects. Any projects you create afterward will have the same Composition mode settings as the current project.

 NOTE You can, of course, customize each project individually, if you prefer. I use different backgrounds for each of my books. To change the backdrop on a per-project basis on the Mac, select View, Composition Backdrop from the menu, and then select an image or texture.

Customizing the Editor

Now that you've set up the window dressing for your writing environment, it's time to think about the writing itself. Scrivener for Mac has two preference tabs to set up the Editor and Formatting elements.

 NOTE Scrivener for Windows combines these into one Options tab for the Editor.

The Editor tab, shown in Figure 2.9, controls the flow of text in the Editor. The formatting of the text itself is the purview of the Formatting tab, covered in the next section of this chapter.

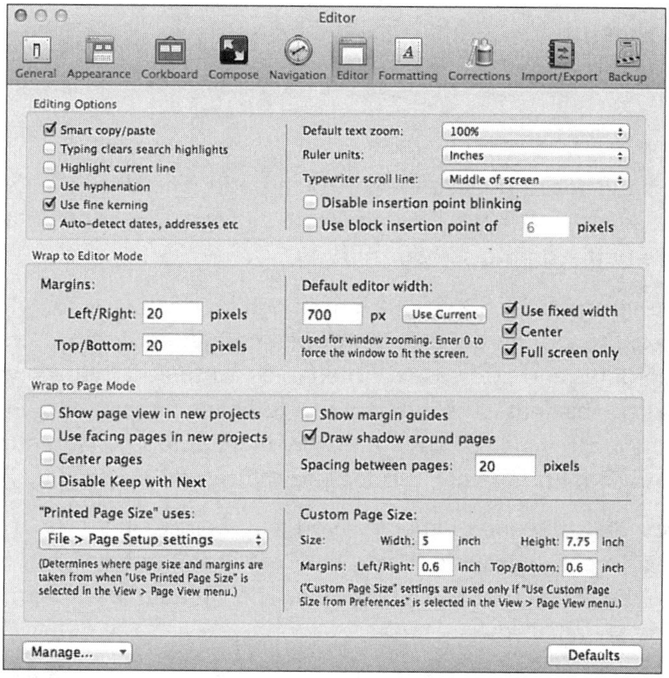

FIGURE 2.9

Tell the Editor how to handle text using the Editor preferences tab.

Editing Options

The Editing Options control the major functions of the Editor. When Smart Copy/ Paste is selected, Scrivener automatically removes extraneous whitespace and inserts a single space to separate the pasted text from any surrounding text, if necessary.

When you search your project, Scrivener highlights any text that matches your search criteria. Enable the Typing Clears Search Highlights check box if you want these highlights to disappear when you resume typing in the document.

As with the similar feature in Composition mode, you can choose to highlight the current line in the document to make it easier to find your place. Set the highlight color in the Customizable Colors panel of the Appearance tab; choose Editor and then Current Line Highlight.

Hyphenation is disabled by default and is rarely necessary in Scrivener. If you use full (left and right) justification, you may want to select Use Hyphenation to automatically hyphenate long words at the end of a line.

NOTE Your margin, page size, and font settings in Scrivener may not carry over onto the printed page, which would change the hyphenation, so this feature only affects readability while you are working.

Kerning is the space between letters on a page. The Use Fine Kerning setting enables Scrivener to make finer adjustments when you zoom in and out of text so it appears better on the screen.

If you are using Mac OS X 10.7 (Lion) or higher, the Auto-Detect Dates, Addresses, Etc. option enables the operating system's data detection tools to recognize dates and addresses and enable you to add them to your calendar or contacts list. This feature is rarely of use to fiction writers, and, in fact, having your character's locations or dates in the story highlighted for potential use may be quite annoying. Fortunately, this feature is disabled by default.

When you draft a scene or chapter, you may want to increase or decrease the size of the text to ease eyestrain. Using the Text Scale tool, you can do this without changing the actual font size of the text. The Default Text Zoom can be adjusted to provide an initial scale setting.

The Editor and QuickReference panels can display rulers to make it easier to set tabs and indents in a document. The Ruler Units setting allows the ruler to use centimeters, inches, picas, or points as its unit of measure.

The Typewriter Scroll Line setting controls the current insertion point's position within the Editor window when typewriter scrolling is enabled for that specific editor. The default setting is Middle of Screen, but you can change this to the top or bottom quarter or third of the screen if you want.

As with Composition mode, the insertion point blinks by default unless you select Disable Insertion Point Blinking. Likewise, the Use Block Insertion Point Of setting controls the width of the insertion point to make it easier to locate in the Editor window. In Windows, this setting affects both the Editor window and Full Screen mode.

Wrap to Editor Mode

Scrivener can use either an Editor or Page View mode. In Editor mode, text wraps to the width of the Editor window. This is similar to using a text editor such as TextEdit on the Mac or Notepad in Windows.

The Margins settings control the space between the text and the edge of the window. Adjust the Left/Right margin to set whitespace between your text and the Binder and Inspector. The Top/Bottom setting is only useful at the top and bottom of a document, so the default is usually fine.

On the Mac, the Default Editor Width controls the size of the Editor. If you resize the window using the Zoom command in the Window menu, Scrivener maintains the Default Editor Width for the Editor and adjusts the Binder and Inspector accordingly. Click the Use Current button to make your current Editor width the default. If you set the default to zero, Scrivener always makes the Editor as large as possible on the screen.

If you enable the Use Fixed Width setting, Scrivener maintains the default width of the page even if the Editor is wider. Any extra space is filled with a background color. If you use this option, set the background color in the Customizable Colors panel of the Appearance tab. Choose Editor and then Fixed Width Background.

The page is centered by default, so any background colors appear on both the right and left sides of the Editor. You can align the page to the left side of the Editor by deselecting the Center check box.

If you work in Scrivener in Full Screen mode, the Editor can become quite large, making it harder to focus on a reasonable amount of text in a line. Click the Full Screen Only check box to constrain the width of the page when you're in Full Screen mode, even if you don't choose to use such limits when working in a smaller window.

Wrap to Page Mode

Page mode is similar to a word processor in that it uses preestablished page margins to control the flow of text. The Editor view is used by default, so if you prefer Page view, you need to set it up for future projects and then close your current project and reopen it. This setting affects future new projects but does not affect existing ones. You can toggle the Page view per project by selecting View, Page View, Show/Hide Page View from the menu.

 NOTE Unlike a word processor, the page settings you establish for the Editor do not necessarily mirror those of the printed output. You can create a customized "page" setting while you write and then use the Compile settings to control the final appearance of your text.

To enable Page view, select Show Page View in New Projects. If you want to view two pages across instead of one, select Use Facing Pages in New Projects. You can also choose to Center Pages to align the page in the middle of the Editor. This setting only affects future new projects. To enable it on a per-project basis, select View, Page View, Two Pages Across from the menu.

To view the printable area on the screen, choose Show Margin Guides. This draws a border on the page. You can also add a shadow around the page to form a border between the page and the background color. If you display two or more pages, the Spacing Between Pages option puts the set number of pixels (the default is 20) between pages.

When using Page view, your onscreen page can match either the printed page size or a custom size. For the Printed Page Size option, Scrivener uses either the settings in the Page Setup window (File, Page Setup) or the settings you choose in the Compile options (File, Compile, then choose Page Settings). For the Custom Page Size, set the overall paper size and the margins.

A WINDOWS VIEW: WRAP TO EDITOR

Scrivener for Windows uses the Editor view only. There is no option for Page view. Lest you think that Windows users have lost out, keep in mind that Page view is primarily for display purposes, not an actual representation of the printed page. When given the choice, I find that using Editor view lets me focus on the words themselves rather than how many "pages" I've written.

Setting a Writing Font

The Formatting tab, shown in Figure 2.10, controls how text is formatted in the Editor and Composition mode on the Mac. In Windows, these options are in the Editor tab. The Main Text Style displays a format bar, which allows you to set the font, typeface, alignment, text and highlight colors, and line spacing for your text. To change the font, click the A button to open the Fonts dialog box and then select a font family, typeface, and size. On a Mac, you can move between the Fonts dialog box and the Preferences window to preview your font choice. Click the Close button on the Fonts dialog box when you finish.

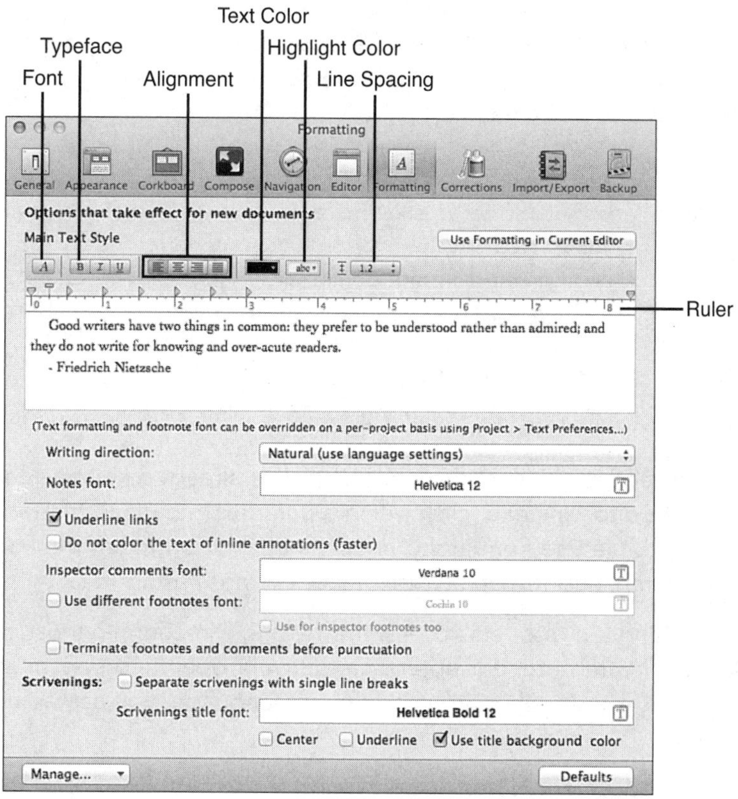

FIGURE 2.10

Tell the Editor how to format your text in the Formatting preferences tab.

Set indents and tabs on the ruler below the formatting bar. You can do this as follows:

- **Change tab position**: Click on one of the right-facing triangles and drag it to the desired position on the ruler.

- **Remove a tab**: Click on a triangle and drag it off the ruler.

- **Add a tab**: Click on the ruler where you want to position the tab. In Windows, double-click to add a tab.

- **Change the first-line indent at the start of a paragraph**: Click on the downward-facing triangle and drag it to the desired position on the ruler.

The Nietzsche quote beneath the ruler displays a preview of your formatting selections. In Windows, the order of options on the formatting bar is different, but the elements are the same.

 TIP Don't resign yourself to endless hours staring at Courier on your screen! Instead, choose a font that's comfortable for you to view onscreen for prolonged periods. You can write in neon green, 14-point Comic Sans, if your eyes can stand it, yet still compile your completed manuscript in 12-point, Times New Roman or Courier for submission to an editor. Learn how to automatically substitute fonts when exporting your manuscript in Chapter 19, "Compiling Your Completed Work."

There's no need to reinvent the wheel if you've already formatted text to your liking in the Editor. Instead, click within a paragraph that's formatted as you want and then click the Use Formatting in Current Editor button in the Formatting preferences tab, and the default text takes on those attributes.

The Formatting tab also lets you set the Writing Direction. In most circumstances, the default Natural setting is appropriate. If your operating system is set to one language but you usually write in a different language, you can adjust this option accordingly.

Project and Document Notes, usually found in the bottom pane of the Inspector, have their own font setting. To change the default, click the current font and choose another from the Fonts dialog box. In Windows, you can use different fonts for both Project and Document Notes, and both are set in the Appearance tab.

If you enter hyperlinks in a document, they are underlined by default unless you deselect the Underline Links option. When you annotate text within the Editor, it changes the color of the text and adds a bubble outline around the selected text. On the Mac, select the Do Not Color the Text of Inline Annotations option if you want annotated text to appear in the default font color. This setting fills the bubble outline with the annotation color.

If you are unsatisfied with the default fonts for comments and footnotes in the Inspector, change them in the Formatting tab just as you made other font adjustments. You can opt to position footnote markers before or after the punctuation of a sentence. The Terminate Footnotes and Comments Before Punctuation option is helpful if your work requires you to add footnotes to text within the punctuation of a sentence instead of following a sentence.

 NOTE Changes in the Main Text Style section of the Formatting tab only affect new documents. They will not alter any previously created documents. You can convert the formatting of existing documents if you want, but choosing this as an option rather than the default behavior allows you to preserve the formatting of already-typed documents.

Scrivenings is the term for viewing multiple items in the Editor at once. This View mode is useful when working on the transitions between scenes or chapters or when you simply want to view a chapter or your entire manuscript at once. The Separate Scrivenings with Single Line Breaks option divides each document with a line break rather than the more obtrusive graphic divider. If you want to see the titles of each document in your Scrivenings (using View, Editor, Show Titles in Scrivenings), set the Scrivenings Title Font and appearance options to control how this is displayed.

 NOTE The Scrivenings options are not available in Scrivener for Windows.

Saving and Sharing Your Preference Settings

After all the thought you put into setting all of Scrivener's preferences, you should preserve your selections. This allows you to recall the settings if you ever need to reinstall Scrivener. You can also use a saved preference file to install your preferences on another computer. To save preferences:

1. Click the Manage button that appears at the bottom of every preference tab, as shown in Figure 2.11.

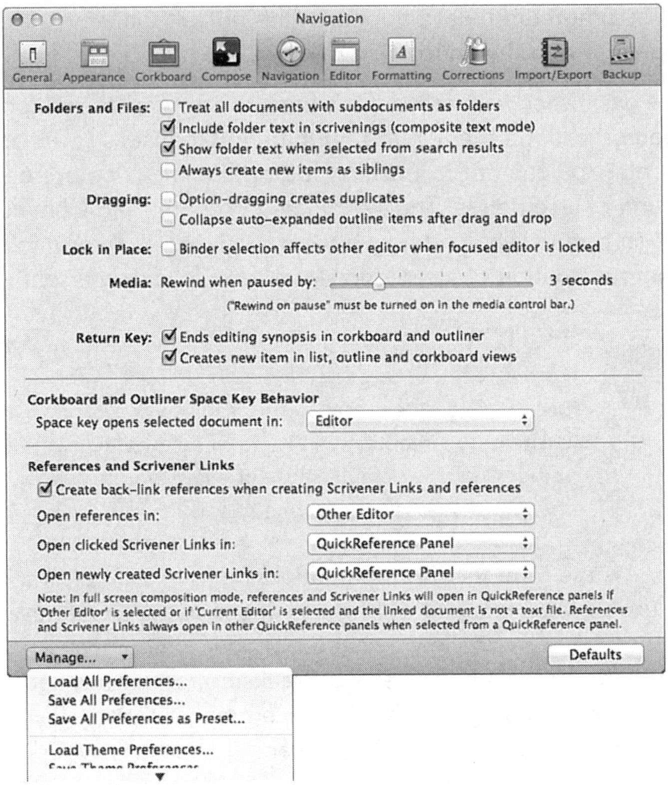

FIGURE 2.11

The Manage button appears at the bottom of every tab in the preferences window.

2. Click Save All Preferences (Save Preferences in Windows) to save all of your preference settings.

3. In the Save dialog box, navigate to the folder where you want to store your preference files.

4. Enter a name for the file. Choose a name that reminds you of any key settings you selected, which makes it helpful to distinguish if you create multiple preference files.

5. Click Save.

> **TIP**   Remember that this chapter has focused primarily on the visual preferences and those that affect how Scrivener operates as a whole. As you work your way through this book, you may change other preference options. If you change your settings, you can overwrite an existing preference file or create a new one.

To load a saved preference file, simply click the Manage button and then choose Load All Preferences (Load Preferences in Windows). Navigate to the .prefs file and double-click on it.

Saving Preference Presets

Some writers may need different settings for varying types of writing projects, such as screenplays and nonfiction. Other writers may use one group of settings during the writing process and another when they're revising. Saving your preferences as a preset saves time when you organize and switch between preference sets. To save a preset:

1.   Click the Manage button at the bottom of the Preferences window.

2.   Select Save All Preferences As Preset.

3.   In the dialog box, shown in Figure 2.12, name the preset.

Please enter a name for this preset:

The preset will be saved in ~/Library/Application Support/
Scrivener/PreferencePresets and will be available in the
"Manage..." menu.

Cancel   OK

FIGURE 2.12

Preference presets are stored differently than other preference files.

4.   Click OK.

CAUTION   When you click the Manage button again, you see your preset appear as a menu option. This makes it faster to load this set of preferences in the future. When you save a preference file using the Save All Preferences command, you can choose where to save the file. Preference presets, on the other hand, are stored in Scrivener's Application Support folders in your Library folder. Choose Scrivener, Reveal Support Folder in Finder from the menu, then double-click on the PreferencePresets folder. If you're comfortable accessing your Library folder, you can copy the .prefs file from there onto a flash drive or another folder for access to the file on another computer. Otherwise, you can save the same preferences using both methods described above so you have a copy of the preferences wherever you need it.

Of course, once you save your preferences, you have the option of sharing them with other Scrivener users. Once you're an experienced Scrivener user, you may want to share your preference files with a newbie to help him or her get started with all the most useful settings already selected.

Saving Theme Preferences

The All Preferences files save all of your settings, including Backup, Navigation, and Import/Export settings. If you use a Mac and all you care to save or share are your color and font schemes, use the Save Theme Preferences option instead. Theme preferences only save the settings that control the appearance of Scrivener. Thus, all of your Customizable Color settings, the Corkboard and Outliner appearance, and Composition mode settings are saved. You can also save fonts in a theme, if you choose.

To save theme preferences:

1. Click the Manage button at the bottom of the preferences window.

2. Select Save Theme Preferences.

3. In the Save dialog box, shown in Figure 2.13, navigate to the folder where you want to store your preference files.

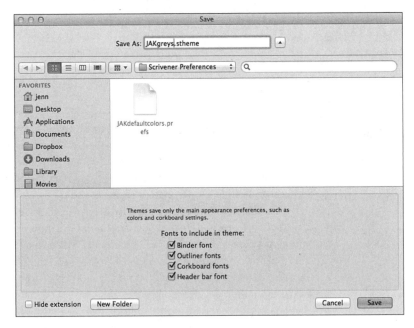

FIGURE 2.13

Theme presets can include the fonts for key Scrivener elements.

4. Enter a name for the file.

5. Select which fonts you want to save with the theme preferences.

6. Click Save.

Save theme presets using the same steps as saving preference presets. When prompted for a filename, you are also prompted to select which fonts you want to save with the theme.

 NOTE Sorry, Windows users, although you can save preference files in Windows, you cannot save theme preference files or presets.

THE CREATIVE PROCESS: YOUR WRITING CANVAS

Now that you know how to customize Scrivener, the actual choices are up to you. Your writing canvas can be a very personal matter. Just as some writers create a music playlist for each book, I create a different color scheme for each project. I know another writer who changes her theme presets on an almost daily basis depending on either her own mood or the type of scene she's writing that day. Feel free to play with your environment—if nothing else, it's a wonderful procrastination tool under the guise of working.

 CAUTION If you've been playing with all of the preferences tabs and changing colors at random and find you've made a muddle of things, you can easily restore order by clicking the Defaults button at the bottom of the Preferences/Options window. This restores all of the settings and colors to their original state. You can also reset individual colors by clicking the Use Default Color button below the color swatches in the Appearance tab. In Windows, click the Use Default Font button to restore individual font settings.

Using Workspace Layouts

Beyond the preference settings, there is much more to Scrivener that can be customized to support your workflow. One of the most useful of these is layouts. When you exit Scrivener, it automatically saves the layout—which elements are visible or hidden, the Group View mode, and which options are being used in each element—so you return to the same settings the next time you open your project. Better still, you can save different layouts to easily switch between them.

When you begin working on a project, you might need only the Corkboard so you can throw ideas up without worrying about their order or tagging it with meta-data. Later, you might use the Binder along with the Corkboard as you tease a story out of all those bits and pieces. At some point, you might want to use the Inspector along with the Binder to add label and status tags, choose which files to include in the compiled manuscript, and view comments and footnotes. When you write a scene, you might want to split the Editor into two windows, so you can refer to research in one while writing in the other. Your needs change as your project progresses.

 TIP Once you save a layout, you can use it in any project without having to start from scratch.

Layouts contain the following elements:

- The size of the Scrivener window, its position on your screen, and the size of each of the open elements

- The visibility of the toolbar, ruler, and format bar

- The toolbar's icon size on the Mac

- The visibility of the Header and Footer bars

- The Binder's status—visible or hidden—and whether the Collection tab is visible or hidden

- The Binder's mode and how it affects documents in the Editor

- The Inspector's status—visible or hidden

- The Editor's layout, how the window is split, and whether the Editor is locked in place

- The Group View mode in the Editor—whether each window in the Editor displays the single text mode, Corkboard, Outliner, or Scrivenings mode

- The auto-load state of the editor—if the editors are linked to that, selecting an item in the Corkboard or Outliner loads it in the other screen

- Whether each split in the Editor is in Page view or the standard view

- The Full Screen status on the Mac (Mac OS X 10.7 Lion and above, only)

- The Corkboard and Outliner settings (optional)

- The use of label and status meta-data on index cards, in the Outliner, and in the Binder, and visibility of keyword chips on index cards (optional)

Creating Layouts

The first step to creating a layout is to adjust all of the interface elements to your liking. When you first begin using Scrivener, you may be fine-tuning and adjusting a lot to see what works for you, but you'll soon find yourself settling into a particular group of features and settings that suit you. To save the layout:

1. Open the Layouts window by choosing Window, Layouts, Manage Layouts (in Scrivener for Windows, choose View, Layout, Manage Layouts), as shown in Figure 2.14.

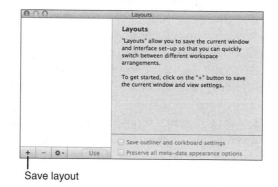

Save layout

FIGURE 2.14

The Layouts window explains the purpose of layouts. If you've previously saved a layout, a preview of the first layout in the list appears in place of the instructions.

2. Click the plus sign (+) button at the bottom of the Layouts window.

3. Enter a name for your layout.

4. Press Return (Enter).

The pane on the right now displays a preview of your layout, as shown in Figure 2.15. The left column lists the name of your new layout.

Saved layout

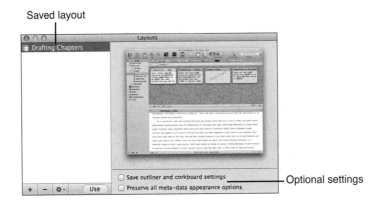

Optional settings

FIGURE 2.15

The preview pane in the Layouts window displays a Snapshot of the selected layout.

Beneath the preview pane are two optional settings you can select with your layout. The Save Outliner and Corkboard Settings option saves the column visibility and sorting in the Outliner and the index card size, ratio, and spacing in the Corkboard. Select Preserve All Meta-Data Appearance Options to save the appearance of keyword chips and the status stamp on the Corkboard and the tinting of documents to match the label tag in the Binder, Outliner, and Corkboard. These settings are optional because you can choose to apply them in a particular instance by toggling the check boxes for the layout before clicking the Use button.

NOTE   The Corkboard and Outliner options are explained in Chapters 6 and 7, "Storyboarding with the Corkboard" and "Plotting in the Outliner," respectively. Learn more about setting visual cues to meta-data in Chapter 12, "Putting Keywords and Meta-Data to Work."

To save additional layouts, adjust the settings in your project and then repeat steps 1–4 above.

Accessing Layouts

Once you create a couple of layouts, switching between them is easy. You can apply a layout using one of the following options:

- Select the layout from the Layouts window and click the Use button at the bottom of the window.

- Choose Window, Layouts, Manage Layouts (or View, Layout, All Layouts if you use Windows) and choose a layout from the submenu.

- Click and hold the Layouts button on the toolbar, and then select a layout from the pop-up menu.

NOTE The Layouts button is on the default toolbar on the Mac. Windows users can add this button by customizing the toolbar, which is explained later in this chapter. When you click the Layouts button in Windows, it opens the Layouts window, from which you can select a layout and click the Use button.

Modifying Layouts

As you work in a layout, your needs may change. Perhaps you're using a different computer with a larger or smaller display and want to resize the entire Scrivener window or adjust which elements are visible. Make the changes you want to your workspace and then do the following:

1. Open the Layouts window.
2. Select the name of the layout you want to modify.
3. Click the gear button at the bottom of the window.
4. Select Update Selected Layout from the pop-up menu.

If you make drastic changes, you notice them in the preview pane.

Renaming Layouts

Many Scrivener users don't realize the Layouts feature even exists, but those who do tend to create layouts for every aspect of their writing process. As you add more layouts, you may find that the name you initially used is not descriptive enough or doesn't fit the naming pattern you've chosen for other layouts. To rename a layout:

1. In the Layouts window, double-click the name of the layout you want to rename.
2. Enter a new name for the layout.
3. Press Return (Enter).

TIP Consider naming your layouts with the phase of writing you're in when you use it. For example, you could save your layouts as Brainstorming, Research, Writing, Story Analysis, and Revisions.

Deleting Layouts

If you no longer wish to keep a layout, you can delete it by following these steps:

1. In the Layouts window, select the name of the layout you want to delete.

2. Click the minus sign (-) at the bottom of the window.

3. A message appears to remind you that you cannot undo this action. Click OK to delete the layout.

 CAUTION As the dialog box warns, you cannot change your mind once you delete a layout. If you're unsure whether you'll need a layout again in the future, consider renaming it to xBrainstorm or something similar, and then see if you find yourself returning to it for a period of time. On the Mac, saved layouts are automatically sorted alphabetically, so prepending an x to the name moves the layout to the bottom of the list.

Exporting and Importing Layouts

Layouts are not project-specific, so you can access them from any project. If you want to use a layout on another computer or send it to another writer, you can export it.

 CAUTION Layouts are platform-specific. You cannot use Mac layouts in Windows, and vice versa.

To export a layout:

1. Open the Layouts window.

2. Select the layout you want to export.

3. Click the gear button at the bottom of the window.

4. Select Export Selected Layout from the pop-up menu.

5. In the Save dialog box (Export Layout in Windows), choose a name for the exported layout.

6. Select where you want to save the exported layout.

7. Click Save.

If you receive a layout from a friend or want to use a layout you exported from a different computer, either copy the file onto your hard drive or insert the flash drive or other media into your computer. Mac layout files have a `.scrlayout` extension while Windows files have a `.scrivlayout` extension.

To import the file into Scrivener:

1. Open the Layouts window.
2. Click the gear button and select Import Layout from the pop-up menu.
3. In the Import dialog box, select the file to import.
4. Click Open.

The imported layout is added to the Layouts window.

Customizing the Toolbar

The toolbar at the top of the Scrivener window contains buttons for the most common features, but you can add or remove buttons to suit your needs. You can customize the toolbar in both Windows and the Mac, although the procedure is different for each.

On the Mac, customize the toolbar as follows:

1. Choose View, Customize Toolbar from the menu. Alternatively, right-click on the toolbar and choose Customize Toolbar from the context menu.
2. Drag icons from the Customize Toolbar window, shown in Figure 2.16, into the toolbar.

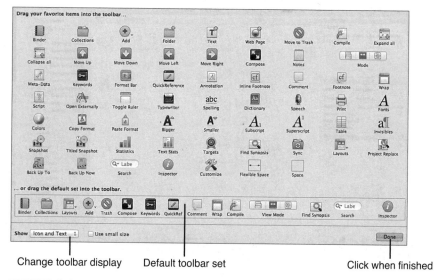

Change toolbar display   Default toolbar set   Click when finished

FIGURE 2.16

The Customize Toolbar window provides many extra tools you can add to your toolbar.

3. Drag icons off the toolbar to remove them.

4. Click the Done button when you finish making changes.

If you want to display the name of the button beneath the icon, click the drop-down menu button at the lower left of the Customize Toolbar window and choose Icon and Text. You can also opt to display only the icon or only text. If you want to hide the toolbar completely, choose View, Hide Toolbar on the Mac or View, Toolbar in Windows.

 TIP   Notice in the figures in this book that I have chosen to display Icon and Text for demonstration purposes. Once you're familiar with the icons, you may choose to hide the Text to save a few pixels of screen real estate. If you forget the name of a button, you can hover over it to view the ToolTip.

You can return to the default toolbar at any time by dragging the default set from the Customize Toolbar window into the toolbar.

If you want to customize the toolbar in Windows, do the following:

1. Select Tools, Customize Toolbars from the menu to open the Customize Toolbars window, shown in Figure 2.17.

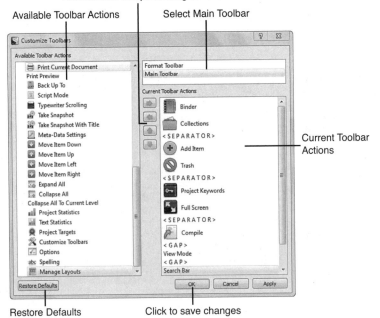

FIGURE 2.17

In Windows, you can add format options to the toolbar.

2. Click Main Toolbar in the upper-right pane.

3. Select an action from the Available Toolbar Actions list to add to the toolbar.

4. Click the right-arrow button in the middle of the window to add the action to the Current Toolbar Actions.

5. Use the up- and down-arrow buttons to position the new button where you want on the toolbar.

6. To remove a button, select the action in the Current Toolbar Actions list and then click the left-arrow button.

7. Click Apply to preview your new setting without closing the dialog box. When you're satisfied with your choices, click OK to save your changes and exit the dialog box.

TIP Consider adding the Layouts button to the Windows toolbar, as mentioned earlier in this chapter.

THE ABSOLUTE MINIMUM

The following are the highlights from this chapter:

- Scrivener automatically saves your project whenever you stop typing for 2 seconds.

- You can change the color of just about every aspect of the interface and control the appearance of the Binder, index cards, the Outliner, and Composition mode.

- On the Mac, the Editor can wrap text to the width of the window like a text editor or to the margins of a virtual page like a word processor.

- The font you choose while working in the Editor can differ from the font you use in your compiled manuscript.

- Layouts allow you to save your workspace and reuse the same layout in multiple projects.

- The toolbar can be customized for quick access to your most-used features.

IN THIS CHAPTER

- Working with files and folders
- Adding documents and folders to the Binder
- Organizing documents and folders in the Binder
- Adding icons to documents and folders
- Importing an existing manuscript
- Focusing on the chapter at hand

3

ORGANIZING THE BINDER

If Scrivener were a bakery, the Editor would be the baker. The Inspector would be the person responsible for labeling and describing the items. The Binder's duties would include taking down all the orders and streamlining the workflow. Without the Binder, the bakery would be in chaos. This chapter covers the Binder, the management system of Scrivener.

As the manager of your project, you create the files for each scene or chapter and choose the order in which all of your documents and folders appear in the Binder. You also choose the order in which you complete each of those documents. One advantage Scrivener has over a word processor is that you don't have to work in a top-down fashion. Before you can come up with a plan for writing your project, however, you need to understand how to use the organizational tools of the Binder.

Working with Files and Folders

As mentioned in Chapter 1, "Getting to Know the Scrivener Interface," files and folders can both be used almost interchangeably to hold text and as a container with subdocuments. Folders are commonly used to provide structure to your project and designate chapters or parts when you compile your work. This is covered in Chapter 19, "Compiling Your Completed Work."

The default icon associated with each type of item varies by its content, as shown in Figure 3.1.

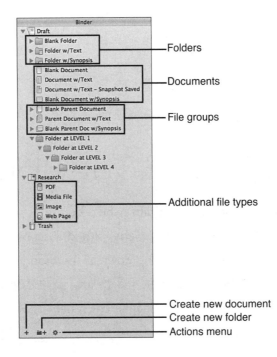

FIGURE 3.1

This Binder shows the various default icons you see for each type of content. The Actions menu (gear icon) at the bottom of the Binder can be used in place of the context menu.

You might discover that terminology of items in Scrivener is almost as fluid as the concept of files and folders itself. The following lists the ways in which you see files and folders referred to within this book, the Scrivener support documentation, and among the user community:

- **Items**: Files or folders of any type, whether empty or containing content.

- **Containers**: Any item that has subitems. This is also referred to as a parent, with any of its subdocuments or folders being referred to as children.

- **Files**: Also referred to as documents or text, these are items that are intended to hold text. In the Binder, the icon for an empty file is a blank sheet of paper. If the file contains a synopsis but no text, it appears in the Binder as an index card. Files with text have an icon showing a page of text; if the document has been saved with a Snapshot, the icon shows a corner of the icon folded down.

- **Folders**: A container for documents or subfolders. In the Binder, an empty folder displays a folder icon, whereas a folder with text displays a folder with a document. Folders with a synopsis but no text display an index card overlay.

- **File groups**: Files containing subdocuments or subfolders. The Binder icons for file groups are similar to those of files, but appear as a stack of papers rather than a single sheet.

 NOTE Folders and file groups can also appear with a folded corner, indicating that it has been saved with a Snapshot.

As you can see in Figure 3.1, the Binder indents files and folders to display the hierarchy of the items. There are three *root folders* that are present at the top hierarchy in every Scrivener project. These folders are as follows:

- **Draft**: This folder contains your actual writing project. For the most part, everything you put into this folder is compiled as part of your manuscript or other completed work.

 NOTE You can exclude files from the compiled work, as discussed in Chapter 11, "Digging into the Inspector."

- **Research**: This folder is intended for research and supporting files related to your project. This may include PDFs, media files, images, and web pages, as well as your own notes and documents.

- **Trash**: This folder holds any item you delete so it is out of sight, but can still be restored.

You can rename these folders to suit your purposes. Some project templates rename the Draft folder to Manuscript, for example. You can also create additional root folders. Some project templates add root folders to store Character and Setting worksheets. On the Mac, you may also discover a Template Sheets folder in certain project templates. I like to add a Pitch folder to my projects so I can work on my synopsis and track submissions.

CAUTION   Although you can add more root folders, you cannot delete the three default folders.

As you add nontext files to the Research folder (or any other folder with the exception of the Draft folder and its subfolders), you see additional file types, each represented by a different icon, as follows:

- **Portable Document Format (PDFs)**: Documents formatted to appear the same on all platforms, complete with layout.

- **Media**: Audio/video files formatted as `.mov`, `.mpg`, `.wav`, or `.mp3`, and so on.

- **Images**: Photographs and graphic images formatted as `.tif`, `.jpg`, `.gif`, `.png`, `.bmp`, and so on.

- **Web pages**: Web archive documents (`.webarchive`) and HTML files.

- **Unsupported formats**: Files that cannot be viewed within Scrivener can still be imported into your Research or other (non-Draft) folder. When you select one of these files in the Binder, the Editor window displays a link to open the file in the appropriate application.

TIP   Discover how to import nontext files into your Research folder in Chapter 8, "Organizing Your Research."

CAUTION   Nontext files cannot be directly placed in the Draft folder. You can, however, embed image files into your documents, such as adding figures to a nonfiction work or illustrations to a children's book. See Chapter 4, "Writing in the Editor," for details on adding images to a document.

THE CREATIVE PROCESS: THINKING ABOUT YOUR FILE STRUCTURE

There is no need to force yourself into a strict act/chapter/scene structure in Scrivener if your actual process is much different. Set up your project to match your workflow.

If you follow the Hero's Journey narrative pattern, consider setting up folders or file groups for The Call to Adventure, Refusal of the Call, and so on, and then add scenes within them. If you use the Snowflake plotting method, you can start with a synopsis on a single index card for step 1, expand it into step 2 in the document text, and move on to creating additional documents and subdocuments as you proceed through the steps.

Nonfiction writers often need to pay more attention to the structure of their project as this type of work may involve parts, chapters, sections, and subsections. The book you hold in your hand is a good example. I've chosen to set up each part as a folder, with subfolders for each chapter within the part folder. Each section within a chapter is a file group, with subsections created as documents within that container.

No matter how you approach your project, you can always move files and folders around later, so organizing your scenes into chapters can come much later in your process.

TIP   When you first set up your file structure, don't worry too much about whether you use folders or file groups, as long as you're consistent, because you can easily convert them from one to the other. Select the item or items you want to switch and then right-click to bring up the context menu and select Convert to Folder (or Convert to File, for the opposite). You can also select the items and click the gear button at the bottom of the Binder to bring up the same menu.

Adding Documents and Folders to the Binder

Once you've thought about how you want to set up your file structure, it's time to start putting it into practice. As with most aspects of Scrivener, you can work in whatever order you want. If you already know your manuscript is going to be 20 chapters long or if you decide to set up your file structure to match the Hero's Journey, you can set up all of your folders at once. If you write by the seat of your pants, you can create folders and documents as you need them.

TIP If you already have an existing manuscript created in another application, read "Importing an Existing Manuscript" later in this chapter before setting up your file structure.

The Blank project template creates an initial Untitled document in the Draft folder. Other templates create an initial folder and file. You can use these items as a starting point.

Adding Text Documents

To add a document:

1. Select the folder, file, or file group under which you want to add the document.

2. Choose one of the following:

   • Press Return (Enter).

   • Click the Add button in the toolbar.

   • Click the Create New Document button, the plus sign (+), at the bottom of the Binder.

   • Right-click the folder and select Add, New Text from the context menu.

   • Choose Project, New Text from the menu.

   • Press Cmd-N (Ctrl+G, N in Windows).

   An Untitled document appears in the Binder, as shown in Figure 3.2.

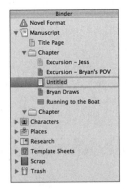

FIGURE 3.2

A blank new document has been added beneath an existing document. Notice that the Draft folder has been renamed Manuscript.

3. Enter a name for the file.

4. Press Return (Enter) .

TIP As you can see in Figure 3.2, your filenames are not important. Choose a name that is meaningful to you, such as the key element of the scene.

NOTE Figure 3.2 shows icons tinted in various colors. Learn how to associate colors with Label meta-data and apply it to various Scrivener interface elements in Chapter 12, "Putting Keywords and Meta-Data to Work."

The position of the new document depends on which item you selected before adding the document. If you select a folder, the new document appears as the last item in the folder. If you select a file or file group, the new document appears right below the file/file group, at the same level in the hierarchy.

Adding Folders

Adding a folder is similar to adding a file. The easiest method for adding a folder is the following:

1. Select a file or folder in the Binder.

2. Choose one of the following:

- Click and hold the Add button in the toolbar and then select New Folder from the pop-up menu. In Windows, click the arrow to the right of the Add button.

- Click the Create New Folder button, the folder with plus sign (+), at the bottom of the Binder.

- Right-click and select Add, New Folder from the context menu.

- Choose Project, New Folder from the menu.

- Press Option-Cmd-N (Ctrl+Shift+N in Windows).

An Untitled folder appears in the Binder, as shown in Figure 3.3.

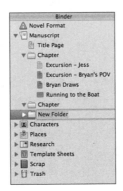

FIGURE 3.3

A new folder has been added to the Manuscript root folder.

3. Enter a name for the folder.

4. Press Return (Enter).

On the Mac, when you select the Draft or Research folder before adding a folder, the new folder is created as a subfolder. When you select any other root folder before adding a folder, the new folder becomes a sibling of the root. When you select a subfolder, file, or file group first, the new folder is added at the same level as the existing item. In Windows, new folders are always created at the same level as the existing item, even if the Draft or Research folder is selected.

Adding a Folder at the Root Level

For some writers, the three default root folders are all you need to organize your project, possibly along with any extra folders included with one of the project templates. As I mentioned, I like to include a Pitch folder in my projects. I also add a Scrap folder to all of my projects so I can move unused scenes or other bits and pieces that I don't want to risk permanently deleting in the Trash. I have accumulated dozens of worksheets at writing conferences over the years, many of which I use to help guide the evolution of my story, so I also create a Plotting folder to store those worksheets in progress (I rarely complete all or even most of them).

To add a root-level folder:

1. Right-click in the empty area of the Binder below the Trash.

2. Select Add, New Folder from the context menu.

3. Enter a name for the folder.

4. Press Return (Enter).

5. Drag the new folder to where you want it positioned in the Binder.

The new folder appears with the default icon. On the Mac, you can apply a custom icon to any item in the Binder. Even if you don't opt to apply custom icons to the rest of your files and folders, you may want to use them with root folders.

Adding a File at the Root Level

Ninety-nine percent of the time, you will only create files within folders. You may notice some project templates, however, have a file at the very top of the Binder containing instructions and tips for using that template. You can add a similar document to your project, but you cannot simply create a text file outside a folder. Instead, use one of these methods:

- Create a new document anywhere in the Binder and drag it to the top of the Binder.

- Create a new root folder (or a folder anywhere in the Binder) and drag it to the top of the Binder. Then right-click on the folder and select Convert to File from the context menu.

- Because files and folders can function in the same way, you could also simply create a root folder, drag it to the top of the Binder, and then add text to it.

Grouping Documents and Folders

If you use a nonstandard file structure while writing your story—or perhaps just write all your scenes before sorting them into any sort of structure at all—you can create a new folder and populate it with selected files and folders in one fell swoop.

Group items into a folder using the following method:

1. Select the items:

- Click the first item and then Shift-click the last item to select consecutive items.

- Cmd-click (Ctrl+click in Windows) each item to select noncontiguous items, as shown in Figure 3.4.

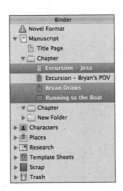

FIGURE 3.4

You can select sequential or nonsequential files and folders.

2.   Use one of the following commands:

   • Right-click and choose Group from the context menu.

   • Select Documents, Group from the menu.

   • Click the gear icon at the bottom of the Binder and choose Group from the pop-up menu.

   • Press Option-Cmd-G (Ctrl+G, G in Windows).

3.   Enter a name for the new folder that appears.

4.   Press Return (Enter).

The new folder appears at the same level in the hierarchy as the selected files or folders.

TIP   This approach is useful when you import a manuscript you wrote in another application. Split your manuscript into scenes (described in the "Splitting and Merging Files" section later in this chapter) and then group appropriate scenes into chapter folders.

Organizing Documents and Folders in the Binder

When you create files and folders, items may not populate exactly where you want them. Others might need a name change somewhere down the road. You inevitably wind up with a handful of untitled files and folders that you created but never used. In short, creating items in the Binder isn't enough; you need to organize and maintain it.

Moving Items

The easiest way to move items around in the Binder is to simply drag and drop them. As explained above in the "Grouping Documents and Folders" section, you can select multiple items at once. To drag and drop items within the Binder:

1. Select one or more items.

2. Holding down the mouse button (or clicking on your trackpad), drag the items over the file or folder into which you want to place them. A bubble appears around the target file or folder as you hover over it. A blue line shows you where the items will be dropped within that container. See Figure 3.5.

FIGURE 3.5

The bubble highlights the target container, while the line designates where the items will be dropped within that container.

3. Release the mouse button.

You can also move items by selecting them and choosing one of the following methods:

- From the menu, select Documents, Move, To, and then choose a location from the submenu. In Windows, select Documents, Move To and then choose a location from the submenu.

- Right-click and select Move To from the context menu; then choose a target location from the submenu.

- Click the gear icon at the bottom of the Binder; then select Move To and choose a target location from the submenu.

- From the menu, select Documents, Move and then Left, Right, Up, or Down to move the selection.

- Use the keyboard shortcuts for the previous commands: Left, Control-Cmd-Left Arrow (Ctrl+Left Arrow in Windows); Right, Control-Cmd-Right Arrow (Ctrl+Right Arrow); Up, Control-Cmd-Up Arrow (Ctrl+Up Arrow); Down, Control-Cmd-Down Arrow (Ctrl+Down Arrow).

These commands move the selection one position in the hierarchy. For example, if you move a selection left, it moves it up one level in the file hierarchy. You can use these commands in combination. Select a file and move it to the left, for example, then move it up. The file is moved above the container in which it was originally located.

NOTE These commands cannot be used on selections of multiple documents that are at different levels or in different containers.

TIP On the Mac, hold the Option key while dragging in the Binder to prevent dropping the selection onto a noncontainer item. If you have set the Option key to duplicate items (in the Navigation tab of the Preferences window), however, this tip will not work. Choose the behavior that you anticipate needing most often.

Duplicating Items

Many project templates contain an initial chapter folder and scene document. A quick method for creating similar containers and items is to duplicate them. As with every other action in the Binder, there are several ways to duplicate items. First select the item, then choose one of the following:

- Select Documents, Duplicate from the menu. Select either With Subdocuments and Unique Title or Without Subdocuments from the submenu.

- Press Cmd-D (Ctrl+D in Windows) to duplicate the selection with any subdocuments, or press Shift-Cmd-D (Shift+Ctrl+D) to duplicate the selection without subdocuments.

- Right-click and choose Duplicate from the context menu to duplicate with subdocuments.

- Click the gear icon at the bottom of the Binder; then choose Duplicate from the pop-up menu to duplicate with subdocuments.

- On the Mac, press the Option key while dragging. This creates a duplicate of the original rather than moving it.

CAUTION   To enable duplicating a file and subdocuments using the Option-drag method, you first need to enable it in the Navigation tab of the Preferences window. Again, this feature is only available on Scrivener for Mac.

After you've duplicated an item, you can give it a unique name.

Renaming Items

As you work, you may decide to rename an item to distinguish it from a similar item elsewhere in the project. For example, in Chapter 1, you create a scene entitled On the Patio. This makes sense as you write Chapter 1, but what if you return to the patio in Chapter 5, and again in Chapter 7? Three scenes entitled On the Patio may cause confusion when you search your project or create collections (covered in Chapter 16, "Searching Your Project"). And of course, if you use the Duplicate command described in the previous section, you need to rename the duplicate items.

To rename an item, double-click the item to select the title and then type a new name. You can also right-click the item and select Rename from the context menu, then type the new name. If you don't like your hands to leave the keyboard, select the item and then press the Esc key on the Mac or the F2 key in Windows, then type over the current name.

NOTE   If you want to navigate the Binder mouse-free, use the arrow keys to move around. The up- and down-arrow keys move as expected, up and down one item at a time. The left- and right-arrow keys toggle the visibility of a container's subdocuments. Press the left-arrow key when viewing a child document to move the focus to the parent container. Press Control-Option-Up Arrow (Ctrl+Shift+Up Arrow in Windows) to go to the previous container or Control-Option-Down Arrow (Ctrl+Shift+Down Arrow in Windows) to go to the next container.

Deleting Items

As you work, you are bound to create unnecessary files and folders. If you are certain you will not need those items again, send them to the Trash.

TIP   You never know when you'll find a use for an abandoned scene or piece of research you think is unimportant. Instead of deleting items that contain text, put them into a separate Scrap folder (you learned how to create an additional root folder earlier in this chapter). Save the Trash can for items that you know are truly garbage, such as blank, untitled documents and folders or a spare duplicate of an item.

To delete one or more items, select the item; then do one of the following:

- Drag the item to the Trash folder.
- Right-click and select Move to Trash from the context menu.
- Select Documents, Move to Trash from the menu.
- Click the Trash icon in the toolbar.
- Press Cmd-Delete (Shift+Delete in Windows).

If you change your mind or move something to the Trash by mistake, you can rescue it. View the Trash folder just like any other folder in the Binder and move items out of it using one of the methods described earlier in this chapter.

The Trash folder can eventually become unwieldy and slow down your project with unnecessary items. To empty the Trash, right-click anywhere in the Binder and select Empty Trash from the context menu. You can also select Project, Empty Trash from the menu.

 CAUTION   Always look through all the items in the Trash folder before emptying the folder! Once you use the Empty Trash command, you cannot recover your deleted files, and this step cannot be undone. Remember, Murphy's Law states that the one file you accidentally deleted instead of moving to a scrap or other holding folder contains the critical piece of research or snippet of dialogue you need to make your story complete.

Adding Icons to Documents and Folders (Mac Only)

Mac users can customize the icons associated with any file or folder. Personally, I leave the file and folder icons in my Draft folder alone, as the default icons convey a lot of useful information. But I create several additional root folders in my projects, and I give each of them a unique icon. I have also personalized the icons for some of the worksheet files I create when brainstorming.

To change an icon:

1. Select the item or items you want to customize. You can change several files or folders to the same icon at once.

2. Choose one of the following options:

   • Right-click and then select Change Icon from the context menu.

   • Choose Documents, Change Icon from the menu.

3. Select an icon from the submenu, as shown in Figure 3.6.

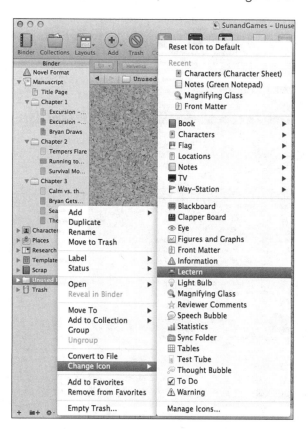

FIGURE 3.6

The Icons submenu contains several colorful options to customize items in the Binders.

Installing Additional Icons

If the preinstalled icons don't quite suit your needs, you can install additional icons you download from the Internet or create yourself. Scrivener accepts files in .png,

.tif, .jpg, or .gif format, and automatically resizes images to the 16×16 pixel icon size, if necessary. To install new icons:

1. Choose Documents, Change Icon from the menu, then select Manage Icons from the submenu.

2. In the Manage Icons dialog box, shown in Figure 3.7, choose from the following:

    - **Icons in Project Package**: Adds icons to the project file, but does not make them available to any other project.

    - **Icons in Application Support**: Adds icons to the Application Support folder in order to make them available to all of your projects.

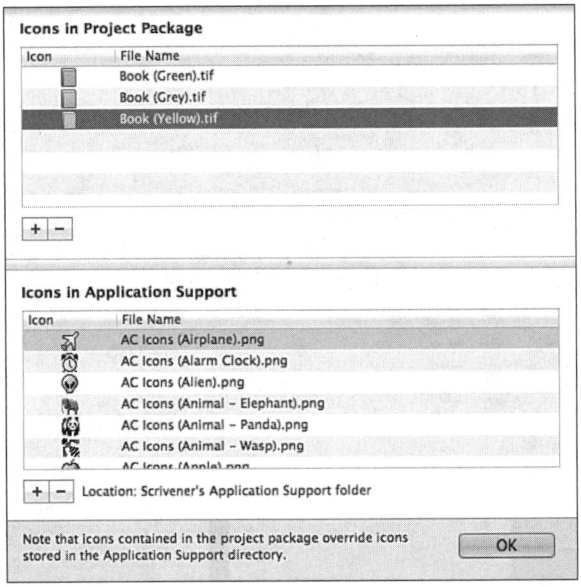

FIGURE 3.7

Add icons to your current project or make them available to all projects.

3. Click the Add (+) button beneath the appropriate list.

4. In the Open dialog box, select the icon or icons you want to add, and then click Open.

5. Click OK to exit the Manage Icons dialog box.

TIP The forum on the Literature & Latte website (http://www. literatureandlatte.com/forum) is a good source for writing-related icons. Many members have uploaded icon file packages. Search the forum for "custom icons."

The new icons are added to the Change Icon submenu. To remove an icon, return to the Manage Icons dialog box, select the icon, and click the Remove (–) button.

Restoring Original Icons

If you are writing a book or blog article about Scrivener and need to show the default settings, or if you simply change your mind about a custom icon, restore the default icon as follows:

1. Select the item or items with the icon.

2. Choose Documents, Change Icon, Reset Icon to Default from the menu. You can also access this command from the context menu.

Importing an Existing Manuscript

If you're new to Scrivener, you may want to import manuscripts you've written in other applications into Scrivener. When you import a manuscript, Scrivener makes a copy of it, leaving the original untouched.

 CAUTION Any changes you make to the imported manuscript in Scrivener are not updated in the original file. Once you import, you have two completely distinct files: the original document and the Scrivener project.

Scrivener converts the following file types in order to import them:

- **Rich Text Format (.rtf):** This is the most Scrivener-compatible option. Scrivener can convert the entire document, including footnotes and comments.

- **Rich Text Format Directory (.rtfd):** This Apple format is used for its proprietary applications, such as Pages. Unfortunately, because Apple does not share this format, other applications have a difficult time converting from it, especially such items as footnotes, comments, and images. If you created your document in Pages, it is best to save as .doc or .docx before importing into Scrivener. If you created your document in TextEdit, you may want to save your document in RTF before importing into Scrivener.

- **Microsoft Word (.doc or .docx)**: When you import a Word document, Scrivener uses a converter to attempt to retain as much formatting as possible. If you encounter trouble importing in this format, return to Word and resave your document in RTF before importing.

- **Open Document Text (.odt)**: Files with this extension were created in OpenOffice. As with Word documents, Scrivener attempts to convert the file, but you may need to try again in RTF if you lose too much formatting. Scrivener for Windows cannot import .odt files, so you should save to RTF or .doc if you are using that platform.

- **Plain Text (.txt)**: Plain text documents don't have much formatting in the first place, so importing them into Scrivener doesn't present any problems.

- **Outline Processor Markup Language (.opml)**: This format is most commonly used by outlining and mind map applications. When you import these files, Scrivener preserves the outline hierarchy in the Binder. If you have text notes attached to the items, Scrivener puts this material in the main text of the item.

- **Mindmap (.mm)**: This format is used by Freemind and other mind map applications. When you import these files, Scrivener preserves the outline hierarchy in the Binder. This option is only available on the Windows platform.

- **Index Card for iPad (.indexcard)**: This format allows you to import cards created in Index Card into your project. This option is only available on the Mac platform.

   NOTE You can also keep Index Card for iPad and Scrivener synced to use your iPad on your Scrivener projects. See Chapter 18, "Taking Scrivener Out and About," for more about using iPad apps with Scrivener files.

- **Final Draft 8+ (.fdx)**: This is the standard Final Draft format. Script writers can import scripts into the Binder to convert them to Scrivener's script formatting.

- **Final Draft 5-7 Converter (.fcf)**: This format converts scripts created in earlier versions of Final Draft into Scrivener. This option is only available on the Mac platform.

- **Fountain (.fountain)**: This format allows you to import scripts created in Fountain and convert it to Scrivener's script formatting. This option is only available on the Mac platform.

- **No extension**: On the Mac, if a document does not have a file extension, Scrivener attempts to import it as plain text. Scrivener treats documents with

MultiMarkdown (`.xml`, `.tex`, `.mmd`, `.md`, or `.markdown`) extensions in the same way. In Windows, files without a file extension are treated as unsupported file types.

Setting Import Preferences

Before importing a document, examine the options in the Import & Export tab of the Preferences (Options) window, as shown in Figure 3.8. Look for the options for the type of file you want to import, paying particular attention to how footnotes and comments are imported.

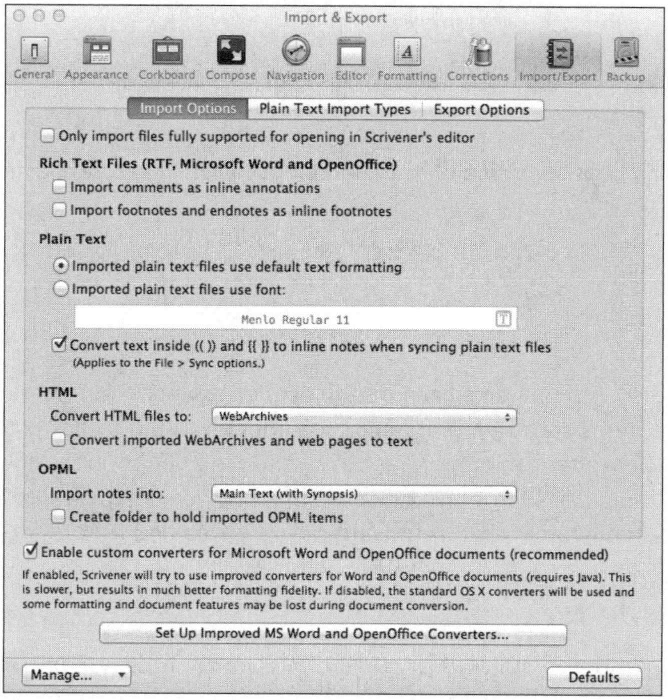

FIGURE 3.8

The import preferences tell Scrivener how to handle comments and footnotes and enable advanced converters for Word and OpenOffice documents.

In Windows, if you choose the Use Microsoft Word or Open Office for DOC and DOCX Conversions option, you must restart Scrivener before your selection takes effect. You must also have Word 2007 or higher or OpenOffice installed on your computer.

Importing Documents

The fastest way to import a text document is to drag and drop it into your Scrivener project. The first time you import a document, a warning dialog box pops up, shown in Figure 3.9. You can also use File, Import from the menu, and then choose a type of file from the submenu. This is best for importing various types of nontext research material because some of the submenu options offer additional options to facilitate the import of that type of data.

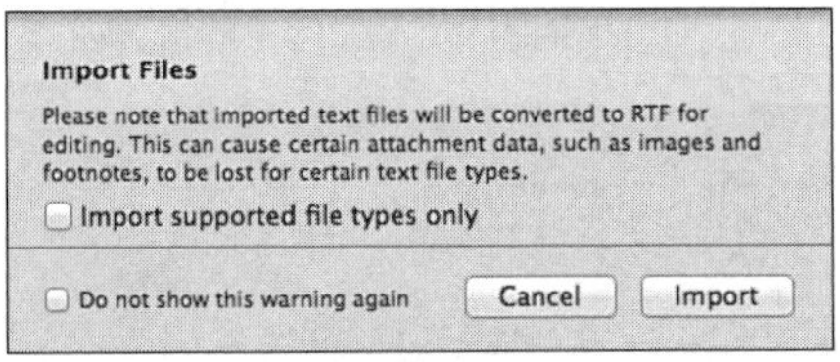

Import Files

Please note that imported text files will be converted to RTF for editing. This can cause certain attachment data, such as images and footnotes, to be lost for certain text file types.

☐ Import supported file types only

☐ Do not show this warning again   Cancel   Import

FIGURE 3.9

This warning pops up whenever you import a document into Scrivener unless you disable it.

NOTE Importing nontext material is covered in depth in Chapter 8.

You can also import items from one Scrivener project into another. To do this, select the items and then drag and drop them into the target project. To import an entire Scrivener project into another, choose File, Import, Scrivener Project from the menu. As with other types of imports, Scrivener creates a copy of the source material rather than removing or merely linking it from the source.

Splitting and Merging Files

When you import a manuscript created in a word processor, you're left with a single file containing the entire work. Continuing to work with the manuscript in this way might be counterproductive now that you have all the tools of Scrivener at hand. Once imported, consider splitting the manuscript into multiple documents.

To manually split a document, you first need to select the document in the Binder. The text appears in the Editor pane. Then do the following:

1. Click in the Editor to position your cursor at the first spot where you want to split the manuscript.

2. Choose one of the following:

- Choose Document, Split, At Selection from the menu.

- Right-click and choose Split At Selection from the context menu.

- Press Cmd-K (Ctrl+K in Windows). This option is particularly useful as this is often a very repetitive task.

3. A new document is created with all of the content after the split point. Enter a name for the new file.

4. Press Return (Enter).

Repeat these steps throughout your manuscript, clicking to put the cursor at the next split point in the new document.

 TIP You can also use the Split with Selection as Title command in the Documents, Split submenu. Select the first few words of text, then choose Documents, Split, With Selection as Title or press Option-Cmd-K (Ctrl+Shift+K in Windows). This splits the selection at the beginning of the selection and automatically uses the selection as the document title.

If you make a mistake and split the document at the wrong point, you can merge files together. Select the documents you want to merge and choose Documents, Merge from the menus or the keyboard shortcut Shift-Cmd-M (Ctrl+M).

Using Import and Split

If your original document already uses dividers between scenes, you're in luck! As long as the separator character is on its own line between scenes, Scrivener can import and automatically split the document. Follow these steps to import and split:

1. Choose File, Import, Import and Split from the menu.

2. In the Import and Split window, shown in Figure 3.10, locate the file you want to import.

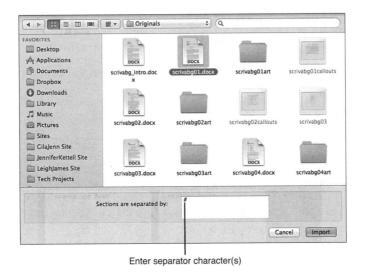

Enter separator character(s)

FIGURE 3.10

Locate the file to import and enter the separator character to import and split in one step.

3. The default scene divider is the pound (#) key. If your document contains a different separator character or a set of characters (such as ###), enter it in the Sections Are Separated By box.

4. Click Import.

The split documents are added to the Binder. The scene dividers are removed as part of the import and split process. It's a good idea to check each of these documents to be certain everything is where you want. You can manually split or merge documents where necessary to clean things up.

Focusing on the Chapter at Hand

Much of this chapter focuses on the early stages of your work, setting up your initial file structure or importing an existing manuscript. Once everything is in place, you will want to focus on the work itself. The Binder can help keep you focused by allowing you to view only the items you currently need.

Revealing and Hiding Items

To the left of any item with subdocuments, you see a triangle. When the triangle points down, the folder or file group is expanded to see any items within it. Click on the triangle to toggle the visibility of items within the container. Use

Option-click (Alt+click in Windows) to expand or collapse all of the items within a container.

 TIP To expand every item in the Binder, select View, Outline, Expand All from the menu (or press Cmd-9 on the Mac). To collapse all of the containers in the Binder, select View, Outline Collapse All (Cmd-0 on the Mac).

If you are moving files and folders around in the Binder, collapsing unnecessary containers can help you pinpoint where to drop an item. You can also drop items into collapsed containers, which can prevent you from accidentally dropping them at the wrong level.

Hoisting the Binder (Mac Only)

When you really want to focus on just a particular chapter or portion of your manuscript, you can block out the distraction of the rest of your manuscript by hoisting the Binder. When you hoist the Binder, it isolates the selected folder or file group in the Binder, as shown in Figure 3.11. You can only access items within the selected container. The name in the Header bar changes from Binder to the name of the isolated container to help you identify which portion of the project you are viewing.

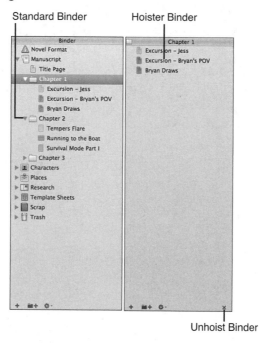

FIGURE 3.11

Hoisting the Binder locks the Binder into the selected container.

To hoist the Binder, select a folder or file group, then choose Documents, Hoist Binder from the menu.

To return to the rest of your project, click the X button at the bottom of the Binder. Alternatively, choose Documents, Unhoist Binder from the menu.

THE ABSOLUTE MINIMUM

The Binder is the management system for all the items in your project. In this chapter, you learned:

- You don't have to conform to a fixed act/chapter/scene structure when drafting your work. You can reorganize your work into chapters and other groupings later.

- The root level of every project contains Draft, Research, and Trash folders. You can add other folders to the root level, but you cannot delete the three default folders.

- On the Mac, you can change the icon associated with an item. You can add extra icons you create yourself or find online.

- You can move files between folders, including the root folders, and convert files to folders or folders to files.

- You can store nontext files such as PDFs, images, movies, and web pages in your project, but they cannot be added to the Draft folder.

4

WRITING IN THE EDITOR

You might be wondering when you actually learn to write using Scrivener. This is it! Scrivener offers a lot of tools and window dressing, but in the end it's all about getting your words on the page.

The Editor is the element of Scrivener that most resembles a word processor, so it may feel familiar. As you will discover, it's much more than just a word processor, but that's a good starting point. To that foundation, this chapter adds an understanding of how to work in Split Screen mode, work on multiple documents at once, and how to access QuickReference panels and the Scratch Pad to keep you working efficiently.

To begin, select a document in the Binder. The document opens in the Editor window.

NOTE There are other ways in which the Binder and Editor interact as you use other forms of navigation, split the screen, and use other modes, as is explained later in this chapter, but this should do for now.

Examining the Editor Window

The Editor consists of the following major components, as shown in Figure 4.1:

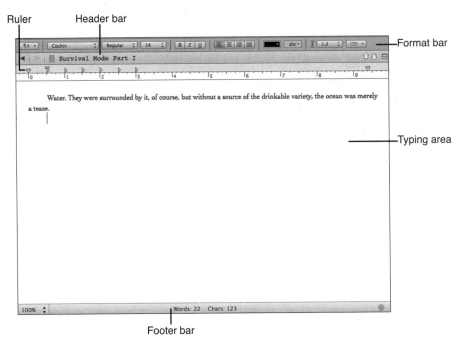

FIGURE 4.1

The Editor is where your manuscript comes to life.

- The **space** where you type your document (or view the Corkboard or Outliner in other view modes). As you soon discover, you can split this area into two screens, each of which works as a fully functional Editor.

- The **Format bar** contains settings for the font, typeface, size, paragraph alignment, color, and spacing of your text. It also contains a Formatting Preset button that allows you to apply a preset combination of formatting options at once.

- The **Header bar** contains navigation buttons, the document title, and buttons to control splitting the Editor. It also includes an Item icon, which provides access to other commands.

- The **Ruler** controls the tab and indent settings for the Editor.

- The **Footer bar** provides different options depending on the type of document you want to view in the Editor. These include the Zoom menu, the document's word and character count, and access to the word count target settings.

Understanding how each of these components works saves you considerable time as you navigate through your manuscript and format your work.

Using the Header Bar

At first glance, the Header bar, shown in Figure 4.2, is rather unassuming. It contains the title of the current document and a few buttons on either end, and that looks to be it. Those buttons can save you a lot of time navigating the Binder, however, so they're worth a closer look.

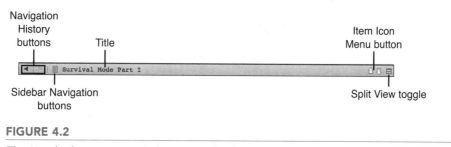

FIGURE 4.2

The Header bar contains navigation and Split Screen controls.

Even the title itself doubles as a tool. If you want to change the document name, select the title, type a new name, and then press Return (Enter). This change is immediately reflected in the Binder and Inspector.

Navigation History Buttons

As you work in the Editor, Scrivener saves a history of which documents you used. On the Mac, the Navigation History buttons on the left side of the Header bar let you access this history. Let's say you were writing a scene in Chapter 5 and then went back to a scene in Chapter 1 in order to change the name of the protagonist's dog. Rather than scrolling through the Binder to find the scene you left in Chapter 5, click the Back button. If you decide Isadora isn't a good dog name, after all, click the Forward button to return to the scene in Chapter 1 once again.

If you want to skip around in the history, click and hold either the Back or Forward button, then select a document from the pop-up menu. Scrivener maintains the history every time you open the project, not just from the current session, so you can use the history menu to access a document you worked on days ago.

CAUTION   When you use the Navigation History buttons, the Binder remains focused on the document you selected in the Binder, even if that is no longer the document open in the Editor. Always look at the title in the Header bar, as opposed to the selection in the Binder, to determine which document is active.

The Item Icon Menu

To the right of the Navigation History buttons is the Item Icon Menu button. This icon looks like the icon representing the file in the Binder. When you click it, the menu with the following options appears (shown in Figure 4.3):

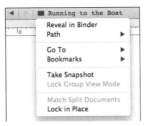

FIGURE 4.3

The Item Icon menu aids in navigation and communication between the Editor and the Binder.

- **Reveal in Binder**: This option solves the problem noted in the Caution above. If you want to see where the active document is located in the Binder, select Reveal in Binder to move the Binder's focus to that document. The keyboard shortcut for this option is Option-Cmd-R (Ctrl+Shift+8 in Windows).

- **Path**: When you select this option, a pop-out menu displays the hierarchy for the current document. You can use this to quickly determine which chapter a scene is located in or move to that container by selecting it.

- **Go To**: Selecting this option opens a pop-out menu that allows you to navigate to any item in your project. As with the Navigation History buttons, the Go To option does not change the focus of the Binder, just the Editor.

Reveal in Binder						
Path ▶						
Go To ▶	△ Novel Format					
Bookmarks ▶	📝 Manuscript ▶		📄 Title Page		
	👤 Characters ▶		📁 Chapter 1 ▶		
Take Snapshot	🖼 Places ▶		📁 Chapter 2 ▶		
Lock Group View Mode	🖼 Research ▶		📁 Chapter 3 ▶		
	📄 Template Sheets ▶				
Match Split Documents	📦 Scrap ▶				
Lock in Place	🗑 Trash ▶				

NOTE When you view multiple documents together in the same Editor pane, known as Scrivenings mode, the Go To menu only displays the items in the group being viewed. When you choose a document from the menu, the Editor focuses on that document's position within the group. Scrivenings mode is covered in more detail later in this chapter.

- **Bookmarks**: In Chapter 16, "Searching Your Project," you learn how to set bookmarks to make it easy to return to marked locations. If you created bookmarks in this document, they are accessible from this menu option.

NOTE Scrivener for Windows does not have the Bookmarks feature, so this option does not appear in the Item Icon menu.

- **Take Snapshot**: This option takes a Snapshot of the active document. Snapshots are explained in Chapter 10, "Editing Your Manuscript."

- **Lock Group View Mode**: On the Mac, this option appears when a container is loaded in the Editor. When selected, it locks the current view mode—Scrivenings, the Corkboard, the Outliner, or single text view—for that container. Whenever you load that container in the Editor, it will always appear in the locked view mode. A small lock icon appears over the selected view mode icon in the toolbar when the locked container is loaded.

- **Match Split Documents**: When you are in Split Screen mode, this feature puts the same document in both panes of the Editor. You can now look at one portion of the document while typing in another portion of the same document.

NOTE This menu option is not available in Scrivener for Windows, although you can still view the same document in each split.

- **Lock in Place**: This option locks the Editor so you cannot change the active document by clicking in the Binder. The Header bar takes on a rust color (red in Windows) as a visual reminder that the Editor is locked.

 NOTE Although Lock in Place prevents you from changing the active document from the Binder, it does not prohibit using the Navigation History buttons or the Sidebar Navigation buttons to navigate to a different document. You can also still drag a document from the Binder into the Header bar to open it. If you use the Go To menu, however, it unlocks the Editor.

 TIP Lock in Place is most commonly used when in Split Screen mode, as you discover in this chapter, but it can also be convenient if you're working on a document and decide to add a new document or change the order of scenes in the Binder. With the Editor locked, you can make your changes in the Binder without losing your place in the active document.

Sidebar Navigation Buttons

The Sidebar Navigation buttons to the right of the title are used to select the next or previous document in the Binder's hierarchy. These buttons not only change the active document in the Editor but also change the Binder's focus.

 TIP Remember, the Navigation History buttons explore the history of the documents you've written, whereas the Sidebar Navigation buttons rely upon and also affect the sidebar to determine the next or previous document to view. The affected sidebar is usually the Binder, but these buttons can be used to navigate search results and collections, as well. You can read about searching and collections in Chapter 16.

Splitting the Screen

The rightmost button in the Header bar is the Split View toggle. This button turns Split Screen on and off. Scrivener for Windows has two separate buttons to split the screen vertically or horizontally.

Split Screen mode lets you divide the Editor into two separate panes. Each pane becomes its own full-featured Editor, complete with Header and Footer bars, so you can work on two documents at once.

THE CREATIVE PROCESS: REASONS TO SPLIT THE SCREEN

There are several reasons why you may want to split the Editor screen:

- To view the Corkboard or Outliner in one pane while working on a document in the other. If you're a plotter, this is helpful because you can see what's coming in your story as you're writing a scene so you can lay the proper groundwork and foreshadowing.

- To refer to your research in one pane while working on a document in the other. If you create worksheets for each of your characters or settings, you can refer to these sheets, as well, so your blonde-haired hero who has an unfortunate rhubarb allergy doesn't meet his downfall by innocently eating a slice of pie, which clings to his brown hair when he falls face-first into it as he expires.

- To view the end of one scene while writing the beginning of the next scene, so your transitions are smooth.

- To compare a Snapshot version of a document with the current version. This is only possible on the Mac.

- To multitask, alternating between working in two documents at once. When writing the book you hold in your hands, splitting the screen has enabled me to work primarily on one chapter while also writing paragraphs of related information in another chapter.

- To scroll to another part of the document you're working on without losing your place. If you can't remember if the hero was eating rhubarb pie or apple, you can split the screen and view the same document in both panes. Any changes you make in one pane will be immediately reflected in the other, and you can make changes to the same document in either or both panes.

Splitting the Editor

To split the Editor, choose one of the following options:

- Click the Split View toggle in the Header bar to split the screen horizontally, divided into top and bottom panes. In Windows, click the Horizontal Split button.

TIP Scrivener for Mac splits the Editor horizontally by default the first time you split the screen using the Split View toggle. After that, it splits the screen either horizontally or vertically depending on which setting you last used.

- To split the Editor vertically, into side-by-side panes, press the Option key while clicking the Split View toggle. In Windows, click the Vertical Split button.
- Choose View, Layout, Split Horizontally (or Split Vertically) from the menu.
- Press Option-Cmd-= (Ctrl++ in Windows) to split horizontally or Cmd-" (Ctrl+Shift+') to split vertically.

When you first split the screen, both panes contain the same document, as shown in Figure 4.4. The color of the Header bar indicates the status of the document— blue for the active pane and gray for the inactive pane.

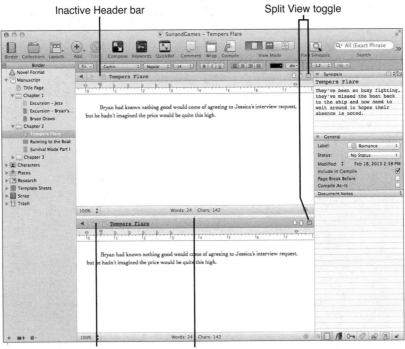

FIGURE 4.4

When you first split the Editor screen, the same document appears in both panes.

Between the two panes is a window sizing handle. The panes are originally equal in size, but you can drag the handle to change the proportions. Each pane also has its own Footer bar, so you can adjust the zoom and see word count information for each document independently of the other.

Selecting an Item in Split Screen

When you first split the Editor, the document that was active in the Single Screen view becomes the active document in Split Screen view. Earlier in this chapter, you learned how to use the Header bar to navigate in your project. Those skills come to good use when you're in Split Screen mode. The Go To option in the Icon Item menu provides a reliable method for opening a document in the desired Editor. You can also use the Navigation History and Sidebar Navigation buttons.

Another way to load a document into one of the Editor panes is to drag it from the Binder and drop it onto the Header bar of the desired pane.

 CAUTION   On the Mac, if you drop the document into the Editor pane itself instead of onto the Header bar, the contents of the document are copied into the document that was previously open in that pane.

You can also click in an Editor pane and then click a document in the Binder. In most cases, the document opens in your chosen Editor pane. You can change this behavior, however, and combine several Scrivener options to create your ideal writing environment.

Binder Affects Menu

Let's say that you like to keep a character sheet handy for the POV (point-of-view) character as you write, as shown in Figure 4.5. You use this to keep track of what you know about the character as you're writing the scene, so you can stay in that character's frame of reference. You then add to this character sheet as other traits become apparent.

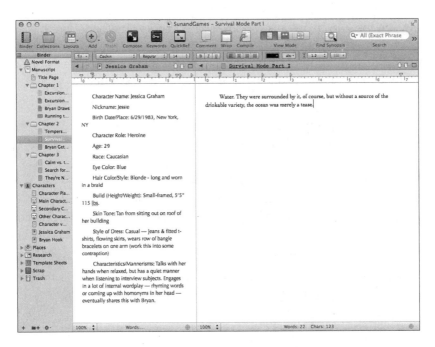

FIGURE 4.5

You can get creative with how you use the Split Screen mode. Here, a character sheet is in the left Editor pane while a scene is being written in the right pane.

No matter which Editor is active—whether you are writing a scene or adding new insight to the character sheet—you want that character sheet to remain in the Editor even as you move items in the Binder or select new documents to edit. To ensure this, use the Lock in Place option from the Icon Item menu, as described earlier. This prevents you from accidentally opening a document from the Binder in that pane even if it's the active Editor.

 TIP   Remember that each Editor pane has its own Header bar, so if you plan to use the Lock in Place option, be sure to select it from the proper Icon Item menu.

But what happens when you click on a document in the Binder when the locked Editor is active? Scrivener has addressed this situation with the Binder Affects menu. If you select View, Binder Affects, you find the following options:

- **Current Editor**: The default setting; any time you select a document in the Binder, it opens in the currently active Editor pane. If the active pane is locked, the document does not open.

- **Other Editor**: This option always loads the selected document into the inactive Editor pane.

- **Left Editor Only**: When the Editor is split vertically, this option always loads the item selected in the Binder into the left Editor pane.

- **Right Editor Only**: When the Editor is split vertically, this option always loads the item selected in the Binder into the right Editor pane.

- **Top Editor Only**: When the Editor is split horizontally, this option always loads the item selected in the Binder into the top Editor pane.

- **Bottom Editor Only**: When the Editor is split horizontally, this option always loads the item selected in the Binder into the bottom Editor pane.

 NOTE   The appearance of the Left, Right, Top, and Bottom options on the Binder Affects menu is determined by the type of split in the Editor. In Windows, the word *Only* does not appear on the menu options.

So to continue our example, if your character sheet is in the left Editor pane, select View, Binder Affects, Right Editor Only to ensure that clicking in the Binder only changes the document in the right Editor pane.

Scrivener for Mac users has an additional setting to control the Binder-Editor interaction in the Navigation tab of the Preferences settings. Select Binder Selection Affects Other Editor when Focused Editor Is Locked if you always want the selected document in the Binder to open in the unlocked Editor pane. If both Editors are locked, selecting a document in the Binder does nothing.

Closing a Split

If you want to return to Single Screen view, choose one of the following:

- On the Mac, click the Split View toggle button in the Header bar of the document you want to remain active in the Single Screen view. In Windows, click the No Split button.

- Choose View, Layout, No Split from the menu.

- Press Cmd-' (Ctrl+' in Windows).

Saving Your Layout

In Chapter 2, "Customizing Your Work Environment," you learned how to use layouts. Once you have everything positioned the way you want in the Editor window, don't forget to save the layout. The layout preserves the Split Screen view, the Binder Affects setting, the sizing of each pane in the Editor, and the visibility of the various Editor bars.

TIP To refresh your memory, select Window, Layouts, Manage Layouts on the Mac or View, Layout, Manage Layouts in Windows to access the Layouts window.

Formatting Text and Paragraphs

Although Split Screen view assigns a separate Header bar, Footer bar, and Ruler to each pane, there is only one Format bar, shown in Figure 4.6. If you want to change the appearance of your text or the alignment of a paragraph or list, you make those changes using the Format bar.

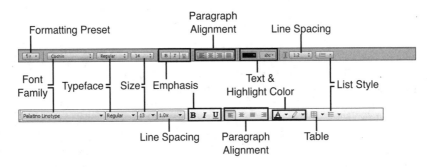

FIGURE 4.6

The top Format bar is from the Mac platform. The bottom Format bar is from the Windows platform.

NOTE The Format bar is also used to apply formatting to the Notes pane in the Inspector. The font and size options can also be used to format comments and footnotes in the Inspector.

The Format bar contains the following options:

- **Font family**: You can choose from any font you have installed on your computer.

NOTE Remember, the font you use while drafting your manuscript does not have to be the same font you choose when you compile. Use a font that's comfortable for your eyes.

- **Typeface**: Some fonts have variations, such as Light or Condensed. If these are available for your chosen font, you can select one of these alternatives here.

- **Size**: Change the size of the font here.

TIP Instead of increasing the font size, consider using the Zoom feature in the Footer bar to increase the appearance of text on your screen. This gives you the option of decreasing the Zoom at other times during your writing process so you can see more words on the screen without having to adjust the font size.

- **Emphasis**: Choose from Bold, Italic, or Underline if you want to add emphasis to your text. Remember to check the submission guidelines for your publisher; some publishers prefer underlining while others accept italic in manuscripts. If you submit to multiple publishers, you can convert from one emphasis style to another in the Compile settings, as explained in Chapter 19, "Compiling Your Completed Work."

CAUTION On the Mac, if you cannot set bold or italics, it is likely because the font you are using does not have a bold or italic variant. You can confirm this by looking at the options in the Typeface drop-down menu. If this emphasis is necessary to your project, change to a similar font with those variants installed.

- **Text color**: Change the color of the text. Click the button to apply the displayed color. Click and hold the button to choose a different color from the available swatches, and then click the Show Colors option to open the Colors dialog box. Windows users, click the down arrow to the right of the Text Color button to access additional color swatches, then click the More button to access the Select Color dialog box.

- **Highlight color**: To highlight text so it stands out from the surrounding text, click the Highlight Color button. As with the Text Color option, you can choose from additional colors, if desired.

- **Paragraph alignment**: The Paragraph Alignment buttons allow you to choose left, center, right, or justified alignment. When you use the justify option, text is aligned to both the left and right margins.

- **Line spacing**: Line spacing adjusts the spacing between lines of text. The line spacing you choose while working on your project can be changed automatically when you compile it, so choose the spacing that is most comfortable for your eyes right now. Choose Other (More in Windows) to open additional options.

- **List style**: To create a bulleted (unordered) or numbered (ordered) list, click the List Style button and then select a list format. In Windows, click the down arrow to the right of the List Style button. Once you select a list style, you can type your list by pressing the Tab key to increase the indent of the bullet or number in order to demote the item or Shift-Tab to reduce the indent in order to promote the item. Press the Return (Enter) key twice to end the list and return to the previous paragraph style.

- **Table**: Windows users can select the down arrow to the right of the Table button and insert or adjust the properties of an existing table. You can also click the Table button itself to open the Table Properties dialog box, shown in Figure 4.7, for an existing table. Mac users can add a table from the Format, Table menu (which Windows users can also access). Mac users can also add a Table option to the toolbar (but not the Format bar) by choosing View, Customize Toolbar in the menu and then dragging the Table icon onto the toolbar.

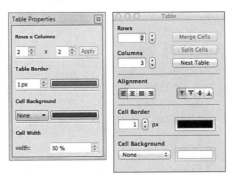

FIGURE 4.7

The Table Properties dialog box is accessible from the Format bar in Windows or the Format, Table menu on the Mac and Windows. The Windows dialog box is shown on the left and the Mac on the right.

 NOTE Table options are limited by the operating system. Scrivener is not intended to be a layout program, so more elaborate tables should be created in an appropriate third-party application.

To apply formatting, you can select the options you want and then start typing. You can also select a block of text and apply the formatting only to the selection. Paragraph alignment and line spacing are applied to entire paragraphs.

TIP   All of the Format bar options are also available from the Format menu.

Preserving Formatting

If you have formatted a block of text with specific attributes that you want to preserve even when you compile your manuscript, you can designate it as exempt from any formatting changes during compilation. To do this, select the text and then choose Format, Formatting, Preserve Formatting. Preserved text is designated with a dashed outline and a light-blue background.

 NOTE   This feature is not available in Windows.

To remove preserved formatting, select the text and choose Format, Formatting, Preserve Formatting to deselect that option.

Using Formatting Presets (Mac Only)

If you're a Mac user, you can save time selecting formatting options. If you use the same combination of formatting options on a regular basis, consider saving them as a formatting preset. A preset applies several formatting options at once, such as adding a section heading in 14-point Helvetica, bold, with center alignment. Presets are also good for portions of your work that need to be set apart from standard paragraphs, such as a block quote.

 CAUTION   Formatting presets do not work in the same manner as styles in Microsoft Word or other word processors. A formatting preset simply applies a group of formatting options at once for convenience. If you change the formatting preset, it will not update any text to which the preset was previously applied.

THE CREATIVE PROCESS: PUTTING FORMATTING PRESETS TO WORK

Formatting presets are particularly useful if you need to use a number of different headers and other formatting styles consistently throughout your project. For this book, for example, I created presets for each type of section heading, figure captions, callouts, and sidebars. Although I still had to apply styles for each of these when I compiled my project into Word documents in order to apply Que's template, it made drafting chapters much faster and sped up the find-and-replace process in Word.

If you are adding a lot of formatting to your text, you may also opt to set up your compile settings so that they do not override your formatting. See Chapter 19, "Compiling Your Completed Work," for more information about preserving or overriding compile settings.

To apply a formatting preset:

1. Select the text to which you want to apply the preset.

2. Click the Presets button in the Format bar. This is the leftmost button on the bar.

3. Select a preset from the drop-down list, as shown in Figure 4.8.

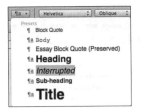

FIGURE 4.8

The Formatting Preset menu lists all of the presets included with Scrivener and that you create yourself.

Creating a Formatting Preset

Scrivener's presets include a few common options, but the more complex your project, the more likely you will want to create your own presets. To create a preset:

1. Select text and format it as you require. If you already have a block of text formatted as you want, you can select that.

2. Choose Format, Formatting, New Preset from Selection. This opens the New Style dialog box, shown in Figure 4.9.

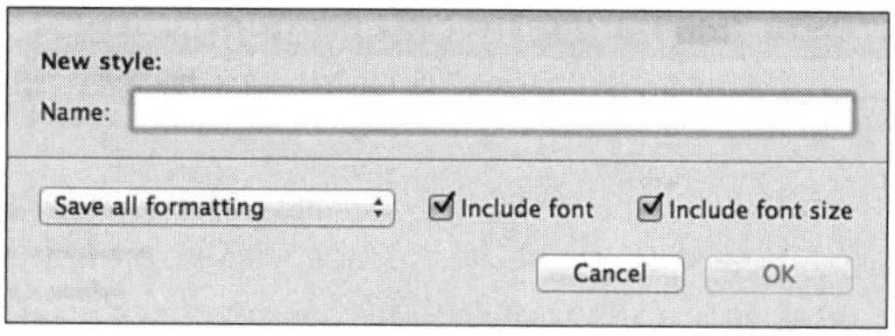

New style:

Name:

Save all formatting ▾   ☑ Include font   ☑ Include font size

Cancel   OK

FIGURE 4.9

Name your preset in the New Style dialog box.

3. Enter a name for the preset.

4. Select an option from the drop-down menu at the lower left of the New Style dialog box:

    • **Save All Formatting**: This is the default and saves both character and paragraph attributes.

    • **Save Character Attributes**: Saves only the character attributes of the selected text.

    • **Save Paragraph Style**: Saves only the paragraph attributes of the selected text.

5. Select the Include Font and Include Font Size check boxes if you want to preserve the font settings along with the other formatting attributes.

6. Click OK to close the New Style dialog box.

7. Click the Presets button in the Format bar to view your preset in the drop-down menu. Presets are automatically alphabetized.

TIP   Presets that contain character attributes display a lowercase *a* before their entries. Presets containing paragraph styles display a paragraph icon (which resembles a backwards *P*). If a preset has both character and paragraph formatting, it displays both icons.

To make changes to a preset, adjust the formatting options on a block of text, select it, and then choose Format, Formatting, Redefine Preset from Selection from the menu. Choose the preset you want to redefine from the submenu.

Deleting a Formatting Preset

Once you create a formatting preset, it is available in all of your projects. If you no longer need a preset, choose Format, Formatting, Delete Preset from the menu, and then select the preset you want to delete from the submenu.

 CAUTION Deleting a preset does not change the formatting of any text to which that preset has been applied. It only prevents you from applying the same preset to additional text. If you delete a preset accidentally, you can simply re-create it.

A WINDOWS VIEW: CREATING A STYLE GUIDE

Although Windows does not offer formatting presets, you should still be consistent in applying formatting options. If your project requires a lot of different formatting, I suggest creating a style guide in your Research folder. In this document, enter every different type of formatting you apply. As an example, if you create a section subheading, enter "Heading 2 – Helvetica 14-point, Bold, Center Aligned" and add that formatting to the entry as a visual clue. You can use the Format, Text, Copy Ruler/Paste Ruler and the Format, Font, Copy Font/Paste Font commands to copy and paste formatting into your style guide. When you create a new heading, you can copy and paste this entry into your document and then type over the wording. Alternatively, you can turn to this style sheet as a reference to manually apply the proper formatting options to your text.

Accessing the Ruler

Below the Format bar is the Ruler. You can choose whether or not to display the Ruler. If the Ruler is not visible, choose Format, Show Ruler or press Cmd-R (Ctrl+Shift+R in Windows). If you are in Split Screen mode, each Editor pane has its own Ruler, and you can show or hide each pane's Ruler independently.

The Ruler, shown for both Mac and Windows in Figure 4.10, usually provides default tab stops every half-inch for the first few inches, although some templates may provide different tab stops.

 TIP You can change the default tabs and indents from the Formatting tab of the Preferences window on the Mac or the Editor pane of the Options window in Windows.

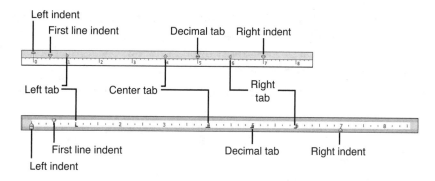

FIGURE 4.10

The Ruler gives you control over tabs and indents. The Mac Ruler is shown on top and the Windows ruler on bottom.

The Ruler can be completely modified. You can add or remove tab stops and adjust the types of tab stops. You can also adjust the location of tab stops and indents. If you want Ruler settings to apply to the entire document, set the tab stops and indents before you begin typing. Select paragraphs before modifying the Ruler to apply tab and indent changes to only those paragraphs without affecting the rest of the document. When you press Return (Enter) to begin a new paragraph, it takes on the Ruler settings of its predecessor.

TIP If you want to change the Ruler for the entire document after it has been typed, press Cmd-A (Ctrl+A in Windows) to Select All and then modify the Ruler.

Setting Tabs

To add a tab stop:

1. Right-click the position on the Ruler at which you want to add the tab stop.

2. Select one of the tab stop options from the pop-up menu.

To adjust the position of a tab stop, drag it to a new location on the Ruler. To remove a tab stop, drag it off the Ruler completely.

There are four types of tab stops available:

- **Left**: Aligns text to the left beginning at the tab stop. This is the most common tab stop.

- **Center**: Centers the text to the tab stop.

- **Decimal**: Aligns text with the decimal point at the tab stop, with text before the decimal point aligned to the right and text after the decimal point aligned to the left. Decimal tabs are most often used with columns of numbers, but they can also be used to interesting effect with poetry.

- **Right**: Aligns text to the right, with the right side of the text culminating at the tab stop.

Adjusting Indents

There are three types of indents in Scrivener:

- **Left**: Specifies how far the text is indented from the left margin. Unless you are typing a block quote or other exception to the margin, the left indent should generally be positioned at the margin itself.

- **First line indent**: Indicates how far the first line of a paragraph is indented from the left margin. To eliminate first line indents, move the first line indent marker to the left margin.

- **Right**: Determines how far the text is indented from the right margin. If you are creating a block quote or other exception to the margin, slide this marker to the desired position. In general, however, the right indent defaults to the right margin.

Using the Footer Bar

At the bottom of the Editor window, you find the Footer bar, as shown in Figure 4.11. If you are in Split Screen mode, each pane has its own Footer bar. In Document view, the Footer bar contains the following information:

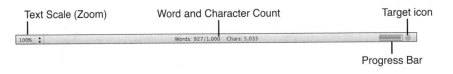

FIGURE 4.11

The Footer bar displays your word count and controls the Zoom setting. Other options appear depending on your settings and mode—Document or Script.

- **Text scale**: This is the zoom control. A pop-up menu provides settings to make the text appear larger or smaller in the Editor window while preserving the actual font settings.

- **Word and Character count**: This shows the number of words and characters in the document. If you set a document target (as explained in Chapter 15, "Tracking Your Progress"), the word count displays as a fraction—the current number of words divided by the target. If you make a selection in Scrivener for Mac, the word and character count turn blue and reflect the counts for the selection.

 TIP   The word count displayed in the Footer bar includes all text displayed in the Editor, including inline annotations and comments. On the Mac, you can refine the word count by clicking the word count in the Footer bar and selecting Include Footnotes and/or Include Comments and Annotations. These options will include Inspector footnotes and Inspector comments and annotations as well as inline notations.

 NOTE   If you are in Script mode, covered in Chapter 21, "Screenwriting in Scrivener," the word and character count do not appear in the Footer bar. If you open a media or other non-text file in the Editor, the Footer bar displays the current playing time or provides other tools for working with that file type.

- **Progress bar**: If you set a document goal for the current document, a progress bar appears in the Footer bar to provide a visual cue of your progress. The bar fills as you reach your goal.
- **Target icon**: This button opens the Target for This Document dialog box, which enables you to set a document goal.

Checking Spelling

Even if you previously took first place at the National Spelling Bee, you will inevitably make typos as you work. Scrivener provides two methods for checking your spelling, either automatically as you work or manually whenever you choose.

Automatic Spell Checking

To turn on automatic spell checking for a project, choose Edit, Spelling and Grammar, Check Spelling While Typing. If you want to always check spelling automatically, choose Scrivener, Preferences from the menu, and then select the Corrections tab. From there, select the Check Spelling as You Type in New Projects check box. If you want Scrivener to also check your grammar, select the Check Grammar with Spelling in New Projects check box as well.

To enable automatic spell checking in Windows, choose Tools, Options to open the Options window, and then select the Corrections tab. From there, select the Check Spelling as You Type check box.

 NOTE Scrivener for Windows does not perform grammar checking. This is not necessarily a bad thing, however, particularly if you write fiction. Grammar checkers are rigid constructs that don't adapt to the more conversational tone of fiction, particularly when it comes to dialogue.

With automatic spell checking enabled, Scrivener marks misspelled words with a red dotted underline. Right-click on the word to open a context menu, as shown in Figure 4.12. If Scrivener has spelling suggestions, they appear at the top of the menu. If the spelling is correct, click Learn Spelling to add the word to the dictionary. You can also Look Up or Ignore the spelling from this menu.

 TIP Both the Mac and Windows provide several other dictionary and search tools. On the Mac, choose Edit, Writing Tools to access the full Mac Dictionary app, perform a Spotlight search, or search Google or Wikipedia. In Windows, choose Tools, Writing Tools to look up words and other information from various research sites. In Windows, you can even access the Translator feature on the Reference.com site (http://translator.reference.com) to translate the selected word or phrase into another language.

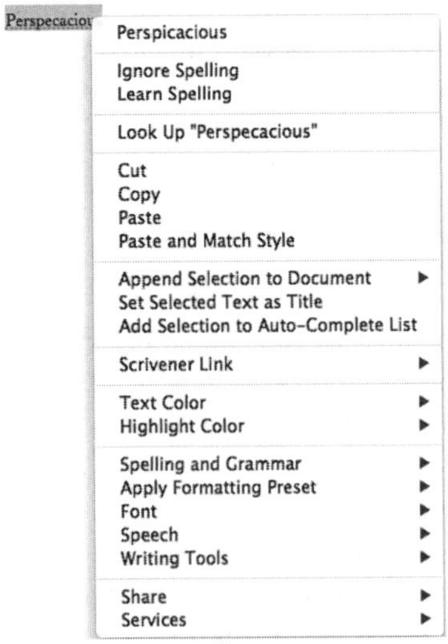

FIGURE 4.12

Did you misspell perspicacious? Scrivener points out the error and offers the correct spelling in the context menu.

Manually Checking Your Spelling

If you find automatic spell checking to be distracting, you can disable it in the Preferences/Options window so Scrivener no longer performs this service. In Windows, this disables automatic spell checking for all projects, but on the Mac you need to choose Edit, Spelling and Grammar, Check Spelling While Typing from the menu to turn it off on existing projects. You can still check spelling when you want.

On the Mac, choose Edit, Spelling and Grammar, Show Spelling and Grammar from the menu to open the Spelling and Grammar dialog box, shown in Figure 4.13. Scrivener moves through your document showing misspellings and allowing you to change each in turn.

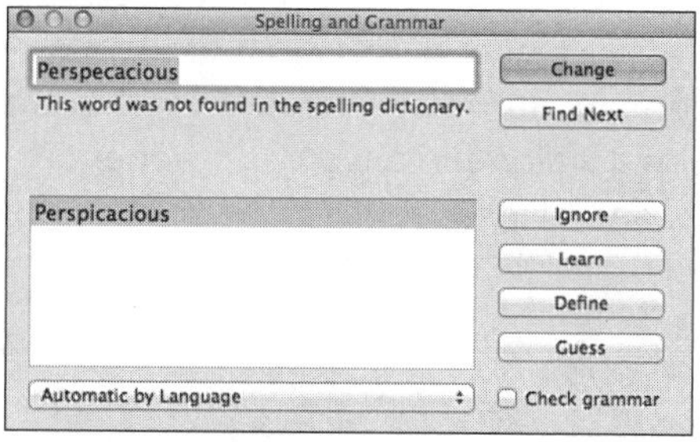

FIGURE 4.13

The Spelling and Grammar dialog box on Scrivener for Mac displays the misspelled word in the top pane and suggests corrections in the lower pane.

In Windows, choose Tools, Spelling from the menu to open the Spelling dialog box, shown in Figure 4.14.

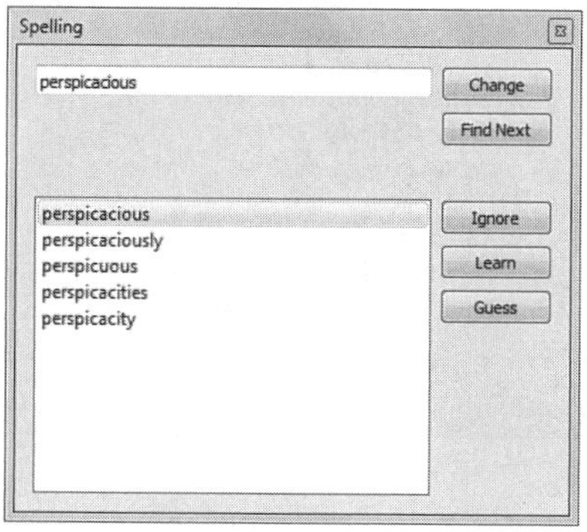

FIGURE 4.14

The Spelling dialog box on Scrivener for Windows tends to provide more suggested spellings than that of the Mac version.

TIP If you prefer to check spelling all at once before you compile your project, disable the automated spelling option. When you want to check the spelling, select the Draft folder in the Binder and choose View, Scrivenings to put the complete manuscript into the Editor as one long document. Then initiate the manual spell check. In Windows, the spell-check stops at the end of each document in Scrivenings. Click into the next document in the Scrivenings session in the Editor to continue spell checking.

Automating Corrections as You Type

Scrivener can automate certain common corrections as you type. Choose Scrivener, Preferences from the menu (Tools, Options in Windows) and then click the Corrections tab (see Figure 4.15). Most of the auto-corrections are selected by default. Among them are automatic capitalization of the first word in a sentence and the letter *i* when it's alone in a word. Scrivener can also substitute smart quotes, em dashes, and ellipses for straight quotes, double hyphens, and triple periods, respectively.

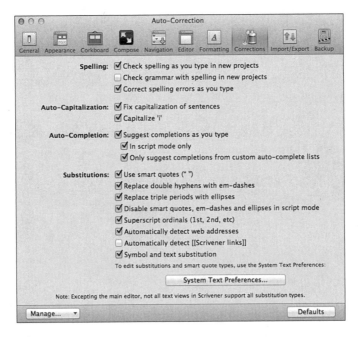

FIGURE 4.15

The Corrections tab in the Preferences window controls spelling and automatic substitutions.

Scrivener can also suggest word and phrase completions for you with custom phrases you add on a per-project basis. Let's say your characters have long names or you use scientific terms in your project. Add those names and terms to the Auto-Complete List, and you no longer have to worry about typing those long words or spelling them correctly.

If you want to enter words or phrases to the Auto-Complete List as they arise, select the word or phrase in your document, then right-click and select Add Selection to Auto-Complete List. To add several words or phrases to the list at once:

1. Select Project, Auto-Complete List from the menu. The Auto-Complete List dialog box for the current project opens, as shown in Figure 4.16.

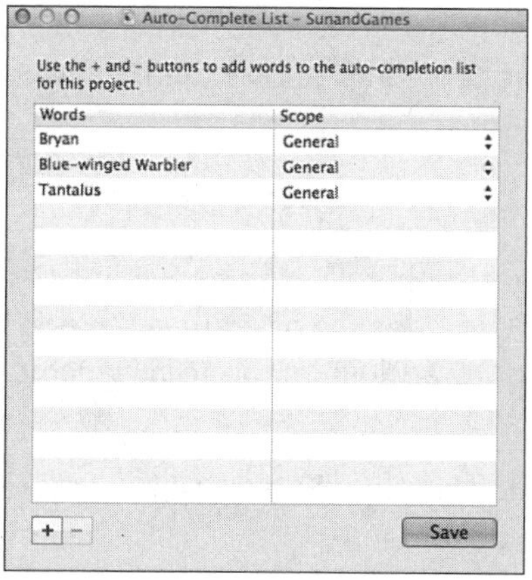

FIGURE 4.16

Create a custom list of words and phrases to automatically complete as you type.

2. Click the Add button (the plus sign).

3. Enter a word or phrase.

4. Select the Scope for the auto-completion on the Mac, as follows:

    • **General**: This is the default and applies to all projects except screenwriting documents.

    • **All (Text & Scripts)**: If you work on a screenwriting project, this option makes the entry available in all scripting elements.

    • **Script**: The remaining options apply to specific scriptwriting elements. Words and phrases are generally added to these scopes automatically as you work on your script. See Chapter 21 for more information about this feature.

5. Repeat steps 2–4 to add more words to the list.

6. Click Save (OK in Windows) to save your entries and close the dialog box.

 TIP Although Auto-Complete Lists are project-specific, you can copy entries between projects by opening both projects simultaneously and then dragging and dropping terms from one Auto-Complete List dialog box to the other. This tip only applies to the Mac, however.

To use your list, Scrivener can automatically suggest completions as you type if you choose Suggest Completions as You Type in the Corrections tab of the Preferences/Options window. If these automatic suggestions distract you, you can use a keyboard shortcut to activate the completion menu when you want Scrivener to complete the word for you. On the Mac, use either the Esc key or Option-Esc to activate the completion menu. In Windows, press Alt+=.

Adding Images to a Document

Although fiction authors generally don't have images in their manuscripts, nonfiction authors and academics often need to add figures and illustrations to their work. If you want to add an image to a document, choose from the following methods:

- Drag an image file from the Finder (Windows Explorer in Windows) or the desktop into the document.

- Paste an image from the clipboard.

- Drag an image from the Binder, Outliner, or Corkboard into the document.

- Choose Edit, Insert, Image from File from the menu.

When you place an image into a document, Scrivener creates a copy of the image, even if it was dragged into the document from another area in the project. This means, however, that if you modify or swap the original image, the change is not reflected in your document.

If you need to resize an inline image, double-click on it to bring up the Resize Image dialog box, shown in Figure 4.17. Use the sliders to increase or decrease the size of the image or enter an exact size in the dimensions fields. Click OK to save your settings and exit the dialog box.

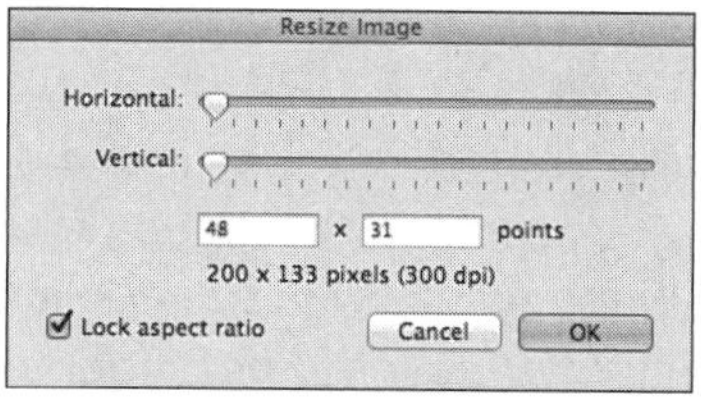

FIGURE 4.17

The Resize Image dialog box on the Mac controls the size of an inline image.

In Windows, right-click on the image and choose Edit Image from the context menu to open the Edit Image dialog box shown in Figure 4.18. Enter the new dimensions for the image and click OK to exit the dialog box.

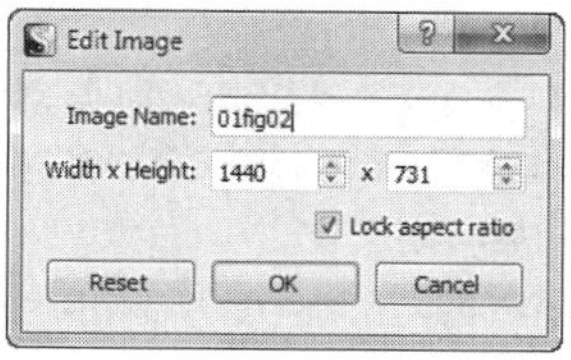

FIGURE 4.18

The Edit Image dialog box in Windows controls the size of an inline image.

Inserting Linked Images (Mac Only)

If you're using Scrivener for Mac and you want the option of being able to change your image file without holding up your project, use linked inline images. Linked images use placeholders within your document so you can determine placement and size, but the actual image file remains outside your project. To create a linked image, choose the Edit, Insert, Image Linked to File command from the menu.

CAUTION If you downloaded Scrivener from the Mac App Store, you may need to authorize Scrivener to access the directory where your image is stored. To do this, choose Scrivener, Authorize Directory Access from the menu.

When using linked images, Scrivener updates the placeholder with the current image. When you compile your draft, the current version of the linked image is embedded into the document.

Embedding PDF Images (Mac Only)

On the Mac, you can also embed PDF files into a document. Although you cannot embed a multipage PDF document, this option is useful for inserting graphics that have been saved in PDF format. As with other inline images, simply drag the PDF file from the Finder (Windows Explorer) or Binder into your document.

CAUTION The PDF file must fit within the page margins of your document. If necessary, crop the PDF file using Preview or Adobe Acrobat Pro before embedding it into your document in Scrivener.

Viewing Scrivenings

When you write a scene, it's generally enough to focus on just that one scene. When you write the transition from one scene or chapter to the next, however, or if you are editing your manuscript, you may want to see how all those bits and pieces in the Binder flow together. This is where *Scrivenings* comes in.

If you are working on one document on a single screen in the Editor, you're in Document view. If you are working with two or more documents on a screen, you're in Scrivenings view. To enter Scrivenings view:

1. Select a container or series of items in the Binder. Select the Draft folder (which may have been renamed to Manuscript or some other title) to see your entire manuscript in one long document.

2. Choose one of the following options:

    - Click the Scrivenings icon in the Group mode of the toolbar.

    - Choose View, Scrivenings.

    - Press Cmd-1 (Ctrl+1 in Windows).

When you are in Scrivenings mode, as shown in Figure 4.19, the title displays the name of the container if you are viewing an entire container or the words *Multiple Selection* if you selected multiple separate items. As you move the insertion point on the Mac, the title is appended with the name of the current active file. On the Mac, files are divided by graphic horizontal rules. In Windows, files are divided by dashed lines.

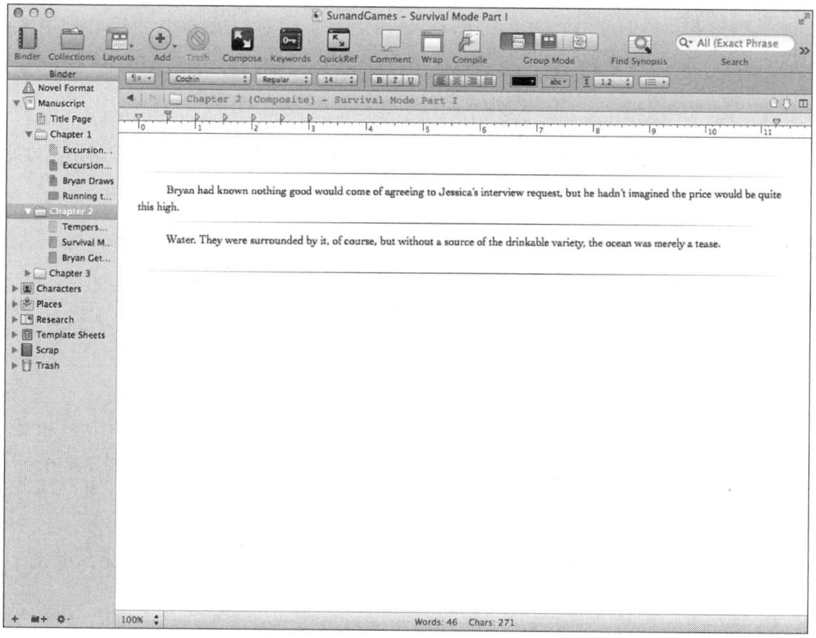

FIGURE 4.19

View all of Chapter 2 at once in Scrivenings mode.

You can edit in Scrivenings mode just as you would in single Document view. Changes are immediately reflected in the proper file. When you want to exit Scrivenings mode, select a single document in the Binder.

> **NOTE** If you select the Go To menu in the Icon Item menu while in Scrivenings, your options are limited to the containers and files in that view. When you make a selection, the insertion point is moved to the top of the selected file within the Scrivenings view.

Using QuickReference Panels (Mac Only)

You're hard at work on a scene. You already have the Editor split into the Corkboard and the current scene, but you need to look up a piece of information in one of your research files or make a quick change to another scene. Open a QuickReference panel, and your problem is solved!

QuickReference panels are extra windows you can open to access additional files at once. Editable and repositionable, they are very flexible. Some writers may even prefer using QuickReference panels instead of splitting the Editor screen.

NOTE Sorry, Windows users! QuickReference panels are currently only available on the Mac.

To open a QuickReference Panel (also referred to as QuickRef panels), choose one of the following options:

- Drag a file from the Binder, Corkboard, or Outliner onto the QuickReference icon on the toolbar.

- Select a file or files from the Binder, Corkboard, or Outliner and then click the QuickReference icon on the toolbar.

 CAUTION Selecting a file this way may change the active document in the Editor if the Editor pane is not locked in place.

- Select one or more files in the Binder, then press the spacebar to open a QuickReference panel for each file.

- Click the QuickReference icon on the toolbar to open the active document in a QuickReference panel.

- Choose View, QuickReference from the menu and then select a file from the submenu.

 TIP This method bypasses the Binder, Corkboard, and Outliner, so you do not risk inadvertently changing the focus of your Editor pane.

QuickReference panels, shown in Figure 4.20, can appear as typical windows or as HUD panels (see Chapter 2 for details on changing this preference). When they are in the traditional window style, you can add a Format bar and Ruler to the display by choosing those options in the Format menu or using the appropriate keyboard shortcuts (Cmd-Shift-R and Cmd-R, respectively). In the HUD display, you can choose to add the Ruler, but not the Format bar. All the formatting options available on the Format bar are still available via the Format menu or keyboard shortcuts.

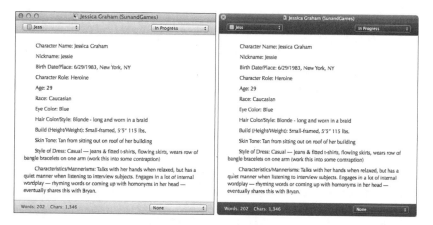

FIGURE 4.20

QuickReference panels are editable, repositionable, and provide access to a file's meta-data. The panel on the left is the standard window, whereas the one on the right uses the HUD display setting.

The upper-left corner of the panel displays the label for the file. The upper-right corner displays the status for the file. You can change these settings here, and those changes are reflected in the Inspector for the file. The Footer bar of the panel displays the word and character count. The drop-down menu in the lower right provides access to additional meta-data, such as the Synopsis and Document Notes.

By default, QuickReference panels automatically hide behind the main Scrivener window when you return to the Editor. If you prefer to have them float on the screen, so that they can remain visible even if you return to the Editor, choose Window, Float QuickReference Panels or press Control-Cmd-Q.

Taking Notes in the Scratch Pad

Whereas QuickReference panels are linked to your project, the Scratch Pad is an editing area that is not project-specific. You can use it to jot down ideas about other projects, accumulate research from web pages and other applications, and later assign those notes to a specific project. Or use the Scratch Pad to write out your To Do list or notes about non-writing-related tasks, just to get them out of your head so you can continue working.

TIP On the Mac, an application can remain running even if no documents are open. Scrivener takes advantage of this by making the Scratch Pad available whenever the Scrivener application is open, even if you don't have a project visible on the screen. To open the Scratch Pad, right-click the Scrivener icon in the Dock and choose Scratch Pad. You can also use the keyboard shortcut, Cmd-Shift-Return.

To open the Scratch Pad, choose Window, Show Scratch Pad or press Shift-Cmd-Return (Tools, Scratch Pad or Ctrl+Shift+0 in Windows). The Scratch Pad window is shown in Figure 4.21.

FIGURE 4.21

The Scratch Pad is not project-specific, so you can take notes on a wide range of topics and link them to a project later.

In Windows, the Scratch Pad (shown in Figure 4.22) contains options to change the split of the window from horizontal to vertical. You can also capture a screenshot.

FIGURE 4.22

The Scratch Pad in Windows has some additional features, including the ability to change the split of the window to a vertical layout.

Adding and Deleting Notes

When you first open the Scratch Pad, your note is called Untitled Note. Double-click this name in the top pane of the window to change it. Enter the text of your note in the bottom pane. If you want to add another note, click the plus sign (+) at the bottom left of the window. The new note is added to the list in the top pane.

If you want to delete a note, select it and press the Delete key (Shift+Delete in Windows) or click the Delete button at the bottom of the Scratch Pad window.

Sending a Note to a Project

To send a note to a project:

1. Open the project (or projects) to which you want to assign a note.

2. Select the note from the list in the top pane of the Scratch Pad.

3. Click the Send to Project drop-down list.

4. Choose the appropriate project from your open projects.

5. Choose one of the following options:

- If you want to add the note to an existing file, choose Append Text To and then select the file to which you want to append the note's content.

- If you want to create a new document for the content of the note, choose Import as Subdocument Of and then select the container to which you want to add the new file.

To close the Scratch Pad, click the Close box in the upper-left corner (the upper-right corner in Windows) or click the OK button at the bottom of the window.

THE ABSOLUTE MINIMUM

The key points to take away from this chapter are as follows:

- The Editor is where you write your manuscript.

- You can select a document in the Binder to open in the Editor. The Editor also has its own navigation system.

- Splitting the Editor enables you to work on two documents at the same time or refer to a research file while you work.

- QuickReference panels (Mac only) are repositionable windows that give you quick access to research or other documents.

- The Scratch Pad is a great place to take notes that belong in other projects or jot down ideas for your current project and later incorporate them into your work.

WRITING IN FULL SCREEN

Scrivener has so many features and options that it's easy to get caught up tweaking preference settings, moving index cards around on the Corkboard, and adding meta-data in the Inspector. If you ever sought an application that secretly supported your procrastination habit under the guise of getting work done, Scrivener is it. At some point, however, you must hone in on your manuscript.

Composition mode, called Full Screen mode in Scrivener for Windows, was made to eliminate onscreen distractions and provide a very simple interface—an editing screen and a cursor. So, get typing!

Using Composition Mode

Launch Composition mode by choosing View, Enter Composition Mode from the menu or press Option-Cmd-F. In Windows, choose View, Enter Full Screen or press the F11 key. On both Mac and Windows, you can also use the Enter Full Screen/Composition Mode button on the toolbar.

Composition mode opens whichever document or Scrivenings is in the active Editor. If you want to work on a single scene, select that scene in the Binder, Corkboard, or Outliner view before you launch Composition mode. If you want to work on a group of documents, select a container or a group of selected documents in the Binder and then click the Scrivenings button in the Group View Mode grouping on the toolbar (or select View, Scrivenings from the menu) before you launch Composition mode.

CAUTION If you select a container but enter Composition mode without first entering Scrivenings mode, only the text of the container itself appears.

TIP If you select multiple documents on the Mac but enter Composition mode without first entering Scrivenings mode, only one document is visible at a time. However, all of the selected documents are loaded into the Composition mode navigation history, so you can switch between them by pressing Cmd-[and Cmd-] (the bracket keys).

Composition mode, shown in Figure 5.1, consists of a single Editor and a Control Strip. Notice the absence of menus, toolbars, sidebars, Rulers, or Format bars. After appearing on the screen when you initially enter the mode, even the Control Strip disappears, leaving you with just a large screen on which to type.

Editor

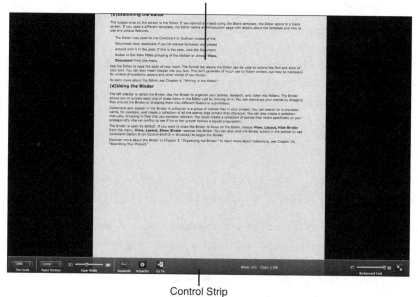

Control Strip

FIGURE 5.1

The Composition mode display lets you focus completely on your text.

As you can see in Figure 5.1, the default background is solid black, with gray paper and black text. Although this certainly blocks everything out, it's a rather bland working environment. Fortunately, you can customize the appearance of all the elements in Composition mode from the Compose tab in the Preferences window (the Appearance tab in the Options window in Windows). The Background can be customized with either a solid color or a texture. The Paper can be customized with a solid color in Windows or with a solid color or texture on the Mac. You can also change the text color to make it readable against a custom paper setting or in order to ease eyestrain.

TIP On the Mac, you can set a backdrop image on a per-project basis. Choose View, Composition Backdrop from the menu. Backdrop images do not tile; rather, they expand to fill the screen. When a backdrop is set, the Background Fade slider in the Composition mode Control Strip changes to a Paper Fade slider.

CAUTION Changing the Text Color setting does not affect the font color of your text. When you view the document in the standard Editor window, the text returns to its actual color.

NOTE If you need a refresher on how to customize colors or modify the other Composition mode preferences, see Chapter 2, "Customizing Your Work Environment."

Composition mode uses *typewriter scrolling* by default. This means that the line of text you type remains vertically centered on the paper. Once your text is long enough to reach the middle of the screen, the preceding text continues to scroll up the screen, but your cursor remains centered. You can disable typewriter scrolling by pressing Control-Cmd-T (Windows Key+Ctrl+T in Windows) while in Composition mode.

Making Adjustments in the Control Strip

The Control Strip at the bottom of the screen allows you to make adjustments to the view and provides access to panels you may need while you work. The Control Strip automatically hides when not in use. To make it appear, move your mouse to the bottom of the screen and wait a moment.

TIP If you want to keep the Control Strip open, adjust your Paper Height, explained below, so the Control Strip doesn't obscure the paper, and then leave your mouse pointer positioned at the bottom of the screen.

On the Mac, you can also access the menu bar while in Composition mode. Move your mouse pointer to the top of the screen, and the menu bar appears after a moment. You can access formatting tools and even turn on the Ruler without leaving Composition mode. Once you move the mouse pointer away from the top of the screen, the menu bar disappears.

Although Windows users can't access the menu bar in Composition mode, many keyboard shortcuts still work for features that could logically be used within this mode, such as formatting, the Go To menu, and toggling the Ruler at the top of the screen.

The Control Strip, shown in Figure 5.2, provides the following options:

| 100% | Center | | | | | Words: 555 Chars: 3,188 | | |
| Text Scale | Paper Position | Paper Width | Keywords | Inspector | Go To | | Background Fade |

FIGURE 5.2

The Control Strip only becomes visible when you hover at the bottom of the screen.

- **Text Scale**: Adjusts the size of the text on the screen. As with the Text Scale setting in the standard Editor, this does not change the font size itself. Only its appearance is affected.

- **Paper Position**: Positions the paper on the left, right, or center of the screen. If you plan to access QuickReference panels or the Inspector panel, you may want to move the paper to the right or left so you can leave the panels open without obscuring the paper.

- **Paper Width**: Adjusts the width of the paper. The paper can be expanded as wide as the entire screen or minimized to a very narrow column.

- **Paper Height**: Adjusts the height of the paper. Hold down the Option key (Alt key in Windows) to change the Paper Width slider into the Paper Height slider. By default, the paper is set to the full height of the screen, but you can make it much smaller, allowing the background to show around all four sides.

- **Keywords**: Opens the Keywords panel (see Figure 5.3) to enable you to add keywords to the document. You can also add and delete keywords for the project.

FIGURE 5.3

The Keywords panel can be repositioned on the screen.

 NOTE Keywords are explained in Chapter 12, "Putting Keywords and Meta-Data to Work."

- **Inspector**: Displays the Inspector panel, shown in Figure 5.4. Click the drop-down menu to change the view from the Synopsis to Document Notes or one of the other Inspector screens. To view (or change) the label and status of the document, go to the bottom of the panel.

Close panel

Inspector View drop-down menu

Label   Status

FIGURE 5.4

The Inspector panel, shown on the Mac, can be repositioned on the screen.

 NOTE Learn more about the Inspector in Chapter 11, "Digging into the Inspector."

- **Go To**: Opens a pop-up menu to select a new document without leaving Composition mode.

- **Word and Character Count**: Displays the word and character count for the document. If you make a selection within the document on the Mac, the selection count turns blue and provides the word and character count for the highlighted text. In Windows, right-click to open the context menu; the selection count is visible at the bottom of the menu.

- **Background Fade**: When you use a background color, this slider controls how the background fades into the desktop behind it. At the lowest setting, the background becomes transparent so you can see your desktop and any open application windows. At the highest setting, the background color is completely opaque.

- **Paper Fade**: If you are using a background texture (image) instead of a solid color, the Background Fade slider is replaced with a Paper Fade slider to control the visibility of the background through the paper.
- **Exit Composition (Full Screen) Mode**: Returns to the standard Editor. You can also press the Esc (Escape) key or Option-Cmd-F (F11 in Windows).

TIP   On the Mac, click the icons at either end of a slider to jump directly to the extreme end of the slider.

In Figure 5.5, notice just how much you can customize the Composition mode using a combination of the Compose tab in the Preferences window and the Control Strip in Composition mode. I've added a tiled image to the background and changed the paper color. In the Control Strip, I narrowed the paper height and width and increased the text scale. I can write for hours in this environment; and if ever I don't like it, I can change it.

TIP   On the Mac, after you have customized the settings on the Control Strip to your liking, you can set them as the default for new projects. Go to the Compose tab in the Preferences window and click the Use Current Composition Settings for New Projects button.

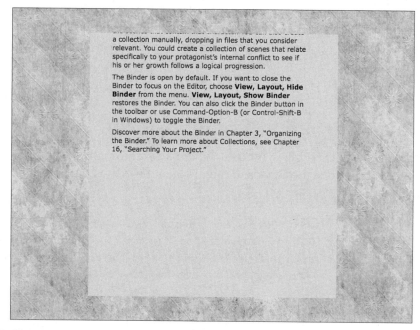

a collection manually, dropping in files that you consider relevant. You could create a collection of scenes that relate specifically to your protagonist's internal conflict to see if his or her growth follows a logical progression.

The Binder is open by default. If you want to close the Binder to focus on the Editor, choose **View, Layout, Hide Binder** from the menu. **View, Layout, Show Binder** restores the Binder. You can also click the Binder button in the toolbar or use Command-Option-B (or Control-Shift-B in Windows) to toggle the Binder.

Discover more about the Binder in Chapter 3, "Organizing the Binder." To learn more about Collections, see Chapter 16, "Searching Your Project."

FIGURE 5.5

An example of Composition mode fully tricked out.

TIP If you are of an artistic bent and have Photoshop or some other graphics application, you can create your own background image, such as a collage of photos of how you envision your characters and setting. On the Mac, set this image using View, Composition Backdrop to avoid tiling. Scrivener automatically scales the backdrop image to fit the screen. In Windows, make the image dimensions the same as your screen resolution to avoid tiling.

Consider your paper height and width settings when creating your image so the elements of the collage flow well around your paper.

Using Composition Mode with Multiple Displays

If you are a Mac user and have dual monitors hooked up to your computer, you can configure Scrivener to use your secondary display for Composition mode while leaving other apps available in your primary display. In the Compose tab in the Preferences window, select Use Secondary Screen If Available. In addition, deselect Blank Out Other Screens.

If you want the standard Scrivener window to remain open while you're in Composition mode, deselect Hide Main Window in Composition Mode. You can then use the Binder to open items in Composition mode by pressing the Option key while selecting items. To form a Scrivenings group in Composition mode, press Option-Cmd while selecting noncontiguous items or Option-Shift while selecting contiguous items in the Binder.

Using the Mac's Full Screen Mode

In addition to Composition mode, Mac users also have a Full Screen mode. Full Screen mode hides the Dock and menu bar and expands the application window to fill the entire display.

NOTE Full Screen mode is only available on Macs running OS X 10.7 (Lion) and higher. See Chapter 2, "Customizing Your Work Environment," for details on setting Full Screen preferences in the Appearance tab of the Preferences window.

To enter Full Screen mode, choose one of the following:

- Click the double-sided arrow button in the upper-right corner of the Scrivener window.

- Choose View, Enter Full Screen from the menu.
- Toggle between Full Screen mode and the standard application window by pressing Control-Cmd-F.

NOTE   If you use multiple displays, Full Screen mode blacks out all your other displays. This is not a Scrivener problem; it's inherent in the operating system.

CAUTION   Yes, the name of this feature is confusing! Scrivener's Composition mode was originally called Full Screen mode, just as it is in Scrivener for Windows. When Apple came out with Mac OS X Lion, it introduced its own Full Screen mode for all applications. Scrivener changed the name of its own feature on the Mac, but Windows still uses the original naming convention.

THE ABSOLUTE MINIMUM

Here are the highlights from this chapter:

- Composition mode is a distraction-free environment that allows you to focus on a single document or Scrivenings.

- Scrivener for Mac's Composition mode and Scrivener for Windows' Full Screen mode are the same feature.

- Open the Inspector panel to see your document and project notes without leaving Composition mode.

- Scrivener for Mac's Full Screen mode hides the Dock and menu bar to give you more space for the standard Scrivener interface.

6

STORYBOARDING WITH THE CORKBOARD

From multicolored index cards and post-it notes to foam-core plotting boards and decoupage collages, the process of planning a story can become quite an artistic adventure. Seeing a visual representation of your story engages the creative side of your brain while also appeasing your logical side by potentially highlighting dangling plot threads, the balance of point-of-view (POV) characters, and other story elements.

If you like to storyboard your books before you begin writing, the Corkboard will prove to be an invaluable tool in your writer's toolkit. Even if you are a pantser, you may find that viewing the Corkboard when you're blocked can help you see the flow of your story to discover what should come next. It can also be used as an editing tool to analyze your completed draft before undertaking revisions.

Academic and nonfiction writers can also benefit from using the Corkboard. Viewing your project in such a visual manner can ensure you have established enough supporting elements for your thesis and put your sections in proper order to provide the most impact.

Scrivener's Corkboard is based on the concept of index cards tacked up to a board, but without the mess of glue sticks or dropped pushpins. Each item in the Binder is represented by an index card, and cards can be color-coded and moved around the Corkboard, just like their nonvirtual counterparts. Unlike a physical corkboard, however, Scrivener's Corkboard travels with your work in progress; anywhere you use Scrivener, you can view your Corkboard.

Opening the Corkboard

As with Scrivenings, the Corkboard is another way to view multiple items from the Binder together as a group. To open the Corkboard:

1. Select the container you want to view from the Binder.

2. Choose one of the following options:

   - Click the Corkboard icon in the Group mode on the toolbar.

   - Choose View, Corkboard from the menu.

   - Press Cmd-2 (Ctrl+2 in Windows).

The Editor window displays the Corkboard view, as shown in Figure 6.1. The standard Corkboard displays a single level of your project hierarchy. Each file at that level is represented by an index card. Folders or file groups containing subdocuments are represented by a stack of index cards, indicating content at a lower level in the hierarchy.

 CAUTION You can view multiple folders, file groups, or nonsequential files and folders. You can also select a collection (which are explained in Chapter 16, "Searching Your Project"). The appearance of the Corkboard and the actions you can perform with the index cards change depending on the selection. If you select a container, for example, you can rearrange the index cards, whereas you cannot move or add cards when the Corkboard displays a selection of multiple items from various folders.

 NOTE See Chapter 3, "Organizing the Binder," for more information about establishing the file and folder hierarchy for a project.

Selected container

Image added in Inspector

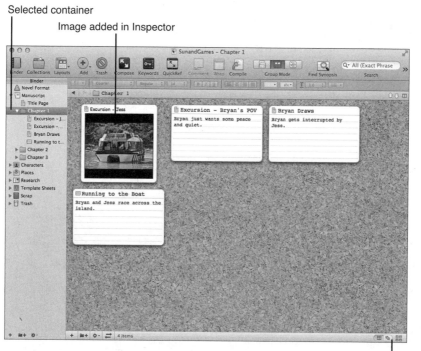

Corkboard Options menu

FIGURE 6.1

The Corkboard displays index cards of each document in the selected container. The Synopsis area displays either text or an image, as added in the Inspector.

The Corkboard is not a fixed view of your documents. If you loaded a container into the Corkboard, you can move cards around to change their order within the container, and these changes are reflected immediately in the Binder. To move a card, just click and drag it to its new location. You can also drag the card from the Corkboard into a different container in the Binder.

Viewing Multiple Containers in a Stacked Corkboard

When you click on a single container in the Binder, the Corkboard displays all of the documents within the top level of that container. If you select multiple containers on the Mac, however, you can stack Corkboards in order to view them all at the same time, as shown in Figure 6.2. To do this, hold down the Cmd key on the Mac while clicking on multiple containers in the Binder.

CAUTION Be careful not to click individual documents while making this selection. If any individual files are in the selection, the standard Corkboard appears, instead of the stacked Corkboard.

NOTE Unfortunately, this feature is not available in Windows.

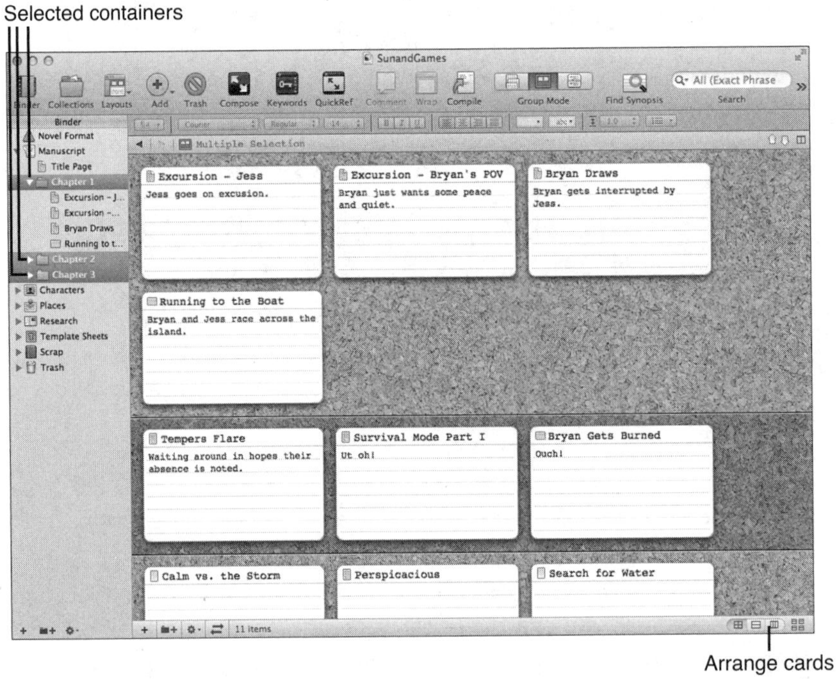

Selected containers

FIGURE 6.2

A stacked Corkboard displays two or more containers simultaneously.

When the Corkboard is stacked, each container's contents appear on the Corkboard. A line appears between the cards for each container, and the shading of the background changes. By default, the cards for each container wrap within the window, as you can see in Figure 6.2, and the containers are stacked horizontally. Change the arrangement of the cards using the three buttons on the right side of the Footer bar. Your options are as follows:

- **Wrap Cards**: The default view. The cards for the container wrap as they do in the standard Corkboard view, and the Corkboards are stacked horizontally on top of each other.

- **Arrange Cards in Rows**: The cards within a container appear in a single row, with the Corkboards stacked horizontally.
- **Arrange Cards in Columns**: The cards within a container appear in a single column, with the Corkboards arranged side by side vertically.

Adding Documents to the Corkboard

If you get an idea for a new scene or concept in your writing project, you can add a new document within the Corkboard. Click the Add button in the toolbar, and a new card appears on the Corkboard. You can also use any of the other methods for adding a new document you learned in Chapter 3. If you want to add a new card directly after an existing card, select that card before adding the new one.

CAUTION You cannot add new items to the Corkboard when displaying a multiple selection.

When you are viewing a stacked Corkboard, if no card is selected when you add a new card, it gets added to the end of the final stack. If a card is selected, the new card is added immediately after it.

TIP If you use the Corkboard as a plotting/planning tool and frequently add new documents while in this view, change your Preferences/Options to add a new document when you double-click in the background. Open the Corkboard tab in the Preferences/Options window. On the Mac, click the Double-Clicking Corkboard Background drop-down menu and select Creates a New Card. In Windows, click the Empty Space Double-Click Will drop-down menu and select Create a New Card.

THE CREATIVE PROCESS: WHICH CAME FIRST—THE BINDER, THE INSPECTOR, OR THE CORKBOARD?

Just as there is no one way to approach a writing project, there is no one way to use Scrivener. I've laid out the chapters in this book so that those who want to proceed quickly to creating documents and getting to work in the Editor have the tools they need to do so without having to wade through a lot of extra steps. Many other writers prefer laying out scenes on the Corkboard (or the Outliner, covered in the next chapter), possibly in conjunction with the Inspector before writing a single line of text. You can also use the Inspector and the Binder together and avoid the Corkboard and Outliner completely. Play with the options to discover how you and Scrivener work best together.

Examining Index Cards

Index cards represent your files, but they do not display the content of the document itself. Rather, the index card contains elements of the meta-data for the file. Imagine it as a physical index card you paper clip to each document describing its content.

As shown in Figure 6.3, there are three mandatory elements on every index card, as follows:

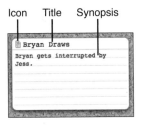

FIGURE 6.3

An index card displays the icon, title, and synopsis of the document.

- **Icon**: The item's icon, matching the one that appears in the Binder. You can easily see if the file contains document text or has been saved as a Snapshot, for example, by looking at the icon. The icon has a functional purpose, as well: to open a document in the Editor window in order to work on the document itself, double-click the icon on the index card.

 NOTE   Icon types were explained in Chapter 3.

- **Title**: The title of the document, as it also appears in the Binder. Double-click the title to highlight and rename it. If you change the title of the document on the index card, it is updated in the Binder and the Inspector.

- **Synopsis**: The synopsis of the document. Double-click to type or edit the synopsis on the index card. You can also enter the synopsis in the Inspector. If you want to use an image in place of a text synopsis, as shown in Figure 6.1, you must add it in the Inspector. You are not required to enter a synopsis; if you do not, this area of the card remains blank.

 CAUTION   The synopsis is not the actual text of your document. Enter your document text by opening the document in the Editor. Do not enter your document text in the Corkboard or Inspector.

NOTE Learn about the Inspector and adding an image in the synopsis in Chapter 11, "Digging into the Inspector."

Adding Index Card Options

In addition to the three core index card elements, there are four optional elements. As shown in Figure 6.4, they are as follows:

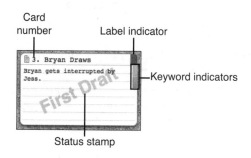

FIGURE 6.4

With additional options, a single index card can tell you a lot about the document at a glance.

- **Label indicator**: Displays the color associated with the Label field in the Inspector. To add label indicators to your index cards, choose View, Corkboard Options, Show Pins from the menu or press Control-Cmd-P (F9 in Windows). If you add a label to the document, it can appear as either a colored chip or pushpin on the index card. To add or change a label on the index card, right-click on the card or cards, select Label from the context menu, and then choose from the submenu. You can also add or change the label in the Inspector, but only for one item at a time.

   NOTE On the Mac, the form of the label indicator—whether color chip or pushpin—depends on the shape of the index card. If the card is rounded, the indicator appears as a color chip on the upper-right side of the card. If the card is square, the indicator looks like a pushpin either on the top center or top right of the card. Change the shape of index cards and the position of the pushpin in the Corkboard tab of the preferences/Options window.

  In Windows, the shape of the index card and form of the label indicator can each be set independently in the Corkboard tab of the Options window. Thus, you can have a rounded card with pushpins or a square card with chips, or vice versa. You cannot, however, change the location of the pushpins from the top center of the card.

TIP You can also apply the label color to the icon or the entire index card, or both. To do this, choose View, Use Label Color In, and select Icons or Index Cards from the submenu. As you can see in the menu, you can also apply the label color to the file in the Binder and the Outliner. If you apply the label color to the icon, the color is visible wherever the icon is used in Scrivener—the Binder, Corkboard, Outliner, and the Header bar in the Editor. If you apply the label color to the index card, adjust the tint in the Appearance tab of the Preferences window on the Mac or the Corkboard tab of the Options window in Windows.

- **Status stamp**: Displays the Status of the document as a watermark across the index card. Choose View, Corkboard Options, Show Stamps or press Control-Cmd-S (F10 in Windows) to enable this feature. Adjust the opacity of the stamp in the Corkboard tab of the Preferences/Options window.

TIP Chapter 12, "Putting Keywords and Meta-Data to Work," offers a neat trick to assign symbols as a status indicator.

- **Keyword indicators**: Displays color swatches associated with keywords applied to the document. Keyword indicators are displayed by default on the Mac but need to be enabled in Windows. To disable or reenable keyword indicators, choose View, Corkboard Options, Show Keyword Colors or press Control-Cmd-K (Ctrl+F12 in Windows). Keyword indicators only appear if keywords have been assigned to the file. Assign keywords from the Inspector or directly on the Corkboard. To add a keyword, click the Keywords button on the toolbar to open the Keywords panel. Drag the desired keyword from the panel onto the index card. You can also select multiple index cards and then drag and drop one or more keywords onto the selection to assign them.

NOTE On the Mac, index cards display up to five keyword indicators by default. In Windows, index cards display all keyword indicators by default. You can change this setting from the Corkboard Options menu accessible in the Footer bar, as explained in the next section of this chapter.

- **Card number (Mac only)**: Assigns numbers to each card based on their order in the container. If you move cards around in the Corkboard, they are renumbered to reflect the new order, and they are reordered in the Binder. To display card numbers, choose View, Corkboard Options, Show Card Numbers from the menu.

TIP When you view a stacked Corkboard, card numbers continue sequentially throughout the visible containers. If you want to start the numbering over in each container, choose View, Corkboard Options, Number Per Section from the menu.

 NOTE To learn more about using labels, status, and keywords, see Chapter 12.

Setting Corkboard Options on the Footer Bar

Aside from the Corkboard options on the View menu, which primarily control the index card elements, the Corkboard Options menu on the Footer bar controls the layout of the index cards and Corkboard. By fine-tuning the size and spacing of the index cards, you can customize this view to maximize the use of your screen real estate. The options on the Corkboard Options menu, shown in Figure 6.5, are as follows:

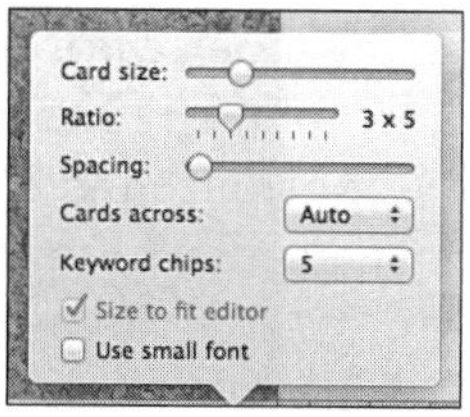

FIGURE 6.5

The Corkboard Options menu controls the size and positioning of index cards on the Corkboard.

 NOTE In Windows, click the Layout Options icon in the Footer bar to open the Corkboard Options menu.

- **Card Size**: Determines the size of index cards by using this slider and then letting the Corkboard determine how many cards fit across the window.

 TIP Another method to determine card size is to set the number of cards you want in each row in the Cards Across option on this menu and let the Corkboard determine the size of the cards required to meet this criteria. In this case, the Size control is disabled.

- **Ratio**: Sets the ratio between the height and width of the cards. The default is 3×5, the ratio of a physical index card. On the Mac, cards displaying images are always 5×5.

- **Spacing**: Adjusts the space between columns and rows of index cards. If space is at a premium, move this slider to the left to minimize the space between cards.

- **Cards Across**: Determines the number of cards to place in each row on the Corkboard. Use Auto to allow the size of the cards to regulate this setting.

- **Keyword Chips**: Sets the maximum number of keyword indicators to be displayed on index cards. If this number is lower than the number of keywords assigned to a card, the additional keywords are ignored.

- **Size to Fit Editor**: Resizes cards to fit the current width of the Editor window if this check box is selected in conjunction with a fixed number set in the Cards Across option. If this option is deselected, you may need to scroll to see the contents of the Corkboard. If Cards Across is set to Auto, this option is disabled. If this option is selected, the Size slider is disabled.

- **Use Small Font**: Instructs the index cards to make use of the Small Text setting in the Corkboard tab of the Preferences window. To access this setting in Windows, choose the Appearance tab of the Options window, then select Corkboard in the Fonts pane and choose Index Text Small.

You can immediately see how changes on this menu affect the Corkboard, so it is easy to fine-tune your settings. To close the menu on the Mac, click outside it. In Windows, click the X button at the top of the menu.

Using the Corkboard in Split Screen

In Chapter 4, "Writing in the Editor," you learned how to use Split Screen mode to divide the Editor window into two separate panes. If you're a planner who likes knowing what's coming next while working in a document, keeping the Corkboard visible in Split Screen mode, as shown in Figure 6.6, can help.

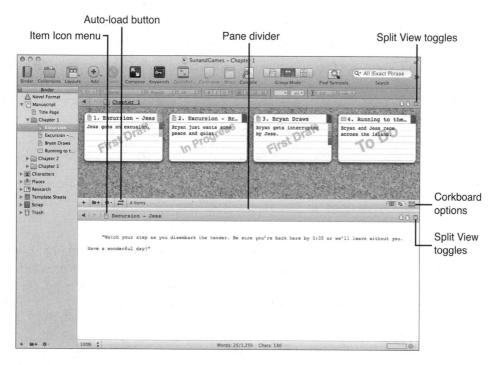

FIGURE 6.6

This split screen allows you to view the Corkboard in the top pane while working on a document in the lower pane.

To split the screen in Corkboard view:

1. Open a container in Corkboard view, if you don't already have one open on the screen.

2. Click the Split View toggle in the Header bar of the Corkboard. The Corkboard appears in both panes.

3. Click in the pane in which you want to work in the Editor. The Header bar turns blue to indicate this is the active pane.

4. Choose one of the following options to open a file in the Editor:

   - Select a file in the Binder.

   - Select an item in the Binder or Corkboard and choose Documents, Open from the menu, then select the desired Editor from the submenu.

   - Click the Item Icon button in the Header bar, then select Go To and choose a file from the submenu.

- Right-click on an index card in the Corkboard, then select Open and choose the Editor in which the document should open.

If you are currently in Document view in the Editor and want to split the screen and add a Corkboard to one pane, you can do this, as well. Split the screen and then open a container in one pane and choose Corkboard view from the toolbar or menu.

TIP You may need to adjust the Corkboard options to position your index cards exactly as you want in the smaller real estate of the Split Screen pane. You can also adjust the amount of space allocated to each pane by sliding the divider bar between panes.

In step 4 above, you had the option of using the Corkboard to control the Editor. You can automate this by clicking the Auto-load button in the Footer bar of the Corkboard. On the Mac, the icon turns blue to signify the feature is enabled. In Windows, the button appears depressed. Whenever you select an index card in the Corkboard, the document opens in the other Editor pane.

CAUTION If you are clicking around in the Corkboard, it's easy to lose track of which document is open in the other Editor. If you have the Auto-load option enabled, get into the habit of looking at the Header bar before typing in your document to ensure you are in the correct document.

Putting Split Screen to Work

You can combine your knowledge of several Scrivener options and commands to build a custom layout. Figure 6.7 shows my usual writing layout when drafting a project. This layout works well on a widescreen display because it makes use of the extra horizontal space while showing as much text in the document as possible.

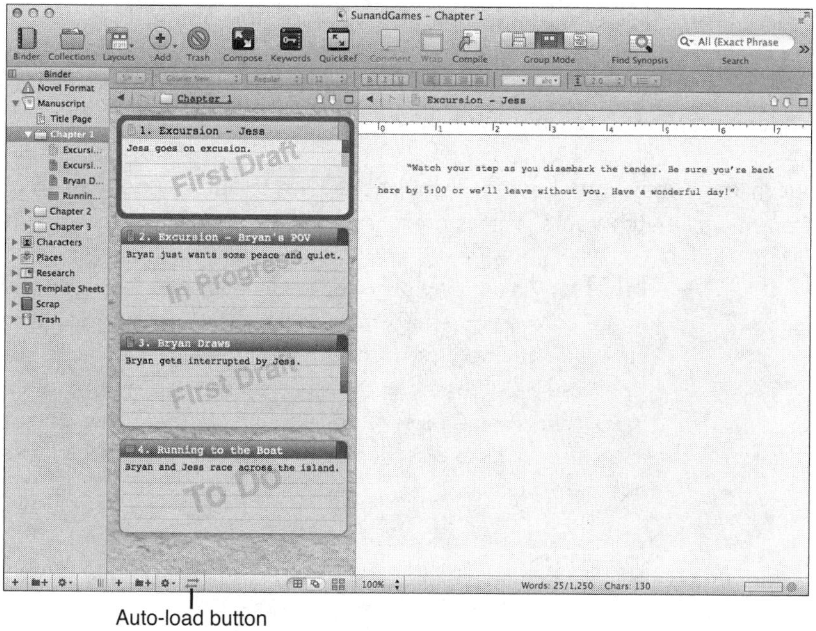

Auto-load button

FIGURE 6.7

Using multiple settings in conjunction with each other allows you to create a unique workspace.

This is how it works:

- The screen is split vertically. Press the Option key while clicking the Split View toggle to change the orientation of the split on the Mac. In Windows, click the Vertical Split button.

- The Corkboard is loaded into the left pane. The width of the Corkboard pane has been adjusted to fit one index card across, and the Corkboard options have been adjusted to change the size and ratio of the index cards to suit the space.

- The Binder Affects (View, Binder Affects) option has been set to Left Editor, so anything selected in the Binder opens in the left Editor pane.

- The Auto-load option in the Footer bar of the Corkboard has been enabled, so any item selected in the Corkboard automatically opens in the right Editor pane.

- If you want to move items in the Binder without affecting the Corkboard, use the Lock in Place option (View, Editor, Lock in Place). This can be toggled as needed.

- To maximize screen real estate, you can hide the Binder completely (View, Layout, Hide Binder on the Mac or deselect View, Layout, Show Binder in Windows). You can also hide the toolbar (View, Hide Toolbar on the Mac or deselect View, Toolbar in Windows).

Your mileage may vary. Each of the options I set to suit my needs can be set differently to match yours. This is merely one example of how to work in Scrivener.

 NOTE As an example of how Scrivener's features can work together, this figure also shows customized Appearance preferences and the application of the Label field to the color of the icons in the Corkboard and Binder and the background of the index cards. See Chapter 2 to learn how to customize colors and Chapter 12 to discover how to use the label color in various elements.

 CAUTION Don't forget to save your layout and preferences settings when you get things arranged as you like!

Using Images to Your Advantage

If you add images to your synopsis in the Inspector (explained in Chapter 11), you can use the Corkboard as a reference tool of a different sort. Figure 6.8 shows a container from the Research folder in Corkboard view in the top pane and an open document in the bottom pane. The images aid in describing the objects in the document. If you need to access the content of the research document, right-click the index card and choose Open, As QuickReference from the context menu.

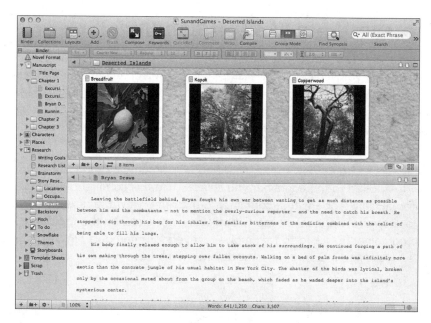

FIGURE 6.8

Using multiple settings in conjunction with each other allows you to create a unique workspace.

NOTE Windows users, Scrivener for Windows does not provide QuickReference panels, but you can opt to open the document in either Editor window from the same Open submenu.

You can apply images to any item, not just Research documents. If you add images representing different characters or the action in your story to key scenes, you can view the Corkboard as a visual storyboard.

TIP Looking for images to use in your project? Use your Internet browser to do a web search for the object or theme you seek, and then select the Images link. Because you are downloading these images strictly for your personal reference and not to distribute as part of your completed project, you don't need to worry about licensing or rights issues.

Locking the View Mode (Mac Only)

The Group View mode that is applied to a container depends on the last Group View mode you selected. For example, if you select a container and view it in the Outliner, the next time you select any container, it automatically opens in the Outliner. If you want to set a container to always open in a particular View mode, you can change this default behavior. Select View, Editor, Lock Group View Mode in the menu.

When Lock Group View mode is selected, it remembers the last Group View mode applied to the container you select while this command is enabled, and automatically reopens that container in the same view the next time it is selected. A lock symbol appears on the Group View mode icon in the toolbar to signify the container is locked to that mode. Scrivener remembers which containers have been locked to a Group View mode and which have not.

Working with the Freeform Corkboard (Mac Only)

The standard Corkboard is also called the Linear Corkboard because it displays items in a fixed order. Scrivener for Mac also offers a Freeform Corkboard. This view allows you to move cards around the background without the constraints of document order or a grid. Best of all, you can group your index cards into different arrangements without changing the order of the documents in the Binder. This gives you a different view of your project, without risking any permanent changes.

To access the Freeform Corkboard, shown in Figure 6.9, open a Corkboard for a single container and then select the Freeform Corkboard button in the Footer bar. You can also toggle the Freeform Corkboard by choosing View, Corkboard Options, Freeform from the menu. The background of the Freeform Corkboard is different by default so you can easily tell which type of Corkboard is active.

NOTE You can also use the Freeform Corkboard if you open a standard collection. Learn more about collections in Chapter 16, "Searching Your Project."

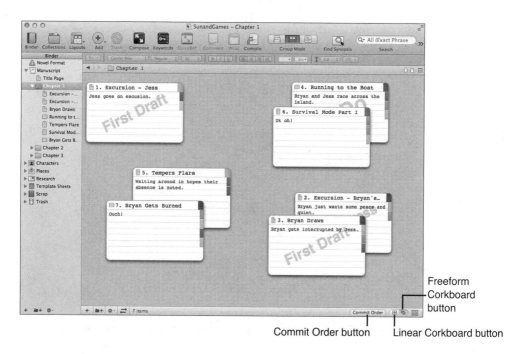

Freeform
Corkboard
button

Commit Order button   Linear Corkboard button

FIGURE 6.9

The Freeform Corkboard lets you move cards freely around the screen without committing to change the order of your documents.

Rearrange cards as you desire by dragging them around the Freeform Corkboard. If you want to return to the Linear Corkboard, click the Linear Corkboard button. Scrivener remembers the card position so you can return to the Freeform Corkboard later.

TIP Even if you don't use card numbers on your index cards as a matter of course, you may want to turn them on when you are in the Freeform Corkboard. The numbering remains the same as you move cards around the Freeform Corkboard, so you can still tell where the scene falls in your project sequence.

You can also use the Reveal in Binder command (View, Reveal in Binder from the menu or right-click on an index card and choose Reveal in Binder from the context menu) to select the document in the Binder so you can see it within the context of your project hierarchy.

If you decide you like the order in which the cards appear in the Freeform Corkboard, you can commit this card order to the Binder. Take the following steps:

1. Click the Commit Order button in the Footer bar. The Commit Freeform Corkboard Order dialog box opens, as shown in Figure 6.10.

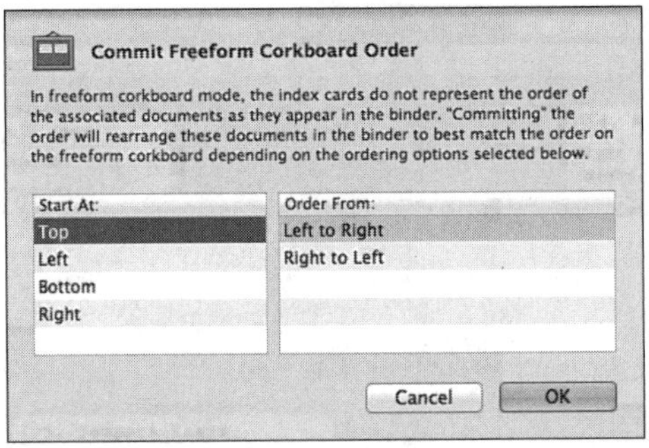

FIGURE 6.10

The Commit Freeform Corkboard Order dialog box confirms the order in which Scrivener should scan cards on the Freeform Corkboard to change the card order.

2. In the Start At column, select the location Scrivener should look for the first card in the new sequence.

3. In the Order From column, select the direction in which Scrivener should scan the index cards to determine the new card order.

4. Click OK.

If you enabled card numbers, you can see that the number assigned to each card has changed to reflect the new order. Your items are also reordered in the Binder. Confirm that each card was positioned as you want; you can rearrange items in the Binder if anything is out of place.

If you change your mind about committing the new card order, use the Undo command (Edit, Undo, or Cmd-Z).

THE CREATIVE PROCESS: PLOT-TESTING YOUR MANUSCRIPT OR PROJECT

The Freeform Corkboard excels at allowing you to look at your project in different ways. For fiction writers, you can move your cards into groups based on POV character, subplot, setting, and so on. This can make it easier to see if your story is unbalanced—having too many scenes in one character's point-of-view or leaving a subplot without resolution.

For nonfiction writers, consider grouping index cards based on the type of information you are providing. If your project contains a mix of quantitative, observational, and interactive research, for example, you can group your index cards by these categories to ensure you have the proper balance. For an analytical paper, you can group items by those that support a thesis statement and those that may disprove or run counter to that thesis and need to be argued against.

Windows users, don't feel left out! You can use labels, status stamps, and keyword chips to get a visual overview of various elements of your project. You can also use collections to gather groups of documents in one place, as explained in Chapter 16.

Printing Index Cards

Although Scrivener provides great flexibility in the Corkboard, there is still something about the feel of holding a stack of physical index cards in your hands and quickly arranging them in various ways. You can print index cards directly from the Corkboard to bring the virtual into physical form.

 NOTE The instructions here are for the Mac platform. If you use Scrivener for Windows, see "A Windows View: Printing Index Cards from Scrivener for Windows," later in this section.

The settings for printing index cards are optimized to work with Avery Perforated Index Card stock, but you can print on plain paper or card stock and cut the cards yourself.

Before printing index cards, ensure that the virtual index cards contain the proper titles and synopses you want to print. If a synopsis is too long for a 3×5 index card, the additional text prints on subsequent cards. If this is the desired behavior, you're all set. If you want each virtual index card to be limited to a single physical index card, however, you may need to edit your synopses to fit. If an index card is displaying an image rather than text on the Corkboard, the image is used when printing. If this is not what you intend, use the Inspector to change the item to the synopsis text view.

 TIP   Before you potentially waste expensive card stock, you can save your index cards to PDF so you can view the layout exactly as it will appear on the printed cards. In the Print window, click the PDF button, then select either Save as PDF or Open PDF in Preview from the drop-down menu.

Before you print index cards, you need to set up the print options by doing the following:

1. Go to File, Page Setup.

2. In the Page Setup dialog box, click the Settings drop-down list and select Scrivener. The window changes to display margin settings.

3. Click Options below the list of margin settings.

4. In the Print Options dialog box, click Index Cards in the center, as shown in Figure 6.11.

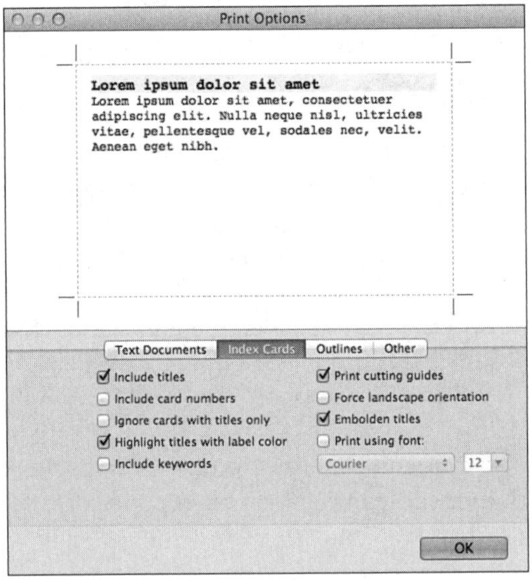

FIGURE 6.11

The Print Options dialog box displays a sample preview of your printed index cards based on the options you select.

5. Choose from the following options:

- **Include Titles**: Selected by default, this prints the document title at the top of each card.

- **Include Card Numbers**: This includes the card number with the title.

 NOTE Cards are numbered based on their order within the selected container on the Corkboard. Without this context, printing card numbers on physical index cards may be of limited use to you.

- **Ignore Cards with Titles Only**: If a card contains only a document title and no synopsis, the card will not be printed.

- **Highlight Titles with Label Color**: Selected by default, this uses the label color in the title. The label name is also added in parentheses after the title.

- **Include Keywords**: This adds keywords below the title. Keywords are underlined and separated by commas on the card.

- **Print Cutting Guides**: Selected by default, this adds dashed lines around the card to guide cutting them with scissors or a cutting block. This option is not necessary if you are printing on perforated card stock.

- **Force Landscape Orientation**: If you are printing to regular sheets of paper or card stock instead of perforated index cards, you can opt to print in landscape orientation. This increases the number of cards per page from three to four.

- **Embolden Titles**: Selected by default, this prints document titles in bold typeface.

- **Print Using Font**: This allows you to override the Corkboard fonts you set in the preferences window and print in a different font and font size.

6. Click OK to close the Print Options window.

7. Click OK to close the Page Setup window.

Once the print options are configured, you are ready to print your cards. If you are printing on perforated index cards or another specialty paper, load the stock into your printer's paper tray. To print:

1. Select the container or files you want to print by loading them into the Corkboard.

2. Choose File, Print Current Document from the menu.

3. In the Print window, shown in Figure 6.12, click Print.

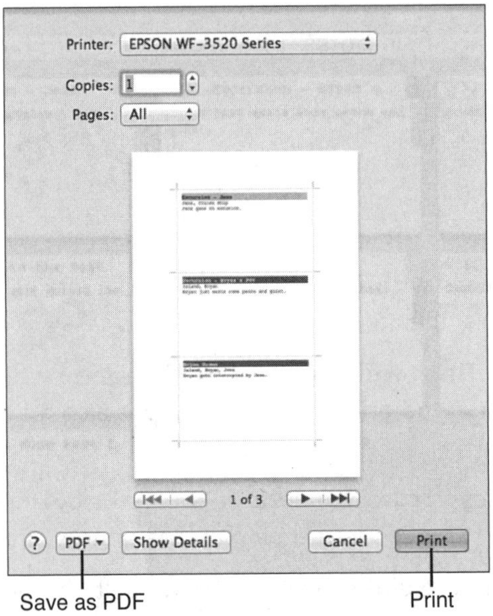

Save as PDF   Print

FIGURE 6.12

Use the Print dialog box to print your index cards or save them as a PDF file.

A WINDOWS VIEW: PRINTING INDEX CARDS FROM SCRIVENER FOR WINDOWS

The procedure for printing index cards in Scrivener for Windows is a bit different from that of the Mac. To print index cards in Windows, view the cards on the Corkboard and then choose File, Print Preview from the menu. The print settings use the last printer settings from your project. Thus, if you previously printed other portions of your project, the settings may not be conducive to printing index cards. Click the Page Settings icon to adjust the settings.

Paper orientation

Scroll through pages

Page settings

Print

If you want to change the margins or print in landscape orientation, make those changes in the toolbar at the top of the Print Preview dialog box. When you are ready to print, click the Print button in the right corner of the Print Preview toolbar.

THE ABSOLUTE MINIMUM

The following are the highlights from this chapter:

- Double-click the icon on an index card to open the document itself. Double-clicking on the title or synopsis areas of the index card allows you to edit those entries.

- Index cards can hold both a synopsis and an image.

- When you adjust the appearance of labels, status, and keywords on index cards, a single card can tell you a lot about your project.

- Lock the View mode (Mac only) to set a container to always open in the Corkboard (or Outliner or Scrivenings) view.

- If you want to use the Freeform Corkboard layout (Mac only) to determine your card order, use the Commit Order command. You can use the Freeform Corkboard, however, without committing to change the order of your cards.

- You can use the Corkboard in conjunction with Document view in Split Screen mode to create a streamlined workflow from Binder to Corkboard to Document.

7

PLOTTING IN THE OUTLINER

Does your writing process lean more to the logical than the visual? Do you need more information about your project than a color-coded index card can provide? Do you want to see your entire project's hierarchy at once instead of one container at a time? If so, the Outliner is the tool for you.

The skeuomorphic Corkboard can be very useful for storyboarding or when you want to hone in on a particular container, but the Outliner offers additional flexibility to give you an overview of your project.

Exploring the Outliner

As with the other Group View modes, Scrivenings and the Corkboard, the Outliner is used to view multiple items at once. Thus, before you can open the Outliner, you must select a container or group of files in the Binder. If you want to see your entire Draft (or Manuscript) folder at once, select this root folder in the Binder. Then choose one of these options to open the Outliner:

- Click the Outliner button in the Group Mode grouping on the toolbar.
- Choose View, Outline from the menu.
- Press Cmd-3 (Ctrl+3 in Windows).

The Outliner, shown in Figure 7.1, resembles a spreadsheet. Each row represents a document or folder. Each column displays meta-data associated with the item, such as Title, Synopsis, Label, and Status. On the Mac, the Title and Synopsis appear in one column, along with the item icon, with the synopsis appearing below the title.

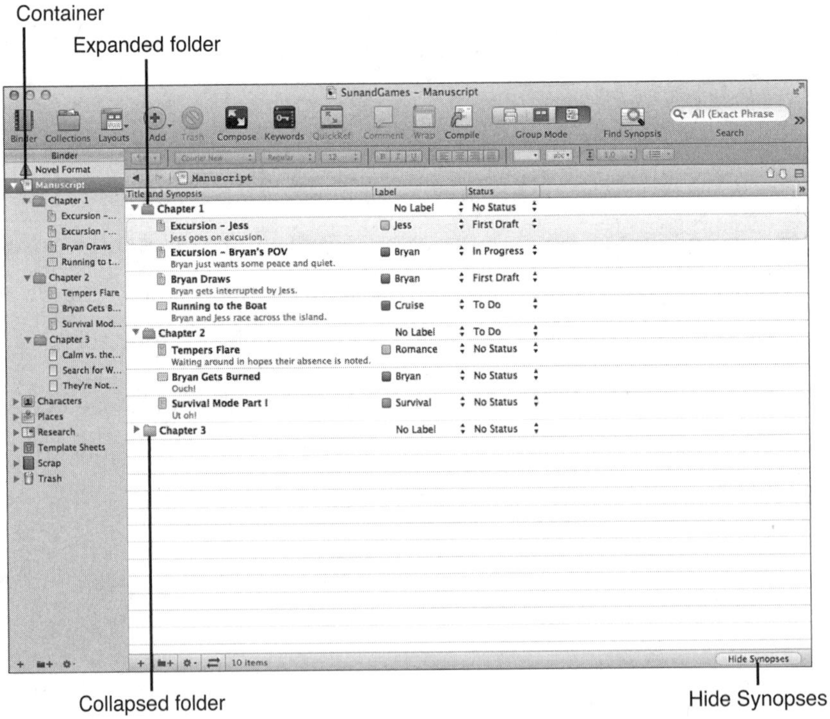

FIGURE 7.1

The Outliner displays multiple levels of your project on a single screen.

On the Windows platform, the Title and Synopsis fields are in separate columns, as shown in Figure 7.2. The item icon appears by default with the title.

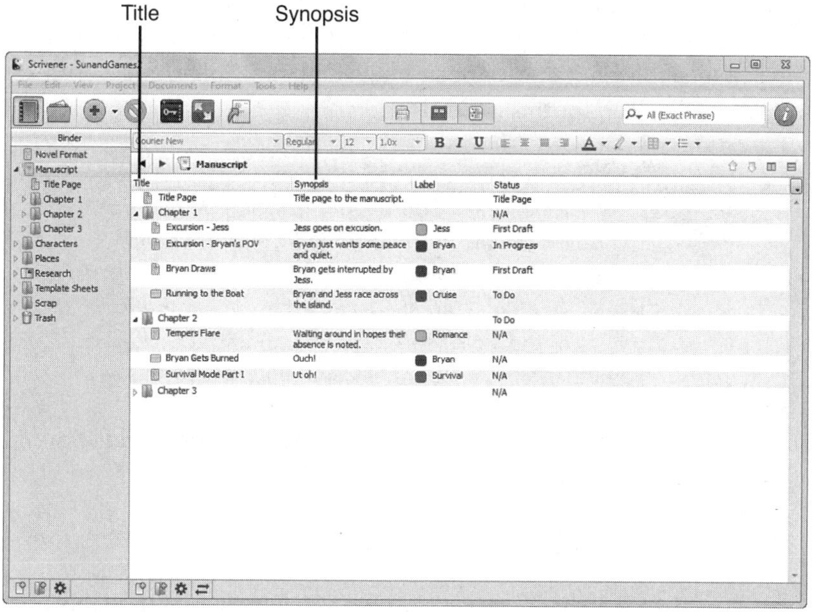

Title   Synopsis

FIGURE 7.2

The Outliner in Windows separates the Title and Synopsis into two fields.

NOTE You can also use the Outliner in Split Screen mode. Refer to Chapter 4, "Writing in the Editor," and Chapter 6, "Storyboarding with the Corkboard," to learn more about Split Screen mode. As with the Corkboard, if you want to open a document in the Editor, double-click its item icon in the Outliner.

Customizing the Outliner

By default, Scrivener displays the Title and Synopsis, Label, and Status fields, but you can customize the columns to add or remove fields. In fact, you can customize just about everything in the Outliner. You can expand and collapse folders and adjust the column width. On the Mac, you can also change the sort order of items.

Expanding and Collapsing Containers

As you can see in Figures 7.1 and 7.2, the Outliner displays the entire contents of the container you selected in the Binder. Items with subitems appear with a disclosure triangle next to the item icon. Toggle the triangle to expand and collapse the subfolder or file group in order to view its contents.

If you want to expand all of the items in the Outliner at once, choose View, Outline, Expand All. On the Mac, you can use the Cmd-9 keyboard shortcut. To collapse all of the items, choose View, Outline, Collapse All. The keyboard shortcut on the Mac for this is Cmd-0.

 TIP If you want to set a keyboard shortcut for these commands in Windows, select Tools, Options from the menu and then select the Keyboard tab. Begin typing the word *expand* (or *collapse*) in the Filter text field at the top of the Keyboard options to narrow the list of menu commands, and then select the Expand All command (or the Collapse All command) and set a keyboard shortcut combination. Click OK to close the Options window.

You can also expand a single item and all of its subfolders and file groups. To do this, press the Option key (Alt key in Windows) while clicking the disclosure triangle.

Adding and Removing Columns

Arguably the most powerful feature of the Outliner is the ability to see all of the meta-data for an entire container on one screen. If you view your Draft folder in the Outliner, you can see all of the meta-data for your entire project, including every subfolder and file group. Of course, you won't want to limit this power to just the title, synopsis, label, and status for your items.

To add or remove columns from the Outliner:

1. Click the Columns Menu button on the right end of the field headers, as shown in Figure 7.3. In Windows, the button is a single down-facing triangle on the far right of the header row.

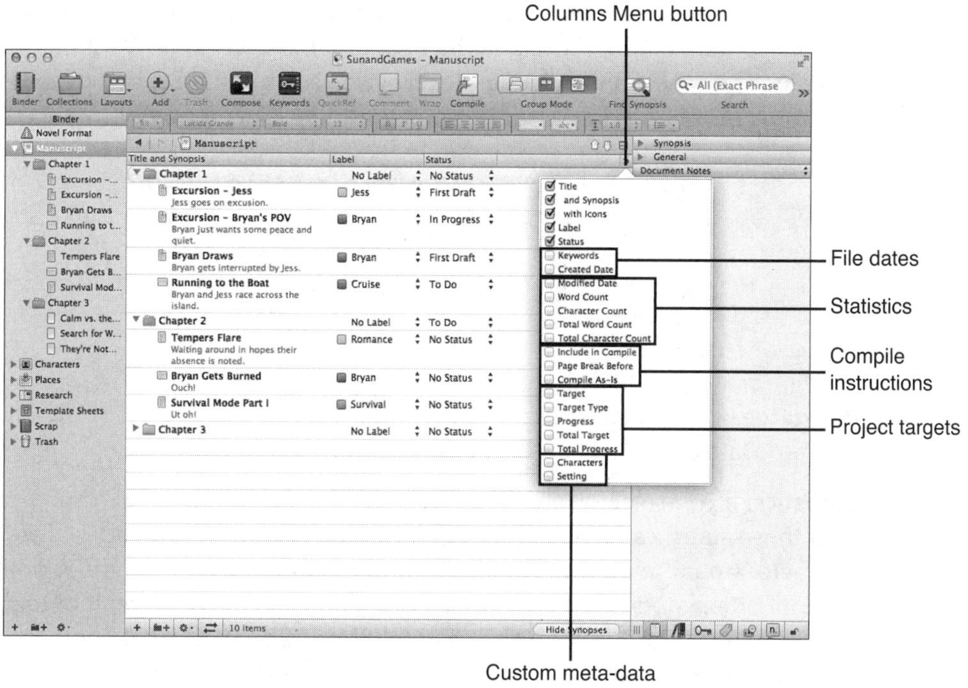

Columns Menu button

File dates

Statistics

Compile
instructions

Project targets

Custom meta-data

FIGURE 7.3

Add or remove columns from the Outliner using the Columns drop-down menu.

2. Select the field you want to add to the Outliner or deselect the field you want to remove.

3. On the Mac, you can continue selecting or deselecting multiple items at once. In Windows, repeat steps 1 and 2 as needed.

4. Click outside the drop-down menu when you are finished.

Alternatively, you can configure Outliner headers by choosing View, Outliner Columns and selecting or deselecting from the submenu. On the Mac, you can also right-click anywhere in the Outliner column headers to select or deselect items from the pop-up menu.

You can display the following types of meta-data fields in the Outliner:

*   **Basic item information**: On the Mac, the default first column is labeled Title and Synopsis and also displays the item icon. You can deselect the And Synopsis and With Icons options if you want to only see the Title field. As with the Corkboard, you can also choose to view the Label and Status. On the Mac, you can view Keywords, as well. You can edit the title and synopsis

by double-clicking in those entries and modifying the text. Change the label or status of an item by clicking in the field (double-clicking in Windows) and selecting from the pop-up menu. Add keywords (on the Mac) by opening the Keywords panel and dragging keywords onto the Outliner entry.

 CAUTION You cannot delete a keyword directly within the Outliner. To delete keywords from an item, open the Inspector, click the Keywords icon at the bottom of the sidebar, and then select the keyword and press Delete. See Chapter 12, "Putting Keywords and Meta-Data to Work," to learn more about using keywords.

- **File dates**: If you want to see when files were created or last modified, choose Created Date and Modified Date.

- **Statistics**: If you select Word Count and/or Character Count, you can view these statistics for each item. Choose Total Word Count and/or Total Character Count to view the statistics for any subitems within a folder or file group. For example, if a folder (or file group) contains a paragraph of text of its own, that word count appears in the Word Count column. The total number of words in that folder plus all of its subfolders and subdocuments appears in the Total Word Count column.

 NOTE The two Word Count options are displayed on the Mac in the colors of the progress bar. You can see how close you are to reaching your target goal from the color of the number in these fields, even if you do not choose to display the project targets in the Outliner. To learn more about project targets, see Chapter 15, "Tracking Your Progress."

- **Compile instructions**: The Include in Compile, Page Break Before, and Compile As-Is settings are used when compiling a project. They are based on the settings in the Inspector. You can modify them by selecting or deselecting the check boxes in either the Outliner or Inspector. Press the Option key on the Mac or Alt key in Windows while clicking to select or deselect all visible rows.

- **Project targets**: If you set document targets, as explained in Chapter 15, the project target fields display how close you are to reaching your goals in each item or container.

  - **Target**: Displays the target goal for the item.

  - **Target Type**: Displays whether the displayed target is a word or character goal. Click in this field and choose from the pop-up menu to change the Target Type.

- **Progress**: Displays a bar showing your progress toward your target goal. The bar changes color as you approach your goal.

- **Total Target (Mac Only)**: Displays the target goal for the item plus any subitems based on the individual document targets set for these items.

- **Total Progress (Mac Only)**: Displays a bar showing your progress toward your target goal for the entire folder or file group based on the individual document targets set for the container and its subdocuments.

- **Custom Meta-Data (Mac Only)**: If you set up custom meta-data, as explained in Chapter 15, you can display these fields in the Outliner. Figure 7.3 shows two custom fields in the Columns menu. A common use of custom meta-data is to add a field to display the date of a scene to use the Outliner as a timeline.

> **TIP** If you're a lawyer using Scrivener to prepare case material, adding a custom field can help you track when you've filed briefs and motions or note references to case law.

You can return to the Columns menu whenever you want to reconfigure the Outliner. New columns are added to the right of previously selected columns, but they do not have to remain in that position.

Arranging Columns and Items

Once you determine which fields you want to display, you can arrange the columns in the header row. To move a column, click on the header and drag it to its new position.

To adjust the width of a column, position your cursor to the right of the column you want to modify. The cursor changes to a two-sided arrow. Click and drag the cursor to the new position. You can also double-click the cursor to automatically resize the column.

> **TIP** If you use multiple configurations of Outliner columns, consider saving each configuration as a workspace layout, as explained in Chapter 2, "Customizing Your Work Environment." Outliner columns and their arrangement are both saved in the layout.

Items can also be rearranged within the Outliner. Simply drag and drop the item to its new location. Changes within the Outliner are immediately reflected in the Binder. If you drop an item into a different folder or file group, you immediately see the statistics update in the Total Words field and the project targets if you have made those fields visible in the Outliner.

Hiding the Synopsis

The Outliner is great for giving you a broad overview of your project. You can look down the Status column, for example, and immediately see which items are unwritten, are in progress, or are ready for revision (if you use the Status field with the default settings and have not repurposed it to track some other aspect of your project). In those instances, you don't need to see the synopsis for each item. In fact, the synopses may take up extra lines of screen real estate when you would prefer to see as many items as possible without scrolling.

There are two ways to hide the synopsis in the Outliner, as follows:

- As noted earlier, you can deselect the And Synopsis option in the Columns menu (deselect the Synopsis option in Windows).
- Click the Hide Synopses button in the Footer bar of the Outliner, as shown in Figure 7.1. This option is only available on the Mac.

To display the synopses again, reselect the option in the Columns menu or click the Show Synopses button (on the Mac).

Sorting by Outliner Columns (Mac Only)

Just as the Freeform Corkboard (on the Mac) allows you to manually group index cards together, the Outliner enables you to sort by any column. If you write your work out of order, for example, you may want to sort by Status to group items that are In Progress, To Do, or have been through a First Draft and are ready for revision.

 TIP Because items may have multiple keywords attached, it is rarely useful to sort by the Keywords field.

To sort, click the header for the column by which you want to organize your items. As you can see in Figure 7.4, a triangular sort indicator appears in the header column to show by which field and in which order the Outliner is sorted. The triangle points upward to signify an ascending (A to Z) sort order and downward when the sort is descending (Z to A). As you can see in the figure, each container is sorted independently. In other words, all of the items in Chapter 1 are sorted, and then all the items in Chapter 2, and so on.

TIP If you change the sort order of items in a container and want to make the change permanent, select the items in the Outliner and drag them back into their container in the Binder. You can also right-click on the selection and then choose Move To from the context menu and select the original container from the submenu.

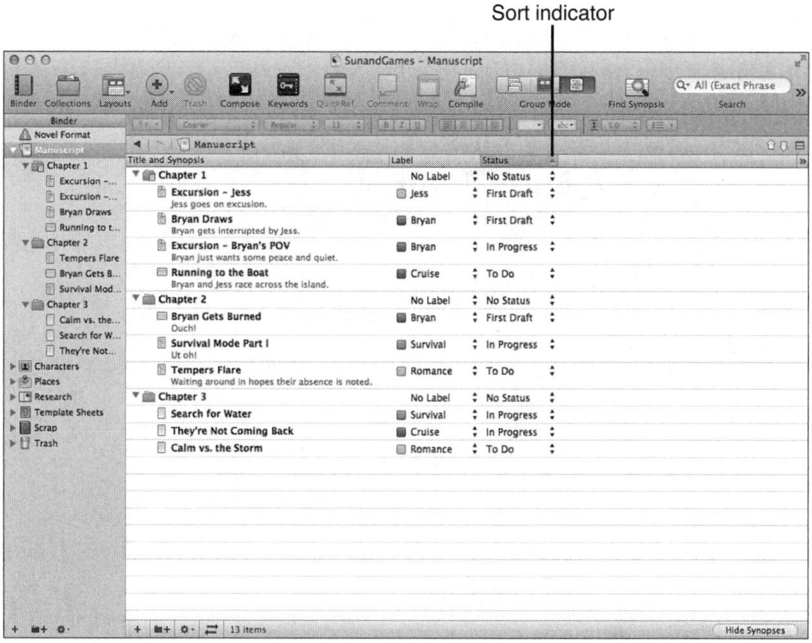

Sort indicator

FIGURE 7.4

Sorting the Outliner by Status can help you determine which items need attention in order to finish a complete first draft.

 NOTE Changing the sort order does not change the arrangement of items in the Binder.

THE CREATIVE PROCESS: IDEAS FOR CUSTOM META-DATA (MAC ONLY)

Sorting is particularly useful when you create custom meta-data fields, as described in Chapter 12, "Putting Keywords and Meta-Data to Work." You can create a rudimentary timeline in Scrivener by adding a custom Timeline field where you can enter the date of each scene in a manuscript. Sort by the created timeline to see the progression of your story by date and time.

Lawyers can sort by a custom date field to note when motions and briefs were filed with the court. You can also add a custom field to note which items cite certain case law.

In this book, I created a custom field to note which sections contained the Creative Process and Windows View sidebars to ensure they were scattered throughout the project.

Printing an Outline on the Mac

Some writers like to do all their work on the computer. But for those times when you need to work the old-fashioned way, with pen and paper, it's convenient to have your project outline available.

To print your outline on the Mac:

1. Select File, Page Setup.

2. Click the Settings option and select Scrivener from the drop-down menu. The dialog box displays margin settings.

3. Click Options. The Print Options dialog box opens.

4. Click Outlines to display the options for printing from the Outliner, as shown in Figure 7.5.

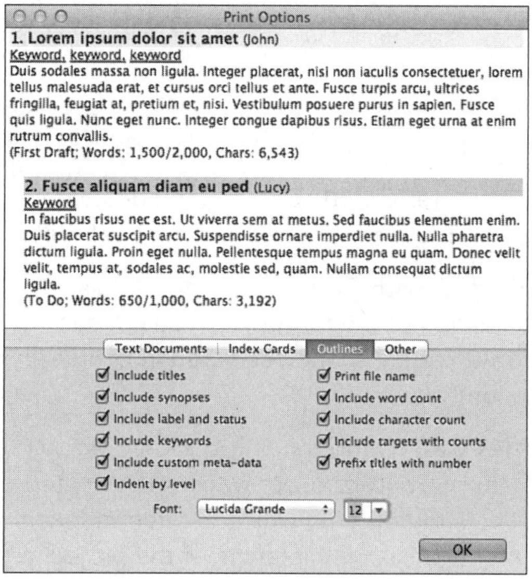

FIGURE 7.5

The preview pane of the Print Options window shows where each selected option appears in the entry.

5. Select from the following options. The top half of the dialog box displays a preview showing how the options you select will appear in the printout:

    - **Include Titles**: Selected by default, this prints the document title for each item.

    - **Include Synopses**: Selected by default, this adds the synopsis to each item.

    - **Include Label and Status**: This option highlights the title in the label color and appends the label name in parentheses next to the title. It adds the status in parentheses below the synopsis.

    - **Include Keywords**: This option adds the keywords beneath the document title. Keywords are underlined and comma separated.

    - **Include Custom Meta-Data**: This option adds the field name and contents of any custom meta-data for the entry below the title and keywords.

    - **Indent by Level**: Selected by default, this indents subitems for each container.

    - **Print File Name**: This option adds the name of the selected container for the outline to the header of the printed outline. For example, if you select the Draft folder in the Binder to open in the Outliner, the header displays the word Draft along with the print date of the outline. If you choose a different container, the header displays the title of that folder or file group.

- **Include Word Count**: This option adds the word count below the synopsis, within the same parentheses as the status.

- **Include Character Count**: This option adds the character count below the synopsis, within the same parentheses as the status and word count.

- **Include Targets with Counts**: This option displays the word count for each item as a fraction of the target word count, such as 647/1,000. This item only affects the outline when selected in conjunction with the Include Word Count option.

- **Prefix Titles with Numbers**: This option prepends a number to the title of each item showing its order within the selected container. This number simply reflects the order in which the item appears within the parent container, not within the hierarchy of the project as a whole.

- **Font**: This option determines the font and font size for your printed outline.

6. Click OK to close the Print Options dialog box.

7. Click OK to close the Page Setup dialog box.

8. Choose File, Print Current Document (or press Cmd-P) from the menu to open the Print dialog box.

9. Click Print.

When you are in the Print dialog box in step 9, you have the option of printing a hard copy of the outline or saving it as a PDF file. To save as a PDF:

1. In the Print dialog box, click the PDF button in the lower-left corner of the window.

2. Select Save as PDF in the drop-down menu.

3. Name the file and navigate to where you want the file to be stored in the Save As dialog box.

4. Click Save.

You can also preview your outline as a PDF before printing. In step 2, above, select Open PDF in Preview from the drop-down menu. You can then print or save the file from within the Preview app.

A WINDOWS VIEW: PRINTING AN OUTLINE IN WINDOWS

In the Windows version, you can print the Title and Synopsis fields using File, Print Current Document (or press Ctrl+P), but the remaining fields cannot be printed in this manner.

The best way to access all of your meta-data into a format that can be printed is to export the Outliner to a CSV file, which can then be opened in a spreadsheet program. You can adjust column widths and formatting in the spreadsheet and then print. Exporting the Outliner is explained in the next section of this chapter.

TIP   Another approach for both Windows and the Mac is to compile your project using the Outliner or Enumerated Outline compile presets. See Chapter 19, "Compiling Your Completed Work," to learn how to use the Compile features in Scrivener.

Exporting an Outline

Another method for using your Outliner data outside Scrivener is to export it to a file. This file can be opened in other applications, such as a spreadsheet or mind map, where you can manipulate and format the data as you require. You can also print from these applications with more flexibility and control over formatting than the Scrivener Outliner options.

For Windows users, this is the only way to access the word count or target goal meta-data fields so you can print them in your outline. Even Mac users may find this approach is preferable, however.

Exporting to a Spreadsheet (CSV Format)

If you want to access your outline in a spreadsheet, such as Microsoft Excel, Apple Numbers, or OpenOffice Calc, you first need to export it to a CSV file. CSV stands for Comma-Separated Values, and that's exactly what this file contains—a text document with each item on its own line and each field separated by a comma.

NOTE   You can also save your file in Tab-Separated Values (TSV) or Semicolon Separated Values (TXT) formats.

To export a file to a spreadsheet-accessible format:

1. Open the container you want to save in the Outliner.

2. If you only want to include specific fields in your spreadsheet file, select those columns from the Columns menu and hide any that you want to exclude.

3. Choose File, Export, Outliner Contents as CSV. This opens the Save As dialog box on the Mac or the Export Outliner dialog box in Windows, shown in Figure 7.6.

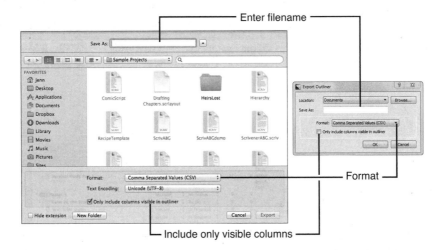

FIGURE 7.6

The Export Outliner Contents as CSV options appear in the Save As dialog box on the Mac and the Export Outliner dialog box in Windows.

4. Navigate to the folder where you want to store your file and enter a filename.

5. Click the Format drop-down list and choose from CSV, TSV, or TXT format.

6. You can include all possible meta-data fields in your file or only those currently visible in the Outliner. Select or deselect the Only Include Columns Visible in Outliner as necessary.

7. Click Export on the Mac or OK in Windows.

To view your outline, open the file within your spreadsheet application.

Exporting to OPML Format

You can also export your outline to a dedicated outliner or mind map application. A dedicated outlining program, such as OmniOutliner, is similar to the Scrivener

Outliner, but with more flexibility for a wider range of projects. A mind map is a brainstorming tool whereby you start with a single idea and branch other concepts off of it, as shown in Figure 7.7. Most of these apps use OPML format. This format stores item headings and tracks the relationships between items, such as parent, child, and siblings.

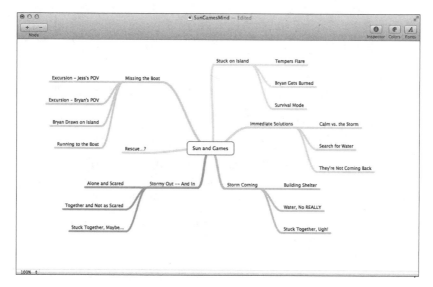

FIGURE 7.7

Here is a mind map laid out in MindNode Lite.

NOTE If you want to give mind mapping a try, FreeMind and XMind are free, cross-platform applications. There are also many Mac-specific applications, including Scapple or OmniOutliner. A more full-featured, yet pricier, option for Mac and Windows is MindManager.

To export your outline to OPML format:

1. Open the container you want in the Outliner.

2. Choose File, Export, OPML File (File, Export, OPML or Mindmap File in Windows). This opens the Export Save As dialog box, as shown in Figure 7.8.

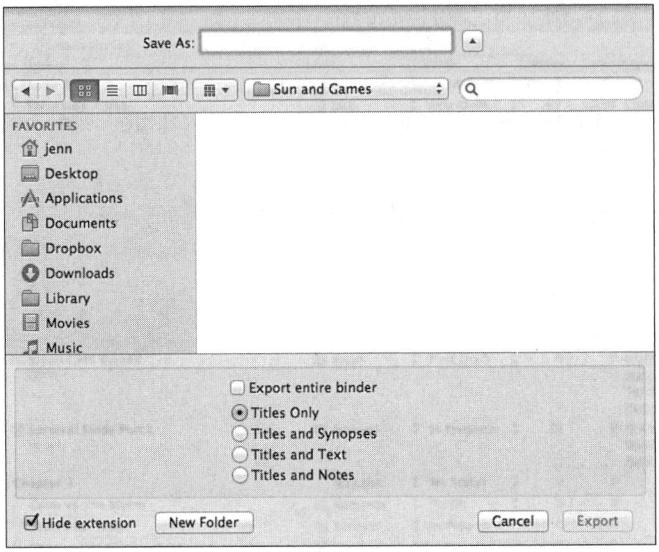

FIGURE 7.8

The Export Save As dialog box provides options for saving only the title or the title plus either the synopsis, document text, or notes in OPML format.

3. Navigate to the folder where you want to store your file and enter a filename. In Windows, also select whether you want to save the file with the `.opml` or `.mm` (FreeMind) extension or save just the titles in an indented plain-text outline.

4. Select the Export Entire Binder option if you want your entire project exported into the OPML file.

> **CAUTION** The Export Entire Binder option includes all of the root folders from your entire project, including the Trash. This can result in an extremely crowded and ultimately useless mind map, so be sure this is the result you want before selecting this option.

5. Choose the information to be included in the OPML folder. The options are as follows:

- **Titles Only**: Includes only the titles of each document in the selected container.

- **Titles and Synopses**: Saves the titles and synopses for each item.

- **Titles and Text**: Saves the titles and document text for each item.

NOTE The Titles and Text option only preserves the text of an item, not any images or formatting that may be included in the document. If you export the entire Binder, the titles of PDFs, images, and other file types in your Research folder will appear in the OPML file, but not the content of those items.

- **Titles and Notes**: Saves the titles and document notes for each item. Document notes are entered in the Inspector, as explained in Chapter 11, "Digging into the Inspector."

6. Click Export on the Mac or Save in Windows.

 CAUTION Not all mind map applications allow you to view synopses, text, or notes. Some of these apps simply ignore this data while others cannot open files containing it. If you have trouble opening an OPML file with this data included, try exporting with the Titles Only option.

Importing an OPML or Freemind Outline

If you get hooked on mind mapping, you may choose to map out your story before using Scrivener. Just as you can export to OPML format (and MM for Freemind in Windows), you can also import from both OPML and Freemind into Scrivener. To import an OPML or Freemind file:

1. In your mind map or outlining application, save or export your file in OPML or MM format.

2. In Scrivener, open the project into which you want to import the file.

3. Select File, Import, Files (in Windows, choose File, Import, OPML or Mindmap File). This opens the Import dialog box.

4. On the Mac, navigate to the file and click Import. In Windows, browse to the file, select where you want Scrivener to place attached notes, and then click OK. The Windows Import dialog box is shown in Figure 7.9.

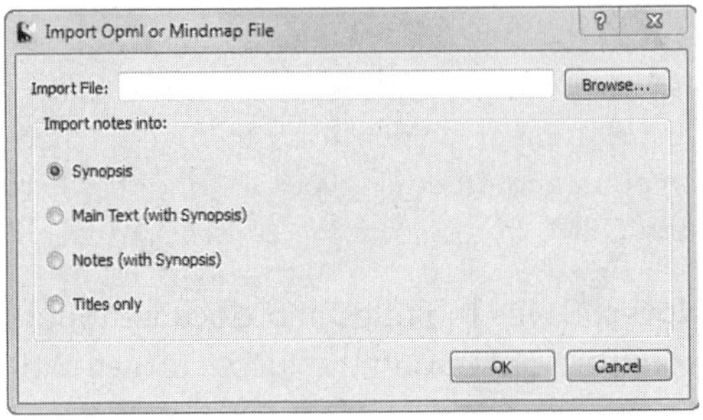

FIGURE 7.9

In Windows, you can select where to import notes attached to mind map items.

When you import a mind map, Scrivener creates a new item for each entry, organizing items into file groups according to the hierarchy of the mind map nodes. Figure 7.10 shows the mind map that was displayed in Figure 7.7 after being imported into Scrivener.

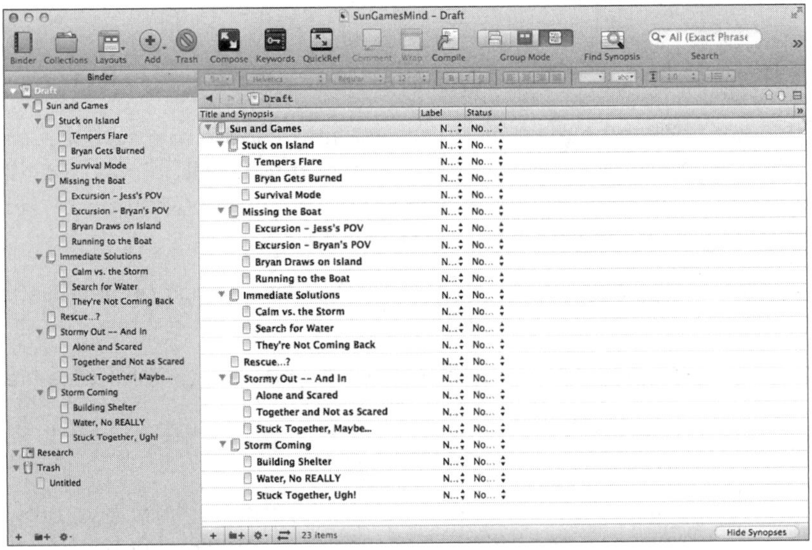

FIGURE 7.10

The mind map from Figure 7.7 is imported into a Scrivener project.

THE ABSOLUTE MINIMUM

The takeaways from this chapter are as follows:

- Like the Corkboard, the Outliner is another Group View mode that provides an overview of your project.

- Unlike the Corkboard, the Outliner can display your entire, multilevel project instead of just a container.

- You can add and remove columns from the Outliner to focus on information that is important to your workflow.

- You can print the outline of your project in much the same manner as you can print index cards from the Corkboard.

- You can also export your outline to a spreadsheet or save in PDF or OPML formats for use in other applications.

IN THIS CHAPTER

- Importing research files
- Using PDFs
- Accessing media files
- Importing web pages

8

ORGANIZING YOUR RESEARCH

Every writing project has certain similarities. If you are writing a novel, you collect information about characters, settings, occupations, and other details to enhance your story. If you are writing an academic thesis, you collect data and published works to support your thesis. Lawyers collect information about a case, their clients, and case law. Cooks collect information about techniques and ingredients. Yes, the common element we cover in this chapter is research.

Scrivener can keep all of your research together with your project. This makes it easy to find exactly what you need. As you learned in Chapter 4, "Writing in the Editor," you can even view a research file in one pane in Split Screen mode while you work on a document in the other pane.

The Research folder is one of the default root folders added to every Scrivener project (as if you needed further proof that research is a key element of any form of writing). You can rename the folder or create additional folders to hold research, as you require. If you are gathering a lot of research on various topics, you might want to create subfolders for each topic within the Research folder.

TIP When working on a novel, I create a root folder called Reference in addition to my Research folder. The Reference folder holds worksheets and notes I've collected from writing workshops and books on writing that I tend to refer to with every project. The Research folder is where I collect research information specific to the work in progress.

Importing Research Files

The easiest way to add most types of files to your Research folder is simply to drag the file from Finder or Windows Explorer and drop it into the location you want in the Binder.

CAUTION Remember, the Draft folder only holds text files. You cannot add other file types to this folder.

Using File Import

You can also import files using the menu. To import a file into your Research folder:

1. In the Binder, select the Research folder or another folder into which you want to import the file.

2. Choose File, Import, Files from the menu or press Cmd-Shift-I (Ctrl+Shift+J in Windows). This opens the Import Files dialog box.

3. Select the file you want to import.

4. Click Import on the Mac or Open in Windows.

When you import, you see a warning about possible loss of footnotes and images if converting a text file, as shown in Figure 8.1. On the Mac, this warning also offers the option to only import supported file types. If you select this option, Scrivener only imports files that can be viewed within the application. If you intend to import files that require viewing in another application, do not select this option. Click the check box beside Do Not Show This Warning Again to disable the warning for future imports.

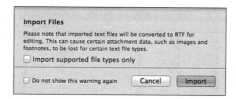

FIGURE 8.1

This warning appears when you import a file.

 NOTE Chapter 3, "Organizing the Binder," explained the different file types and default icons that appear in the Binder when you import nontext files.

Opening Files in an External Editor

Scrivener can display many file types directly within the application. You can read PDFs, listen to audio files, and view videos and images. Some formats, such as spreadsheets, are unsupported by Scrivener, but can still display a Quick Look view of the file on a Mac.

 NOTE If you are using Mac OS X 10.6 Snow Leopard or earlier, you must click the Quick Look icon in the Footer bar to open a Quick Look panel. In OS X 10.7 Lion or higher, the Quick Look automatically opens in the Editor. You also still have the option of opening a Quick Look panel in Lion or higher.

If Scrivener cannot open a file, the Editor displays an icon representing the application in which the file was created, as shown in Figure 8.2. In Windows, the Editor displays a link to open the file in the default application associated with that file type, as shown in Figure 8.3.

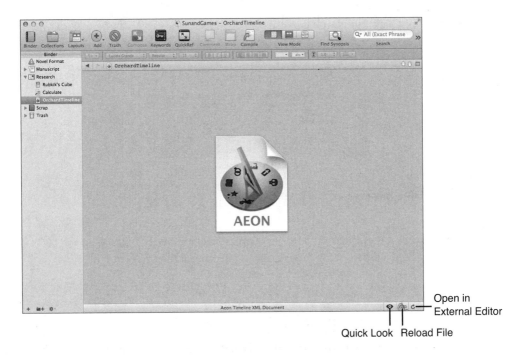

FIGURE 8.2

Scrivener cannot directly display Aeon Timeline files.

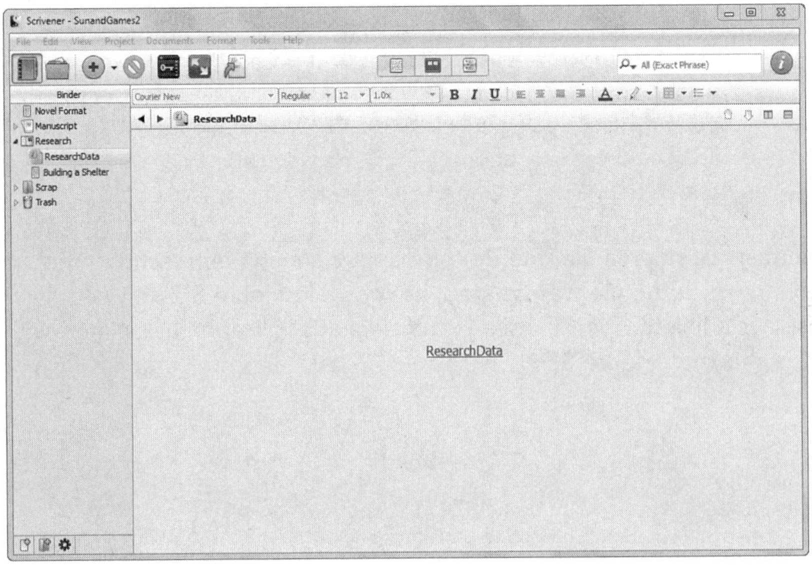

FIGURE 8.3

Scrivener cannot display an Excel file in Windows, so it provides a link to open the file in an external editor, namely Microsoft Excel.

TIP You may also want to open a file in an external editor in order to make changes to the file. You can open an image file in a graphics package, for example, to crop the image or add a callout to a figure.

To open a file in an external editor, choose one of the following options:

- In Windows, click the link in the Editor.

- On the Mac, click the Open in External Editor button in the Footer bar to open the file in the default application for that file type. Alternatively, click and hold or right-click the Open in External Editor button to choose the application with which you want to view the file.

- Choose Documents, Open, Open in External Editor in the menu.

- Right-click on the file in the Binder and then select Open, In External Editor (Open, Open In External Editor in Windows).

- Press Control-Cmd-O on the Mac or Ctrl+F5 in Windows.

 NOTE If you edit a file in an external editor on the Mac, click the Reload File button in the Footer bar when you return to Scrivener so the file is updated in your project. In Windows, switch to a different item and then back to the file to refresh the display.

Linking to an Alias

Sometimes your research material is itself a work in progress. When you import a file into Scrivener, a copy is made that becomes an inherent part of your project. If you make changes to the original file, those changes are not reflected in the copy that resides in Scrivener.

Some of your research files may also be quite large. Importing these items significantly increases the file size of the project, which could slow down automatic backups and even fill up your backup storage with multiple copies of such large files.

If you face either of these challenges on the Mac, you can link to the file as an alias rather than using the standard import options. To do this, select File, Import, Research Files as Aliases from the menu. When you link to a file as an alias, the icon for the item in the Binder displays a small arrow on the lower left to indicate that the file is stored externally. Whenever you access that item in your project, Scrivener checks for the most recent copy of the external file. If you move or rename the file, Scrivener can locate it, but if you move your Scrivener project to another computer, your links will not function on that computer.

CAUTION If you obtained your copy of Scrivener from the Mac App Store, you may see an error message when you try to open files linked with an alias. This is due to security limitations on file access that Apple has put on apps sold through the Mac App Store. If you want to grant Scrivener access to these files, choose Scrivener, Authorize Directory Access from the menu, and then click the Add Directories button. In the Open dialog box, select the directories to which you want Scrivener to have access.

NOTE You can only link to a nontext document as an alias. You cannot link to a text document or supported word processor file, such as a Microsoft Word document.

In Windows, the process is a bit different. Rather than creating an alias within the Binder to link to a source file, Scrivener for Windows requires using the References table in the Inspector to create an external reference. References are covered in detail in Chapter 11, "Digging into the Inspector." But, briefly, to use this feature specifically for use in linking to your research files:

1. Create a new file in the Research folder.

2. Open the Inspector, if it is not already visible in your Scrivener window. Click the Inspector icon in the toolbar (the italicized *i* in a blue circle), or select View, Layout, Show Inspector from the menu, or press Ctrl+Shift+I.

3. Click the References button at the bottom of the Inspector.

4. Click the Add (+) button at the top of the Document References pane of the Inspector.

5. Select Look Up & Add External Reference from the drop-down menu, shown in Figure 8.4.

NOTE You can also drag files from Windows Explorer into the Document References pane in place of steps 4 and 5.

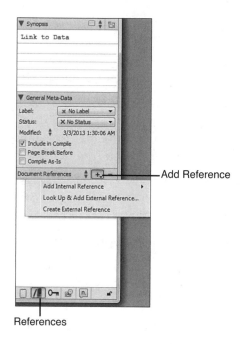

Add Reference

References

FIGURE 8.4

In Windows, create links to external documents using the Document References pane of the Inspector.

6. Select the file in the Add References dialog box, and click Open.

To open a reference, double-click it in the Document References pane of the Inspector. You can also right-click it and choose Open in Default Editor from the context menu.

As with many other procedures in Scrivener, there are several ways to approach this. Instead of creating a file just to hold a reference, for example, you can click the toggle to the right of the Document References heading in the Inspector and switch to Project References. Then you can attach a reference to the project as a whole rather than one document. This does not give you a point of reference within your Research folder, however, making it easy to forget the link is available.

 TIP   Although on the face of it, this process may seem more convoluted than the Mac method of linking to external files, there are actually several advantages to it. You can add notes to the document you create to hold the references. You can also add references to multiple external files from that document. Thus, this approach can serve as a way to collate and organize your research material. Mac users may want to take note, as this trick works on both platforms!

Using PDFs

Portable Document Format (PDF) is a popular way to save files so they can be accessed on multiple platforms while preserving the formatting of the document.

You can view PDF documents directly in Scrivener. Zoom in and out using the View, Zoom menu or the Cmd-> and Cmd-< keyboard shortcuts (Ctrl+= and Ctrl+- in Windows). You can also control the appearance of PDF documents from the View, Media, PDF Display submenu. The options on this menu are as follows:

- **Automatically Resize**: Mac only. Automatically resizes the document if you adjust the Editor window. In Windows, the Size to Fit option works the same way.

- **Actual Size**: Mac and Windows. Displays the document in its actual size.

- **Size to Fit**: Mac and Windows. Sizes the document to fill the Editor window. In Windows, this option automatically adjusts the size of the document if you change the Editor width.

- **Single Page**: Mac only. Displays a single page of the document at a time.

- **Facing Pages**: Mac only. Displays two pages of the document side by side.

- **Continuous**: Mac only. Displays the document as a continuous page.

- **Page Breaks**: Mac only. Displays the document with page breaks.

The Footer bar of the Editor changes when viewing PDFs. In Windows, the sizing controls appear in the Footer bar in addition to the PDF Display submenu. Use the arrows on the left side of the Footer bar to move forward and backward through the pages of the document. The center of the Footer bar displays your current page as well as the length of the document.

Click the Open in External Editor button in the Footer bar to open the document in another application. You can highlight selections of text in a PDF from within Scrivener for Mac by selecting Format, Highlight, Highlight Text or pressing Shift-Cmd-H. To add comments or make any other changes to a PDF, however, you need to use an external editor such as Adobe Acrobat.

TIP PDFs are not meant to be edited. You can highlight sections in Scrivener and make comments or add other annotations in Adobe Acrobat or Preview, but the document itself is meant to remain formatted as is. If you need to quote a block of text from a PDF, you can copy and paste it into a text document in your Draft folder. On the Mac, you can choose Documents, Convert, PDF File to Text from the menu to convert the document, and then copy and paste. If you're viewing the PDF in another application on the Mac, use the Services submenu in that application to create a clipping for Scrivener, as described in Chapter 2, "Customizing Your Work Environment." This converts the pasted or clipped selection into text, which you can then format to suit your project. If the content of the PDF document is not your original work, however, be sure to attribute the source in your project.

Accessing Media Files

Scrivener uses a multimedia view to play movie and sound files. When you select an audio or video file in the Binder, a control panel appears above the Footer bar in the Editor window, as shown in Figure 8.5.

Rewind by a Few
Seconds on Pause

0:00   –4:49

FIGURE 8.5

The media control panel in Scrivener provides a typical set of tools to control the playback of audio and video files.

Most of the controls should be familiar, as they control the volume, play/pause the file, and fast-forward or rewind. In the lower-right corner of the control panel, the Rewind by a Few Seconds on Pause toggle instructs Scrivener to automatically rewind whenever you pause. The number of seconds for the rewind is set in the Navigation tab of the Preferences/Options window. This feature is useful if you are transcribing the audio or video file. When you are transcribing or taking notes on a media file, you do not have to leave the document editor to pause the playback. Use Cmd-Return (Ctrl+Enter) to pause and resume playback in the other editor.

Importing Web Pages

Importing a web page requires a slightly different process than importing other types of research. When you import a web page, any links on the page open your default web browser. If you click the Reload File button on the right side of the Footer bar, the web page view is updated to reflect any changes to the page. The Footer bar also displays a link to the page so you can quickly open it in your default web browser.

To import a web page:

1. Click File, Import, Web Page from the menu. This opens the Import Web Page dialog box, shown in Figure 8.6.

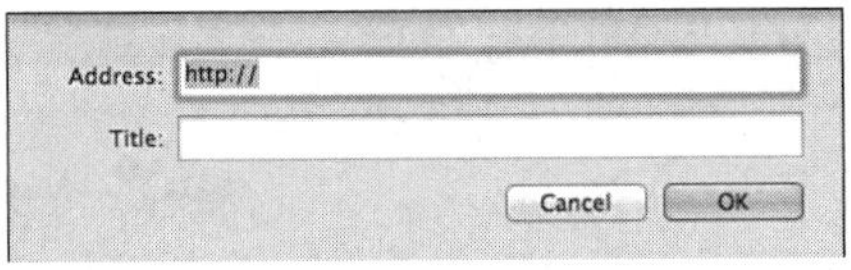

Address:	http://
Title:	
	Cancel OK

FIGURE 8.6

To import a web page, enter the URL in the Import Web Page dialog box. The title you supply appears in the Binder.

2. Enter the URL for the page.

3. Enter a title for the page. The title appears in the Binder.

4. In Windows, click the Import As drop-down menu and choose the format in which you want to import the web page. On the Mac, web pages are imported in .webarchive format by default. You can choose to import web pages as text in the Import/Export tab of the Preferences dialog box.

 TIP If you are working on a project on both Scrivener platforms, it is best to convert imported web pages on the Mac to text, as Windows does not support the .webarchive format. You can convert web pages on import using the Import/Export tab of the Preferences dialog box or after importing by choosing Documents, Convert, Web Page to Text from the menu.

5. Click OK.

THE ABSOLUTE MINIMUM

In this chapter, you learned the following:

- Add research files to your project by dragging and dropping, using the Import command, or linking to an external file.

- Use the References panel in the Inspector to add links to multiple external files from a single document. You can add your own notes to this document, as well.

- You can import PDFs and other nontext files into any folder except the Draft folder.

- You can view PDFs within Scrivener, but you cannot edit the files.

- You can make clippings from PDFs (with permission) and edit those clippings.

- Scrivener has audio and video playback controls within the application.

- You can link to other types of files and automatically open them in the proper application.

IN THIS CHAPTER

- Using the Name Generator
- Creating a sketchpad
- Using Aeon Timeline with Scrivener

9

BRAINSTORMING WITH SCRIVENER

Although Scrivener can be used for all manner of writing projects, a large percentage of its user base is composed of fiction writers. With that in mind, this chapter is all about using brainstorming tools with Scrivener to come up with your story.

In Chapter 7, "Plotting in the Outliner," you learned how to import and export Outline Processor Markup Language (OPML) files to work in conjunction with mind map applications. Mind mapping is one of many ways to brainstorm your plot and characters. Hopefully, this chapter gives you other ideas and shows you how to work both within and beyond Scrivener in a cohesive manner.

Using the Name Generator

To butcher Shakespeare, there's a lot in a name. A name can make your character approachable (or not), convey a sense of time and place, motivate, or be a burden to its bearer. In some cases, the choice of name for your protagonist is one of the most important decisions you make at the start of your novel.

To help you with this task, Scrivener includes a Name Generator. This tool contains thousands of names ranging from the common to the unique. There are names from classic literature as well as regional and cultural names.

The Name Generator works very differently in the Mac and Windows versions, so each is covered separately here.

Searching for Names on the Mac

To open the Name Generator on the Mac:

1. Select Edit, Writing Tools, Name Generator from the menu. The Name Generator appears, as shown in Figure 9.1 (shown with the Options Drawer open).

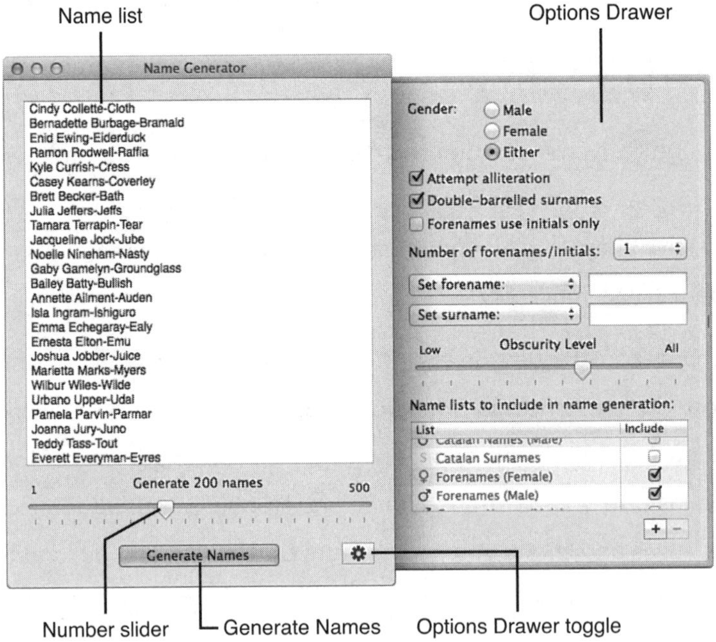

FIGURE 9.1

The Name Generator on the Mac utilizes an Options Drawer to narrow down the types of names you seek.

2. Click the Options Drawer toggle button (the gear) to open the Options Drawer.

3. Select options in the Options Drawer to hone in on the type of name you want to generate, as follows:

- **Gender**: The default setting is Either, but you can select to display only Male or only Female names.

- **Attempt Alliteration**: This option instructs the Name Generator to attempt to find alliterative names, such as Kelsey Clemson or Hector Hawkins. This option works best with Romance (Latin-based) languages because the sounds of the letters are more consistent among them, but try it with other languages and see what you get.

- **Double-Barrelled Surnames**: This option generates hyphenated surnames, such as Louise Minus-Peddle.

 TIP Try using the Attempt Alliteration and Double-Barrelled Surnames options together. The results can be quite humorous. Dusty Danks-Dither makes me want to create a character that would have that name, just to figure out what makes him or her tick!

- **Forenames Use Initials Only**: Select this option in conjunction with the Number of Forenames/Initials drop-down below it to generate surnames preceded by one to three initials, such as S. A. Crabwise.

- **Set Forename and Set Surname**: These options limit the search for a forename and/or surname by allowing you to enter one or more letters in the name. Click the option to open a drop-down menu with additional settings, as follows:

  - **Set Forename/Surname**: Enter a complete name. This allows you to enter a specific forename and use the Name Generator to match it with potential surnames, or vice versa.

  - **Forename/Surname Starts With**: Enter one or more letters, and the Name Generator provides names that begin with those letters.

  - **Forename/Surname Ends With**: Enter one or more letters, and the Name Generator provides names that end with those letters.

  - **Forename/Surname Contains**: Enter one or more letters, and the Name Generator provides names that contain those letters anywhere within the name. If you enter more than one letter here, the Name Generator only returns names that contain those letters grouped together in the specified order.

- **Obscurity Level**: Use the slider to set the level of obscurity in the names you seek. If you want a common name, such as Bobby Walker, move the slider all the way to the left. If you want an obscure name, such as Cluny Ruscoe, move the slider all the way to the right. The obscurity of a name often resides in the eyes of the beholder, as names with a strong cultural or regional tie may appear more obscure to those outside that community.

- **Name Lists to Include in Name Generation**: The Name Generator has several name lists built in from a variety of languages and sources. To the left of each name list is an icon indicating whether it is a male or female list of names. Lists of surnames appear with a yellow S icon. To select or deselect a list, click the check box in the Include column for that entry. You may select multiple lists for a wider range of names or narrow down the lists to a specific type of name.

NOTE   You must select at least one list of the gender you chose at the top of the Options Drawer and at least one surname list in order to generate names.

4. Below the Name list pane on the left, use the number slider to limit the number of names generated.

5. Click Generate Names.

Names fitting the criteria you selected in the Options Drawer appear in the list pane. As you view the list, you will undoubtedly come up with your own combinations of forenames and surnames, as well.

TIP   If you want to research the origin of a name, return to the main Scrivener interface—you can leave the Name Generator open in the background—and enter the name in the Editor. Select the name and use the search options in the Writing Tools submenu (Edit, Writing Tools or the context menu) to search for the name. You can search in Spotlight for files on your computer or search in Google or Wikipedia to open your web browser and access those sites. These search tools are helpful when conducting other project-related research, as well.

Adding Names to the Mac Name Generator

Although there are several lists from which to choose in the Name Generator, it is by no means complete. You can add your own name lists by creating a CSV (comma-separated value) file. All of the names in the file should be on one line, with each name separated by a comma but no spaces, such as

name1,name2,name3,name4

NOTE   Don't worry if your application automatically wraps long lines, but do not add any manual line breaks or carriage returns.

Save the file with a `.csv` extension. If you have both male and female names, separate them into their own lists. Consider creating lists of names with a common cultural or regional origin, popularity during a particular historical period, or with a similar meaning. This makes it easier to select or deselect lists when generating names to meet specific criteria. Enter names in order from least to most obscure (that is, most common to least common) so you can use the obscurity slider on the list.

TIP   You can find preformatted name lists created by other Scrivener users online. Search the forums on the Literature & Latte site (http://www.literatureandlatte.com).

To add lists to the Name Generator:

1. Open the Options Drawer in the Name Generator.

2. Click the Add (+) button below the Name lists.

3. In the Open dialog box, select the `.csv` file, then click Open.

4. In the Name List dialog box, shown in Figure 9.2, enter a descriptive name for the list.

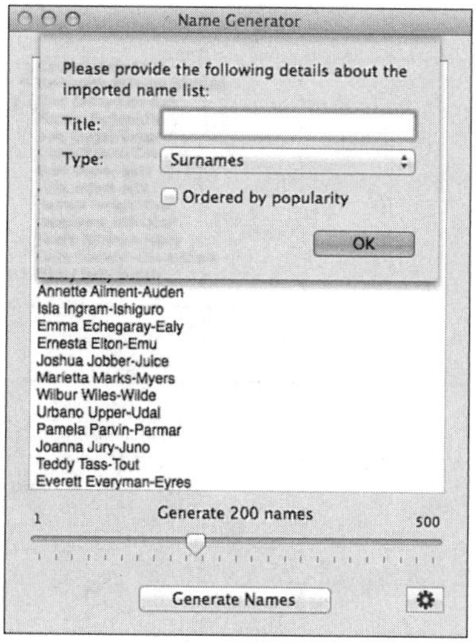

Name Generator

Please provide the following details about the imported name list:

Title: [ ]

Type: Surnames ▾

☐ Ordered by popularity

OK

Annette Ailment-Auden
Isla Ingram-Ishiguro
Emma Echegaray-Ealy
Ernesta Elton-Emu
Joshua Jobber-Juice
Marietta Marks-Myers
Wilbur Wiles-Wilde
Urbano Upper-Udal
Pamela Parvin-Parmar
Joanna Jury-Juno
Teddy Tass-Tout
Everett Everyman-Eyres

1   Generate 200 names   500

Generate Names   ⚙

FIGURE 9.2

Enter a description for your new name list and select the type of list.

5. Select the list type, whether Male Forenames, Female Forenames, or Surnames.

6. If the list has been ordered from the most common to most obscure, select the Ordered by Popularity check box. This affects the Obscurity slider when using this list.

7. Click OK. The list appears in the Name lists options.

 NOTE If you want to delete a list, select the list and click the Remove Custom Name List (–) button. You cannot delete any of the built-in lists.

Searching for Names in Windows

Scrivener for Windows has many features that do not exist in the Mac version. In Windows, select Tools, Writing Tools, Name Generator to open the Name Generator, as shown in Figure 9.3.

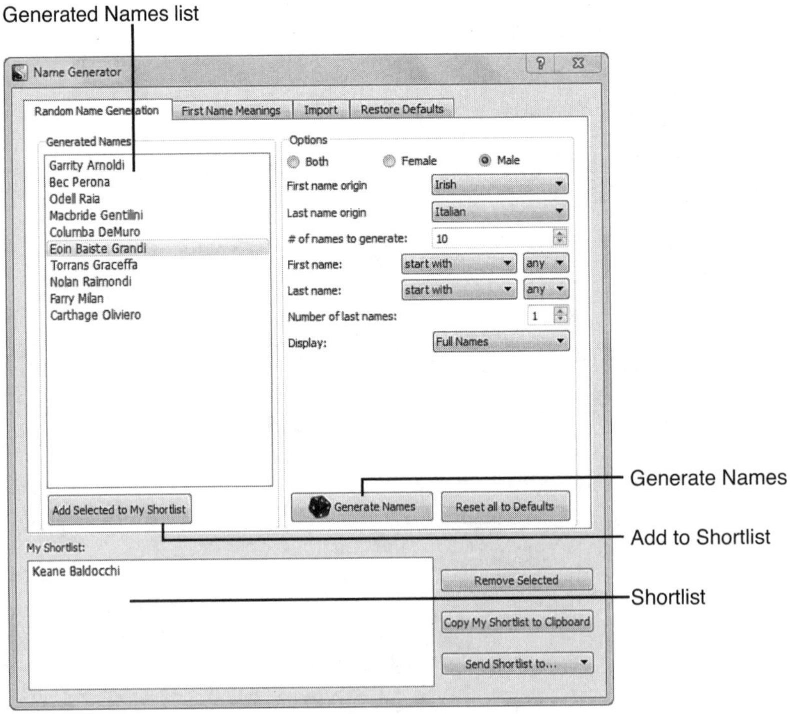

Generated Names list

Generate Names

Add to Shortlist

Shortlist

FIGURE 9.3

The Name Generator in Windows allows you to create a shortlist of names you want to consider for characters.

The Windows Name Generator has the following options:

- **Gender**: The default is Both, but you can choose to view only Male or only Female names.

- **First/Last Name Origin**: Open the drop-down menu for the first and last name to choose the language of origin for that name. If you have an Irish-Italian hero, for example, you can choose Irish for the First Name Origin and Italian for the Last Name Origin to come up with a unique name that explains your character's heritage upon the reader's first introduction to him. The default for both Name Origin options is All.

- **Number of Names to Generate**: This option controls how many names the Name Generator displays in the Generated Names list.

- **First Name/Last Name Start With**: Choose a letter from the drop-down list to limit the names to those that start with, end with, or both start and end with the chosen letter.

- **Number of Last Names**: This option determines the number of hyphenated surnames for each name in the list. Choose from 1 to 3.

- **Display**: Choose from displaying full names or only first or only last names.

Once you have set the options for your list, click Generate Names. The Generated Names list is populated with options that fit your criteria. When you discover a name you like, select it in the Generated Names list and then click Add Selected to My Shortlist. You can Shift+click to select multiple contiguous names at once from the list or Ctrl+click to select multiple noncontiguous names.

When you have created a shortlist of possible names, click Copy My Shortlist to the Clipboard to copy the list, and then open a document in your project to paste it. You can also paste the list from the Clipboard to a program outside Scrivener. Click the Send Shortlist To button to open a submenu of options in order to copy or append the list to a specific file in your Scrivener project.

 CAUTION If you close the Name Generator, your shortlist is erased. Always copy or send your shortlist to a file before closing the Name Generator.

Often, the meaning of a name can be used as a characterization element. To view the meaning of a name in the Windows Name Generator, click the First Name Meanings tab, shown in Figure 9.4. Most, but not all, of the names in the database have defined meanings.

FIGURE 9.4

The origin of most names listed in the Name Generator in Windows can be found in the First Name Meanings database.

Each name in the database is listed by gender, origin, and meaning. Search for names using the following criteria:

- **Exact Match**: Searches for the specific name you enter.

- **In Name Meaning**: Searches for a term in the Meaning column of the database. For example, a search for the word *flower* brings up a list of all the names that include the word *flower* in their meaning, such as Ardath, which means flowering field.

- **Anywhere in Name**: Searches for names containing the letter or letters you enter, grouped together in the order you specify. Thus, entering "LP" as the search criterion causes the name Alphonse to appear among many others matching that criterion.

- **At the Start/End of Name**: Searches for names beginning or ending with the letter or letters you enter.

- **Use Gender & Origin Only**: Searches for names matching your search term and meeting the Gender and Origin criteria you set in the First Name Meanings tab.

TIP You can also search for name meanings and conduct other project-related research using the Writing Tools submenu (Tools, Writing Tools or the context menu). These options open your browser and automatically search for any term you select in the Editor using Google, Wikipedia, and various other sites. The Translate to Another Language option opens your default web browser and enters the search criteria on the Dictionary.com Translator website (http://translate.reference.com). Translating a name or common word to another language can help you come up with an interesting variation of a name.

Adding Names to the Windows Name Generator

You can add names to the Name Generator in Windows by formatting them in a `.csv` or `.txt` file. Create separate lists for first and last names. For Last Name lists, format them as follows, with each name on its own line followed by the origin of the name, separated by a comma:

Name1,English

Name2,Polish

For First Name lists, enter each name on its own line followed by M or F to indicate gender, the origin of the name, and the meaning. The meaning must appear in double quotations. The list should appear as follows:

Name1,M,English,"Meaning of Name"

Name2,F,Irish,"Meaning of This Name"

 CAUTION Because of the formatting differences, name lists for the Mac and Windows versions are not interchangeable.

To add the list to the Name Generator:

1. Open the Name Generator and click the Import tab, shown in Figure 9.5.

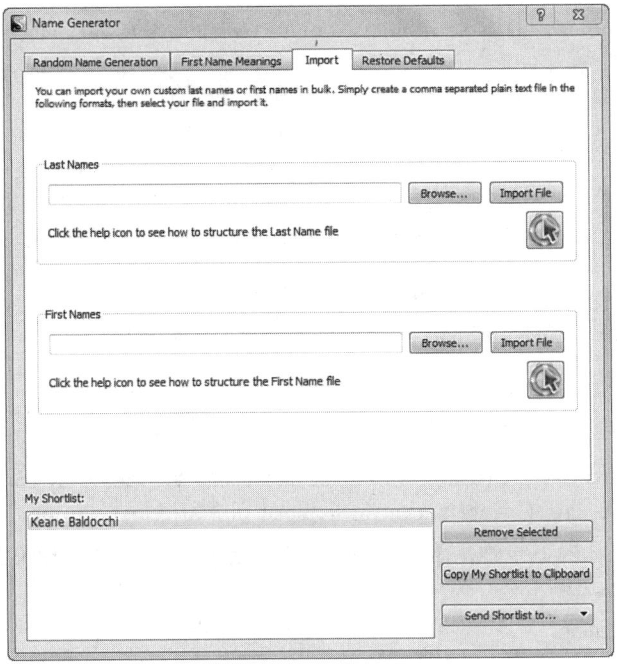

FIGURE 9.5

The Import tab allows you to add names to the lists.

2. Click the Browse button for either First or Last Names.

3. Locate the file in the Open dialog box, then click Open.

4. Click the Import File button.

5. A message tells you how many names were added to the database. Click OK.

If you want to reset the Name Generator to the default list, open the Restore Defaults tab and click the Restore Defaults button.

Creating a Sketchpad

In Chapter 8, "Organizing Your Research," you learned how to open a file in an external editor. You can take full advantage of this feature to connect brainstorming tools to your project. In this example, you see how to create a sketchpad. If you have an artistic bent and like to draw anything from house floor plans to sketches of your characters, this may be of use to you. You can also use a sketchpad to create collages with photographic images that represent elements from your book.

First, determine which drawing application you would like to use to create your artwork. I use AutoDesk SketchBook on both my Mac and PC. Then take the following steps:

1. Open your drawing application and create a blank file.

2. Save the file under a name such as sketchpad or whiteboard to remind yourself of its purpose.

3. Import the file into your Scrivener project by dragging it from the Finder or Windows Explorer into the project.

   NOTE On the Mac, I suggest dragging this file into your Templates folder. This makes it easily reusable. Template sheets are covered in Chapter 13, "Creating and Using Template Sheets."

   In Windows, you can create a root folder for documents like this and other pseudotemplates. To use them, select Documents, Duplicate (Ctrl+D) from the menu to duplicate the file and drag the duplicate into your Research or another folder.

4. To use the sketchpad, create a new sketchpad file in your Scrivener project, either using the template sheet on the Mac, as shown in Figure 9.6, or duplicating the file in Windows.

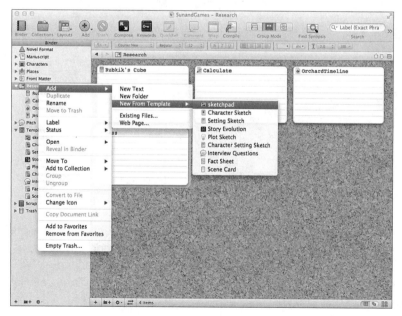

FIGURE 9.6

Create one blank file in a drawing app, and use it to create multiple sketchpads in your projects.

5. In the Editor, click and hold the Open in External Editor button in the Footer bar.

6. In the pop-up menu on the Mac, select the application in which you want to open the file.

7. Create your drawing or collage in your drawing application.

8. Save the file.

9. In Scrivener for Mac, click the Reload File button to update the link, as shown in Figure 9.7. In Windows, open a different file in the Editor and then return to the sketchpad document to reload it.

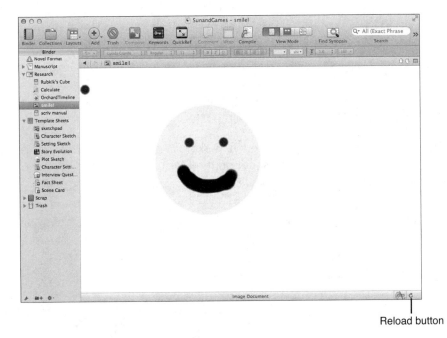

Reload button

FIGURE 9.7

Your new sketchpad can be used to add drawings to brainstorm your project or just remind you to smile when you're in the thick of it.

You can use this same process to create template sheets (or pseudotemplates in Windows) for other applications, such as mind maps and timelines, as well. If you save these items into a project template, as you learn in Chapter 14, "Creating and Using Project Templates," you can have them immediately available whenever you begin a new project.

Using Aeon Timeline with Scrivener (Mac Only)

Although Scrivener offers many tools for writers, one area some authors find missing is the lack of a timeline feature. If you use a third-party timeline application, you can import a timeline into your project and open it in an external editor, but actually integrating your timeline's components into your project requires considerable duplication of efforts.

One Mac timeline application has addressed this need for integration. Aeon Timeline was designed by Scribble Code, the company created by a Scrivener user with the express purpose of creating a writer-friendly timeline application that synchronizes with Scrivener. Much like importing an OPML file into your project, Aeon Timeline creates items in Scrivener based on timeline entries. Better still, it keeps these links synchronized. If you change a date in the custom meta-data in your Scrivener project, it is updated in Aeon Timeline, and vice versa. You can also view this meta-data in Scrivener's Outliner, so you can sort files by date or other fields.

TIP   Aeon Timeline was designed by a third party and is not included in Scrivener. You can obtain it from the Scribble Code website (http://www.scribblecode.com) or the Mac App Store for $40. Download a 30-day trial from the Scribble Code website. It is worth evaluating this application not just because of its Scrivener integration but because it is designed for use by writers. You can use it to create fantasy calendars, explore the relationships between characters and events, and create concurrent storylines and character arcs.

NOTE   Explaining the details of how to use Aeon Timeline is beyond the scope of this book, but the application provides a tutorial and a manual.

To synchronize an Aeon Timeline file with a Scrivener project:

1. Create your timeline in Aeon Timeline.

2. Either create a new project in Scrivener or determine which project you want to synchronize with Aeon Timeline.

3. Close the chosen project in Scrivener.

4. In Aeon Timeline, select File, Synchronize. The Synchronize Timeline dialog box opens, as shown in Figure 9.8.

NOTE The first time you select this option, you'll see a warning to back up your timeline project before syncing. Click the Do Not Show This Again button to prevent the warning from reappearing.

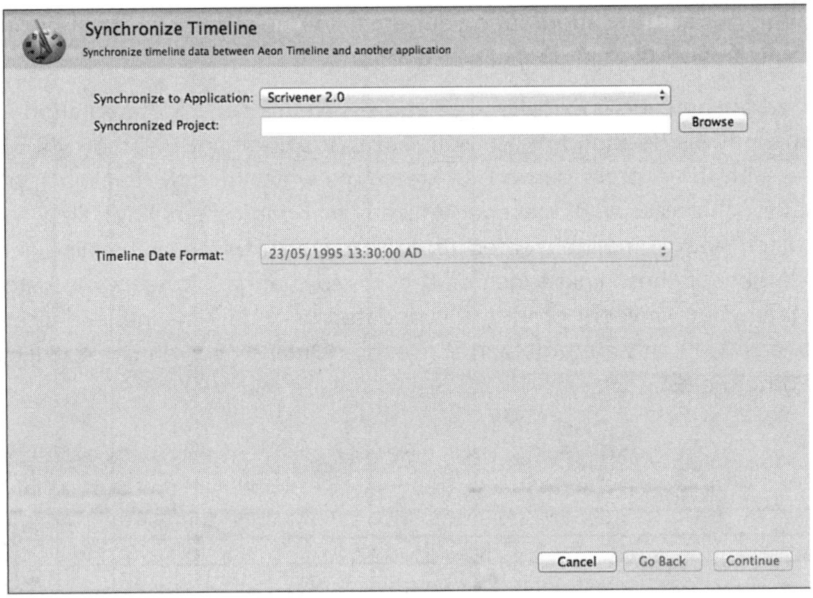

FIGURE 9.8

The Synchronize Timeline dialog box in Aeon Timeline creates the link between your timeline and your Scrivener project.

5. In the Synchronize to Application drop-down menu, select Scrivener 2.0.

6. Click the Browse button to navigate to your Scrivener project.

CAUTION If you did not close the project in Scrivener in step 3, a warning appears reminding you to close the project and try again.

7. Choose a date format from the Timeline Date Format drop-down menu.

8. Click Continue. This opens the Action window in the Synchronize Timeline dialog box, as shown in Figure 9.9.

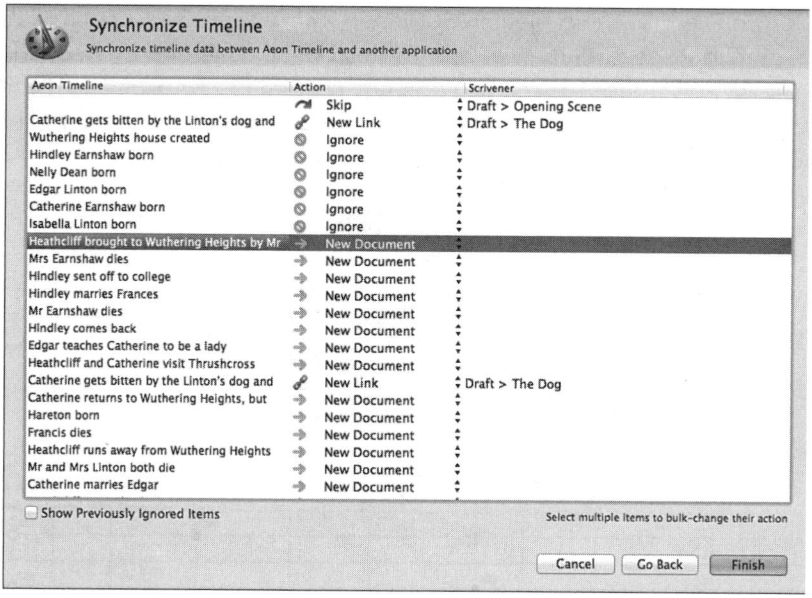

FIGURE 9.9

The Action window controls how each event in your timeline is synchronized.

9. For each event in your timeline, click the Action setting and choose from the following options:

- **New Document**: Creates a new document in the Scrivener project to which the timeline entry is linked

- **New Link**: Creates a link between the timeline entry and an existing document in the Scrivener project, as selected from a sheet that appears with a list of documents

- **Ignore**: Ignores this timeline entry in the Scrivener project by not linking it to any document

- **Skip**: Does not link the timeline entry to a Scrivener document at this time, but continues to prompt for a link when you synchronize in the future

10. Click Finish. The selected timeline events and documents are linked.

When you reopen the project in Scrivener, if you open the Custom Meta-Data pane in the Inspector, you can see the custom fields added by Aeon Timeline, as shown in Figure 9.10. You can edit any custom field in Scrivener (with the exception of the Aeon ID and Aeon Sync fields), and your changes will be synced back to Aeon Timeline.

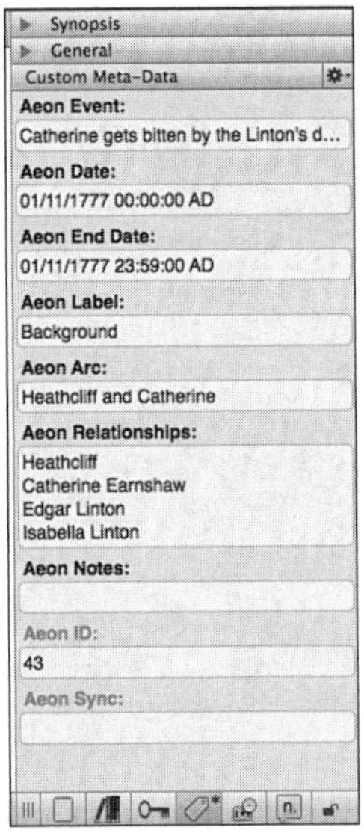

FIGURE 9.10

Aeon Timeline has synchronized with a document in Scrivener and created custom meta-data, which can be used in both applications.

A WINDOWS VIEW: A SCRIVENER FOR WINDOWS EASTER EGG

If you're a Scrivener for Windows user who writes or simply appreciates science fiction, you're in for a treat. Scrivener can be used in many languages, and localization efforts are always expanding. Scrivener user Pigfender took advantage of this effort to create a Science Fiction localization of the Scrivener interface. The menus, toolbar, dialog boxes, and tooltips all contain science fiction references.

To access this Easter Egg, select Tools, Options from the menu. On the General tab, click the Languages drop-down menu and choose Science Fiction. Click OK to accept the change and close the Options window; then exit and restart Scrivener. To return to English or another language, select Engineering, Options to reopen the Options window.

THE ABSOLUTE MINIMUM

The following are the highlights from this chapter:

- Scrivener's Name Generator creates lists of potential character forenames and surnames.

- The Windows version of the Name Generator provides the origin and meaning of many of the first names in its database.

- You can add names to the Name Generator in both the Mac and Windows versions, but you cannot share name files between the two platforms.

- Use Scrivener's ability to open an external editor in conjunction with its template sheet or Duplicate command to create updateable sketchpads, timelines, and mind maps to facilitate brainstorming your project.

- Aeon Timeline synchronizes with Scrivener to integrate timeline capabilities with the application.

EDITING YOUR MANUSCRIPT

No matter what you write, first drafts generally consist of descriptions that need to be fleshed out, topics that need more research, citations that require verification, or scenes consisting completely of dialogue without any narrative. As you write, you need tools to mark up these areas so you can find them easily later.

Unless you are the perfect first-draft writer of legend—and I think they're almost as mythical as unicorns—your writing process likely involves two or more drafts. When you've worked so hard to craft a paragraph, a page of dialogue, or a legal argument, however, you may hesitate to delete what you have in the hopes that your revisions will actually improve on the original.

Scrivener has tools to address the need to mark up your project as you work and to track revisions and preserve your documents along the way. This chapter introduces annotations, comments, Revision mode, and Snapshots.

Using Inline Annotations

Inline annotations are notes inserted into your document text. As Figure 10.1 demonstrates, they appear surrounded by a colored bubble to make them stand out from the document text itself.

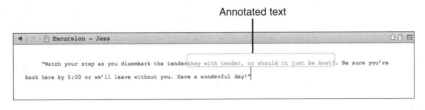

Annotated text

◄ | ⌐ | 🗋 Excursion - Jess

"Watch your step as you disembark the tenderokay with tender, or should it just be boat?. Be sure you're back here by 5:00 or we'll leave without you. Have a wonderful day!"

FIGURE 10.1

Inline annotations appear within the text of the document.

Because annotations don't warrant opening a separate sidebar or dialog box, they are quick to add and don't disrupt the flow of your work. They can be used to mark spots where you want to find a better word, as in Figure 10.1, or to remind you to weave a key plot element into a later scene. The key is to add these notes on the fly and forget about them so you can continue working unabated.

You can optionally remove annotations from your compiled project so they do not appear in the compilation. You can also use the compile settings to format inline comments as margin comments in Rich Text Format (.rtf) and the two Word formats (.doc and .docx). See Chapter 19, "Compiling Your Completed Work," for details on how to change the formatting of comments and annotations.

Adding Annotations

To add an inline annotation:

1. Position the cursor where you want to add the inline annotation.

CAUTION Do not add extra spaces before or after the annotation, as they will appear in your compiled project even if you remove the annotations themselves. If you want to create whitespace between your document text and the annotation, enter extra spaces within the annotation bubble.

2. Choose Format, Inline Annotation from the menu or press Shift-Cmd-A on the Mac or Ctrl+Shift+A in Windows.

TIP This is a keyboard shortcut worth memorizing as it enables you to add your annotation without lifting your fingers from the keyboard and continue typing.

3. Type the content of your annotation.

4. Choose Format, Inline Annotation from the menu or press Shift-Cmd-A (Ctrl+Shift+A in Windows) to close the annotation. You can also just click outside the annotation bubble.

If you want to convert existing text into an annotation, select the text and use the keyboard shortcut or menu command listed in step 2. This command acts as a toggle, so if you select an annotation and then use the keyboard shortcut or menu command, the annotation converts to regular text.

Your annotation does not have to consist of text. You can add hyperlinks, bulleted lists, tables, and even images to an annotation, although these may be stripped out when you compile to certain output formats. Anything you type or insert in step 3 above appears within the annotation.

Editing Annotations

Edit annotations just as you would any other text in your document. Position the cursor within the annotation and type to add text. Select text and type over it to modify the annotation. To replace the complete text of the annotation:

1. Position the insertion point within the annotation.

2. On the Mac, choose Edit, Select Annotation from the menu. Alternatively, right-click to bring up the context menu, and choose Select Annotation. In Windows, select the full text of the annotation with your mouse or keyboard as you would select regular text.

3. Type over the selection.

If you paste text into an annotation, the original formatting of the text is pasted, as well. Thus, if you paste document text into the middle of an annotation, it splits the annotation and inserts the document text between the two annotations. Similarly, if you paste text from an annotation into your document text, it creates a new annotation. If you want to paste text within an annotation and have it formatted as an annotation, copy or cut the source text and then select Edit, Paste and Match Style from the menu or press Option-Shift-Cmd-V (Ctrl+Shift+V in Windows). Use this same procedure to paste text from an annotation into your document text while removing the annotation formatting.

To delete an annotation, select the entire annotation as you saw in the step-by-step above, and press Delete or the backspace key.

Changing the Appearance of Annotations

Annotations appear as red text with a red bubble by default. In Windows, change the default color in the Appearance tab of the Options dialog box (Tools, Options). Choose Editor in the Colors list and then select Annotation Text and choose a new color. Both existing and new annotations appear in the new color.

To change the annotation color on the Mac:

1. Position the insertion point within an existing annotation.

2. Choose Format, Font, Show Colors from the menu or press Shift-Cmd-C.

3. Select a color from the Colors dialog box.

4. Click the Close button to close the Colors dialog box.

When you change annotation colors on the Mac, only the annotation you selected changes. Other existing annotation colors retain their original color. New annotations use the new color. You can take advantage of this behavior in interesting ways. If you are editing your work in a group setting, assign each contributor a color for his or her annotations. You can also use different annotation colors for different types of comments, such as red when you can't think of the proper word and purple when you're skipping over writing a portion of a scene, and so on. Although it is a manual process to change the annotation color every time you switch, the following trick will help you remember the purpose of each color choice:

1. Position the insertion point within an annotation.

2. Choose Format, Font, Show Colors from the menu.

3. In the Colors dialog box, select the Color Palettes option, as shown in Figure 10.2.

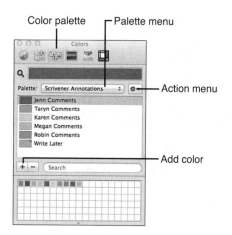

FIGURE 10.2

Use the Color Palette tool to create a custom color palette for your annotations and comments.

4. Click the gear button to open the Action menu, and choose New. A new palette called Unnamed is created.

5. Open the Action menu again, and choose Rename.

6. Enter a descriptive name for your new palette, such as Scrivener Annotations.

 NOTE If you obtained your copy of Scrivener from the Literature & Latte website or on CD, you can add your custom colors to the Scrivener palette instead of taking steps 4–6. To do this, click the palette drop-down menu and choose Scrivener. If you obtained Scrivener from the Mac App Store, however, you must create a new custom palette as described in steps 4–6 to preserve your colors.

7. Click the Color Wheel option, as shown in Figure 10.3.

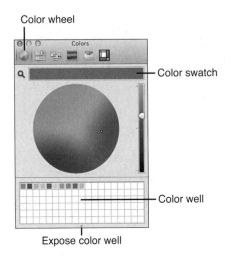

Color wheel

Color swatch

Color well

Expose color well

FIGURE 10.3

Use the color wheel to choose colors to add to your custom palette.

8. Select a color for your annotations from the color wheel. The color appears in the swatch above the wheel.

9. Drag the color from the swatch into an empty position in the color well. If the color well is not open in your Colors dialog box, click and drag the Expose Color Well bar.

10. Repeat steps 8 and 9 to select other colors for your new palette.

11. Click the Color Palette icon to return to your new palette.

12. Click on a color in the color well.

13. Click the Add Color (+) button below the palette.

> If you inadvertently add the wrong color, click the Delete Color (–) button.

14. Click the name automatically assigned to the color and enter a unique name, such as `Word Choice` or `Write Later`. This reminds you of the purpose of the annotation color.

15. Repeat steps 12–14 to fill your palette.

16. Close the Colors dialog box.

Once you have created your custom palette, whenever you need to change annotation colors, select Format, Font, Show Colors from the menu, and then choose the appropriate color from your custom palette in the Color Palettes tab.

Adding and Reviewing Comments

Comments serve the same purpose as inline annotations, but they appear separately in a sidebar instead of within the document text, as shown in Figure 10.4. You can use comments and annotations interchangeably, and each has its advantages. Comments can be tucked out of the way so as not to distract from your work, but entering them in the Comment text box requires using the mouse and can pull you out of the moment. Annotations are easy to enter, especially if you use the keyboard shortcut, but they can leave your Editor window looking like a battlefield.

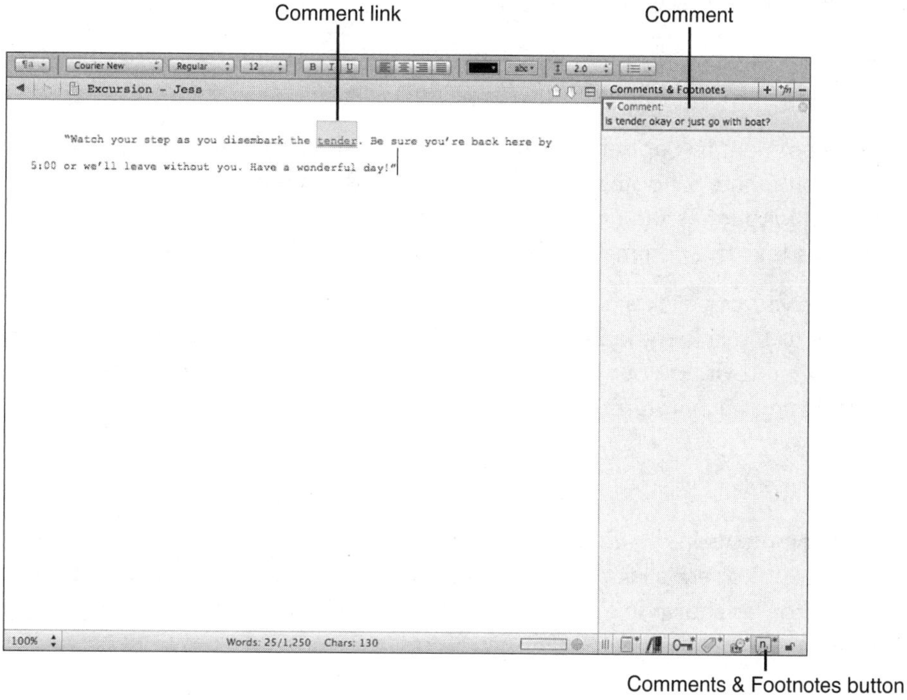

FIGURE 10.4

Comments create links from your document text to the Comments & Footnotes pane in the Inspector.

Adding Comments

To add a comment:

1. Select where in your document text you want to link a comment. You can select a single word or multiple words.

NOTE If you do not select text, Scrivener automatically links the comment to the word just prior to the insertion point.

2. Choose Format, Comment from the menu. You can also press Shift-Cmd-8 (Shift+F4 in Windows).

3. Type the content of your comment. You can add formatted text and hyperlinks to comments. The project author name and current date and time automatically appear in the comment box. They are highlighted so you can type over these items. If you want to retain them, press the right-arrow key before adding your comment.

4. Click outside the Comment box. You can also press the Esc key to exit the comment and return to the Editor window.

The comment link appears highlighted in the document text. If you click the link, the Comments & Footnotes pane opens in the Inspector. Although the comment link no longer has the same appearance as the document text, it serves double duty as text and comment link.

Just as you can click a comment link to view the comment, clicking on a comment jumps to the link in the Editor window. You can use this behavior as a navigational tool when revising your project, moving down the list of comments and addressing each in turn.

Editing Comments

Edit comments in the Comments & Footnotes pane of the Inspector. If this pane is not open, click the Comments & Footnotes button at the bottom of the Inspector, as shown in Figure 10.4. You can also click a comment link to open the pane.

NOTE An asterisk to the right of an icon in the Inspector Footer bar indicates the presence of content in that pane, such as a comment or footnote in the Comments & Footnotes pane.

To edit a comment, double-click in the comment box, shown in Figure 10.5, and then make the changes.

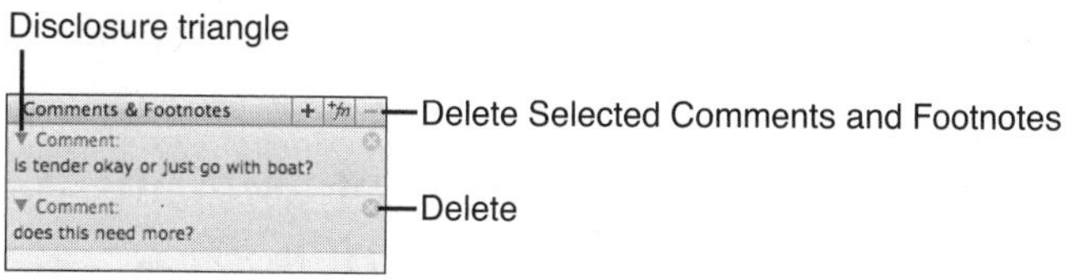

Disclosure triangle

Comments & Footnotes ——Delete Selected Comments and Footnotes

Delete

FIGURE 10.5

Edit comments by double-clicking within the comment box.

If you have multiple comments in a document and want to focus on one or more at a time, toggle the disclosure triangle in the upper left of each comment box to minimize their appearance.

To delete a comment, click the X in the upper right of the comment box. Deleting a comment box also deletes the comment link. The document text to which the comment was linked returns to its original formatting.

You can also delete multiple comments by selecting the comments and then clicking the Delete Selected Comments and Footnotes button at the top of the pane.

Changing the Appearance of Comments

The comment link is highlighted in yellow by default, and the background of the comment text box in the Comments & Footnotes pane matches it. To change the highlight color, right-click on the comment box and select a new color from the context menu. Scrivener remembers this color choice for new comments. Both the Mac and Windows versions allow for comments to appear in multiple colors.

 TIP If you created a custom palette for annotations on the Mac earlier in this chapter, you can use the same colors for comments. Select Show Colors from the context menu to open the Colors dialog box, and then choose a color from your palette.

Moving Comments

As you revise your project, you may want to move a comment to a different word in a paragraph so you can view a particular sentence without the distraction of the highlighted comment link.

To move a comment to a new comment link on the Mac:

1. Select the text to which you want to link the comment.

2. Right-click the comment you want to move in the Comments & Footnotes pane.

3. Choose Move to Selection from the context menu.

THE CREATIVE PROCESS: MULTIPASS REVISIONS

As I work, I color-code my annotations and comments—word choice questions in one color, awkward dialogue that will need tightening in another, reminders about loose plot threads in a third, research questions in a fourth, and so on. When I begin revisions in my projects, I make multiple passes through each document, looking at different elements with each pass. Before beginning this undertaking, I create a comment in a unique color stating, "Begin Here." I position this comment on the last line I edit in the current pass through the document. As I return to the document for another revision session, I move the comment to the new ending point. The unique color allows me to quickly locate it in the Comments & Footnotes pane and then use it as a navigation tool to pick up where I left off.

An alternative to using a comment to mark the ending/beginning point on the Mac would be to set bookmarks, which are explained in Chapter 16, "Searching Your Project," but the comment approach works best for me.

Removing All Document Notations

As your document comes closer to completion, you may no longer have a use for any of the comments and annotations you made along the way. Instead of deleting notations individually, you can remove them from the entire document in one fell swoop.

CAUTION This process removes all notations in the document, including footnotes. If you need to preserve your footnotes, which are covered in Chapter 22, "Using Scrivener for Academic Writing," do not use this procedure!

You should also consider taking a Snapshot of your document before stripping the notations. If you realize you removed an important comment, you will then have the means to retrieve it.

To remove all comments, annotations, and footnotes:

1. In the document text, choose Edit, Select All from the menu or press Cmd-A (Ctrl+A in Windows).

2. Choose Edit, Copy Special, Copy Without Comments or Footnotes.

3. Choose Edit, Paste from the menu or press Cmd-V (Ctrl+V in Windows).

What you have just done is copied and pasted the entire document without notations over the document that contained notations.

Converting Annotations to Comments (and Vice Versa)

Comments and annotations are essentially interchangeable in their usage, so it is a simple matter to convert from one to the other. If you begin working on a document using annotations and then find them too distracting, convert them to comments to get them tucked away in the Comments & Footnotes pane. To convert annotations to comments:

1. Open the documents you want to convert in the Editor. If you want to convert a series of documents, save time by using Scrivenings mode to open all of them together instead of converting each document separately.

2. Click anywhere in the Editor window.

3. Choose Format, Convert, Inline Annotations to Inspector Comments.

The converse also works. If you are working on a small display and find the Comments & Footnotes pane takes up too much screen real estate or you don't like going back and forth between the Editor and sidebar, convert your comments to annotations by choosing Format, Convert, Inspector Comments to Inline Annotations.

 NOTE Although you can use a combination of annotations and comments in your documents, the Convert options cannot be applied to an individual notation.

 CAUTION If you are using a custom palette to mark your comments and annotations, you may find that the conversion process changes these colors. Scrivener recognizes that each notation has a unique color, but it does not necessarily retain the same color you applied.

Searching for Annotations and Comments

The advantage of using annotations and comments is that you can make a note for yourself while you write, such as "Pick up this thread again in Chapter 6," and continue working. When you get to Chapter 6, however, you may have a vague notion that you were supposed to mention something but can no longer remember what it was or where you made that note. The solution for this problem is to search your notes.

To find a notation in your project:

1. Choose Edit, Find, Find by Formatting in the menu. This opens the Formatting Finder dialog box, shown in Figure 10.6.

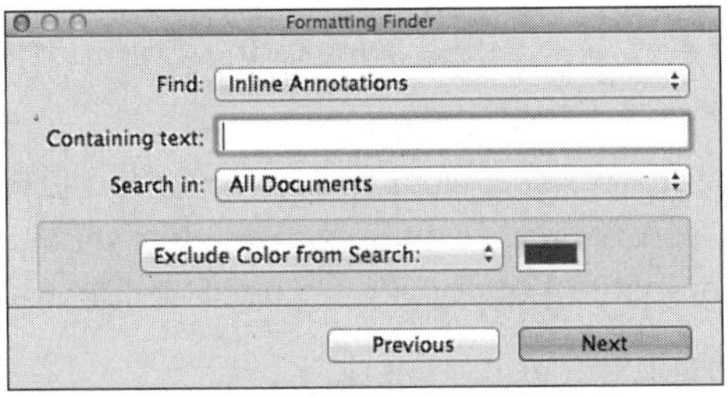

FIGURE 10.6

Search your entire Draft folder or selected documents for a comment or annotation.

2. In the Find drop-down menu, select either Inline Annotations or Comments & Footnotes.

3. Enter the text you seek in the Containing Text field.

4. In the Search In drop-down menu, select where to search. You can choose to search All Documents to search your entire Draft folder or Selected Documents to search documents selected in the Binder.

5. Mac users, in the drop-down menu to the left of the color swatch, choose from the following options:

   - **Any Color**: Searches all notations

   - **Limit Search to Color**: Searches only for notations that contain the search term and match the selected color

   - **Exclude Color from Search**: Searches for the search term in all notations except for those formatted with the selected color

6. If you chose to Limit or Exclude the search by color, click the color swatch and select a color from the Colors dialog box.

7. Click Next to begin the search.

 NOTE Windows users cannot use color to limit the search. After step 4, continue directly to step 7.

Exporting Annotations and Comments

If you use notations to mark areas where you need to do more research or locate a source to validate a statement, you may want to be able to view your notes as a complete research list. If you print the list, you can then use it as a reference for offline research.

To export your comments and annotations into a document that can be edited and printed outside Scrivener:

1. Scrivener exports notations from your entire Draft by default. If you want to limit the export to specific documents, select them in the Binder.

2. Choose File, Export, Comments & Annotations.

3. In the Save As dialog box, enter a name for the file and navigate to the folder in which you want to save it.

4. If you selected documents in the Binder to limit the export, click the Selected Documents Only check box.

5. If you want the notations listed underneath the title of the document in which each is located, click the Include Titles check box.

6. Click Export.

The exported document is saved in Rich Text Format (.rtf), which can be opened in almost any word processor. When you open the file, inline annotations are indented while comments are not. If you opted to see the titles of each document, these titles appear in bold.

Using Revision Mode (Mac Only)

Mac users have an additional editing tool in their Scrivener arsenal. As you edit your document, you can use Revision mode to track added and modified text. You can use different colors for each revision pass or assign a color to each member of a work group or writing team.

CAUTION Although Revision mode has its uses, it is not comparable to the Track Changes feature in Microsoft Word or Apple Pages. You cannot compare versions, accept or reject changes, or mark where text was deleted. Use caution and understand the limits of Revision mode before using it.

Although Revision mode is limited to essentially color-coding passes through your document, it does provide a couple of advantages. You can search for revision levels to quickly locate all changes made to a document. You can also strip all of your revision markings with one command when you have finished editing the project.

Marking Text

Revision mode works as a toggle. When it is on, any new or modified text appears in the selected revision color. When it is off, text appears in the normal color.

To turn on Revision mode, select Format, Revision Mode from the menu, then select a revision level from the submenu, as shown in Figure 10.7. Although these levels are labeled First Revision, Second Revision, and so on, you can use them for different purposes. If you work with a writing partner or on a project team, for example, one of you can edit using First Revision and the other using Second Revision so you can differentiate between each contributor's changes.

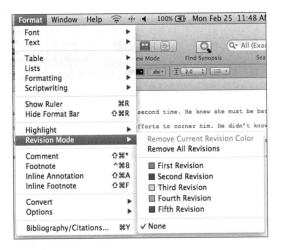

FIGURE 10.7

To enable Revision mode, select a revision level from the Revision Mode submenu.

The first time you enter Revision mode, a warning appears to ask if you're sure you want to proceed. Once you enable Revision mode, any additions or changes you make in the document are marked with the selected revision level color, as shown in Figure 10.8. If you paste text into the document, use the Edit, Paste and Match Style command to mark the text.

 NOTE The Paste and Match Style command matches all of the pasted text to a uniform style, eliminating bold, italic, and underlining.

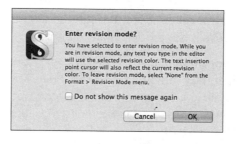

Inserted text

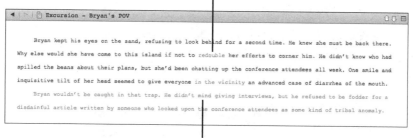

Added text

FIGURE 10.8

Changes you make in the document are marked with the selected revision level color.

To change to another revision level, choose Format, Revision Mode, and then select a different revision level from the submenu.

 NOTE Any revision level can be used to overwrite another. If you or a writing partner makes changes in the document using the First Revision level, you or a different contributor can add to or modify the original text or the First Revision–marked text with your own changes. Scrivener does not track layers of changes, so there is no way to revert to the original or a prior revision level once the text has been modified. If you need this level of control, use the Snapshots feature, either on its own or in conjunction with Revision mode, as explained later in this chapter.

To exit Revision mode, choose Format, Revision Mode, None. You can also choose the revision level currently selected to toggle it off.

Marking Text for Deletion

Revision mode only marks text you add or modify. If you delete text—including deleting a word or phrase to replace it with another—that text is lost without a trace. If you need to track deleted text, you can work around this issue by formatting text with a strikethrough typeface instead of deleting it. Select the text you want to format, then choose Format, Font, Strikethrough from the menu or press Shift-Cmd--. This draws a line through the text, colored to match the current revision level because it is a modification of the text.

This workaround does not actually delete any text. It remains in your document unless you later manually remove it. You can, however, use the transformation options when compiling your work to remove text that's been marked for deletion. Details on this process can be found in Chapter 19, "Compiling Your Completed Work."

Customizing Revision Mode

The colors assigned to each level in Revision mode are set in the Appearance tab of the Preferences dialog box, shown in Figure 10.9. To change the assigned colors:

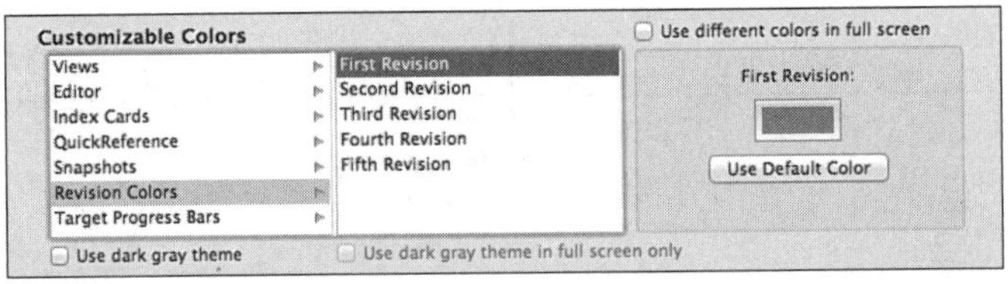

FIGURE 10.9

The Customizable Colors section of the Appearance tab lists all of the revision levels.

1. Choose Scrivener, Preferences from the menu.

2. Click on Appearance.

3. In the Customizable Colors pane, select Revision Colors from the left column.

4. Choose the revision level you want to modify from the middle column.

5. Click the color box on the right to open the Colors dialog box.

6. Select a color.

7. Repeat steps 4–6 for each revision level you want to modify.

8. Close the Preferences dialog box.

There is an important caveat to changing revision colors. If you have previously applied revision markings using a different color, they will no longer be associated with that revision level when you search or remove revisions. This also affects sharing a project with other contributors. If their revision colors are set to different preferences, Scrivener will not see them as revisions. If you are working with others, be sure all of you are using the same color palette and preference settings.

Finding Revisions

Earlier in this chapter, you learned how to use the Find by Formatting feature to search for comments and annotations. To search by revision level using the Find by Formatting feature:

1. Choose Edit, Find, Find by Formatting from the menu to open the Formatting Finder dialog box, shown in Figure 10.10.

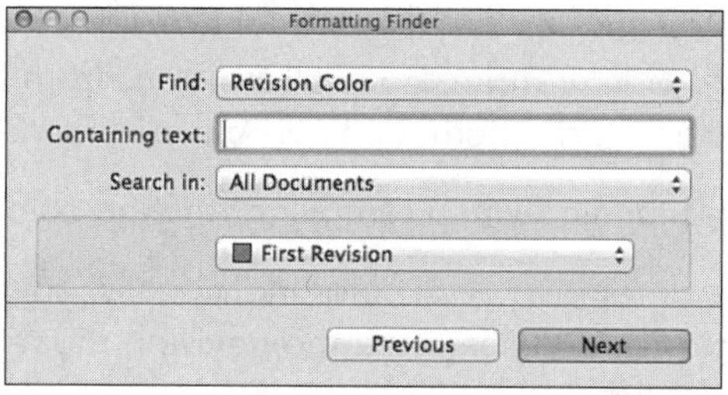

FIGURE 10.10

Search for revisions by level using the Find by Formatting feature.

2. In the Find drop-down menu, select Revision Color.

3. Enter a search term in the Containing Text field. If you simply want to search for all of the revisions at a particular level, leave this field blank.

4. From the Search In drop-down menu, select to search for All Documents in the project or only Selected Documents in the Binder.

5. In the Revision drop-down menu, choose which level of revisions you want to search.

6. Click Next.

Removing Revisions

If you use Scrivenings to view your entire Draft folder or multiple documents at once, you can remove the revision colors when you finish revising your document(s) or project(s). You can remove each revision level individually or all at once. When you remove revision colors, Scrivener changes all of the text back to regular text. To remove a specific revision level:

1. Open one or more documents in the Editor. Use Scrivenings mode to view multiple documents. Click in the Editor if you are not already working in it in order to place the focus on this pane.

2. Choose Format, Revision Mode, and then the revision level you want to remove.

3. Select Format, Revision Mode, Remove Current Revision Color from the menu.

4. Choose Format, Revision Mode, None to turn off Revision mode or select a different revision level to work in that mode or to repeat step 3 on a different level.

To remove all revision levels at once, click in the Editor to make it active, and then choose Format, Revision Mode, Remove All Revisions from the menu. You can also select a block of text and remove all revisions from within the selection using the Format, Revision Mode, Remove Revisions command from the menu.

Keep the following in mind when removing revision colors:

- If you choose to remove each color individually, any revisions you made in a different color before changing the Revision mode color preferences will remain in that color.

- If you remove revision colors, any text marked for deletion with strikethrough formatting is formatted in the default text color. The strikethrough typeface remains.

- If you remove an individual revision color, any other text in the same color, even if used for other purposes, returns to the default text color.

 NOTE For this reason, you should use unique colors for your revision levels that you do not need for any other purpose in your project.

- If you choose to remove all revision colors at once, all text, including any other text you may have formatted in a different color for other purposes, returns to the default text color.

Taking Snapshots

As you can see throughout this chapter, there are many tools to aid you in the revision process. Some, particularly the Revision mode, come with a level of risk that text may be deleted without your awareness if co-workers edit the project. Even when you're working independently, the notion of making extensive changes to text already on the page can cause anxiety. After all, the new version may be better than the original, but you may find you preferred your first draft. The best way to leave your options open and create a virtual paper trail throughout the revision process is with the use of Snapshots.

A Snapshot is essentially just a copy of a document. Rather than forcing you into the multistep process of copying, pasting, and then moving the copied document to a different folder, however, the Snapshots tool stores the copy within the document itself, hidden from view until you call upon it. A Snapshot preserves all of the formatting in the document, including revision marks and notations.

In short, Snapshots have your back so you can revise with impunity.

CAUTION Snapshots are not a substitute for backing up your entire project. See Chapter 17, "Backing Up Your Work," to learn how to perform a complete project backup and set automated backup preferences.

Creating Snapshots

To create a Snapshot, choose one of the following options:

- Select a document or multiple documents in the Binder, Corkboard, or Outliner, and then choose Documents, Snapshots, Take Snapshots of Selected Documents from the menu.

  NOTE In Windows, if only one item is selected in the Binder, Corkboard, or Outliner, the menu option is Take Snapshot.

- Click inside a document in the Editor window, then choose Documents, Snapshots, Take Snapshot.

- If the Snapshots pane of the Inspector is open, click the Take Snapshot (+) button at the top of the pane to take a Snapshot of the active document.

- Press Cmd-5 on the Mac or Ctrl+5 in Windows to take a Snapshot of the active document.

Snapshots are untitled by default. You can store multiple untitled Snapshots or sort through them later and give them proper titles, if you want. If you wait, however, it can be difficult to find exactly what you seek or remember why you took a particular Snapshot. Another approach is to create a Snapshot with Title. This option prompts you to name the Snapshot as you take it, so you can remind yourself that you changed a paragraph or used a particular Revision mode.

To save a Snapshot with Title, choose one of the following:

- Select the item or items you want in the Binder, Corkboard, or Outliner and then choose Documents, Snapshots, Take Titled Snapshots of Selected Documents. Enter a title in the Snapshot Title dialog box.

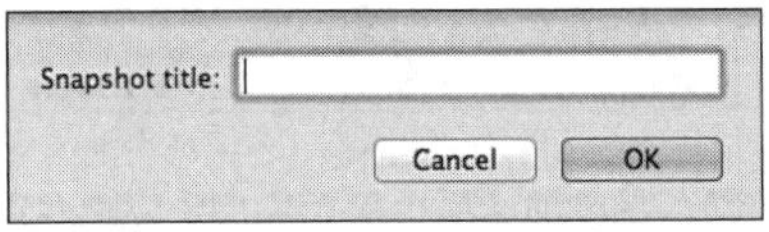

- From an active Editor window, choose Documents, Snapshots, Take Snapshot with Title. Enter a title in the Snapshot Title dialog box.
- Press Shift-Cmd-5 (Ctrl+Shift+5 in Windows).

After you take a Snapshot of an item, its icon bears a folded corner to signify that it contains a Snapshot, as was explained in Chapter 3, "Organizing the Binder." This icon also appears in the Header bar of the Editor, on index cards in the Corkboard, and to the left of the document title in the Outliner. You can also see an asterisk appear next to the Snapshots button at the bottom of the Inspector. Thus, you can tell if a document contains Snapshots from any of the major interface elements.

Viewing Snapshots

To access your Snapshots, click the Snapshots button at the bottom of the Inspector. If the Inspector is not open, select Documents, Snapshots, Show Snapshots from the menu. On a Mac, you can also press Control-Option-Cmd-K.

The Snapshots pane, shown in Figure 10.11, lists all of the Snapshots for the selected document. The list is sorted by date and time. Click the Date heading to invert the sort order (from newest to oldest instead of the default oldest to newest). If you created Titled Snapshots, you can click the Title heading to sort by title.

FIGURE 10.11

Compare   Take Snapshot Delete Snapshot

Date	Title
30 March 2012, 13:37	Pre-Sync External File Version
24 February 2013, 16:22	Untitled (In Progress)
24 February 2013, 16:22	Added tribal anomaly
24 February 2013, 16:25	Untitled (In Progress)
24 February 2013, 16:36	In a trap...tribal anomaly

— Roll Back

— Snapshots list

— Text of selected Snapshot

        Bryan kept his eyes on the sand,
refusing to look behind for a second
time. He knew she must be back there.
Why else would she have come to this
island if not to redouble her efforts
to corner him. He didn't know who had
spilled the beans about their plans,
but she'd been chatting up the
conference attendees all week. One
smile and inquisitive tilt of her head
seemed to give everyone in the vicinity
an advanced case of diarrhea of the
mouth.

— Snapshots button

The Snapshots pane in the Inspector displays a list of all the Snapshots for the document and the contents of the selected Snapshot.

NOTE The Windows Snapshots pane does not have a Compare button, as that feature is not available in Windows.

If you have untitled Snapshots in the list, double-click the title to rename the Snapshot. To delete a Snapshot, select it and then click the Delete (-) button at the top of the pane. On the Mac, you can also press the Delete key.

Select a Snapshot from the list to view its contents in the lower portion of the Snapshots pane. You cannot edit this text, of course, but you can select and copy it. If you are simply looking to recover content you deleted in a prior revision, copy the text in the Snapshots pane, then paste it into the document in the Editor window.

TIP Drag the splitter between the Editor and the Inspector to the left to widen the Inspector pane to view more of the Snapshot at once. If you do this frequently, consider saving a workspace layout with the widened Inspector.

Comparing Snapshot Versions (Mac Only)

On the Mac, Snapshots afford you the opportunity to compare different versions of your document. To compare the current version of your document with a Snapshot:

1. Select the Snapshot you want to compare with your current document.

2. Click the Compare button.

3. View the differences in the lower portion of the Snapshots pane, as shown in Figure 10.12.

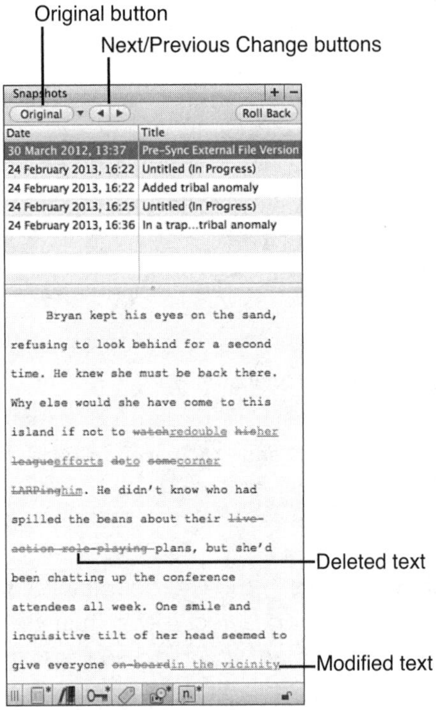

FIGURE 10.12

Compare two versions of your document in the Snapshots pane.

Text that appears in the Snapshot but is no longer in the current document is displayed in red with strikethrough typeface, indicating that it was deleted between the Snapshot and the current version. Text that appears in the current document but was not in the Snapshot version is blue and underlined, indicating it was added between the Snapshot and the current version. Click the Next or Previous Change buttons at the top of the pane to navigate through the comparison one difference at a time. You can also navigate to the next or previous change by choosing Documents, Snapshots, Show Changes from the menu and selecting from the submenu or pressing Control-Cmd-] or Control-Cmd-[.

NOTE You can also compare two Snapshots with each other. Cmd-click two Snapshots in the list, then click the Compare button.

Scrivener can compare documents on three levels of granularity. By default, comparisons are made word by word. If you want a broader view of the changes, click the down arrow to the right of the Compare/Original button or choose Documents, Snapshots, Show Changes, Comparison Granularity and then select one or more of the following options from the submenu:

- **By Paragraph**: If anything within a paragraph has changed, the entire paragraph is marked. For example, if you add a word anywhere within the paragraph, the entire paragraph is marked in blue. If you delete anything within the paragraph, the entire paragraph is marked as deleted and then the current paragraph is marked as new.

- **By Clause**: If anything within a clause has changed, it is marked. For example, if you add a word within a sentence or clause within a sentence, that clause is marked in blue. If you delete anything within the clause, the clause is marked as deleted and then the current clause is marked as new.

- **By Word**: Marking is done word by word, as was shown in Figure 10.12.

The Compare button changes to an Original button when you are comparing versions. To turn off the comparison, click Original at the top of the pane. When you are comparing versions, the Snapshot appears in plain-text, but the actual formatting of the text is preserved.

Reverting to a Prior Snapshot

During the revision process, you may find yourself going off on quite a tangent. You completely change the staging or motivation of a scene or decide to argue an obscure point of a supporting element of your thesis, and suddenly you realize that you're going nowhere. The best solution to undo the damage is to simply revert to a prior version of the document.

TIP Before you begin revisions on a document, take a Snapshot. You may think you have an idea of where your writing will take you that day, but until you see the changes on the screen, you can't be sure you'll be happy with the results.

To roll back to a prior Snapshot, select the version to which you want to revert from the Snapshots pane, then click the Roll Back button at the top of the pane.

CAUTION Snapshots are stored with the document, not as a separate element in the Binder. If you delete a document, any Snapshots of that document are also deleted.

Scrivener asks if you want to take a Snapshot of your current document before rolling back. You should always take a Snapshot of the current document, warts and all. Even in madness, there may be a few glimmers of brilliance, and having a Snapshot gives you the opportunity to tease out those bits and pieces later. If nothing else, you'll have a record of the carnage to laugh at later!

THE CREATIVE PROCESS: REVISING BY COMMITTEE

If you have a critique partner or group who all use Scrivener, you can use the features mentioned in this chapter as a critique tool. Send your project to your critique partner and ask him or her to use inline annotations or comments to mark up your work. Use Snapshots to preserve the original work before addressing the suggested changes, and create a Post-Critique Revision mode to use when making the edits. If you critique with a group, each member can use a different annotation and comment color, and each member can pass the project along to the next member in turn to avoid receiving multiple copies of the project in return.

Be sure you and your writing partners back up the project religiously throughout the critique and revision process!

THE ABSOLUTE MINIMUM

The following are the highlights from this chapter:

- Inline annotations and comments allow you to make notes as you write.

- Annotations and comments can contain formatted text, hyperlinks, and images.

- Annotations on the Mac and comments on both the Mac and Windows can be color-coded to aid in working with a group, parsing through different types of notes, and searching for notations.

- Revision mode on the Mac allows you to track added or modified text.

- Although Revision mode is not a full-featured version tracker, it does allow you to search for changes based on revision level.

- Snapshots protect you from accidental deletions within a document by making a hidden copy of the document, which you can then use to compare with other versions.

11

DIGGING INTO THE INSPECTOR

All of the chapters so far have focused on getting you up and running so you can write. Now that you know how to get your words on the screen, it's time to dig deeper into what Scrivener can do. Many of the prior chapters have mentioned being able to use data from the Inspector. This chapter explores the Inspector properly.

Navigating the Inspector

To begin this exploration, open the Inspector pane in Scrivener using one of the following methods:

- Choose View, Layout, Show Inspector from the menu.

- Click the Inspector icon on the toolbar (the italicized *i* on the far right).

- Press Option-Cmd-I on the Mac or Ctrl+Shift+I in Windows.

The Inspector sidebar, shown in Figure 11.1, consists of a series of panes. By default, the Synopsis, General, and Notes panes are visible. As you work with the Inspector, it remembers the pane settings you last used and automatically reopens those panes.

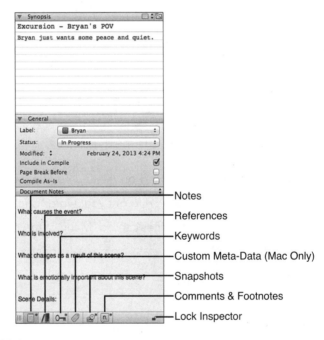

FIGURE 11.1

The Inspector sidebar contains multiple panes to record meta-data for your documents.

At the bottom of the Inspector is a Footer bar containing icons to access additional panes. If an asterisk appears with the icon, the pane contains data pertaining to the selected item.

The Inspector reflects the meta-data for the item in the Editor window. If you are in Split Screen mode, you can lock the Inspector to always display the data for a particular Editor screen, which is explained later in this chapter. Otherwise, the Inspector displays the data for the active Editor screen, as follows:

- If you are in the Corkboard or Outliner views, the Inspector shows the meta-data for the selected index card or Outliner item.

- If you load a container in the Corkboard or Outliner but do not select an index card or row, the Inspector shows the meta-data for the container.

- If you select multiple items in the Corkboard or Outliner, the Inspector displays the Project Notes and References.

- If you are in Scrivenings view, the Inspector displays the meta-data for the document that currently has the focus in the session.

 NOTE The three root folders—the Draft, Research, and Trash folders—do not have meta-data associated with them. If you select one of these folders, you see only the Project Notes and References, as those are associated with the entire project.

Adding a Synopsis in the Inspector

In Chapter 6, "Storyboarding with the Corkboard," you learned how to enter a synopsis on an index card. The synopsis also appears on a similar index card at the top of the default Inspector panel. The Synopsis pane, shown in Figure 11.2, consists of a title, which is the same as the item's title in the Binder, and the synopsis itself. The disclosure triangle to the left of the Synopsis pane header can be used to open and close the pane.

 NOTE If you have been following this book chapter by chapter in your copy of Scrivener, the Inspector may open in the Snapshots or Comments & Footnotes pane, both of which fill the entire Inspector. Click the Notes button at the bottom of the Inspector to open the Synopsis, General, and Notes panes.

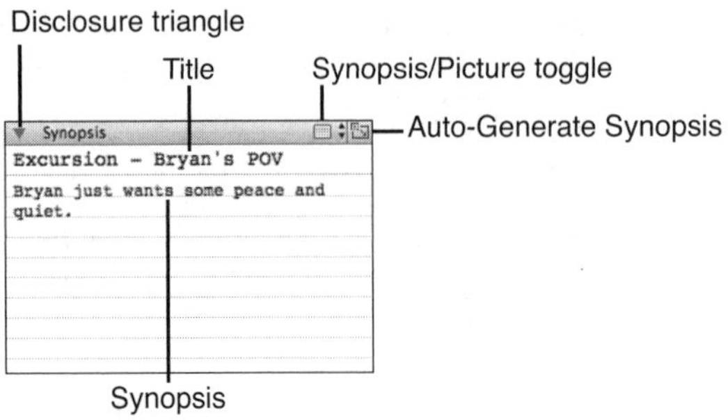

Disclosure triangle

Title   Synopsis/Picture toggle

———Auto-Generate Synopsis

Synopsis

FIGURE 11.2

The Synopsis pane contains the document's title and a synopsis describing the contents of the document.

CAUTION Remember, the synopsis is not the same as the document text. Enter the content of your document in the Editor window. The synopsis is purely meta-data to help you organize your work.

To change the title of the document, select the current title and type over it, then press Return/Enter. The title immediately changes in the Binder as well as in the Inspector. If you have the Corkboard or Outliner open, you can view the title change there, as well.

To add or edit the synopsis, click in the text area below the title. You can enter as much text as you want, but it's generally best to keep it brief, as the text you enter here also appears on the index card in the Corkboard and in the Title and Synopsis column (the Synopsis column in Windows) in the Outliner.

NOTE You cannot format text in the synopsis; thus you cannot use bold, italic, or bullets. You can, however, use asterisks or hyphens to emphasize text or make a bulleted list. On the Mac, press Alt-8 to create a round bullet using the standard keyboard layout.

Automatically Generating a Synopsis

If you don't want to manually enter a synopsis, Scrivener can automatically generate one for you based on text in the Editor. If you want to use specific lines of your document as your synopsis, select that particular text in the document and then click the Auto-Generate Synopsis button at the upper right of the Synopsis pane in the Inspector.

You can also click the Auto-Generate Synopsis button without preselecting any text. Scrivener uses the shorter of the first 500 characters or up to the first paragraph break of your document as the synopsis. On the Mac, you can select multiple documents in the Binder, Corkboard, or Outliner and choose Documents, Auto-Generate Synopses from the menu to generate synopses for all of the selected documents at once.

 CAUTION The Auto-Generate Synopsis feature overwrites text that you have already entered into the Synopsis pane. This is a good way to update the synopsis if you have made changes to your document since you last used the Auto-Generate Synopsis tool, but be careful not to use this feature if you have manually entered a synopsis.

 TIP The Auto-Generate Synopsis feature is best used in nonfiction and academic work, where it is more likely that the first few lines of text will contain an introduction and possibly even a thesis statement about what follows in that section. In a fiction setting, the first few lines of your text are not likely to give you much of a clue of the purpose of the document.

Adding an Image to the Synopsis

As mentioned in Chapter 6, the synopsis can hold text or an image. In fact, the index card can serve double duty. You can add a text synopsis and also add an image to the "other side" of the index card. To add an image to the Synopsis pane:

1. Click the Synopsis/Picture drop-down menu at the top of the Synopsis pane to switch to the Picture view. You can also press Cmd-7 on the Mac. A black box appears in the Synopsis pane.

2. Drag an image from the Binder, desktop, Finder (on the Mac), or Windows Explorer (in Windows) and drop it in the Synopsis pane. On the Mac, you can also drag an image that has been inserted into a text document in your project.

 TIP On the Mac, right-click on the image after adding it to the index card to open a pop-up menu with options to scale and align the image.

When you are in the Picture view of the Synopsis pane, the Auto-Generate Synopsis button changes to a Clear Picture button. If you want to delete the image, click this button.

Although you cannot view synopsis text and an image at the same time, both are preserved on the index card. Use the Synopsis/Picture toggle to switch the view between the synopsis and the image. The Outliner always displays the synopsis text, whereas the Corkboard displays either the text or the image depending on which view you used the last time you viewed that item in the Inspector.

Toggling the Created and Modified Date

Below the Synopsis pane, you see the General pane, shown in Figure 11.3. See Chapter 12, "Putting Keywords and Meta-Data to Work," to learn about the Label and Status fields. The Modified field displays the date the document was last edited. Click the drop-down arrows to the right of the Modified field name and select Created if you would prefer to see when the item was created.

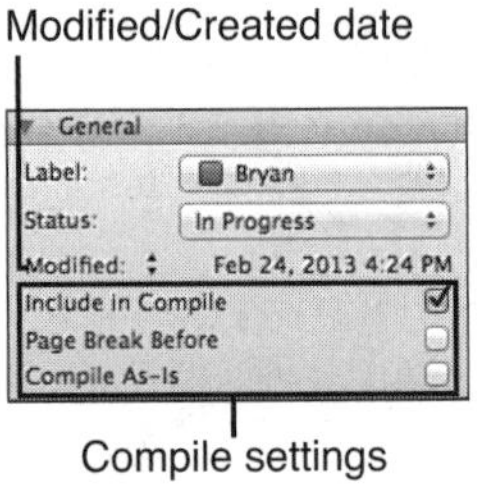

Modified/Created date

Compile settings

FIGURE 11.3

The General pane contains information about the creation/last modification date for the file and the Compile settings.

Selecting Compile Settings

The General pane contains three options to control how Scrivener handles the document when you compile your project to export or print it. They are as follows:

- **Include in Compile**: By default, when you add a file to the Draft folder, it is marked for inclusion when you compile. If you do not want to include the file, deselect this check box.

TIP   Using Scrivener to prepare a presentation with handouts would be an example of when this may be useful. Deselect any files in the Draft folder that contain your speaking points and notes so you can compile the handouts, then return to the project and select the Include in Compile option for those files, and then recompile the project so you have a working copy of the presentation for yourself.

- **Page Break Before**: When selected, this option inserts a page break before the document when it's compiled.

TIP   Use this option to add a page break before a document that would otherwise use a different separator in the compile settings. For example, you can set your compile settings to separate files in the same folder by a line break. If you have a title page followed by a dedication page, however, you want them each to appear on a different page. The Page Break Before option ensures that happens. For routine separations between files, file groups, and folders, use the Separators tab in the Compile window, as you learn in Chapter 19, "Compiling Your Completed Work."

- **Compile As-Is**: Select this option to preserve the formatting and layout of the file instead of using any text and notes formatting settings in the Compile window. See Chapter 19 for more information about formatting options in the Compile window.

These settings can be changed at any time. Thus, if you are compiling and printing a draft of your project for editing purposes, you may want to deselect the Page Break Before check box to save on paper and then reselect it before compiling the final version.

Adding Project and Document Notes

The Notes pane, shown in Figure 11.4, provides space for you to enter notes and ideas about the document or the project as a whole. The Notes header has a toggle button to switch between Document and Project Notes. Document notes are attached to a specific document and are only visible when that document is selected in the Editor, Corkboard, or Outliner. Project notes apply to the entire project and can be viewed at any time.

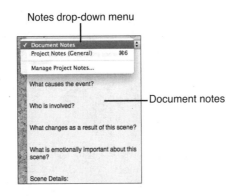

FIGURE 11.4

The Notes pane provides space for you to enter notes about the project as a whole or a specific document.

To enter a note, simply click in the pane and type. Although the Synopsis pane does not allow formatting, the Notes pane is more flexible. Format notes using the Format bar, menus, or keyboard shortcuts, just as you do in the Editor. You can also add an image to a note, either alone or along with text.

 CAUTION Just as with the synopsis, the text you enter in the Notes pane is meta-data, information about your work rather than the work itself. Enter the actual text of your project in the Editor, not in the Inspector.

Adding Images to Notes

When you add an image to the Synopsis pane, you are forced to choose between viewing the image and viewing your synopsis text (if you have chosen to enter any). In the Notes pane, you can view both text and images together. This allows you to either view both a Synopsis pane image and the Notes image in the Inspector at the same time, or to keep your Synopsis pane in text view while adding images to the Notes pane.

To add an image to the Notes pane:

1. Select either the Document or Project Notes pane.

2. Position the insertion point in the note in which you want the image to appear.

3. Choose Edit, Insert, Image from File from the menu or drag an image from the Binder, desktop, Finder (on the Mac), or Windows Explorer (in Windows). On the Mac, you can also drag an image that has been inserted into a document in your project.

4. Drop the image into the Notes pane. The image is added at the insertion point.

On the Mac, images are automatically scaled. In Windows, you should scale the image before inserting it into a note.

To delete an image, position the insertion point after the image and press the Delete/Backspace key.

THE CREATIVE PROCESS: THE MYRIAD NOTE OPTIONS

Scrivener provides several places for you to take notes about your project. You can choose from the Synopsis or Document and Project Notes panes in the Inspector, the Scratch Pad (covered in Chapter 4, "Writing in the Editor"), or creating a file in your Research or other non-Draft folder. While this makes Scrivener extremely flexible, it is easy to forget where you entered some critical piece of information. Thus, some organization may be in order.

To give you an example of how to put each of these options to work in a consistent, logical manner, here is how I use them for a novel:

- **Synopsis (Inspector, Corkboard, and Outliner):** Contains a synopsis of the scene, brief enough to fit comfortably on the index cards in the Corkboard view.

- **Document Notes (Inspector):** Contains questions I use when determining the purpose of every scene. In Chapter 13, "Creating and Using Template Sheets," and Chapter 14, "Creating and Using Project Templates," you learn how you can add these questions to document notes to use as a template sheet (Mac only) or as part of a project template.

- **Project Notes (Inspector):** Used as a quick method to jot down a line or dialogue or idea that I might want to incorporate into another scene later. You cannot compile or export project notes, so this is generally not the best place for an entire story synopsis.

- **Scratch Pad (Floating Pane):** Used for taking notes about other book ideas or completely unrelated topics, so they can be moved to a more appropriate home later. You can also use the Scratch Pad to take or paste notes when browsing the Web or using another application so they can be moved into the appropriate project later.

- **Non-Draft Files (Binder):** Used for a complete synopsis of my story, research notes and interviews, character and setting worksheets, a query letter draft, and to track submissions.

Your mileage may vary, of course, but think about what types of notes you take in the course of your work and which of the many options is the best container for that information. As long as you are consistent within a project, you will find the right workflow for your notes.

Managing Project Notes (Mac Only)

Project notes are both limited and extensive in their use. As mentioned in the sidebar above, you cannot compile project notes, so unless you manually cut and paste them into a document, they are not of any use outside the Scrivener interface. On the other hand, if you do all your work within Scrivener, this limitation does not matter because the information is exactly where you need it. On the Mac, you can also expand the Project Notes to a separate, resizable notepad window so that you can enter more extensive notes and create additional Project Note sheets.

To open project notes in a window, choose one of the following options:

- Click the Notes header to open the drop-down menu and select Manage Project Notes.

- Choose Project, Project Notes from the menu.

- Press Option-Cmd-P.

The Project Notes window, shown in Figure 11.5, can be repositioned and resized. To add a new note:

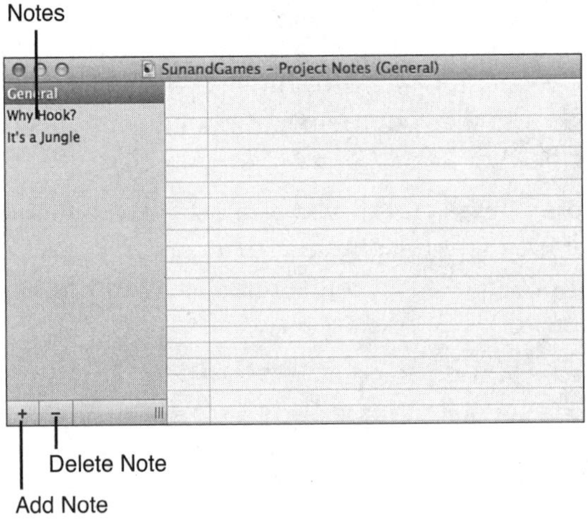

FIGURE 11.5

The Notes pane provides space for you to enter notes about the project as a whole or a specific document.

1. Click the Add (+) button.

2. Enter a title for the new note.

If you want to rename a note, including the default General note, double-click the title and enter a new name. To delete a note, select it in the sidebar and then click the Delete (–) button at the bottom of the window or press Cmd-Delete. A warning pops up to remind you that you cannot undo this action.

Once you have created additional notes, they are accessible even when the Project Notes window is closed. To switch between notes, click the drop-down menu in the Notes pane header in the Inspector. Your new notes are automatically added to this menu. You can also press Cmd-6 and Control-Cmd-6 to cycle forward or backward through the available document and project notes in the Notes pane.

Using Reference Links

As you are working on a document, you may refer to the same supporting material again and again. You may be writing a scene in a novel and keep referring back to an earlier scene to get the details correct. You may refer to specific pieces of research or data in each section of an academic paper. Perhaps you access the same website repeatedly while working on a project. In any of these or similar situations, rather than browsing through the Binder in Scrivener, Finder or Windows Explorer on your computer, or the bookmarks in your web browser, you can add reference links to these relevant resources in the Inspector.

Reference links provide access to material relevant to your document or project without cluttering the project itself. Reference links appear in the References pane of the Inspector and can be attached to either a single document or available on a projectwide basis. To access the References pane in the Inspector, click the References button at the bottom of the Inspector. The References pane header acts as a toggle between Document References and Project References.

 TIP On the Mac, you can also use Cmd-6 to switch between Document References and Project References when the References pane is open.

There are two types of reference links, as follows:

- **Internal references**: Link to an item within the Scrivener project
- **External references**: Link to items outside the Scrivener project, either stored on your computer or on the Internet

Adding Internal References

It may seem counterintuitive to link to an item within your project, but there are several reasons why internal references can be helpful. Internal reference links are particularly useful document references, as they can help you link the vast amount of items in your Research folder to the documents where that material is pertinent. This makes it easier to quickly access this material instead of repeatedly searching for the item you need.

Link related items within your Draft folder in order to make it easier to refer back and forth. If you write mysteries, for example, adding reference links to the scenes where you plant red herrings can help you quickly access those scenes when writing the villain's denouement in order to tie up all the loose ends.

To add an internal reference link:

1. Click the References header and choose between Document References and Project References. Most internal reference links are created as document references because all internal items are already available on a projectwide basis from the Binder.

2. In the References pane, click the Add (+) button at the top of the pane.

3. Hover over Add Internal Reference, then select an item from the submenus that appear, as shown in Figure 11.6.

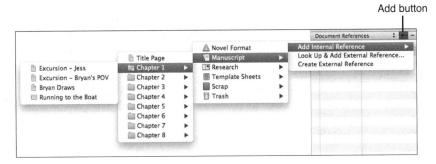

FIGURE 11.6

The Add menu of the References pane provides options for linking to internal and external references.

 TIP You can also drag and drop an item from the Binder into the References pane in place of steps 2 and 3. If you are adding multiple items to the References pane, Cmd-click (Ctrl+click in Windows) or Shift-click to select them all at once and drag them to the References pane. You might want to lock the Editor when dragging items to the References pane to avoid accidentally switching the active document.

The internal reference link appears in the References pane, as you can see in Figure 11.7.

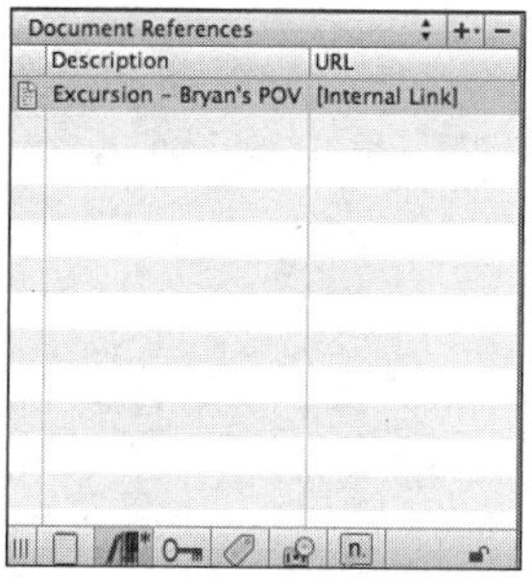

FIGURE 11.7

Links appear in the References pane.

TIP In Windows, the URL appears as a tooltip when hovering over the reference rather than in a URL column.

NOTE On the Mac, internal reference links are automatically cross-referenced. Thus, if you are working in a document titled "The Villain Gets His," and create an internal link to a document titled "Mr. Smith Is Poisoned," a similar link is added to the References pane for "Mr. Smith Is Poisoned" linking back to "The Villain Gets His."

Adding Internal References to the Item Icon Menu (Mac Only)

Scrivener for Mac has a trick that can add internal references to the Item Icon menu in the Header bar of the Editor. This provides access to the internal reference link when the Inspector is closed. To add internal references to the Item Icon menu:

1. In the References pane, double-click on the words [Internal Link] in the URL column.

2. Type an asterisk (*).

3. Press Return.

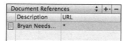

When you open the Item Icon menu, you see a link to the reference at the top of the menu, as shown in Figure 11.8.

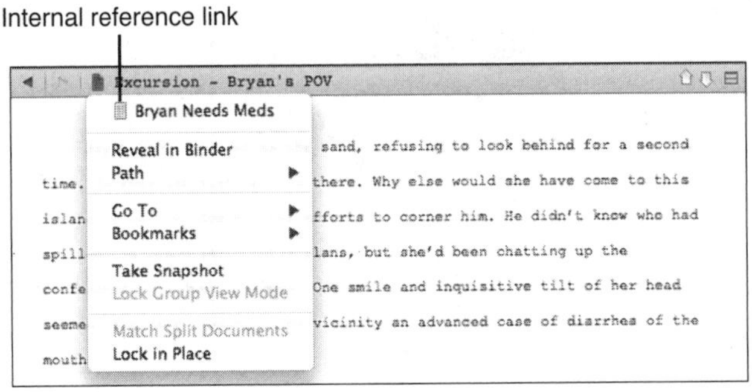

Internal reference link

FIGURE 11.8

Replacing the [Internal Link] URL in the References pane with an asterisk adds an internal reference to the Item Icon menu.

Adding External References

External references link material outside your project, whether you're using computer storage, the Cloud, or the web. Although you can import research material into your project, as you learned in Chapter 8, "Organizing Your Research," doing so can potentially explode the file size of the project. You also have to ask yourself if there's a reason to add everything to your project if it is readily available elsewhere. When researching Victorian clothing, for example, it is just not practical to import dozens of images when you can simply link to a website that has already compiled and organized those resources.

External references are also convenient for linking files created in other applications, such as spreadsheets and timelines. You can add these files to the Research folder of your project, but such items function solely as a link to open an external editor (the original application). Adding an external reference link in the Inspector is often a more practical and space-saving approach to such files.

 CAUTION   If you move a file or access your project from a different computer, your links will be broken. If you need to access information from multiple computers or if the path of the file may change, import the material into your project, instead.

There are three ways to add an external reference link, two of which are accessible from the Add (+) menu:

- **Look Up & Add External Reference**: Used to link to a file in Finder or Windows Explorer. Select the file to which you want to link, and then click Open.

- **Create External Reference**: Used to link to web pages. Enter a title for the reference in the Description field. Copy and paste the URL from your web browser into the URL field. You can also use this option to link to a file on your computer if you know the path.

You can also add an external reference link by dragging and dropping a file from Finder or Windows Explorer to the References pane. For web pages, drag and drop the URL icon from your browser's address bar to the References pane. Figure 11.9 shows both internal and external reference links.

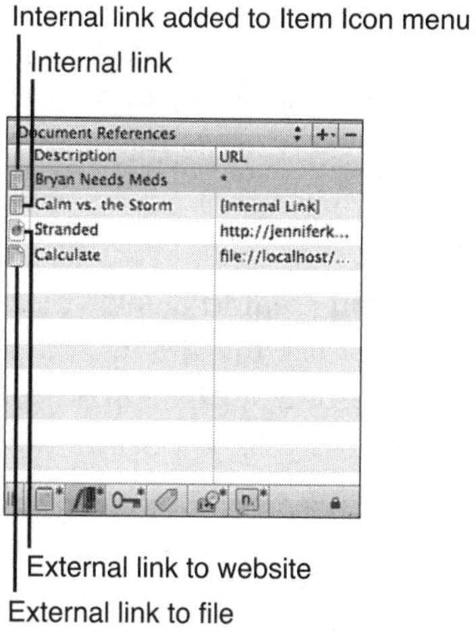

Internal link added to Item Icon menu

Internal link

Document References		
Description	URL	
Bryan Needs Meds	*	
Calm vs. the Storm	[Internal Link]	
Stranded	http://jenniferk...	
Calculate	file://localhost/...	

External link to website
External link to file

FIGURE 11.9

Here is an example of a populated References pane, containing a mix of internal and external links.

TIP On the Mac, if you have created an external reference link for a file or web page and decide you want to import it into your project, drag and drop the link from the References pane into the Binder.

Viewing References

Once you've added a reference link, view the item by double-clicking the icon to the left of the description in the References pane. Scrivener displays the reference differently depending on the type of reference link:

- Internal reference links open in the other editor of the Split Screen view. On the Mac, if you right-click on the icon in the References pane, you can opt to open the link in the Current Editor, Other Editor, or as a QuickReference. You can also change the default settings in the Navigation tab of the Preferences window.

- External reference links open in the application in which the file was created or in your default web browser. Right-click on the icon in the References pane to open a pop-up menu with options to locate the file in Finder or Windows Explorer or to view the item in a QuickLook pane (Mac only).

Editing and Deleting References

As you add links, the References pane may need some organization. To sort links alphabetically, click either the Description or URL heading. On the Mac, a triangle to the right of the heading tells you which column is the basis of the sort order, and the direction in which the triangle is pointing designates if the sort is ascending or descending. You can also manually drag entries to a new position in the References pane.

If you move a file to which you created a link, you need to update the URL in the References pane. Double-click the URL for the reference and enter the new path or URL. In Windows, the URL appears in a tooltip. To edit the title or URL in Windows, double-click on the title. A pop-up field appears below the title allowing you to change the URL, and the title itself becomes editable.

 TIP To change the title of a reference on the Mac, double-click it. Changing the title of an internal reference does not affect its title in the Binder or elsewhere.

To delete a reference, select it in the References pane and then click the Remove (–) button at the top of the pane or press Cmd-Delete on the Mac or Delete in Windows.

 TIP If the path or URL of a reference has changed, you can delete the original reference and drag and drop an updated reference to save time.

Locking the Inspector

When you are in Split Screen mode, you can lock the Inspector to the current Editor pane so even if you switch the Editor focus to the other pane, the Inspector remains focused on the first document. This can be helpful when you are creating internal references and need to review the contents of several files to determine which ones should be linked to a particular document. To use this feature in this manner:

1. Open the document in which you want to create internal references.

2. Split the screen.

3. Click the Lock Inspector button at the bottom of the Inspector, as shown in Figure 11.1.

4. In the other pane, open an item you want to review. You can select items from the Binder or the Item Icon menu in the Editor.

5. When you find an item you want to link to the original document, choose View, Reveal in Binder from the menu or press Option-Cmd-R (Ctrl+Shift+8 in Windows) to see where in the Binder hierarchy the item appears.

6. Drag the item from the Binder to the References pane.

 CAUTION   The Inspector is locked to the Editor pane, not specifically to the document itself. If you change documents in that Editor pane, the Inspector shows the meta-data of the new loaded document.

The Lock Inspector button is a toggle. When the Inspector is locked, the lock icon appears closed. In Windows, the lock button also appears depressed. To disable the lock, click the button again or close the split screen.

THE ABSOLUTE MINIMUM

The following are the highlights from this chapter:

- The Inspector contains meta-data about a selected item.

- The Synopsis pane contains the same synopsis that appears on index cards in the Corkboard and in the Title and Synopsis column (the Synopsis column in Windows) of the Outliner view.

- You can add an image to the Synopsis pane.

- Project and Document Notes offer a place to make project- or document-specific notes as you work.

- You cannot format text in the Synopsis pane, but you can format text in the Notes pane.

- Reference links connect your documents to other information within your project or to external files and web pages.

- External reference links are an alternative to importing large files into your project.

PUTTING KEYWORDS AND META-DATA TO WORK

When you undertake a writing project, the words that will compose the finished work are of utmost importance. The journey from beginning to end can be made easier, however, by the tools you use behind the scenes. Meta-data is arguably the most powerful of these tools because it can be used in so many ways.

Meta-data is all of the information about your file. In Chapter 11, "Digging into the Inspector," you learned how to work with the title, synopsis, document and project notes, and reference links in the Inspector. These are all forms of meta-data. This chapter takes meta-data a step further into the various types and methods of tagging your files with labels, status, keywords, and additional fields so they can be searched or categorized.

For those of you with a visual bent, this chapter also explains how to assign colors to each of these meta-data types and apply them to the Binder, Corkboard, and Outliner so you can take in all of this information at a glance.

Setting Status and Labels

The General pane in the Inspector has two fields that were not covered in the previous chapter: the Label and Status. These fields are important for the following reasons:

- Labels have an associated color that can be applied to items in the Binder, Corkboard, and Outliner. The status can be applied as a watermark across index cards in the Corkboard.

- Label and Status values can be set from multiple interface elements.

- The list of values for both the Label and Status fields can be completely customized.

- The titles of the Label and Status fields can themselves be customized, and the terms *Label* and *Status* will be replaced throughout the interface to reflect your field names.

- You can search the project and make collections based on Label and Status values.

As you can see, the Label and Status fields are extremely flexible and accessible.

To assign a label or status to an item, choose from the following options:

- In the General pane of the Inspector, click in the Label or Status field and select a value from the drop-down menu.

- In the Outliner, be sure the Label and/or Status columns are visible (see Chapter 7, "Plotting in the Outliner"), and click the drop-down menu in that column for the item to which you want to assign a value.

- From the context menu in the Binder, Outliner, or Corkboard, right-click on the item and then choose Label or Status and select a value from the submenu. This option allows you to select multiple items using Shift-click or Cmd-click (Ctrl+click in Windows) and assign a label or status to all of them at once.

- In the QuickReference panel on the Mac, click the drop-down menus at the top of the panel and select a value.

- In the floating Inspector panel in Composition mode on the Mac, click the drop-down menus at the bottom of the panel and select a value. In the floating Inspector panel in Full Screen mode in Windows, click the Label and Status drop-down menus in the General pane.

Changing the Label and Status Titles

The Label and Status fields consist of two customizable parts: the field title and the values that can be assigned to the field. You can rename the field titles to suit your needs. When deciding how to use these fields, keep in mind that the Label field can apply color to items in the Binder, Corkboard, and Outliner, making it the most visually predominant option. The Status field appears as a stamp across index cards in the Corkboard and in a column of the Outliner, so it is powerful, but not as immediately eye-catching.

THE CREATIVE PROCESS: REPURPOSING THE STATUS AND LABEL FIELDS

The following are some of the uses you may find for the Label and Status fields:

- **Storyline**: Create a value for each of your subplots so you can see if each subplot is fully resolved.
- **Scene type**: Create values to describe the types of scenes in your novel, such as action, love scene, backstory, black moment, and resolution.
- **Point of view (POV)**: Create values for each character who has scenes in his or her point of view so you can see if your characters' viewpoints are well balanced throughout the book or if your use of a character's POV in only one scene is gratuitous or signifies a weakness in your story. This field only works effectively if you limit each scene to one point of view.
- **Sets**: For scripts, create values noting in which set each scene takes place, such as the village square, tavern, Belle's home, or the Beast's castle. Fiction authors can also use this to track settings.
- **Recipe type**: For a cookbook project, create values for each course or category of food, such as breakfast, proteins, vegetables, and desserts.
- **Filing**: For lawyers, create values such as brief, motion, deposition, and witness list to organize your case files.
- **Lesson**: For teachers, create values such as worksheet, lecture, reading, and homework to organize your lesson plans.
- **Blog category**: For bloggers, create values such as Six-Sentence Sunday, Wordless Wednesday, Friday Five, or whatever categories you use on your blog.

I use different field titles depending on the type of work I'm writing. For novels, I rename the Label field to Storyline and use it to track subplots. I rename the Status field to POV and use it to track the point-of-view character for each scene.

For nonfiction, I rename the Label field to In-House to signify which sections I have in progress and which are completed or yet to be done. I rename the Status field to Production and add values such as Submitted, Tech Edited, and so forth. Although the actual editing is done in a word processor to accommodate my publisher's template, tracking the progress of the chapters throughout production in Scrivener reminds me of where the project as a whole stands and lets me know if I can sneak in any last-minute changes to an earlier chapter before it completes the editing cycle.

To change either the Label or Status field titles:

1. Open the Inspector if it is not already visible.

2. In the General pane, click either the Label or Status field to open the drop-down menu.

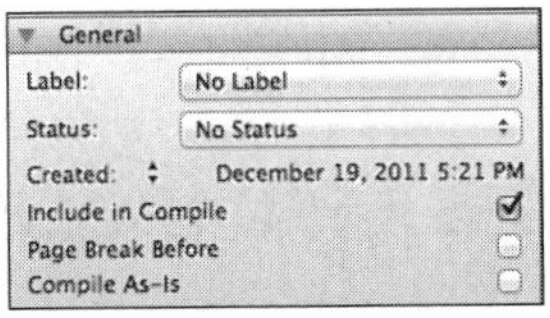

3. Select Edit to open the Meta-Data Settings dialog box (Figure 12.1).

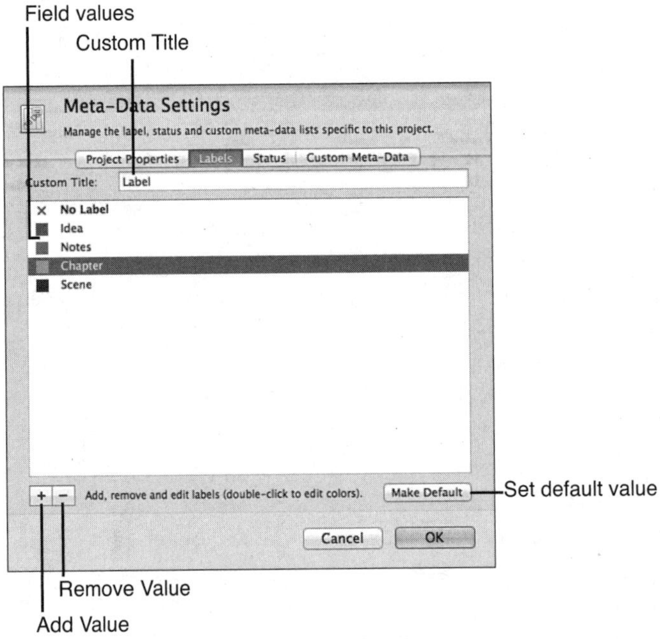

FIGURE 12.1

Change the Label and Status field titles and values in the Meta-Data Settings dialog box.

4. In the Custom Title field, enter a name for the field title.

5. If you want to change the field title for the other field, click the tab for Label or Status at the top of the Meta-Data Settings dialog box and repeat step 4. Otherwise, continue to step 6.

6. Click OK to close the window.

TIP You can also open the Meta-Data Settings dialog box by choosing Project, Meta-Data Settings from the menu or pressing Option-Cmd-, on the Mac or Ctrl+Shift+M in Windows.

In Figure 12.2, you can see that the titles for the Label and Status fields have been changed. These title changes are universal throughout the Scrivener interface. The headings in the Outliner, the context menus, and the main Scrivener menus all reflect the new titles. If you open the View menu, for example, the Use Label Color In command has been updated with the new title for the former Label field (for example, Use Storyline Color In).

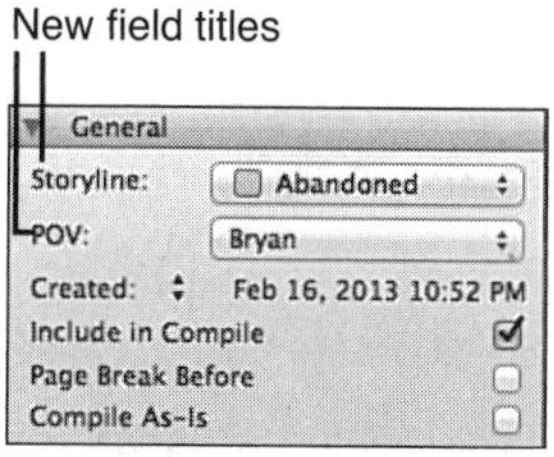

New field titles

General	
Storyline:	☐ Abandoned ⬍
POV:	Bryan ⬍
Created: ⬍	Feb 16, 2013 10:52 PM
Include in Compile	☑
Page Break Before	☐
Compile As-Is	☐

FIGURE 12.2

The Label and Status fields are now titled Storyline and POV.

 NOTE For consistency, I will continue to refer to these fields as Label and Status. Remember that you may have changed them in your own project. Also note that the Meta-Data Settings dialog box continues to refer to Labels and Status in the tabs at the top of the dialog box.

Removing Status and Label Values

Once you have determined how you want to use the Label and Status fields, you can populate them with values that reflect their purpose. If you have decided to use the Label field to track storylines, for example, you'll want to delete the default values and create a unique value for each subplot in your manuscript.

To delete the current values:

1. In the Inspector, click to open the Label or Status drop-down menu, as appropriate, and select Edit.

2. In the Meta-Data Settings dialog box, select the value you want to delete. On the Mac, Cmd-click to select multiple values at once. In Windows, you must select values one at a time.

3. Click the Remove (–) button at the lower left of the window.

4. Repeat step 3 as needed. You can switch from the Labels to the Status tab, or vice versa, to remove all of the unnecessary values from both fields.

5. Click OK to close the Meta-Data Settings dialog box.

 NOTE If you delete a value previously assigned to an item, the label or status for that item changes to the default value. You cannot delete the No Label and No Status values, although you can rename them.

You can remove values at any time. If you decide to eliminate a subplot when you are tracking storylines or realize that you are never going to participate in Wordless Wednesday on your blog, remove the unneeded values from your project.

Adding Status and Label Values

If you delete the default Label and Status values, you will want to add new ones. You can also add new values as you work. If you are tracking storylines and add a new subplot to your manuscript where the hero's past catches up with him, for example, you will want to add a new value called "Hero's Past."

When you add values to the Status and Label fields, they appear in the drop-down lists for that field throughout the interface. To add a value:

1. Open the Meta-Data Settings dialog box using one of the methods described earlier in this chapter. If necessary, click the appropriate tab for either Labels or Status.

2. Click the Add (+) button at the lower left of the dialog box.

3. Enter the name of the new value, as shown in Figure 12.3.

New values

> **Meta-Data Settings**
>
> Manage the label, status and custom meta-data lists specific to this project.
>
> Project Properties | Labels | Status | Custom Meta-Data
>
> Custom Title: Storyline
>
> ✕ No Label
> ■ Avoiding Contact
> ■ Abandoned
> ■ Romance
> ■ Real Life
>
> + − Add, remove and edit labels (double-click to edit colors).   Make Default
>
> Cancel   OK

FIGURE 12.3

The values in the Labels tab are now appropriate for the Storyline field title.

4. Repeat steps 2 and 3 to add more values. You can also use the Labels and Status tabs at the top of the dialog box to modify values for the other field.

5. Click OK to close the dialog box.

Writing projects tend to evolve. If you are keeping a blog, you may decide Wordless Wednesdays will now be called Witless Wednesday. If you're writing a novel, perhaps you decide your protagonist hangs out at a pool hall instead of a coffeehouse. To modify existing values:

1. Open the Meta-Data Settings dialog box. If necessary, click the appropriate tab for either Labels or Status.

2. Double-click the value you want to modify. In the Label field, be sure to double-click the name of the value and not the color swatch.

3. Enter a new value.

4. Click OK.

 TIP To rearrange the order of values, click and drag them to the desired location. The order in which values appear in the Meta-Data Settings dialog box is the order in which they appear on any of the drop-down lists for those fields (in the General pane of the Inspector, context menus, the Outliner, QuickReference panels, and the floating Inspector pane in Composition/Full Screen mode).

Setting a Default Status or Label

Every item is automatically assigned a default status or label. The default value for the Label field is initially No Label. The default value for the Status value is, you guessed it, No Status. Once you have populated the values for each field, however, you may want to change the default to the value you intend to use most often. For example, if you are writing a romance novel, the romance subplot is going to dominate your story. If you are writing a foodie blog, most of your posts are going to be about food, with only occasional forays into other events in your area or your personal life.

To set a new default value, open the Meta-Data Settings dialog box (use the drop-down menu for either the Label or Status field in the Inspector), select the value you want to choose as the default, and click the Make Default button at the lower right of the dialog box. The default value always appears in bold in the Meta-Data Settings dialog box.

NOTE Existing items are not automatically updated when the default value is changed. Items with the No Status or No Label values remain designated as such until you manually change their values.

TIP There are two ways of thinking about the default values for the Status and Label fields. If you leave the defaults at No Status and No Label, you can see at a glance if you neglected to assign those fields to an item, particularly if you are in the Outliner. If you assign the most common value as the default, however, you will not have to manually set these fields for every file, as most of them correctly remain at the default values.

Associating Color with Labels

Every value in the Label field is automatically associated with a color. To change the color assigned to a value:

1. Click the Label drop-down menu in the General pane of the Inspector and select Edit.

2. In the Meta-Data Settings dialog box, double-click the color swatch to the left of the value you want to change. On the Mac, this opens the Colors dialog box, shown in Figure 12.4. In Windows, the Select Color dialog box opens (Figure 12.5).

Color selection options

Color wells

FIGURE 12.4

The Colors dialog box on the Mac provides multiple color selection options. Use the color wells to store favorite colors or create your own palettes.

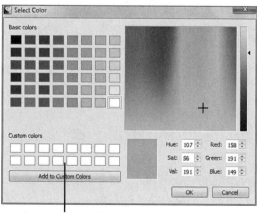

Custom color wells

FIGURE 12.5

In Windows, use the custom color wells to store your favorite colors for use in other Scrivener appearance options.

3. Choose from the following, depending on your platform:

- On the Mac, choose a color selection option, such as the color wheel shown in Figure 12.4 or the Color Palettes tool described in Chapter 10,

"Editing Your Manuscript," and choose a color. You can also select a color from the color wells. Click the Close button in the upper-left corner to close the Colors dialog box.

- In Windows, click on one of the Basic Colors, choose from the spectrum and the color slider, select a Custom Color that has already been added to the dialog box, or enter the RGB values for a specific color. Click the Add to Custom Colors button to add a color to one of the empty color wells if you want to keep the color readily available to apply to other appearance options in the future. Click OK to exit the Select Color dialog box.

4. Repeat steps 2 and 3 to change the colors for other Label values.

5. Click OK to close the Meta-Data Settings dialog box.

Applying Label Color to Interface Elements

The color that is associated with each label can be applied to items in the Binder, Corkboard, and Outliner. This provides a visual cue to the item's label, which in turn can help you analyze your project. If you use the Label field to track subplots, you can tell if one plot has been dominating the manuscript by the preponderance of that color in the Binder, Corkboard, or Outliner. Are you using Scrivener to draft your blog posts? You can tell at a glance if you've been avoiding Wordless Wednesday when the hot-pink color you assigned to that value is nowhere to be seen in this month's posts.

To apply the label color, choose View, Use Label Color In from the menu, and then select where you want to use the color from the submenu. You can choose any or all of the four available options, as follows:

 CAUTION If you changed the title of the Label field, this menu option reads Use [Title] Color In.

- **Binder**: Highlights the item name in the Binder, as shown in Figure 12.6.

FIGURE 12.6

The label color has been applied to the Binder.

- **Icons**: Adds the color to the item icon in the Binder (shown in Figure 12.7), the Corkboard, the Outliner, and the Header bar in the Editor.

Binder
Novel Format
Manuscript
Title Page
Chapter 1
Excursion - Jess
Excursion - Bryan's POV
Bryan Draws
Running to the Boat
Chapter 2
Tempers Flare
Bryan Gets Burned
Survival Mode Part I

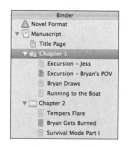

FIGURE 12.7

The label color has been applied to icons. Here, you can see how the icons appear in the Binder with this option selected.

- **Index Cards**: Adds the color to the background of index cards in the Corkboard, as shown in Figure 12.8, and the Inspector. If you opt to show pins on your index cards (see Chapter 6, "Storyboarding with the Corkboard"), the pin or chip also reflects the label color.

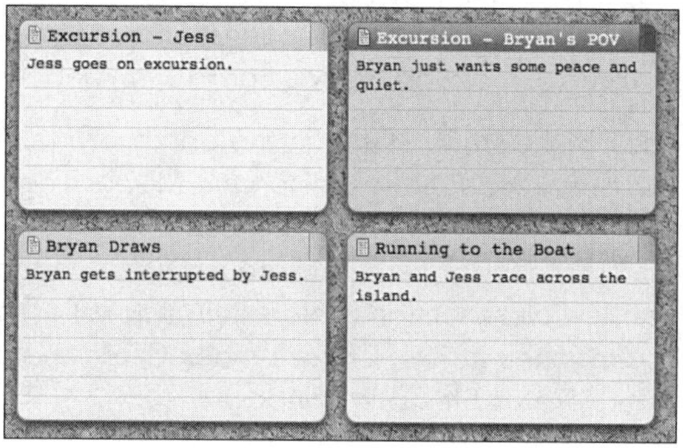

Excursion - Jess
Jess goes on excursion.
Excursion - Bryan's POV
Bryan just wants some peace and quiet.
Bryan Draws
Bryan gets interrupted by Jess.
Running to the Boat
Bryan and Jess race across the island.

FIGURE 12.8

The label color has been applied to the index cards in the Corkboard.

- **Outliner Rows**: Adds the color to the background of each row in the Outliner, as shown in Figure 12.9.

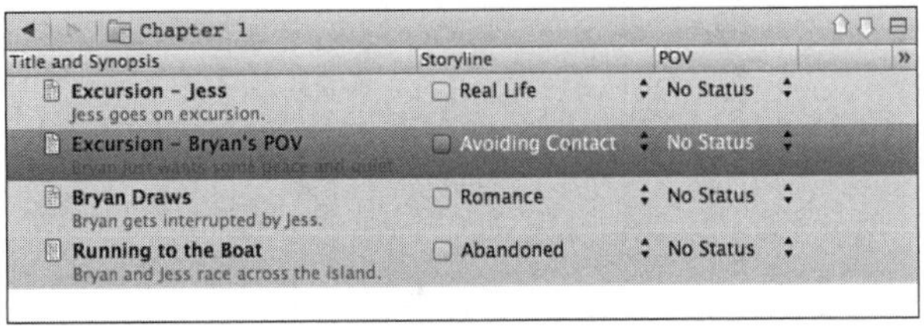

Title and Synopsis	Storyline	POV	»
📄 **Excursion – Jess** Jess goes on excursion.	☐ Real Life	⬍ No Status ⬍	
📄 **Excursion – Bryan's POV** Bryan just wants some peace and	☐ Avoiding Contact	⬍ No Status ⬍	
📄 **Bryan Draws** Bryan gets interrupted by Jess.	☐ Romance	⬍ No Status ⬍	
📄 **Running to the Boat** Bryan and Jess race across the island.	☐ Abandoned	⬍ No Status ⬍	

FIGURE 12.9

The label color has been applied to the rows of the Outliner.

NOTE Personally, I apply the label color to icons and the Corkboard. I find the bars of color to be distracting in the Binder, and seeing the color in the icon and in the Label column of the Outliner is plenty for me in that view. Your mileage may vary, of course!

Applying a Status Stamp to Index Cards

The Status field is not associated with a color, but it can be applied to items in the Corkboard as a watermark across the card. To add the Status field to your index cards, choose View, Corkboard Options, Show Stamps from the menu. You can also press Control-Cmd-S on the Mac or F10 in Windows.

Adjust the opacity of the status stamp in the Corkboard tab of the preferences/ Options window (Scrivener, Preferences on the Mac or Tools, Options in Windows). Use the Status Stamp Opacity slider to make the status stamp fade into or stand out against the index card background. Change the color of the stamp in the Customizable Colors section (Colors in Windows) of the Appearance tab of the Preferences/Options window. Choose Index Cards and then Index Card Status Stamps (Index Card Status Stamp in Windows).

Using Glyphs as a Status Stamp on the Mac

If you don't like the idea of a word appearing across the index cards, consider using symbols instead.

CAUTION If you use glyphs to indicate status, don't forget what each symbol means to you. If you are using the Status field to indicate POV, for example, and only have one male and one female POV character in your novel, it's fine to use male and female symbols in place of the words *Male* and *Female*. If you have several POV characters, however, this gets more complicated. The glyph serves as the only character in the Status field value, so there is no key to what the symbols mean to you unless you create one—which you may want to do in a document in your Research or other non-Draft folder.

To add a symbol as a value in the Status field on the Mac:

1. Choose Edit, Special Characters from the menu.

2. In the Characters dialog box, shown in Figure 12.10, locate a symbol.

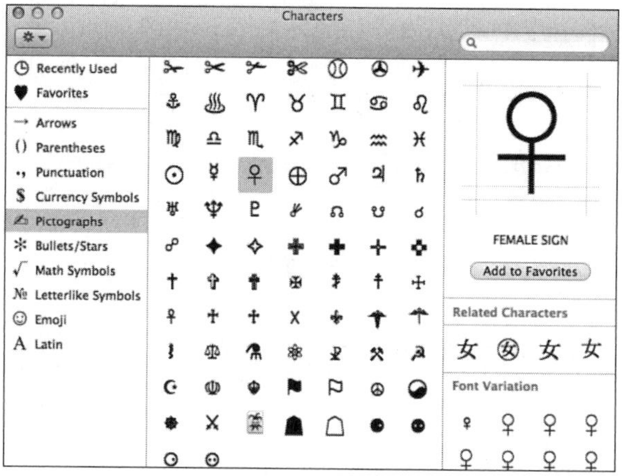

FIGURE 12.10

The Characters dialog box in Mac OS X 10.8 Mountain Lion displays symbols to use as glyphs.

 NOTE The Characters dialog box is a Mac tool rather than a Scrivener-specific tool. Thus, the interface might be slightly different depending on the version of OS X you are using.

3. Click the Status drop-down menu and select Edit to open the Meta-Data Settings dialog box.

4. Click the Add (+) button.

5. Double-click or drag and drop the symbol from the Characters dialog box into the empty Status field value.

6. Press Return.

7. Click the Close button on the Characters dialog box.

8. Click the OK button in the Meta-Data Settings dialog box to exit.

To see the glyph in action, open the Corkboard view for a container and apply the glyph as a status for one of the index cards, as shown in Figure 12.11.

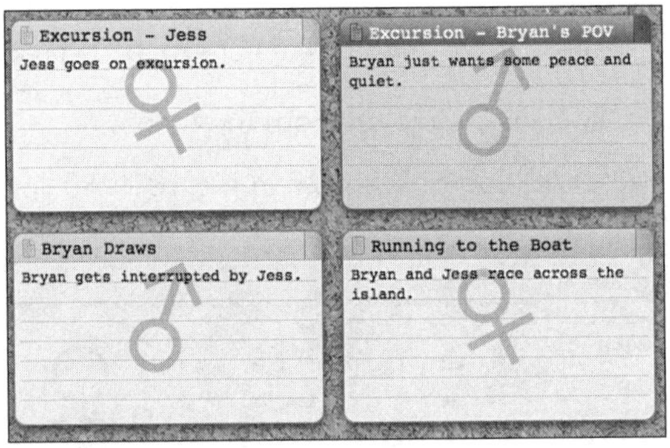

FIGURE 12.11

The male and female symbols have been applied as status stamps.

The status stamp is automatically scaled to fit the index card. Certain fonts, however, appear larger or more noticeable than others. To change the appearance of the glyph:

1. Choose Scrivener, Preferences from the menu.

2. Click on the Corkboard tab.

3. In the Fonts area of the dialog box, click on the Status Stamp field.

4. In the Fonts dialog box, choose a different font family and typeface.

5. Click the Close button in the Fonts dialog box.

6. Click the Close button in the Preferences dialog box.

Adding Glyphs as a Status Stamp in Windows

To add a symbol as a value in Windows:

1. Choose Edit, Character Map from the menu.

2. In the Character Map dialog box, shown in Figure 12.12, click on the symbol you want to use. Make note of the font from which you choose the symbol, and as you add symbols as other values, be sure to select from the same font.

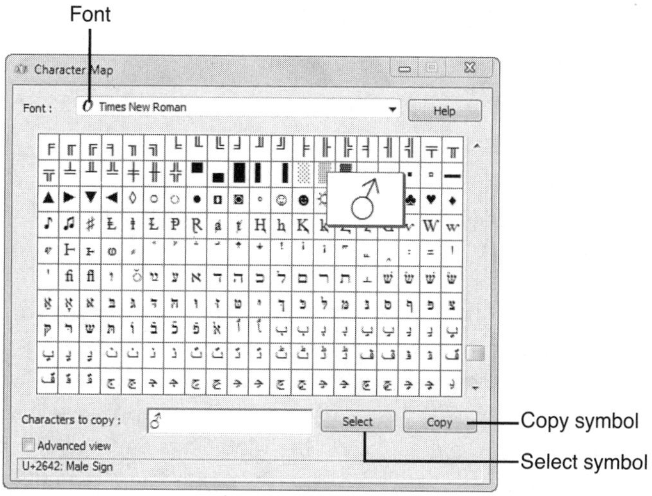

FIGURE 12.12

The Character Map in Windows allows you to choose symbols from any font installed on your system.

3. Click the Select button. The symbol appears in the Characters to Copy field below the Symbols list.

4. Click Copy to copy the symbol.

5. In Scrivener, click the Status drop-down menu and select Edit to open the Meta-Data Settings dialog box.

6. Click the Add (+) button.

7. Press Ctrl+V to paste the symbol into the empty Status field value.

8. Press Enter.

9. Click the OK button in the Meta-Data Settings dialog box to exit.

Once you have created the glyph values, you may have to adjust the status stamp font so the symbol renders properly on the index cards. To do this:

1. Select Tools, Options from the menu.

2. Click on the Appearance tab.

3. In the Fonts pane, click the disclosure triangle to the left of Corkboard, then select Status Stamp.

4. Click the Select Font button in the right column.

5. In the Select Font dialog box, choose the font in which the symbol(s) you chose originated.

6. Click OK to close the Select Font dialog box.

7. Click OK to close the Options window.

When you apply the new Status value to an index card in the Corkboard, the glyph should appear.

CAUTION To ensure the widest support for your glyphs, choose Unicode characters rather than a symbol font, such as Wingdings. If you select a symbol font, the symbol will appear correctly on index cards, but it will not appear as that symbol in drop-down menus or in the Meta-Data Settings dialog box, which can make it very difficult to locate and apply the desired status.

Using Keywords

The Label and Status fields are useful when you only need to apply a single value to an item. If you need to apply multiple values to an item, however, keywords are a better option. You can create keywords to track any details you want, including multiple categories of information.

For example, if you want to track not only the POV character for each scene but all of the characters that appear in the scene, you need keywords to attach multiple characters to the scene. You can attach keywords to the same item to note the setting of the scene. Or if you are creating a recipe file, you can designate a recipe as being both Lunch and Pork.

You can search your project based on keywords (see Chapter 16, "Searching Your Project"). This gives you an advantage over searching the text of your documents. Let's say you have a scene that affects a character's story arc, but the character himself is not in the scene. If you attach the character's keyword, the scene appears when you search for that name.

Like labels, keywords are color-coded. Keywords and their associated colors are used in the following elements:

- On index cards in the Corkboard, if you enable them (View, Corkboard Options, Show Keyword Colors or press Control-Cmd-K on the Mac or Ctrl+F12 in Windows)

- On the Mac, underlined in their associated color in the Keywords column of the Outliner, if the Keywords column is visible
- In the Keywords pane of the Inspector

Viewing the Keywords Inspector Pane

To view keywords in the Inspector, click the Keywords button at the bottom of the Inspector, as shown in Figure 12.13.

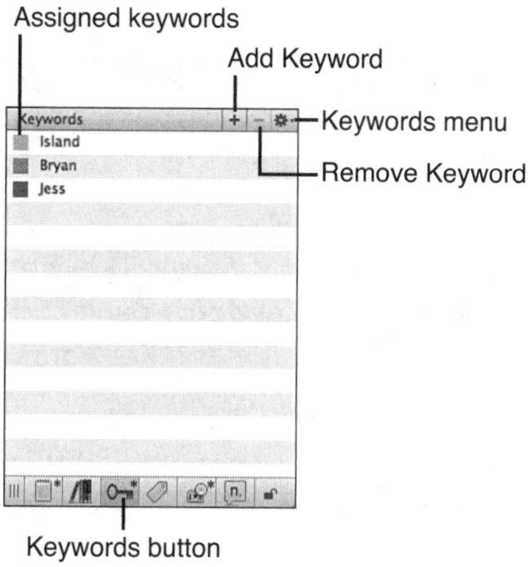

FIGURE 12.13

The Keywords pane lists any keywords that have been attached to the selected item.

Any keywords that have been applied to the item are listed in the Keywords pane, along with the associated color.

Adding Keywords to Documents

To create keywords directly within the Keywords pane, apply them to the item, and add the keyword to the Project Keywords window in one process:

1. Open the Keywords pane in the Inspector if it is not already visible.
2. Click the Add Keyword button (+) in the header of the Keywords pane.
3. Enter the name you want to give the new keyword.
4. Press Return/Enter.

The keyword appears with a color swatch to the left of it. You can customize keyword colors, but only from the Project Keywords window, explained below.

You can also add keywords that have already been created, whether in another item or in the Project Keywords window. To add a preexisting keyword:

1. Open the Keywords pane in the Inspector.

2. Click the Keywords menu (the gear icon) in the header of the Keywords pane.

3. Hover over the Add Keyword option on the drop-down menu, and then select a keyword from the submenu.

Removing Keywords from a Document

As you enter a recipe into your cookbook project, you decide that it is more of a Lunch or Dinner meal than the Breakfast keyword with which you tagged it. Or suppose a scene to which you assigned the Boathouse keyword now takes place in the back room of a seedy bar.

If your document takes a turn and an assigned keyword no longer applies, remove it by selecting the keyword in the Keywords pane and either pressing Delete or clicking the Remove Keyword button in the Keywords pane header.

Although the keyword is removed from the document, it remains in the project. This holds true even if the keyword is not applied to any other item in the project. To manage keywords on a projectwide basis, you need to open the Keywords panel.

Using the Keywords Panel

The Keywords panel is the brain center of keyword meta-data. Here, you can add and remove keywords from your project, change the color associated with a keyword, group keywords into parent-child relationships in order to organize them, and search your project by keyword.

Open the Keywords panel using one of the following methods:

- Click the Keywords button in the toolbar.

- Choose Project, Show Project Keywords from the menu.

- Press Option-Shift-Cmd-H on the Mac or Ctrl+Shift+O in Windows.

- From the Inspector, click the gear icon in the Keywords pane header, and choose Show Project Keywords from the drop-down menu.

- In Composition/Full Screen mode, press the Keywords button in the Control Strip.

NOTE Keywords are created on a per-project basis. If you want to preserve your keywords for other projects, save them as part of a custom project template. Learn how to create project templates in Chapter 14, "Creating and Using Project Templates." You can also copy keywords from one project to another by opening the two projects side-by-side, opening the Keywords panel in each, and then dragging and dropping selected keywords from one panel to the other.

You can use the Keywords panel, shown in Figure 12.14, for all of your keyword-related tasks. To add a keyword to a document, drag and drop the keyword from the panel to the item name in the Binder, onto the index card in the Corkboard, onto the item's row in the Outliner, or into the Keywords pane in the Inspector. To apply multiple keywords at once, Cmd-click (Ctrl+click in Windows) or Shift-click to select the keywords and then drag them to a document. To apply keywords to multiple documents at once, Cmd-click (Ctrl+Click in Windows) or Shift-click to select the documents and then select the keyword or keywords and drag them onto the selected documents.

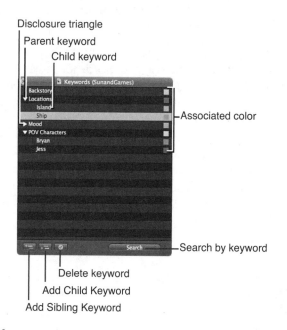

FIGURE 12.14

The Keywords panel floats above your project.

Organizing Project Keywords

When you create keywords from the Keywords pane in the Inspector, they are immediately added to the Keywords panel. As you continue to add more keywords, the Keywords panel can become very disorganized, with some keywords relating to characters and others to setting, or other dissimilar ideas relating to your project. To add a measure of organization to the Keywords panel, create parent-child relationships to sort keywords by category. To do this:

1. Click the Add Sibling Keyword button at the bottom of the pane to create a new keyword.

2. Enter a descriptive name for the keyword, such as Locations.

3. Drag and drop any keywords relating to the category onto the new keyword. For example, in Figure 12.14, Island and Ship have been dropped onto the Locations keyword.

You can add new keywords directly into a parent category by selecting the category keyword and clicking the Add Child Keyword button at the bottom of the pane. To create another keyword on the same level as the selected keyword, click the Add Sibling Keyword button.

As the Keywords panel fills up, the disclosure triangles to the left of each parent keyword can be used to hide the child keywords for easier navigation. On the Mac, choose View, Outline, Expand All or Collapse All or press Cmd-9 or Cmd-0 to toggle the disclosure state of all of the parent items in the Keywords panel at once.

NOTE In Windows, you can sort keywords in ascending or descending order. Click the Enable Sorting of Keywords check box at the bottom-center of the Keywords panel. This adds a header at the top of the panel, from which you can click to sort in ascending or descending order. Not only are parent keywords sorted, but any child keywords within them are also sorted in the same order.

TIP To change the color associated with a keyword, double-click on the color swatch and choose a new color from the Colors (Mac) or Select Color (Windows) dialog box.

Searching by Keyword

Once you add keywords to the items in your project, you can search by keyword to view only the documents that have a specific keyword applied. This can be helpful if you want to see how many blog posts covered a certain topic or how many recipes are tagged for a particular meal, if you have created keywords for those purposes.

To search for items by keyword:

1. In the Keywords panel, select the keyword you want to use for your search criteria.

2. Click the Search button at the bottom of the panel.

3. View the Search Results in the left sidebar of the Scrivener window, in place of the Binder, as shown in Figure 12.15.

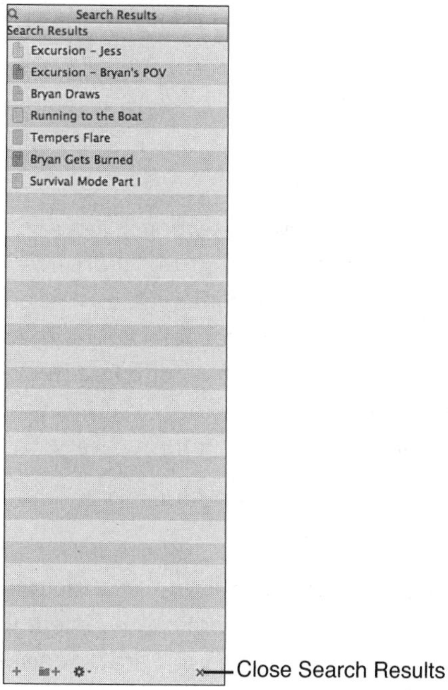

FIGURE 12.15

Use the results of a keyword search to view the items individually or grouped as Scrivenings, in the Corkboard, or in the Outliner.

Use the Search Results in much the same manner as the Binder. On the Mac, click the Search Results heading and then select a Group View mode to see all of the search results grouped together as Scrivenings, in the Corkboard, or in the Outliner. In Windows, view the search results in a group by pressing Ctrl+A to select them all or press Ctrl+click or Shift+click to select specific items. You can also view items individually in the Editor.

When you are finished using the Search Results, click the X at the bottom of the Search Results list to return to the Binder.

Deleting Keywords from a Project

If you want to remove a keyword from your project, select the keyword in the Keywords panel and then click the Delete Keyword button at the bottom of the panel.

CAUTION This action is permanent. If you delete a keyword that is in use, it is removed from all documents. A warning pops up to confirm the deletion if the keyword is in use. If you proceed and delete a keyword in error, you can re-create it, but you must manually reapply it to your documents.

Adding Custom Meta-Data (Mac Only)

With the Label, Status, and Keyword options, you might think you have enough meta-data fields to support any project, but there are always exceptions. The Label and Status fields are limited to the values you enter, which makes them too restrictive to use as a timeline. Because you can add multiple keywords to an item and those keywords can relate to multiple categories, they are not useful when sorting in the Outliner. Custom meta-data, on the other hand, can accept unlimited values that all relate to a common category.

Here are some uses for custom meta-data:

- Create a custom field for Events and populate it with the parties and social occasions your historical novel heroine attends during the Season year after year as she gets closer to being put on the shelf. Create a field for Cars and use it to track which automobiles your protagonist has stolen as he's chased across the country by the mob. Create a field for Creatures and use it to track the different races your space traveler encounters (and reencounters). You get the idea!

- In a cookbook, create a custom field for Meal. This frees up your Label and Status fields to track information such as the completion status of each item (such as To-Do, In Process, Taste Tested, Directions Tested).

- Students, create Assigned Date and Due Date fields for assignments. This lets you use Scrivener as a planner as well as a place to write your essays and other assignments.

- Create a timeline.

Custom meta-data does not provide the same level of visibility within the Scrivener interface as other types of meta-data. You can view your custom fields in the Custom Meta-Data pane of the Inspector or in the Outliner. You can also use custom meta-data for searches and to create collections. You can then use these collections to filter items when compiling your project.

 NOTE Collections are explained in Chapter 16, "Searching Your Project." Filtering your project as part of the compilation process is explained in Chapter 19, "Compiling Your Completed Work."

Adding Fields

To add a custom meta-data field, you must first open the Meta-Data Settings dialog box:

1. Click the Custom Meta-Data button at the bottom of the Inspector to open the Custom Meta-Data pane, shown in Figure 12.16.

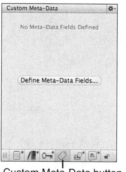

Custom Meta-Data button

FIGURE 12.16

When the Custom Meta-Data pane in the Inspector is empty, it displays a button to begin the process of creating custom fields.

2. Choose one of the following options to open the Custom Meta-Data tab in the Meta-Data Settings dialog box:

    *   If this is your first custom field, click the Define Meta-Data Fields button in the center of the pane.

    *   Click the gear button in the Custom Meta-Data pane header; then select Edit Custom Meta-Data Settings from the drop-down menu.

- Choose Project, Meta-Data Settings from the menu and then click the Custom Meta-Data tab at the top of the dialog box, shown in Figure 12.17.

- Press Option-Cmd-,.

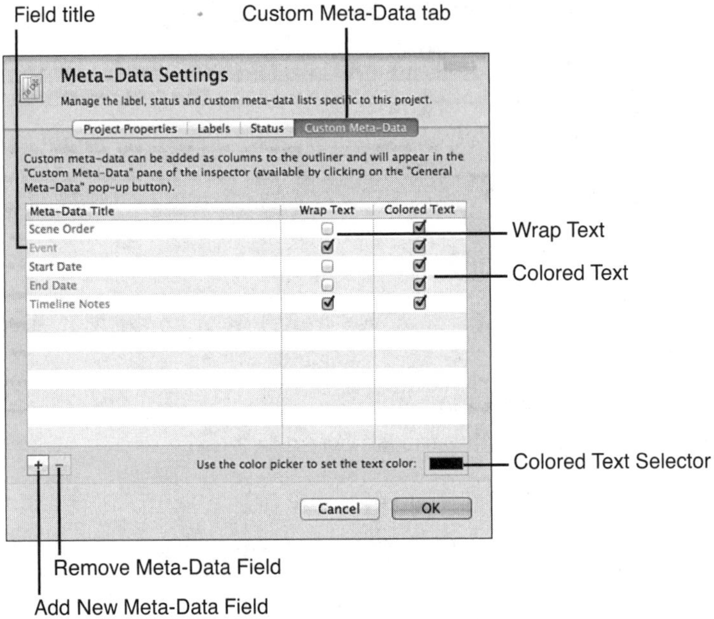

FIGURE 12.17

The Custom Meta-Data Settings dialog box is used to create new meta-data fields.

3. Click the Add New Meta-Data Field (+) button.

4. Enter the title for the field.

5. Click the optional Wrap Text check box if the values for the field are likely to require more than one line.

6. Click the optional Colored Text check box if you want the field values to appear in a different color. If you select this option, click the Colored Text Selector at the bottom of the dialog box to open the Colors dialog box and select a color.

7. Repeat steps 3–6 if you want to add more custom meta-data fields.

8. Click OK to close the Meta-Data Settings dialog box.

Adding Values

Custom meta-data does not use a predetermined list of values. Instead, you enter a value directly in the field in either the Outliner or the Inspector. This allows you to enter a wide range of values, but it can also lead to inconsistencies and typos.

If you are entering values for multiple items at once, use the Outliner, as you can scroll down and enter a value for each item. To do this:

1. Select a container in the Binder to open in the Outliner.

 NOTE See Chapter 7 to learn how to access the Outliner.

2. Click the Columns menu button and select the custom meta-data fields you want to view.

3. Double-click in the empty field for the item to add a value to the field.

4. Press Return.

Figure 12.18 shows the Outliner with several custom meta-data fields visible. In this timeline example, the Scene Order field holds the position in which the scene appears in the story. The Event field is intended to describe the inciting incident in the flashback. The Start Date field provides the chronological timeline of events in the story. The Timeline Notes field can describe why the flashback is important to the story. Creating multiple fields intended to work together like this allows you to sort the Outliner by Scene Order or by Start Date. You can even sort by Event if you want to analyze whether there's a good reason for certain flashbacks.

Columns menu button

Chapter 1				
Title	Scene Order	Event	Start Date	Timeline Notes
Tempers Flare	5	Refers to Ship	2012-11-10 21:00	She refers to him giving her the brush-off
Excursion – Jess	1		2012-11-14 10:23	
Excursion – Bryan's POV	2		2012-11-14 10:24	
Bryan Draws	3		2012-11-14 12:00	
Running to the Boat	4		2012-11-14 17:04	
Survival Mode Part I	6		2012-11-14 19:00	
Bryan Gets Burned	7		2012-11-15 12:00	

FIGURE 12.18

This Outliner demonstrates how custom meta-data can be used to create a rudimentary timeline.

TIP If you are creating a field to store time and date values, use the YYYY-MM-DD HH:MM convention. That way, when you sort on this field, the date goes from broadest unit of time, the year, to the month and day and then to the hour and the smallest unit of time, the minute. If you are using hours and minutes, be sure to enter the time based on a 24-hour clock so your daytime and nighttime events do not get confused.

To add custom meta-data in the Inspector:

1. Click the Custom Meta-Data button at the bottom of the Inspector or press Control-Option-Cmd-M to open the Custom Meta-Data pane in the Inspector.

2. Click in the field into which you want to enter a value.

3. Enter a value and then press Tab to automatically move to the next custom meta-data field or Return to enter the value.

Figure 12.19 shows the Custom Meta-Data pane with values added.

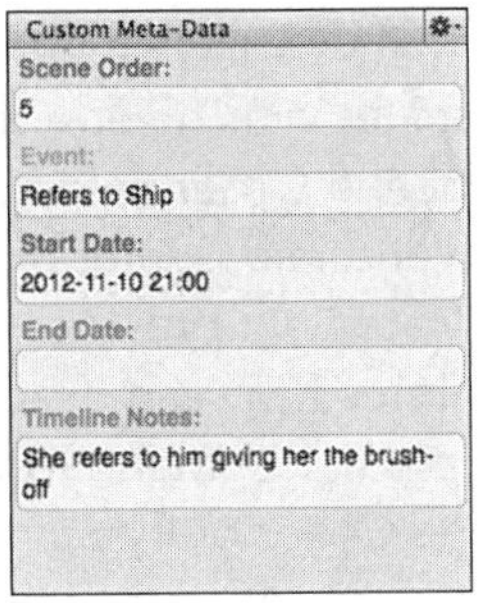

Custom Meta-Data	⚙
Scene Order:	
5	
Event:	
Refers to Ship	
Start Date:	
2012-11-10 21:00	
End Date:	
Timeline Notes:	
She refers to him giving her the brush-off	

FIGURE 12.19

The Custom Meta-Data pane displays the values for an item.

Deleting Custom Meta-Data Fields

Creating custom meta-data fields can be quite empowering, but you may find that some of that power has gotten away from you. If you don't use a custom field, delete the field with these steps:

1. Open the Custom Meta-Data tab in the Meta-Data Settings dialog box using one of the methods described earlier in this chapter.

2. Select the field you want to delete.

3. Click the Remove Meta-Data Field (–) button at the bottom of the dialog box or press Delete.

4. Click OK to exit the dialog box.

When you delete a custom meta-data field, any values entered into that field in any item are removed as well.

THE ABSOLUTE MINIMUM

The following are the highlights from this chapter:

- Scrivener provides many options to tag your documents with meta-data.

- The Label and Status settings are highly customizable and can be displayed in the Inspector, Corkboard, and Outliner. The label can also be displayed by color in the Binder.

- You can change the titles of the Label and Status fields and customize the values for each.

- You can attach multiple keywords to an item.

- On the Mac, custom meta-data can be added and viewed in the Inspector and Outliner.

IN THIS CHAPTER

13

CREATING AND USING TEMPLATE SHEETS

Unfortunately, this chapter begins with a disclaimer. The template sheets discussed here are only available on Scrivener for the Mac. I encourage Windows users to skim through this chapter, however, as I explain other methods of accomplishing similar goals.

If you are using Scrivener for Mac and based your project on one of the Fiction project templates, you may have noticed a root folder in the Binder labeled Template Sheets. A template sheet is a preformatted document that you use as the basis for creating new documents. The template sheet itself remains unchanged, but the document it creates can be added anywhere in the Binder and edited as you desire.

Think of template sheets as worksheets. They are good for documents that you need to use over and over, such as a character sketch. You may create unique profiles for each character in your novel, all based on the same worksheet. You can also use template sheets to prepopulate certain meta-data fields, such as questions or prompts that you want to include in your document notes for every scene. You can even use a template sheet to create a Notes document that uses a different font and font color in the text, is tagged with a Notes label, has a custom icon applied, and has the Include in Compile option deselected in the Inspector. You can then use that template sheet to add Notes documents in your Draft folder that are easily distinguished from the body of your work.

Using Predesigned Template Sheets

Several preformatted Scrivener project templates contain a root folder called Template Sheets. Inside this folder are sheets that relate to the purpose of the project template. The Novel project template, for example, is prepopulated with two template sheets: Character Sketch and Setting Sketch. If you look at these items in the Binder, as shown in Figure 13.1, you see they have a small T badge on their item icons.

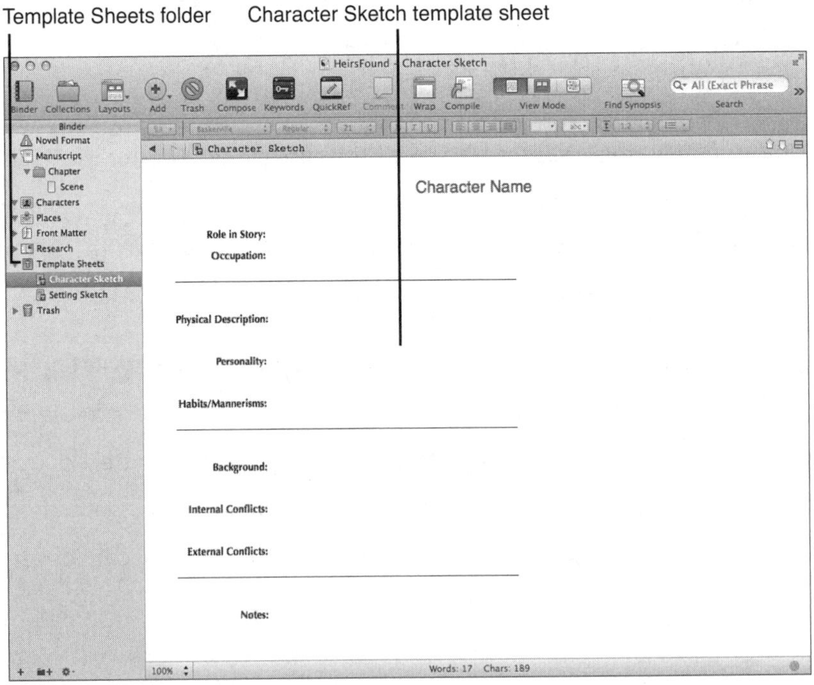

FIGURE 13.1

The Character Sketch template sheet is a worksheet that can be used to create other new documents.

Changing the Template Folder

Each project can only have one Template Sheets folder. Before you can assign a different folder to serve as the container for template sheets, you must first remove this designation from the existing folder. You can, however, remove this designation and choose a different folder to store your template sheets or designate a folder to store template sheets if your Scrivener project did not assign one.

To remove the template sheets folder designation, choose Projects, Clear Templates Folder from the menu. After you click OK in the warning dialog box, the template folder designation is removed from the folder and all of the documents within it.

NOTE   Any documents created from these former template sheets remain unscathed. The folder and documents that formerly acted as templates are likewise unscathed. They no longer function as templates, but they can be edited, duplicated, and otherwise treated as any other item.

To designate a new template sheets folder, select the folder and then choose Project, Set Selection as Template Folder. Any documents within that folder automatically assume the template sheet designation, as well.

TIP   The first item in the Template Sheets folder is automatically assigned a keyboard shortcut to create new documents based on that template. The keyboard shortcut is Shift-Option-Cmd-N. Take advantage of this feature by placing your most-used template sheet at the top of the folder.

Modifying Template Sheets

As the Editor shows, the Character Sketch template sheet contains prompts to enter a name and information about a character. This sketch is a good start, but as every writer has his or her own way of creating a character and determining which traits are important, you are probably already thinking of ways you would change this document. With that in mind, before you actually use the template sheet to create any working documents, you should go ahead and revise the template to meet your needs.

CAUTION   Documents do not remain linked to their template sheet. Once you create a document from a template sheet, the document stands alone, so future changes to the template are not reflected on earlier documents. Thus, it is best to modify template sheets to your liking before you ever use them.

To modify an existing template sheet, select the document in the Binder to open in the Editor. Edit the sheet just like any other document, using the Format bar and menu to change the appearance of the sheet and adding or removing prompts for information. Remember, however, that this is merely a template for future working documents. Do not fill in any information that is specific to a particular character, setting, or other story element.

The template sheet consists of more than just the content in the Editor. Any metadata you add to the item becomes part of the template sheet and is included in the documents you create from it. This means you can add keywords, an initial Label or Status value, reference links, and document notes.

TIP You might have noticed that both the Character Sketch and Setting Sketch template sheets use the image view in the Synopsis pane of the Inspector. Because characters and settings are highly visual, it is assumed that you will want to add an image to these items once you create a document from the template sheet. If you do not want to add images to your sketches, switch the Synopsis pane view in the template sheet before creating documents from the template.

Once you have customized the template sheet, such as in Figure 13.2, you are ready to put it to work.

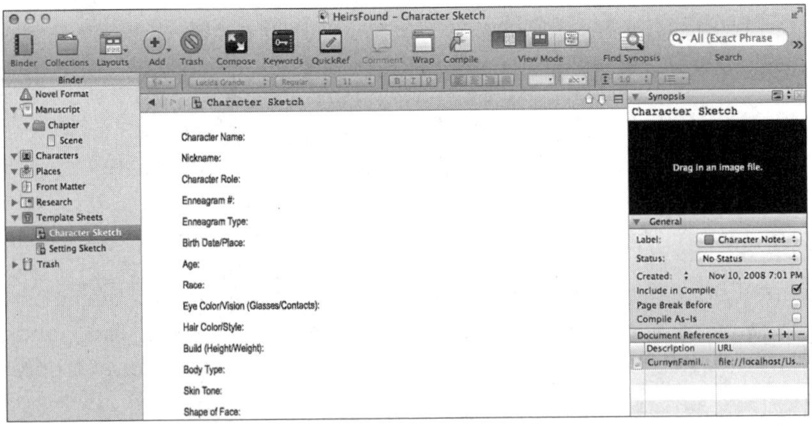

FIGURE 13.2

After much editing, this Character Sketch template sheet is a bit less stylish, but contains prompts for more detail about a character and a reference link to a family tree created in a third-party genealogy application.

Creating a Document from a Template

To use a template sheet:

1. Select the folder into which you want to add the new document.

2. Choose from the following options:

- Right-click the folder and choose Add, New from Template, and then select a template sheet from the submenu.

- Click and hold the Add button in the toolbar and then select the template sheet from the drop-down menu.

- Press Option-Shift-Cmd-N to create a new file from the top document in the Template Sheet folder.

- Choose Project, New from Template from the menu and then choose a template sheet from the submenu.

3. Enter a title for the new document.

4. Press Return.

Figure 13.3 shows the new document created from the Character Sketch template. I have titled the document with the name of the character. To populate the sketch with information, simply type. Documents created from templates are the same as any other Scrivener document. To move from prompt to prompt in the worksheet, click the mouse or use the arrow keys.

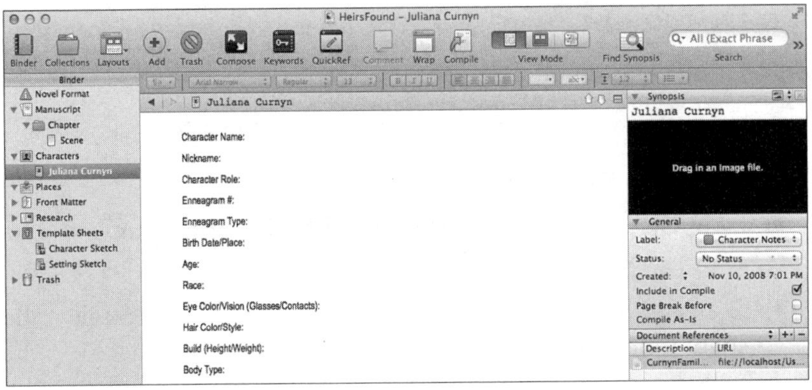

FIGURE 13.3

This character sketch has been added to the Characters folder, titled with the character's name, and is ready to be filled in.

Creating Your Own Template Sheets

Now that you have an idea of how template sheets work, you can create your own from scratch. To create a new template sheet:

1. Select the Templates folder in the Binder. Unless you renamed or created your own, this folder is usually titled Template Sheets.

2. Create a new text file using one of the following methods:

   - Press Cmd-N.

   - Choose Project, New Text from the menu.

   - Right-click on the folder and choose Add, New Text from the context menu.

   - Click the Add button in the toolbar.

3. Type a title for the new template sheet.

4. Press Return. The new document appears in the Template Sheets folder with a small T badge.

5. Open the document in the Editor, if necessary.

6. Type and format the worksheet.

7. Add any default meta-data you want to associate with documents created from your new template sheet.

TIP You can convert any document in your project into a template sheet by dragging the file into the Template Sheets folder. You can also drag template sheets between projects to copy them into another project.

NOTE If you want to use a different font or font color in the text of documents created from the template sheet, you must include some text in the template. For example, if you want to create a Notes template sheet, as I mentioned at the beginning of this chapter, you should type the word *Notes* in the document text and format it as you want the text in the document to appear. If the document text is blank—such as if you are creating a Scene template with a preset label and document notes—the default font is used.

Template sheets can go beyond individual documents. You can create a template subfolder or file group filled with template sheets. When you choose the New from Template command to create working documents from the template, the entire container and all its subdocuments are copied. As shown in the example in Figure 13.4, you can use this to create an entire character builder series of worksheets.

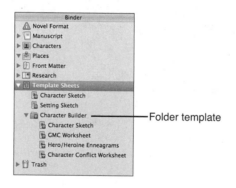

FIGURE 13.4

The Character Builder template folder contains four template sheets. You can create a new document from a single template sheet within the folder or create a new folder containing all of the documents.

THE CREATIVE PROCESS: OTHER IDEAS FOR TEMPLATES

If you are a plotter, template sheets may become your favorite feature in Scrivener. You can create template sheets to organize your research, interview people, and analyze your plot. You can create a shorter character sketch to note details about minor characters or a sheet to compare the traits of two or more characters.

You can also create a Scene template sheet with the Document Notes field containing scene questions, such as what causes the scene and what changes as a result of the scene. If you create new scenes from this template sheet, these document notes appear in the Inspector for every scene.

One of my favorite things to do with template sheets is to create customized sheets based on worksheets I've gathered from books and writing workshops. Whenever I discover a new plotting method, for example, I create a template sheet and try putting it to work to see if it is of value to my work.

Not a fiction writer? That doesn't mean template sheets have nothing to offer you. If you are a student using Scrivener to complete and organize assignments, create an assignment sheet. If you are a teacher or professor, create template sheets for the various types of documents you create—assignments, lecture notes, readings, and so on. If you are using Scrivener to store recipes, create a blank recipe card so all of your entries are consistent. Template sheets are limited solely by your imagination!

 CAUTION If you create custom template sheets based on worksheets published in books or disseminated at a workshop, be sure you have permission from the original author before sharing your Scrivener project or document templates with other Scrivener users.

Setting a Default Document Type

If you look at Figure 13.4, you see a Characters folder and a Places folder. If you add a new document to the Characters folder by selecting the folder and pressing Return, by clicking the Add button in the toolbar, clicking the New Document (+) button at the bottom of the Binder, or by using the Cmd-N keyboard shortcut, it automatically creates a new document based on the Character Sketch template sheet. In the Places folder, the same actions automatically create a new document based on the Setting Sketch template sheet.

To designate a default document type for a container:

1. Select the container to which you want to designate a default document type.

2. Choose Documents, Default New Subdocument Type from the menu, and then select the intended template sheet from the submenu.

When you assign a default subdocument type, the New Text command in the Project menu changes to reflect the type of document created when you invoke the command from that folder. For example, when the Characters folder is selected, the command in the Project menu changes to New Character Sketch.

You can still create other types of documents within a folder that has been designated to create a default subdocument type using the Documents, Move, To command in the menu or the Move To command in the context menu. You can also create a document elsewhere in the project and drag it into the folder.

A WINDOWS VIEW: CREATING FAUX TEMPLATE SHEETS

Although template sheets are not available in Windows, you can apply a similar concept to your workflow. Create a root folder in your project called Worksheets or Templates. Create worksheets and forms to use in your project and add any pertinent meta-data. This folder becomes your home base for creating new items in your project.

When you need a new document based on a faux template, select the template item and choose Documents, Duplicate from the menu or press Ctrl+D. Then drag the duplicate document into place in the Binder or choose Documents, Move To from the menu or Move To from the context menu and select a folder from the submenu.

This is a somewhat clumsy workaround because you have to remember to make the copy so you don't overwrite your faux template, but it will do until the Windows version of Scrivener gains template sheet functionality.

THE ABSOLUTE MINIMUM

The following are the highlights from this chapter:

- Template sheets are preformatted documents, generally intended as worksheets or forms to store project-related information such as character and setting sketches.

- You can edit preexisting template sheets or create your own from scratch.

- Any meta-data you assign to a template sheet is carried over to documents created from that template.

- Template sheets can be edited using the same methods as any other document in your project.

IN THIS CHAPTER

- Creating a project to build a template
- Developing a good template
- Using template placeholder tags
- Saving a project template
- Importing and exporting project templates

14

CREATING AND USING PROJECT TEMPLATES

The first step to getting started in Scrivener is choosing a project template. Unfortunately, this is also the step that causes the most anxiety in new Scrivener users because they don't want to make the wrong choice. Equally unfortunate is that many of these new Scrivener users don't have anyone standing over their shoulder or reassuring them from the pages of a book that there is no wrong choice.

Project templates are merely a starting point for a project. They provide a few files and folders to get your project started, possibly some template sheets, an initial workspace layout, and so on. An important point, however, is that all of these items and settings can be changed. Even if you choose the Recipe Collection template intending to create a cookbook, if you decide to write a novel about eating your way around Europe instead, you can simply modify your project. Although changing all of the settings in a project isn't the most efficient way to work, knowing that it's possible should take some of the stress out of choosing the best project template.

Even if you are writing a screenplay and choose the Screenplay project template, which seems like a perfect match, you might still tweak settings and create supporting documents until you most likely wind up with a project that's quite different from the basic template. Doing this the first time you create a project is fine, but this is not a process you need to repeat every time you start a new work. Thus, the best project templates are usually the ones you create for yourself.

Creating a Project to Build a Template

Project templates are created from a regular project that is customized and saved in such a way as to be available as the basis of future projects. As you have become more familiar with Scrivener, perhaps you have already begun tweaking the original project file you opened, or at least considered what you would change.

If you want to base your custom template on your current project, before you proceed any further in this chapter, save a duplicate copy of the project. To save a copy of your project, choose File, Save As from the menu and provide a name and storage location for the new file. This new project becomes the starting point for your project template.

 CAUTION Do not use the only copy of your current project as the basis for a project template. Creating a template is as much about stripping out unnecessary information as it is about adding and customizing elements. Because Scrivener automatically saves whenever you pause in your work, these changes affect the project upon which your template is based. Always create project templates from a duplicate or "dummy" project file.

If you prefer, you can also create a brand-new project for the purpose of customizing it to create your own template. To create a new project:

1. Click File, New Project from the menu. You can also press Shift-Cmd-N on the Mac or Ctrl+G, N in Windows.

2. In the Project Templates dialog box, shown in Figure 14.1, choose a template as the foundation for your customization efforts. If you want to start truly from scratch, choose the Blank template. Otherwise, choose the project template that provides the best starting point for your customization.

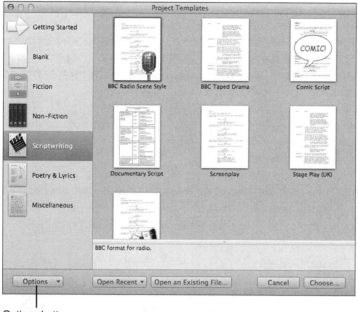

Options button

FIGURE 14.1

Choose a template from the Project Templates dialog box to use as the foundation for your own custom template.

3. Mac users, click Choose and then enter a project name in the Save As dialog box. Windows users, enter a name in the Save As field and select a location to store the project in the Project Templates dialog box.

4. Click Create.

Developing a Good Template

A project template includes every file, folder, and setting that exists in the project upon which it is based. This means that if you want something to appear in projects in the future, add it into your project template so you only need to create it once. It also means if you don't want something in your projects, be certain it is removed before you save your template. The following sections provide a checklist of items to consider when creating a template, which can be addressed in any order you want.

Create a Workspace Layout

In Chapter 2, "Customizing Your Work Environment," you learned how to set up workspace layouts. If you want the project to open in a particular layout, select it from the Window, Layouts menu (or the Layouts button on the toolbar) on the Mac toolbar or the View, Layout menu in Windows.

 TIP If you want new projects created from this template to open in Full Screen mode on the Mac, save the template while in Full Screen mode.

When creating an initial layout for a template, consider how you will use the project. If your workflow necessitates a lot of entering and customization of metadata, for example, be sure the Inspector is visible in the layout.

Set Up the Draft Folder

Your Draft folder contains the body of your work, so give it proper attention when creating your project template. Remove any files and folders that should not become part of the template. If you have already written material within this project, remove it. You did make a copy of the project before beginning this process, right?

Rename the Draft folder. Although purely cosmetic, referring to your work as something other than a draft may appeal. If you plan to share your project template, changing this folder title makes it appear more professional. The Novel project template that is preinstalled in Scrivener renames the Draft folder to Manuscript, whereas the Screenplay template renames it to Screenplay.

If you are using a preinstalled template as the foundation for your own project template, examine your Draft folder for a title page that may contain identifying information. See the "Using Template Placeholder Tags" section later in this chapter to learn how to strip out this personal information and replace it with placeholder tags on the Mac for future projects. In Windows, replace personal information with generic text, such as Name and Address, that can be replaced by the user.

Create an initial folder and file system upon which you can base the structure of your project. If you are writing a novel, you generally want this to be open ended—perhaps a single folder and file to get things started. If you create more structured works, such as academic papers, you can prepopulate the Draft folder with folders for Introduction, Hypothesis, Research Methods, and so on. If you write three-act screenplays, create a folder for each act.

If you are on a Mac and choose to create a template sheet for your Draft documents, select the Draft folder in the Binder and choose Documents, Default New Subdocument Type from the menu to set the default document used when new items are added to the Draft folder. See Chapter 13, "Creating and Using Template Sheets," to learn more about template sheets.

In Windows, or if you don't want to use the template sheet feature on the Mac, you might want to format an initial document file. You can duplicate this document as needed when you create a project from this template.

Add or Modify the Information File

In some templates, you see a file at the top of the Binder that contains instructions on how to use the template. Although you can always veer from how a project is intended to be used, these instructions act as a guideline.

If you base your custom project file on a preinstalled template, modify the instructions file to remind you how to handle new projects created with this project template.

TIP   Even if you have no intention of sharing your project template with other Scrivener users, this information sheet serves a purpose. If you are a fiction author, you may only create one or two new projects a year, if that, so it's easy to forget what you were thinking when you changed the Label field title to Ostentation, even if you had a very good reason at the time. Make a note of it and remove all doubt.

If you used the Blank project template to begin your customization, you may want to create an instruction sheet. To do this, create a new file and move it to the top of the Binder. Note any changes to the meta-data settings, how you intend the Draft folder to be structured, additional folders you created for non-Draft elements of the project, template sheets, and the Compile settings.

TIP   If you create this file as soon as you begin customizing the template, you can add to it as you make noteworthy changes.

Create Non-Draft Folders and Files

As you know, the Draft, Research, and Trash folders cannot be deleted, only renamed, so they remain an integral part of your project template. You might want to create additional folders that will be of use to projects built on this template. To give you an idea of the possibilities, the following is a list of files and folders (shown in Figure 14.2) I use in my novel project template and some of the worksheets or blank files I create within them:

FIGURE 14.2

Adding other folders helps you organize all of the material relating to a project.

- **About Jenn's Novel Template**: This is my information file. It details all of the unique features of my template, both as a reminder to myself and to give insight to others if I decide to share it.

- **Manuscript**: This is my renamed Draft folder. It contains a title page, an empty Chapter folder, and an empty Scene file created from a Scene template sheet.

- **Plotting**: This folder contains worksheets titled Story Overview and Story Evolution, a subfolder for the Snowflake Method created by Randy Ingermanson, and a subfolder for Backstory, all of which I use for plotting. If the project is intended for multiple books in a series, I also add a file for Future Book Ideas.

 NOTE See Chapter 23, "Discovering New Uses for Scrivener," to learn how to use a single project for multiple works.

- **Characters**: This folder is intended to store character sketches for each of the main characters created from a series of template sheets. The default document for this folder is the Character Sketch template sheet.

- **Setting**: This folder is intended to store setting sketches created from a template sheet. The default document for this folder is the Setting Sketch template sheet.

- **Front Matter**: This folder contains front matter for various types of completed work, including a title page for a manuscript, a file to draft a dedication and acknowledgments, and cover art for an e-book.

- **Pitch and Submission**: This folder contains files to begin drafting a synopsis and cover letter to submit with a manuscript proposal. It also contains a blank submission worksheet to track where a book has been pitched.

- **Reference**: This folder contains reference materials pertaining to writing, such as tips on creating a story world and the inherent strengths and weaknesses of various character traits. This folder also contains links to my critique group's private email list and public blog.

- **Research**: This is the default Research folder, used to compile story-related research, to which I add subfolders for Time-Period Research and Book-Specific Research.

- **To Do**: This folder contains an editing checklist to which I refer during revisions and a Progress Sheet, which is a document into which I enter my daily word count and how many hours I've worked that day.

- **Template Sheets**: This folder contains template sheets for character sketches, setting sketches, conflict worksheets, theme development worksheets, and plotting worksheets. I also have a Scene template sheet, which is the default document for my Manuscript folder.

- **Scrap**: This is an empty folder intended to put scenes and bits of information that I cut from the project but don't want to permanently delete.

- **Trash**: This is the default Trash folder, which I only use to hold files and folders I create by mistake or am otherwise certain I want to permanently delete from the project.

TIP If you are a Mac user, you can customize the icons for your files and folders, as shown in Figure 14.2. See Chapter 3, "Organizing the Binder," to learn how to assign a custom icon and add new icon files to Scrivener.

Set Default Meta-Data

In Chapter 12, "Putting Keywords and Meta-Data to Work," you learned how to change the Label and Status field titles and values and use the Keywords panel and custom meta-data to tag your documents with meta-data. Although the values of these fields are likely to be project-specific, you will probably use the same Label and Status field titles in multiple projects. For example, if you changed the Label field to be titled Storyline, the subplots will vary by manuscript, but you still want that field to be titled Storyline. If this is the case, remove the values from the Label field, as follows:

1. In the General pane of the Inspector, click the Label drop-down menu and choose Edit.

2. In the Label pane of the Meta-Data Settings dialog box, select the top value on the list, below the No Label entry.

3. Click the Remove button at the bottom of the dialog box.

4. Repeat step 3 until all of the values are removed. You cannot delete the No Label entry.

5. Click OK to close the dialog box.

Alternatively, you can rename the values to be more generic, such as Storyline 1, Storyline 2, etc.

TIP If you remove or rename the Label and Status values, make a note in the Information document at the top of the Binder to remind yourself to add or modify values when you create a new project from the project template.

For Keywords, the individual keywords you create may be project-specific, but the parent keywords into which you group them are likely to stay more constant. Thus, you can prepopulate the panel with parent keywords titled Settings, POV Characters, or any other general groups that relate to your type of writing, and then add specific child keywords when you create a project based on your template. You may also prepopulate the panel with keywords that apply to any project, as shown in Figure 14.3.

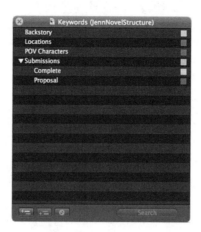

FIGURE 14.3

Create general keyword categories and keywords that apply to all your projects in the project template.

It is easy to include custom meta-data in your project template (on the Mac). These fields do not store any preset values, so it's enough to create the fields. If you use custom meta-data, however, don't forget to go into the Outliner and select those fields from the Columns menu so they are visible when you create a working project.

See Chapter 7, "Plotting in the Outliner," if you need to review the process of setting up columns in the Outliner.

Set Project Targets

If you write novels or academic papers with an upper word count limit, you may want to set word count goals. You may also want to set project targets if you create a custom project template to use every year for writing challenges such as National Novel Writing Month (NaNoWriMo). Refer to Chapter 15, "Tracking Your Progress," to learn more about setting project and document targets.

Create Template Sheets

If you're a Mac user, template sheets can form the core of your project template. Create template sheets for any type of document you use in multiple instances in a project. See Chapter 13, "Creating and Using Template Sheets," for details on how to create template sheets and configure them as default documents in different folders. Figure 14.4 shows all of the template sheets in the Binder of my custom novel template.

TIP Although Windows does not have template sheets, you can create your own folder of base documents and duplicate them in the Binder when you want to use them. See Chapter 13 for more information about this process.

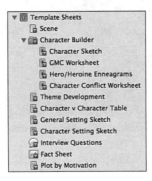

FIGURE 14.4

Forms and worksheets make excellent template sheets.

Create Initial Collections

Although collections are project-specific (see Chapter 16, "Searching Your Project," for details on creating and using collections), you can save the criteria for a collection in your project template. For example, you can create a collection for the first three chapters in your Draft folder and a synopsis and query letter you store in a Pitch and Submissions folder. You can then use that collection to compile a proposal to submit to an editor or agent.

1. Create a keyword in the Project Keywords panel called Proposal.

2. Apply this keyword to the title page in your Draft folder, query/cover letter document, and the synopsis document.

3. In the Search box in the Scrivener toolbar, click the magnifying glass and choose Keywords from the drop-down menu.

4. Enter the word `Proposal` in the Search box. The documents that have been tagged with the Proposal keyword appear in the Search Results pane.

5. Click the magnifying glass and choose Save Search as Collection (Save Search in Windows).

6. Enter a collection name for the New Saved Search Collection.

TIP When you later create a working project from this template, add the Proposal keyword to the files in the first three chapters of your Draft folder and view the collection to update the search results. Once you have created the first three chapters of your manuscript and updated the collection, you can convert the saved search to a standard collection, whereupon you can change the order of the documents.

NOTE Similarly, you could create a standard collection to prepare a proposal, but you would need to prepopulate your template with the files and folders for the first three chapters because standard collections are static and do not update based on changing search results.

You can also create collections to automatically gather all of the documents marked with a Needs Research status or keyword so you can make a list of information you need to look up.

Designate Compile Settings

Configuring Compile settings can be rather confusing and time consuming. If you configure them in your project template, those settings appear in any projects created from the template, saving you time and frustration.

Learn more about how to compile your work in Chapter 19, "Compiling Your Completed Work." If you are using this project template to prepare e-books, see Chapter 20, "Creating E-Books," for information on how to compile and export in various e-book formats.

Using Template Placeholder Tags (Mac Only)

Many types of writing, such as manuscript submissions and academic papers, require a title page with contact information about the author. If you plan to retain the project template solely for your personal use, you can enter your contact information directly into the project. If you intend to share your project template with other Scrivener users, however, you should remove your personal data from the template.

One way to preserve your privacy but make information available within your project is to use placeholder tags. Instead of entering your name on a Title page, for example, use the placeholder tag <$template_fullName> in your project template, as shown in Figure 14.5. When you create a new project based on that template, the placeholder tag is replaced with data from your card in your Contacts or Address Book app.

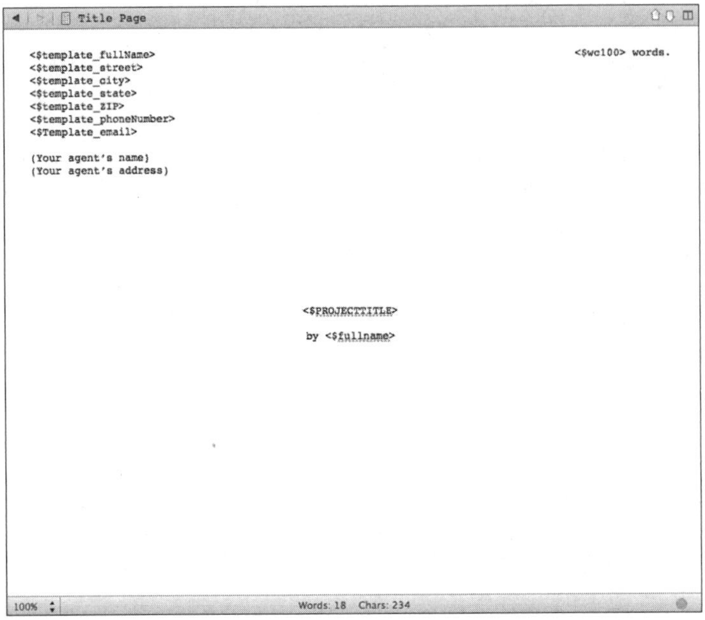

FIGURE 14.5

Placeholder tags can protect your personal data and automatically provide word count and pagination information when you compile your project.

Table 14.1 lists the project template placeholders specific to protecting your contact information.

TABLE 14.1 Project Template Placeholders

Placeholder Tag	Data Acquired from Contacts App
<$template_firstName>	First name
<$template_lastName>	Last name
<$template_fullName>	Combines the first and last name
<$template_initial>	First letter of the first name
<$template_street>	Street address
<$template_city>	City
<$template_state>	State
<$template_ZIP>	Zip code
<$template_country>	Country
<$template_phoneNumber>	Phone number
<$template_email>	Email address

There is an additional project placeholder tag that gathers data from the name of the project rather than your Contacts app. The tag <$template_projectName> enters the filename of the project when it was created.

Scrivener for Mac also offers additional placeholder tags that can be used on title pages and elsewhere in the project. The Project Properties tab of the Meta-Data Settings dialog box, shown in Figure 14.6, automatically fills in the project title based on the filename of the project and the author's surname and forename based on the Contacts app. The placeholder tags to access these values appear to the right of each field.

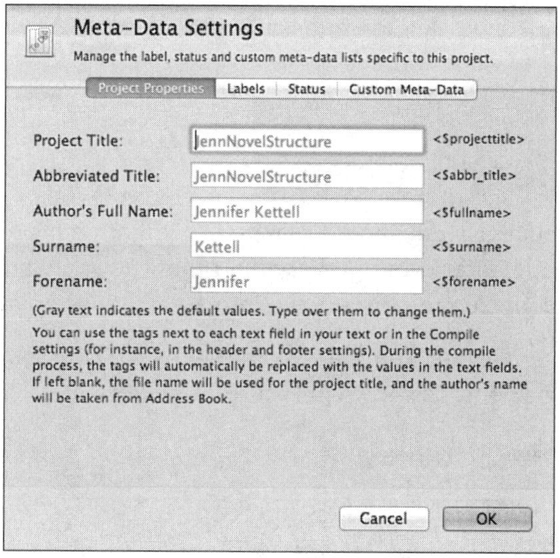

Meta–Data Settings

Manage the label, status and custom meta-data lists specific to this project.

Project Properties	Labels	Status	Custom Meta-Data

Project Title:	JennNovelStructure	<$projecttitle>
Abbreviated Title:	JennNovelStructure	<$abbr_title>
Author's Full Name:	Jennifer Kettell	<$fullname>
Surname:	Kettell	<$surname>
Forename:	Jennifer	<$forename>

(Gray text indicates the default values. Type over them to change them.)

You can use the tags next to each text field in your text or in the Compile settings (for instance, in the header and footer settings). During the compile process, the tags will automatically be replaced with the values in the text fields. If left blank, the file name will be used for the project title, and the author's name will be taken from Address Book.

Cancel   OK

FIGURE 14.6

The Project Properties tab of the Meta-Data Settings dialog box on the Mac contains placeholders for name and project information, which can be added to documents using placeholder tags.

TIP If you write under a pseudonym and want this information saved in your project template, type over the Author's Full Name, Surname, and Forename fields to replace the automatic entries from the Contacts app.

If you save this information as a contact in your Contacts or Address Book app, type (Scrivener:UseMe) in the Note area of the entry; Scrivener will then use this contact entry for the author information.

Whereas the project template placeholders are only available on the Mac, there are other placeholder tags available for both Mac and Windows. Most of these are used in conjunction with the Compile tool, such as <$p> to add page numbers to the header, for example. Another common placeholder tag for the title page of a document is <$wc100>, which is replaced with the word count of the compiled work rounded to the nearest 100. The complete list of placeholder tags is too extensive to print here.

NOTE A complete list of placeholder tags that work on the Mac is available by choosing Help, Placeholder Tags List from the menu. For a list of placeholder tags that work in both Mac and Windows, visit http://scrivener.tenderapp.com/help/kb/windows/placeholder-tags-list.

Saving a Project Template

Rome wasn't built in a day, and it's quite likely that your project template won't be, either. Finally, after getting everything the way you want it, however, you are ready to turn your dummy project file into an actual template. Follow these steps:

1. Choose File, Save as Template from the menu. The Template Information dialog box opens, as shown in Figure 14.7.

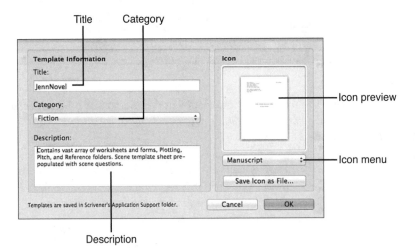

FIGURE 14.7

The Template Information dialog box prompts you to name your template, add it to a template category, and provide a description and icon to be displayed in the Project Templates dialog box.

2. Enter a name for the template in the Title field.

3. Choose a category from the Category drop-down menu.

4. In the Description field, note what makes this project template unique.

5. Below the icon preview, click and choose an existing template from the drop-down menu to use its icon. Choose Custom from the menu to use a custom image.

6. Click OK to save the template.

Once you have saved your project template, you can close the dummy project upon which it was based. You can even delete the entire project if you want, as you now have a template to create new working projects. To create a project with your new template, open the Project Templates dialog box (File, New Project), click on the category in which you placed your project template, and select the template from the options on the right.

Modifying a Project Template

Even when you think you have settled upon the best combination of settings and features for your project template, you may still come up with a new reference sheet or value for a piece of meta-data. The longer you work in Scrivener, the more features you begin to rely upon. Your writing needs may change, as well, necessitating changes in your project template(s). If you begin using Scrivener for short academic essays, you may need to modify your template—or create a new template based on your current template—as you begin writing longer research papers or a thesis. I have been writing for decades and using Scrivener for over five years, and I still tweak my project templates on a regular basis.

 CAUTION Templates do not remain linked to the projects created from them. If you modify your template, you need to make the same changes to your existing projects if you want them to contain the same options and settings.

You cannot edit a project template itself. Instead, you need to repeat the process you undertook to create the initial project template. Follow these basic steps:

1. Create a project with the project template you want to edit. The name and location of this project do not matter because you're using it as a dummy project just to update the template.

2. Make the changes you want to the project. This process should be much more streamlined because you aren't starting from scratch.

3. Choose File, Save as Template.

4. Enter the same name for the project template as you did previously.

5. Update the description and logo, if you want.

6. Click OK to save the new project template over the old one.

 CAUTION   If you remove files and folders from the project in the course of modifying the template, be sure to empty the Trash folder before you select Save as Template.

Setting a Default Project Template

If you use Scrivener primarily for only one type of project, you can set a project template to be the default. When you designate a default project template, the Project Templates dialog box automatically opens to the category in which that template resides and preselects the template.

To set the default project template:

1. In the Project Templates dialog box, select the template you want to designate as the default.

2. Click the Options button at the bottom of the dialog box, as shown in Figure 14.1.

3. Select Set Selected Template as Default from the drop-down menu.

 NOTE   You can set any project template to be the default, whether you created a custom template or consistently use one of the preinstalled templates.

Deleting a Project Template

As you work with Scrivener, you will likely create several project templates. You may create a couple of variations on the same type of template, give each template a different name, and then work with them to see which approach you like best. Or you may import project templates posted on the Internet by other Scrivener users, hoping to discover a new way of working in Scrivener. You then drag and drop the portions you want to use into your own, ever-evolving project template. All of this experimentation can leave behind a lot of unused project templates. To clear out the dead weight:

1. In the Project Templates dialog box, select the template you want to delete.

2. Click the Options button at the lower left of the dialog box.

3. Select Delete Selected Template from the drop-down menu, shown in Figure 14.8.

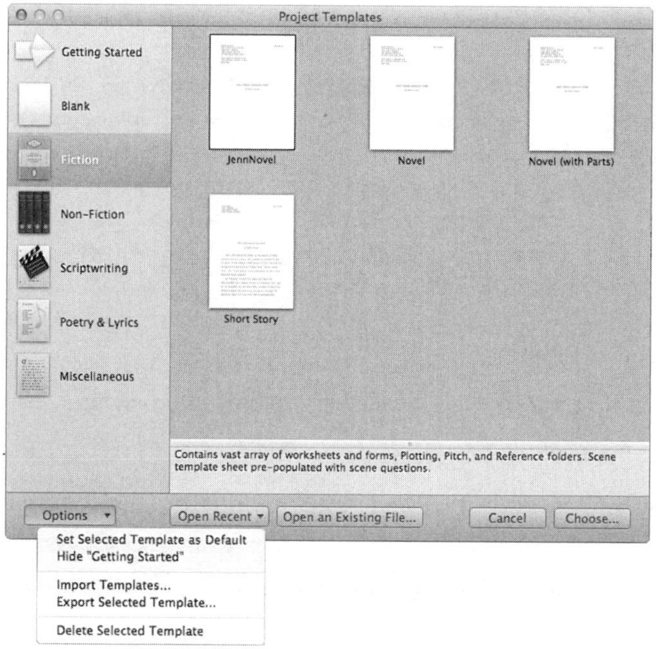

FIGURE 14.8

The Options button in the Project Templates dialog box provides options to set a default template and delete unwanted templates.

4. Click OK on the Mac or Yes on the PC to confirm the deletion.

> **NOTE** You cannot delete the preinstalled templates that came with Scrivener.

Importing and Exporting Project Templates

You now understand how to fend for yourself in the world of project templates. One of the advantages of using project templates, however, is the ability to share them with others. The best way to see how someone else uses Scrivener is to import one of his or her templates and look at how he or she sets up the metadata, template sheets, and overall file and folder system. And if you have created a project template for a specific type of writing task, consider exporting it to share with the Scrivener user community.

Importing a Project Template

If you download a template from the Internet or simply want to use your own project template on another computer, you can import it.

 NOTE You can share templates between the Mac and Windows versions of Scrivener, but certain features are not available from Windows. You can view template sheets in Windows, for example, but they do not function in the same manner as on the Mac. To use them, you need to duplicate the template sheet and move it into the folder where you want it to reside. Windows also cannot use custom meta-data.

To import a template:

1. Download or copy the template file onto your computer.

2. Open the Project Templates dialog box.

3. Click the Options button and select Import Templates from the drop-down menu.

4. Navigate to and select the template file you want to import. The template is automatically imported to the category assigned to it by its author.

5. Click Cancel to close the window or select the project template and create a new project.

On the Mac, templates are saved in the Application Support folder in your Mac's Library folder. In Windows, templates are saved in your local AppData folder. In Windows XP, templates are saved in your Application Data folder. Once you have imported the template, you can delete the copy of the template you saved to your computer in step 1 or retain it as a backup.

 NOTE Scrivener templates have a `.scrivtemplate` file extension. Users sometimes share regular project files with a `.scriv` file extension intended to be used as a template. If you download one of these files, open it as a regular project and then save it as a template to make it available in the New Projects dialog box (Project Templates dialog box in Windows).

Exporting a Project Template

If you want to share your own templates, either with other Scrivener users or to use the template on another computer, export it by doing the following:

1. Open the Project Templates dialog box.

2. Select the template you want to export.

3. Click the Options button and select Export Selected Template from the drop-down menu.

4. In the Export dialog box, navigate to where you want to store the new project template and enter a name for the exported file.

5. Click Export on the Mac or Save in Windows.

THE ABSOLUTE MINIMUM

The following are the highlights from this chapter:

- Project templates have been preformatted with a basic group of files and folders, Compile settings, template sheets, workspace layouts, and meta-data conducive to working efficiently on a specific type of project.

- Anything in a project template can be modified or deleted when you begin working on your project.

- You can modify an existing project template to personalize it or create a new project template from scratch.

15

TRACKING YOUR PROGRESS

There's an awful lot of math involved in writing. We worry about the upper word count of article and novel submissions. We calculate how many words a day we need to write to meet our deadlines. We think about overusing particular words, reading level, and how many words we can write per hour. Some of us even participate in an annual ritual to write 50,000 words in 30 days, which happens to coincide with the start of the holiday season, forcing many a poor soul to calculate how many hours he can spend with Grandma and Grandpa at the Thanksgiving table and still meet his writing goals.

Scrivener makes it easier to do the math by allowing you to set project and document targets. You can even view your progress in the Editor. You can also view project statistics to show word count, calculate estimated page count, and view a word frequency chart. Unfortunately, Scrivener still leaves it up to you to convince Grandma that NaNoWriMo is more important than green bean casserole.

Using Project Targets

Our first math problem involves performing calculations on the entire project. If you are participating in National Novel Writing Month (NaNoWriMo), your goal is to write 50,000 words in the month of November. How many words do you need to write per day if you write all 30 days of the month? What if you can't write on Wednesdays? If you delete a paragraph, how far does that set you back? NaNoWriMo is one month out of the year. What about writing a 90,000-word manuscript in six months, when it's more difficult to know exactly what will keep you away from the computer for a day or more?

 TIP For more information about NaNoWriMo, visit http://www. nanowrimo.org.

Project targets allow you to set those limitations and calculate how many words you need to write in a day and how close you are to your goal. To access project targets, choose Project, Show Project Targets from the menu or press Shift-Cmd-T on the Mac. In Windows, choose Project, Project Targets or press Ctrl+,.

The Project Targets dialog box, shown in Figure 15.1, is divided into two goals:

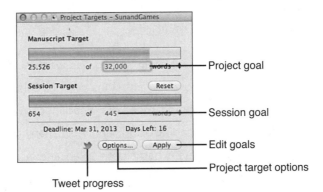

FIGURE 15.1

The Project Targets dialog box shows your progress toward completion of your project and your daily/session goals.

- **Draft Target**: Your goal for the complete project. This goal is usually referred to by the name of your Draft folder, such as Manuscript Target, as you can see in Figure 15.1. Only words you add to your Draft folder count in your progress toward your project target. Documents you import or move into the Draft folder are added to your progress toward the draft target. Documents in your Draft folder that are not included in your Compile settings are excluded from the draft target.

- **Session Target**: Your word count goal for the current day or writing session. You have to really work for these words, though. Documents you import or move into your Draft folder do not count, only text that you type or paste into a document. In Windows, text you add anywhere in the project counts toward your session target, although you still need to type or paste text for it to count.

These goals can be set independently of each other. In other words, if your goal is to write a 90,000-word novel, but you don't care how many words you write a day, set only the draft target. If you want to write 1,000 words per day in order to develop a writing habit, but don't yet know how long the project will be, set only the session target. You can also set these goals to work together. If your goal is a 90,000-word novel, and you want to write 1,000 words per session, set both fields.

Setting Target Options (Mac Only)

The options for project targets directly affect how Scrivener calculates your goal and your progress, so it is best to set these options before setting a target. To set the target options:

 NOTE These options are not available in Windows.

1. Open the Project Targets dialog box, as described above.
2. Click the Options button. The Project Targets Options pane opens, as shown in Figure 15.2.

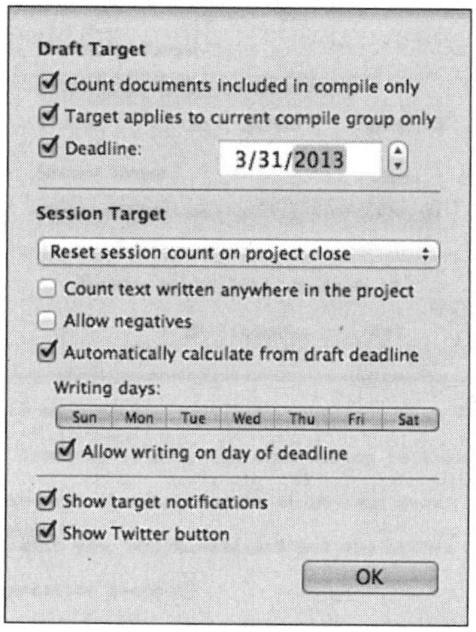

Draft Target
☑ Count documents included in compile only
☑ Target applies to current compile group only
☑ Deadline: 3/31/2013

Session Target
Reset session count on project close
☐ Count text written anywhere in the project
☐ Allow negatives
☑ Automatically calculate from draft deadline
Writing days:
| Sun | Mon | Tue | Wed | Thu | Fri | Sat |
☑ Allow writing on day of deadline

☑ Show target notifications
☑ Show Twitter button

OK

FIGURE 15.2

The Project Targets Options allow you to customize how Scrivener calculates your writing goals and progress.

The Project Targets Options for the draft target are as follows:

- **Count Documents Included in Compile Only**: When selected, as it is by default, this option limits progress tracking to those documents in your Draft folder that are marked to Include in Compile in the General pane of the Inspector. This setting is useful if you have files in your Draft folder that you do not want to include when you compile the project, such as notes or alternative scenes, and don't want to include them in your project's target progress.

 NOTE This option is available in Windows as a check box below the Draft target. It is deselected by default, however, so you must select it if you want to only count documents included in the compile group.

 TIP This setting is not necessary if you keep your Draft folder free from documents that are not intended to be included in the compilation. If you need to take notes but want to limit your Draft folder only to documents you want to include in the compilation, use the Document or Project Notes options in the Inspector. If you prefer to use documents, store them in a non-Draft folder and use reference links to connect them to the appropriate documents in the Draft folder.

- **Target Applies to Current Compile Group Only**: This option limits progress tracking to only those files selected in the Contents pane of the Compile settings. If you only have the first three chapters set to compile at the moment, such as if you're preparing a proposal for an editor or agent, only those chapters are tracked in the target progress.

 CAUTION The Target Applies to Current Compile Group Only setting can become confusing unless you remember exactly which documents you have set to compile. It's easy to forget that you last compiled only a single chapter for your critique group, and then be confused by the lack of progress in your project target. I suggest deselecting this option unless you have a specific reason to use it.

NOTE This setting and the Count Documents Included in Compile Only setting work in tandem. If you select the Target Applies to Current Compile Group Only option without the previous option, and if you have documents that are not marked to Include in Compile but have been added to the current compile group, their word count is added to your progress. If you have selected both these options, the word count of documents that are not marked to Include in Compile is not considered even if they are part of the current compile group. Again, my recommendation is to avoid changing these settings unless you understand exactly what you are including and excluding, and how this affects your project targets.

- **Deadline**: If you have a deadline for this project, selecting this option adds a countdown to the bottom of the Project Targets dialog box. Type the deadline date or use the up-down button to increase or decrease the month/day/year settings.

The rest of the project target options apply to the session target, as follows:

- **Session Target Reset**: Click the drop-down menu to select when you want the session target to reset, as follows:

  - If you want to track your daily progress, choose to Automatically Reset at Midnight. You may write at various intervals throughout the day, all of which contribute to that day's session progress.

  - If you want each instance in which you sit down to write to be considered a separate session, choose Reset Session Count on Project Close.

  - If you are a night owl, select Reset Session Count on Next Day Opened. This compares the current time to the time when you last opened the project, and resets the session if it is the next calendar day. For example, let's say you open the project at 11:00 p.m. on Monday and work until the wee hours of Tuesday morning. When you open the project again on Tuesday afternoon, the session resets because it is the next calendar day after the session you began on Monday. But if you open the project yet again late Tuesday evening, the session does not reset because you last opened it on the same calendar day.

  - If you want to take control over your sessions, choose Never Automatically Reset Session Counts. A session continues until you manually reset it. The Reset button is in the Project Targets dialog box.

- **Count Text Written Anywhere in the Project**: When selected, this option counts text you add anywhere in the Binder, including non-Draft items. If this option is deselected, only documents in the Draft folder are included in your session progress.

   NOTE   Although this option allows you to include text written outside the Draft folder in the session goal, this content does not increase your progress toward your draft target.

- **Allow Negatives**: When this option is selected, text you delete during a session is subtracted from your progress, even if this results in a net loss during the session. If you deselect this option, Scrivener does not track deletions once you reach zero, so even if you have a net loss of words during a session, Scrivener may inaccurately report it as a gain.

- **Automatically Calculate from Draft Deadline**: This option works in conjunction with the Deadline option above. If you set a deadline and a draft target, Scrivener automatically sets the session target based on how many words (or characters) you need to write per day to reach the deadline.

   NOTE   If this option is selected, you cannot manually set a session target.

- **Writing Days**: Scrivener assumes you are writing every day by default. If you take weekends off or have other commitments on specific days of the week, click the days you are unavailable to deselect them. Scrivener can then calculate how many words you need to write per day (session) to reach your deadline based on the actual days you plan to write.

- **Allow Writing on Day of Deadline**: When this option is selected, Scrivener counts the day of your deadline as a writing day, unless it is a day of the week you deselected in the Writing Days setting. If you deselect this option, Scrivener calculates how many words you need to write per day assuming you complete the project by midnight the day before the deadline.

   NOTE   The Writing Days and Allow Writing on Day of Deadline options are only available if the Deadline option is set and the Automatically Calculate Draft from Deadline option is enabled.

If you are using Mac OS X 10.8 Mountain Lion, you see two additional options, as follows:

- **Show Target Notifications**: Scrivener uses the operating system's Notification Center to post a notice when you reach or fall below your project or session goal.
- **Show Twitter Button**: If you use Twitter, select this option to add a Twitter button to the Project Targets dialog box. When you click the Twitter icon (a blue bird, shown in Figure 15.1), you can send a tweet notifying your followers of your progress.

If you are using an earlier Mac OS, you can enable the Show Target Notifications option if you have Growl installed and running when Scrivener is launched. This option sends a Growl notification when you reach or fall below a target.

When you have finished setting the project target options, click OK to return to the Project Targets dialog box. You are now ready to set your targets.

Setting Draft Targets

To set the draft target goal:

1. Open the Project Targets dialog box, as described above.

2. Click in the Project Goal box (refer to Figure 15.1).

3. Enter the expected word, character, or page count of your completed project.

4. Click the Words drop-down menu if you prefer to measure your target in characters. On the Mac, you can also measure your target in pages.

CAUTION   If you use the Pages option on the Mac, be aware that the page count is not always accurate. The page count uses a characters per page calculation based on the compile settings when you open the Project Targets dialog box. When you actually compile your project, however, you may add page padding or other formatting that changes the final page count.

5. On the Mac, click the Apply button to set the goal; this step is not necessary in Windows.

If your project already contains text, the word count and progress bar immediately reflect this.

TIP   The progress bar changes from red to green as you approach your goal. To change these default colors on the Mac, open the Appearance tab of the Preferences/Options dialog box. In the Customizable Colors pane, select Target Progress Bars and then change the Start, End, and Midway colors as you like.

Setting Session Targets

By default on the Mac, the session target tracks how many words you write in a day, resetting your progress to zero at midnight. Thus, a session can be multiple shorter periods of writing throughout a day. In Windows, the session is reset every time you close and reopen the project.

To set the session target:

1. Open the Project Targets dialog box, if it is not already open.

2. Click in the Session Goal box (refer to Figure 15.1).

3. Enter the expected number of words or characters you plan to write during a session. Keep in mind the option you chose for resetting the session if you're on a Mac.

CAUTION If you're on a Mac and you set the Automatically Calculate from Draft Deadline option, you cannot manually set a session goal. Instead, this number is calculated by Scrivener.

TIP On the Mac, if you are over your word count and need to cut, select Allow Negatives and also set your session target for a negative number of words. Although the progress bar will not reflect your progress, the Project Targets dialog box will display the count.

4. Click the Words drop-down menu if you want Scrivener to track characters instead of words. Unlike the project target, you cannot set a session target to track pages.

5. On the Mac, click the Apply button to set the goal; this step is not necessary in Windows.

Resetting Target Sessions

If you want to manually reset a session, click the Reset button. This is a handy cheat if you need to cut material (such as everything you wrote after 3:00 a.m. the night before) at the start of the day, but don't want to begin a session having to overcome a negative in your progress.

If you selected the Never Automatically Reset Session Counts option, Scrivener continues to add to an endless session until you click the Reset button.

TIP One limitation of project targets is that you cannot automatically save a record of your writing sessions. If you need to keep track of how many words you write per session to report to your critique partners or for your own edification, create a document in a non-Draft folder in your project and manually enter the date and word count of your session before closing the project. I also like to keep track of how long I write each session so I can calculate words per hour.

Using Document Targets

Whereas the project targets track your project as a whole, you can also set document targets for individual documents. This is convenient if you are writing a series of essays or articles, each with their own word count. You can also use document targets to attempt to keep the scenes in a novel relatively equal in length.

To set a document target:

1. Open the document for which you want to set the target in the Editor.

2. Click the Set Target button in the Footer bar, as shown in Figure 15.3.

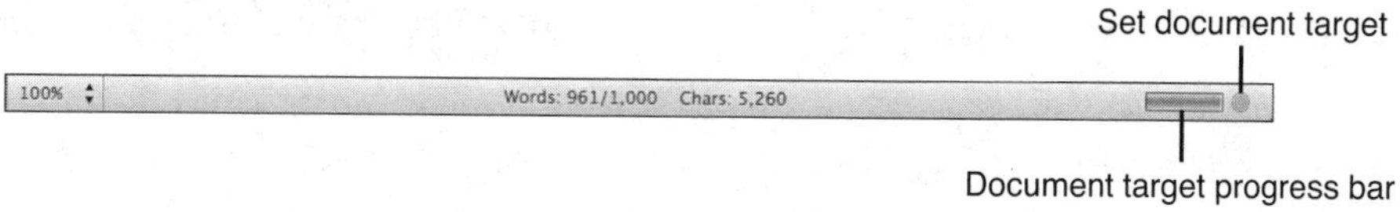

Set document target

| 100% ⟲ | Words: 961/1,000   Chars: 5,260 | ▭▭ |

Document target progress bar

FIGURE 15.3

Set document targets individually from the Footer bar.

3. Enter the target word or character count in the Document Target dialog box, shown in Figure 15.4.

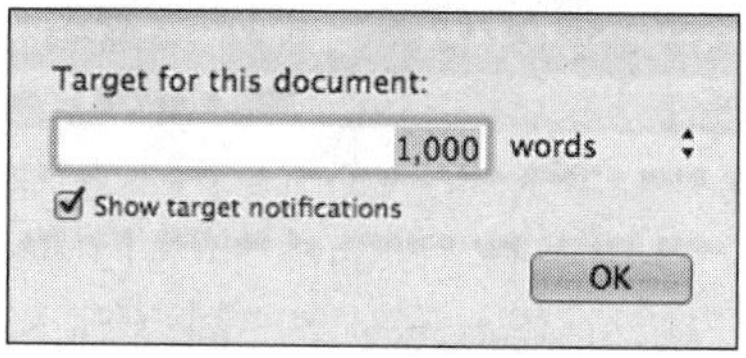

Target for this document:

| 1,000 | words | ⟲ |

☑ Show target notifications

OK

FIGURE 15.4

Enter a target word or character count for a document in the Document Target dialog box.

4. (Mac Only) Select Show Target Notifications if you want Scrivener to post a notification either in Growl or in the Notification Center when you reach or fall below your goal.

5. Click OK.

When you set a document target, a progress bar appears in the Footer bar of the Editor each time you open that document. The word count also changes to display your word count as a fraction of the document target.

You can also set and view document targets in the Outliner. To view document targets, open the Columns menu and choose the Target and Target Type columns. If you want to view the progress bars, as well, select the Progress column. To set a document target from within the Outliner, double-click in the Target column for an item and enter a number; then use the drop-down menu in the Target Type column to select either words or characters.

> **NOTE** The Total Words, Total Target, and Total Progress columns automatically tabulate the total word count and target for all of the documents in a file group or folder. Any text in the file group or folder itself is also included in this total.

THE CREATIVE PROCESS: SETTING NANOWRIMO TARGETS

Scrivener is ideal for participating in National Novel Writing Month or the Camp NaNoWriMo events that have sprung up in the summer months. If you downloaded Scrivener from the link on the NaNoWriMo website, you should see a project template designed specifically for the event, preconfigured with the necessary project targets.

Otherwise, you can use the project template of your choosing and set your own project target options. In the Project Targets options, set the deadline for 11/30/xx (with xx being the current year), and select the Automatically Calculate from Draft Deadline option. Also select the Allow Writing on Day of Deadline option so you can write up until the last minute of the month. In the Project Targets dialog box, set the draft target for 50,000 words. If you're on a Mac, Scrivener automatically calculates the session target. In Windows, you can do the math yourself and set the session target. If you write all 30 days of the month, you will need to write 1,667 words per day. If you miss a day or more, Scrivener automatically adjusts the session target on the Mac to ensure you meet your 50k project target by the deadline. Again, in Windows, you can manually enter a new session target.

If you want to track your progress on a daily basis, consider creating a new file each day with a document target of 1,667. Scrivener's NaNoWriMo project template includes a Daily Target template sheet with this preset.

Project targets are also useful for any other sort of Book-in-a-Month or Week challenge.

TIP   If you are a fan of NaNoWriMo, consider extending the challenge by participating in National Novel Editing Month (NaNoEdMo) in March. This group encourages writers to spend 50 hours editing previously written material, generally the novel you raced to complete in November. For more information, visit http://www.test.nanoedmo.net.

Using Project Statistics

If you want to see an overview of your project's word, character, and page count, choose Project, Project Statistics from the menu. You can also press Option-Shift-Cmd-S on the Mac or Ctrl+. in Windows. The Project Statistics dialog box, shown in Figure 15.5, is divided into two sections. The top section reflects the statistics for the Draft folder, based on the current Compile settings. If your current Compile settings limit the compile to the first three chapters of your project, the project statistics only reflect those chapters.

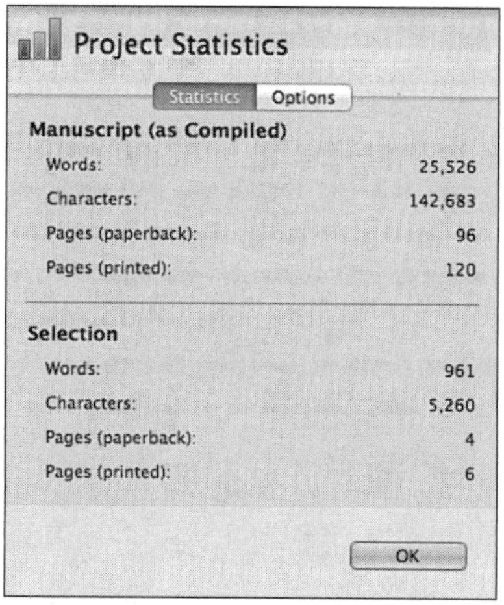

Project Statistics

| Statistics | Options |

Manuscript (as Compiled)

Words:	25,526
Characters:	142,683
Pages (paperback):	96
Pages (printed):	120

Selection

Words:	961
Characters:	5,260
Pages (paperback):	4
Pages (printed):	6

| OK |

FIGURE 15.5

The Project Statistics dialog box displays the word, character, and page count of the entire project or a selection of items.

 NOTE   See Chapter 19, "Compiling Your Completed Work," for details on how to compile your project and select documents to include in the compilation.

The bottom half of the dialog box reflects Selection Statistics for the item or items selected in the Binder, Outliner, or Corkboard. These statistics can reflect non-Draft folder items if they are included in the selection.

The Pages (Paperback) is another example of where Scrivener does the math for you. The number of pages equals the total number of characters divided by the product of characters per word times the number of words per page. This is an industry standard formula, so you can generally rely on it if your project needs to fit a specific page count criteria.

The Pages (Printed) information is calculated based on the formatting and content options you select in the Compile settings. This statistic is recalculated whenever you open the Project Statistics dialog box, so it may take a few seconds for this information to appear if you have a large project.

 CAUTION If you are on a Mac and your project is more than 100,000 words, the Project Statistics no longer automatically update. Instead, an Update Printed Counts button appears at the bottom of the dialog box so you can recalculate the Pages (Printed) data. In Windows, the counts always recalculate when you open the Project Statistics dialog box.

The Options tab, shown in Figure 15.6, of the Project Statistics dialog box controls which elements of the project are included in the calculations.

FIGURE 15.6

The Project Statistics Options tab controls how the project statistics are calculated.

The Project Statistics Options are divided into three sections. The Draft Statistics Options on the Mac apply to the entire Draft folder and are as follows:

- **Count Current Compile Group Only**: When selected, this option limits the calculations to documents that have been chosen in the Contents pane of the Compile settings.
- **Count Footnotes**: Selected by default, this option includes footnotes in the counts.

The Selection Statistics Options apply to how items selected in the Binder, Corkboard, or Outliner are calculated, as follows:

- **Count All Documents**: This option includes all documents in the selection, even if the document does not have the Include in Compile setting selected.
- **Count Only Documents Marked for Inclusion**: This option includes only selected documents that are marked to Include in Compile in the General pane of the Inspector.
- **Count Only Documents Not Marked for Inclusion**: This option includes only selected documents that are not marked to Include in Compile.
- **Exclude Comments and Annotations**: By default, comments and annotations are not included in the statistics calculations. If you want to include them, deselect this option.
- **Exclude Footnotes**: By default, footnotes are included in the calculations. To exclude them, select this option.
- **Count Subdocuments**: With this option selected, the text in a selected container and any of its children are counted in the calculation. If it is deselected, only the text in the container itself is counted.

The Page Count Options sets the words per page number Scrivener uses when calculating Pages (Paperback). Scrivener uses 350 words per page by default, where a word is calculated as six characters (five plus a space).

Viewing Word Frequency

There are certain words you cannot avoid using in abundance, such as *the* and *is*. Every writer also has certain words in his arsenal that he turns to repeatedly out of habit. The Text Statistics dialog box, shown in Figure 15.7, displays a Word Frequency list to help you identify your habitual words.

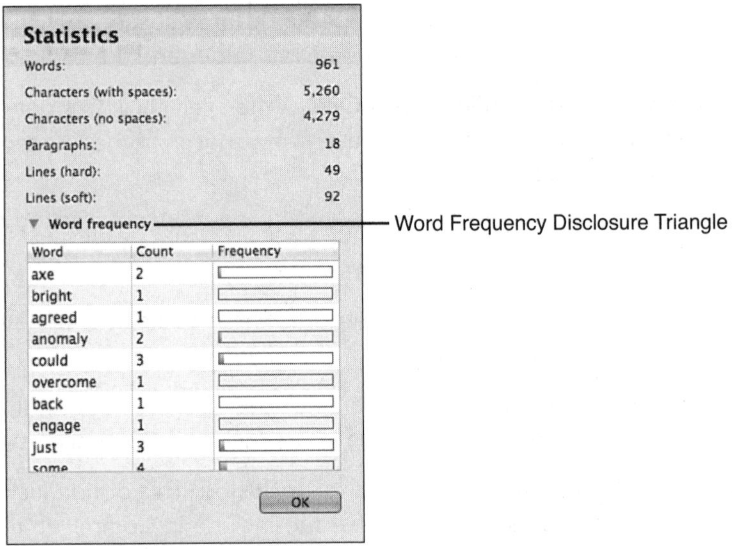

Statistics

Word	Count	Frequency
Words:		961
Characters (with spaces):		5,260
Characters (no spaces):		4,279
Paragraphs:		18
Lines (hard):		49
Lines (soft):		92

▼ Word frequency ——————————————— Word Frequency Disclosure Triangle

Word	Count	Frequency
axe	2	
bright	1	
agreed	1	
anomaly	2	
could	3	
overcome	1	
back	1	
engage	1	
just	3	
some	4	

OK

FIGURE 15.7

The Text Statistics dialog box displays the word, character, paragraph, and line count of a selected document, as well as a Word Frequency table.

Choose Project, Text Statistics from the menu to open the Text Statistics dialog box. You can also press Control-Option-Cmd-S on the Mac or Ctrl+/ in Windows. Click the disclosure triangle next to the Word Frequency title to expand the table. You can sort the table by clicking on a heading.

NOTE The Text Statistics dialog box bases its calculations on the active document in the Editor, so you must first load a document into the Editor before opening the dialog box. The statistics are calculated based on the entire document; you cannot calculate only a selection within a document.

THE ABSOLUTE MINIMUM

Did this chapter hit the mark? Here is what you learned:

- Project targets track your progress as you work to complete your project. Session targets track your progress in a writing session or day.

- Document targets set a goal for an individual document.

- Document targets can be set and viewed in the Editor or the Outliner.

- Project statistics display the word, character, and page counts for the Draft folder.

- You can use the project statistics to display information about a selection of items in the Binder.

- Text statistics display word, character, and paragraph counts for the selected items.

- Text statistics also display a table of words in the selected documents, sorted by frequency.

IN THIS CHAPTER

- Conducting project searches
- Using Document Find and Replace
- Using the Find Synopsis tool
- Searching by format
- Creating and using collections
- Setting bookmarks
- Choosing favorites

SEARCHING YOUR PROJECT

Scrivener projects are like Chia pets. You start with a very nondescript foundation, plant the seeds of an idea, and they take off growing until they bear little resemblance to the original. Once your project has started sprouting with documents, research, template sheets, keywords and other meta-data, comments, annotations, and footnotes—along with its sheer number of words—it can be a challenge to find a single item within the whole.

Fortunately, Scrivener provides tools to search your project for every possible aspect of your content and its meta-data. There are four types of searches in Scrivener:

- **Project Search**: This search is used for finding items in the Binder that match the criteria you specify. Results are listed in a Search Results pane in the left sidebar.

- **Document Search**: This feature searches a selected document or Scrivenings. Scrivener steps through each of the results one at a time, in the same manner as a word processor.

- **Format Search**: This option searches for specific formatting or text that serves a particular function in a project, such as underlined or highlighted text, annotations, or links. Scrivener steps through the results one at a time within each item of the project.

- **Synopsis Search (Mac Only)**: This feature opens the Synopsis Finder to examine synopses that match your search criteria.

Scrivener also allows you to create collections, groups of files that you manually group together or that are gathered as the result of a project search. This can save you considerable time if you tend to repeat the same searches over and over again.

If you need to find a needle in the haystack that is your project, this chapter explains how to do it.

Conducting Project Searches

The fastest and most direct way to search is with the Search tool on the Scrivener toolbar, shown in Figure 16.1. To use the Search tool:

Search results   Search box

Search
constraints

Close search

FIGURE 16.1

A project search lists all of the items that meet your search terms in the Search Results pane, subject to any constraints you put on the search.

1. Click inside the Search box in the toolbar. You can also press Control-Option-F on the Mac or Ctrl+G, Ctrl+S in Windows.

2. Type your search criteria.

3. Click the magnifying glass in the Search box to open the Project Search menu and select constraints for the search, if you want.

Scrivener begins listing items in the Search Results pane as you type your search criteria. To view an item in the Editor, select it in the Search Results pane. If the search criteria appear in the content of the document, every instance of the term or phrase is highlighted in the document. If the search criteria are found in the meta-data, of course you will not see any highlighted text in the document itself. To exit the Search Results pane and return to the Binder, click the Close (X) button at the bottom of the pane.

Narrowing Project Search Results by Element

Scrivener searches your entire project, including the Trash folder, to find an exact match for the word or phrase you enter. Scrivener searches meta-data as well as the content of your documents. If you have a large project, you may wind up with a considerable list of Search Results.

The magnifying glass in the Search box opens a drop-down menu of project search constraints, allowing you to hone in on exactly the type of result you seek. This menu is divided into three sections: Search In, Operator, and Options.

The Search In constraints limit the search to particular project elements, such as text, keywords, title, or other meta-data. In Windows, you can only use one Search In constraint at a time. On the Mac, select an option from the menu and then open the menu again and Option-click another option if you want to search within multiple project elements.

For example, if you want to find all the items using the Island keyword you created in the Project Keywords panel, type `Island` in the Search box and select Keywords from the Search In section of the Project Search menu. You can search by the following elements:

- **All**: Searches for all instances of the search term in every type of project element, including both document text and meta-data.

- **Title**: Searches for matches only within the titles of project items.

- **Text**: Searches only within the document text of each item.

- **Notes**: Searches the Document Notes throughout your project.

- **Synopsis**: Searches the synopsis of each document.

- **Keywords**: Searches for keywords assigned to each item.

- **Label**: Searches the Label field of each item. If you have renamed the Label field, this menu option reflects the current field name.

- **Status**: Searches the Status field. As with the Label option, the menu reflects the current field name for this option.

- **Custom Meta-Data (Mac Only)**: Searches any custom meta-data fields for your search term.

 TIP You can also search by keyword from the Project Keywords panel, as explained in Chapter 12, "Putting Keywords and Meta-Data to Work."

Limiting Project Searches with Operators

The operators on the Project Search menu determine how Scrivener parses your search terms. The operators are as follows:

- **Exact Phrase**: When you enter multiple words as the search criteria, such as *missing part*, Scrivener searches for an exact match of that phrase, in the same word order and without any extra words or characters between words. If a document contains the words *missing participle*, it also appears in the search results because the word *missing* is just before the beginning of the word *participle*.

- **All Words**: Scrivener searches for documents that contain all the words in the search criteria. Unlike the Exact Phrase operator, however, the words can appear anywhere in the document, either together or apart. If the document only contains one of the words, however, it is excluded from the search results. Thus, if you search on *missing part*, documents with phrases such as *missing an essential part* or *missing the party* are included in the search results, but a document containing just *missing* is not included.

- **Any Word**: Scrivener searches for documents that contain any of the words in the search criteria. If you search on *missing part*, documents containing the words *missing* or *part* are included in the search results. Documents containing words such as *party* and *particle* are also included.

- **Whole Word**: This option is intended for single word searches when you want the exact word, not any other words of which that combination of letters may be a part. In Windows, this option is similar to an Any Word search, but only provides search results if the entire word matches rather than a part of a word.

- **RegEx (Mac Only)**: This option allows you to enter Regular Expressions to narrow search results. Regular Expressions use a combination of special characters added to control the search criteria.

 NOTE For more information about Regular Expressions, see http://www.regular-expressions.info.

Narrowing Search Options

The Options portion of the Search menu provides additional means to narrow your search results. You rarely need to search your Trash, for example, so select Exclude Trash Documents to exclude the contents of the Trash folder from the search results. You can select multiple options, from among the following:

- **Search Draft Only**: Limits the search to the Draft folder. If you have renamed your Draft folder, this option is labeled with the name of the folder.

- **Search Binder Selection Only (Mac Only)**: Limits the search to items you select in the Binder prior to performing the search.

- **Exclude Trash Documents (Mac Only)**: Excludes the Trash folder from the search results.

- **Search 'Included' Documents**: Limits the search to items with the Include in Compile option selected in the Inspector.

- **Search 'Excluded' Documents**: Limits the search to only those items that are not included in the Compile settings.

- **Case Sensitive**: Limits the search to results that match the case setting of the search criteria. For example, *Part* is different than *part*.

The last option on the menu is Save Search as Collection (Save Search in Windows). Use this option to save your search options and criteria to reuse them. The search results become a new collection, as you discover later in this chapter.

Using Project Replace

Now that you've found all the items matching your search criteria, what do you do with them? The Search Results pane serves as a subgroup of the Binder, and can be helpful when you want to examine items with similar elements. You can select and edit items just as you would from the Binder. The Search Results pane is not, however, the best way to make global changes to your project. For that, you need to use Project Replace.

For example, if you decide your protagonist should own a bar named Styx rather than a coffee shop named Last Drop, if he swaggers instead of strides, if his name needs a sudden overhaul, it is faster to make these changes universally in your project than to manually wade through each reference. To do this:

 TIP Although you can use Project Replace without first running a Project Search, you may want to use these tools together. Scanning through your Search Results following a Project Search with similar settings allows you to ascertain if you need to modify your search before you run Project Replace to make any changes, particularly because you cannot undo changes made with Project Replace. If you are a Mac user, you can also select documents from the Search Results pane and limit the Project Replace scope to only affect selected documents.

1. Choose Edit, Find, Project Replace from the menu.

2. In the Project Replace dialog box, shown in Figure 16.2, enter the word or phrase you want to replace in the Replace field.

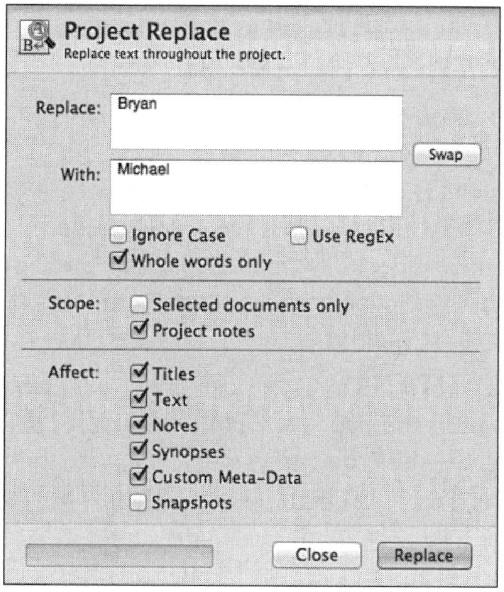

Project Replace
Replace text throughout the project.

Replace: Bryan

[Swap]

With: Michael

☐ Ignore Case   ☐ Use RegEx
☑ Whole words only

Scope: ☐ Selected documents only
          ☑ Project notes

Affect: ☑ Titles
          ☑ Text
          ☑ Notes
          ☑ Synopses
          ☑ Custom Meta-Data
          ☐ Snapshots

[Close]   [Replace]

FIGURE 16.2

Use Project Replace to change character names or similar global changes.

3. Enter the new word or phrase in the With field.

4. Limit the replacement operation with the following options:

- **Ignore Case**: When this option is selected, the name *Pat* is the same as the word *pat*.

- **Whole Words Only**: When this option is selected, the name *Pat* is different from *Patrick*.

- **RegEx (Mac Only)**: When selected, this option allows you to add Regular Expressions to the Replace field.

5. Select the Scope options to further limit the replacement:

- **Selected Documents Only (Mac Only)**: Only replaces the word or phrase if it appears in documents preselected in the Binder, Outliner, Corkboard, Search Results, or a collection

- **Project Notes**: If selected, replaces the search term in the Project Notes

6. Select from the Affect options to constrain the replacement to particular elements of a document.

NOTE Project Replace cannot replace label and status values or keywords. To modify those elements, see Chapter 12.

7. Click Replace. The progress bar at the bottom of the dialog box on the Mac counts the number of changed documents.

8. Click Close to close the dialog box.

NOTE In Scrivener for Windows, the Scope and Affect options are combined. You cannot limit the replacement to only selected documents. Windows also does not offer the ability to limit the scope of the replacement to Snapshots.

CAUTION You may want to create a backup before performing this operation because you cannot undo changes made with Project Replace. If you want to perform the replace in reverse, however, reopen the Project Replace dialog box and click the Swap button.

Using Document Find and Replace

Project Search and Project Replace are intended for large-scale interaction with your project. But what if your needs are more refined and require more oversight before making broad changes? Document Find and Replace work on a much more narrow scale, a single document or Scrivenings session within the Editor.

Performing a Document Find

Document Find and Document Replace are similar to the search tools found in a word processor. Instead of compiling a list of search results, these tools progress through your selected documents from result to result, allowing you to act on each one individually. To perform a Document Search:

1. Select the document or documents upon which you want to search.

2. Choose View, Scrivenings if you selected multiple documents and are not already in that view in the Editor.

3. If you want to search only a portion of a document or Scrivenings, select the text.

4. Choose Edit, Find, Find from the menu or press Cmd-F (Ctrl+F in Windows).

5. In the Find dialog box, shown in Figure 16.3, enter your search term(s) in the Find field.

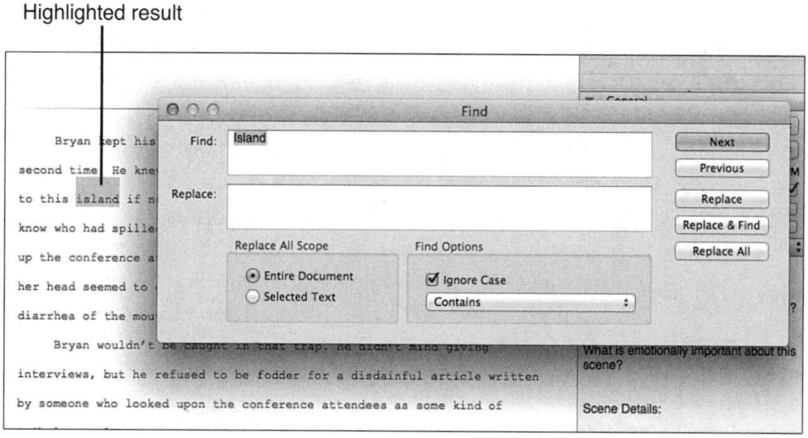

Highlighted result

FIGURE 16.3

Document Find and Replace is similar to that of a word processor.

6. In the Find Options, deselect the Ignore Case check box if your search is case sensitive.

7. Click the drop-down menu below the Ignore Case option to choose from the following options:

   - **Contains**: Finds any text containing the search term.

   - **Starts With**: Finds text that starts with the search term. If you search for *Pat*, it highlights those letters in the words *Pat*, *Patrick*, and *Patrice*, for example.

   - **Whole Word**: Highlights only words that completely match the search term. If you search for *Pat*, it only highlights *Pat*, not *Patrick* or *Patrice*.

   - **Ends With**: Finds text that ends with the search term. If you search for *pat*, it highlights those letters in the word *spat*.

   - **Regular Expression (Mac Only)**: Allows you to use Regular Expression characters in the Find field.

8. Click Next. Scrivener begins to search the document(s) in the Editor and highlights the first match, as shown above in Figure 16.3.

9. Click Next to move to the next match. On the Mac, you can also press Return to close the Find dialog box and move to the next match. In Windows, press Enter to move to the next match, but this does not close the Find dialog box.

If you close the Find dialog box, you can continue to move from match to match through the document(s) with keyboard shortcuts. Press Cmd-G and Shift-Cmd-G to find the Next/Previous matches on the Mac or F3 and Shift+F3 in Windows.

> **TIP** You can edit the document or Scrivenings while you search. Take advantage of this feature not only by changing the highlighted match, but also by editing content around the match. If you can't recall the specific portion of the document you seek but know certain words appear in or around that text, search for what you know and then edit the content when you find the appropriate match.

Using Document Replace with Document Find

You can search a document or Scrivenings for a search term and replace it at the same time. Follow steps 1–7 in the "Performing a Document Find" section earlier in this chapter. Then follow these steps to add Replace criteria:

1. Enter the word or phrase you want to substitute in place of the search criteria.

2. In the Replace All Scope options, select if you want to replace the search criteria throughout the contents of the Editor or only a selection of text.

3. Click the Next button to find the first match.

4. Click one of the Replace buttons to replace the highlighted text, as follows:

   - **Replace**: Replaces the highlighted text.

   - **Replace & Find**: Replaces the highlighted text and finds the next match. If you want to skip a Replace but continue finding and replacing other matches, click the Next button.

   - **Replace All**: Replaces all matches in the document, Scrivenings, or selection. If you want to use this option, skip step 3.

Using the Find Synopsis Tool (Mac Only)

If you make judicious use of synopses, you can use them as a search tool to locate key scenes or sections of your project. The Synopsis Finder, shown in Figure 16.4, allows you to search and view synopses and titles. When you find the scene you need, you can open the document itself in a QuickReference panel. To use the Find Synopsis tool:

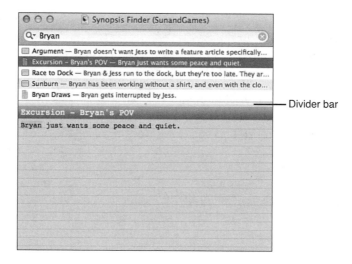

FIGURE 16.4

The Synopsis Finder is a very specific search tool for synopses.

1. Choose one of the following options to open the Synopsis Finder:

   - Click the Find Synopsis icon in the toolbar.

   - Choose Edit, Find, Find Synopsis from the menu.

   - Press Control-Cmd-G.

2. At the top of the Synopsis Finder, enter a search term.

3. If you want to constrain your search with Regular Expressions, click the magnifying glass in the Search field and select Use Regular Expressions (RegEx) from the drop-down menu.

4. Select one of the results at the top of the Synopsis Finder to view the complete synopsis in the lower pane of the dialog box. You can also right-click on a result and choose to view either the synopsis text or image.

5. Adjust the size of the results list or synopsis by clicking the bar between the two panes.

6. Select a result and choose View, Reveal in Binder from the menu to highlight the document in the Binder.

7. Double-click on an item in the search results to open the document in a QuickReference panel.

If you find this search tool helpful, use your synopses wisely. If you are writing fiction, be sure the names of characters that appear in the scene are mentioned in the synopsis. If you are writing an academic paper, note the thesis statement or which point this section of the project supports. The more details you can briefly note in the synopsis, the more useful this tool becomes.

You can edit synopses directly within the Synopsis Finder. If you mention something in one scene that needs to appear again in a later scene, open the synopsis for the later scene in the Synopsis Finder and make a note of it. Then you can continue writing without having to navigate back to your original document.

TIP Because you can open documents from the Synopsis Finder in a QuickReference panel, it's an ideal solution for locating a key scene or supporting topic for reference without losing your place in the current document in the Editor.

Searching by Format

Both the Project and Document Search tools focus on the text and meta-dàta of your document. You can also perform a Format Search to find items such as highlighted text, comments, footnotes, annotations, revision colors, links, and specific character formats. Searching by format allows you to find comments and revisions made by a co-worker or critique partner and double-check your footnotes and links before compiling an academic or nonfiction project.

NOTE If you want to search within selected documents, open them in the Editor before proceeding.

To search by format:

1. Choose Edit, Find, Find by Formatting from the menu. You can also press Control-Option-Cmd-F on the Mac or Ctrl+F3 in Windows.

2. In the Formatting Finder, shown in Figure 16.5, click the Find drop-down menu and select a format. Each option provides additional format-specific selections in the lower portion of the dialog box. Choose from the following options:

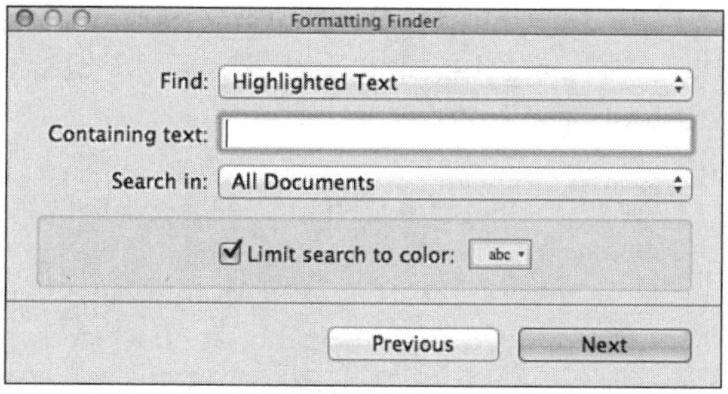

Formatting Finder	
Find:	Highlighted Text
Containing text:	
Search in:	All Documents

☑ Limit search to color: [abc ▾]

[Previous] [**Next**]

FIGURE 16.5

The Formatting Finder lets you search your project for formatted elements such as highlighted text.

 NOTE The Windows version lists these options in a different order, but with the exception of Revision Color and Text with Preserved Style, all options are available on both platforms. The Comments and Footnotes options are listed separately in the Find drop-down menu in Windows.

- **Highlighted Text**: Searches for highlighted text. If you select a specific highlight color, this option searches only for that color; otherwise, it searches for all highlighted text.

- **Comments & Footnotes**: When this option is selected, displays a Type drop-down menu to choose to search for All, Comments, or Footnotes.

- **Inline Annotations**: When this option is selected, click the drop-down menu at the bottom of the pane to select from Any Color to search for all inline annotations, Limit Search to Color to search for only annotations in a specified color, or Exclude Color from Search to search for all annotations except those in a particular color. To select a color to Limit to or Exclude, click the color swatch and choose a color from the Colors dialog box.

- **Inline Footnotes**: Searches for inline footnotes. There are no additional limits for this option.

- **Revision Color (Mac Only)**: Searches for text marked as revised. You can specify a revision color from the drop-down menu.

 NOTE Learn more about annotations, comments, and revision marks in Chapter 10, "Editing Your Manuscript." Learn about footnotes in Chapter 22, "Using Scrivener for Nonfiction Writing."

- **Colored Text**: Searches for text that has been formatted with a specified color. If you deselect the Limit Search to Color option, Scrivener searches for all text that has been formatted with a color.

   NOTE There is a difference between text that has been specifically formatted with the black text color and text that does not have a color applied (even though it may appear black onscreen, depending on your preference settings).

- **Links**: Searches for links within the document text. You can search All, Web/File links to external sources, or Scrivener links to in-project sources.

   NOTE Links within the document text, known as Scrivener links, are not the same as reference links, which are added as meta-data. See Chapter 23, "Discovering New Uses for Scrivener," to learn more about Scrivener links.

- **Text with Preserved Style (Mac Only)**: Searches for text to which you have applied the Preserve Formatting command (Format, Formatting, Preserve Format). There are no additional settings for this option.

- **Character Format**: Searches by text format. Options include Bold, Italic, Underline, Strikethrough, and (on the Mac) Keep with Next.

3. Limit the search to specific text in the selected format by entering text in the Containing Text field. If this field is left blank, Scrivener identifies all instances of the selected formatting.

4. Click the Search In drop-down menu to choose from All Documents or Selected Documents.

5. Click Next. Scrivener highlights the first match.

6. Continue to click Next to browse through the matches. You can edit text in the Editor as you work.

Creating and Using Collections

A collection in Scrivener is a group of files that you pull together—either manually or through a project search—to view and arrange them outside the Binder hierarchy. Let's say you have worked on scenes out of order and now want to focus on the scenes that still need content. You can collect all the items with a To Do status so they all appear in one group that can be easily updated as you pare down the list. You can also use a collection to try a different scene order without changing the Binder hierarchy.

 TIP If you are using Windows, a collection is a good way to play with the order or grouping of scenes or similar items in lieu of the Freeform Corkboard, which is not available in Windows.

Collections can also be used to create a group of documents that you want to compile with different settings rather than the entire Draft folder, such as when printing the first three chapters and a synopsis for a manuscript submission. If you are a teacher or professor, you can create collections of materials you need for each day of a course.

You can also use collections to make portions of your project available through an external folder so non-Scrivener users can access and modify the documents. If you are on a Mac and also have an iPad, use collections to create a sync file to transfer items back and forth between Scrivener and the Index Card for iPad app using Dropbox as an intermediary.

There are two types of collections:

- **Standard Collections**: This type of collection allows you to manually add and remove items in a collection, giving you complete control over its contents. These are static collections, in that the only way to add or remove documents is for you to act to do so.

- **Saved Search Collections**: If you choose the Save Search as Collection option (Save Search in Windows) from the Project Search menu, your search results are saved as a dynamic collection that includes documents only as long as they continue to meet the criteria of the collection. The Search Results pane itself is a special collection, always containing the results of the most recent search.

Creating a Standard Collection

A standard collection is very flexible because you decide exactly which documents to include. To create a standard collection:

1. Open the Collections pane in the left sidebar by doing one of the following:

- Click the Collections icon in the toolbar.

- Choose View, Collections, Show Collections from the menu.

- In Windows, press Ctrl+Shift+9.

2. Choose one of the following methods for selecting files to include in the collection:

    • Manually select files in the Binder.

    • Run a Project Search to pare down the files, and then select the specific files you require from the Search Results.

3. Click the Add Collection (+) button in the header of the Collections pane, shown in Figure 16.6.

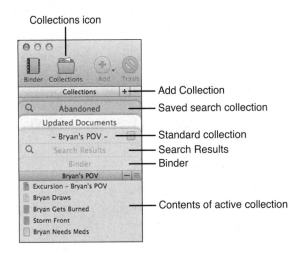

Collections icon

Add Collection

Saved search collection

Standard collection

Search Results

Binder

Contents of active collection

FIGURE 16.6

The Collections pane lists each collection along with the Search Results and Binder tabs.

4. Enter a name for the collection, then press Return (Enter).

As you can see in Figure 16.7, collections appear in the same sidebar as the Binder. If you have several collections, you may need to scroll to view them all. You can increase the number of visible tabs by clicking and dragging the Resize Collections Pane button on the Mac. In Windows, hover on the top edge of the Collections header bar to switch the cursor to a splitter that allows you to drag the pane up or down.

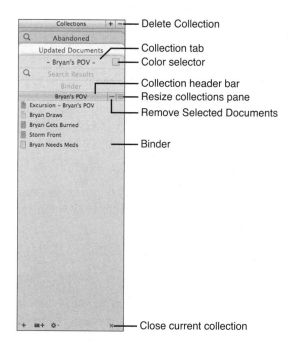

Delete Collection

Collection tab

Color selector

Collection header bar

Resize collections pane

Remove Selected Documents

Binder

Close current collection

FIGURE 16.7

A closer look at the Collections pane shows the Color Selector and the contents of the collection.

Each collection is automatically assigned a color. If you want to change the color on a Mac, double-click on the Color Selector to the right of the collection name, and then select from the Colors dialog box. In Windows, double-click to open a list of options that include the More option, from which you can open the Select Color dialog box.

TIP   When you are viewing collections, any tabs below the currently active collection appear in the same color as the active collection. Do not let that confuse you into thinking those tabs are part of the same collection. If you hover over the tabs, you see their true color and can select a different collection, the Search Results tab, or the Binder.

Once you have created a collection, it performs as a subset of the Binder. You can select documents to write or modify in the Editor or view the collection in the Corkboard or Outliner. On a Mac, to view an entire collection in the Corkboard, Outliner, or Scrivenings, click the header bar for the collection to select it, and then click one of the view buttons from the toolbar.

NOTE The collection tab is used to select it from the collections pane and to change the collection color. The collection header bar controls the documents within the collection.

To close the collection, click the Close (X) button at the bottom of the pane. You can also simply click on another collection tab or the Binder tab.

Adding and Removing Files from Standard Collections

If you forget to include an item when creating a collection, you can add it afterward. You can also create new items directly within the collection (on a Mac) and remove items from a collection.

To add an item to a collection:

1. Select the item in the Binder.

2. Choose Documents, Add to Collection from the menu. You can also right-click the item to open the context menu and choose Add to Collection.

3. Select a collection from the submenu.

You can also drag and drop an item from the Binder tab onto a collection tab to add it to that collection. When you add a container to a collection, its subdocuments are not added unless you specifically select them. On the Mac, choose Edit, Select Subdocuments from the menu or hold the Option key while dragging a container to the collection tab to add the subdocuments of a selected container to the selection.

To remove an item from a collection, select the item within the collection and then click the Remove Item (–) button on the Mac or press Delete (in Windows, press Shift+Delete). When you remove an item from a collection, it remains in the Binder as part of the project.

If you create a new item when you are viewing a collection on a Mac, it is not associated with a particular folder in the Binder because collections stand apart from the Binder hierarchy. Thus, new documents are placed into new root folders in the Binder, with names that correspond to the collection name.

 NOTE You can move new files into the proper position when you return to the Binder or by using the Move To technique covered in the next section.

Moving Files in a Standard Collection

Changes in the order of files in the collection do not affect the Binder; thus you can rearrange the documents to play with a different order without locking it in. For example, when writing some of the chapters of this book, I wasn't sure in which order I should present certain topics. By creating a standard collection containing all of the subheadings for a topic, I could rearrange the documents until I thought they flowed logically.

 NOTE Collections are flat lists, meaning you cannot change the hierarchy of files, only the order of them.

To rearrange files within the collection, simply drag and drop them into the desired location. You can also press Control-Cmd-arrow keys (Ctrl+arrow keys in Windows) to move documents up and down the list.

If you decide you want to retain the order of files you established in the collection, you can move items back into the Binder to preserve that order. To do this:

1. Select the files for which you want to preserve the order.

2. Choose one of the following options:

- Choose Documents, Move, To from the menu and then select a location from the submenu.

- On the Mac, drag the files to the Binder tab to open the Binder, and then drop the files into the desired folder.

- Right-click to open the context menu and then choose Move To and select a location from the submenu.

 TIP This concept may seem confusing at first because of the terminology. Think of it as moving documents from wherever they originally appeared in the Binder into a new location in the Binder. The collection simply serves as the catalyst to bring the items together.

 CAUTION Remember that a collection is a subset of the project whole. If you move a file into a new location in the Binder based on how it flows within a collection, be sure you haven't created a plot or content hole for yourself in another portion of the project.

Creating a Search Collection

Search collections are created by saving the results of a Project Search so you can repeat the search whenever necessary. These collections are dynamic because they automatically update the contents of the collection every time you open it. This ease of use in creating and updating a search collection comes with some compromises, however. You cannot manually adjust the items—no adding, removing, or reordering of files.

Search collections are good for grouping items that may change as you work on your project. If you use the Status field in the Inspector to note the progress of a document, for example, you can create a search collection for all documents with a status of First Draft so you know which items are waiting for you to revise. When you have revised the document, change its status to Second Draft in the Inspector, and that document no longer appears the next time you open the First Draft collection.

To create a search collection:

1. Perform a project search to create the search results you require.

2. Click the magnifying glass in the Search field of the toolbar and select Save Search as Collection (Save Search in Windows).

 CAUTION If you selected the Search Binder Selection Only option in the Project Search menu prior to conducting the search, the Save Search command is grayed out. This is because Binder selections are transient, so the dynamic collection would not be able to update properly.

If you conducted the project search on the Labels or Keywords, the search collection assumes the color associated with that label or keyword on the Mac, although you can change this color in the same manner as a standard collection.

You can distinguish standard collections and search collections in the Collections pane by looking for the magnifying glass that appears on the left side of a search collection tab. The contents of a search collection also appear on an alternating-color background on the Mac.

When you open a search collection in the Collections pane, the Search field in the toolbar reflects the criteria of the project search that created the collection. Click on the magnifying glass in the Search field to see which options and limitations were selected when performing the search. This acts as a reminder of the intent of the collection.

Converting a Search Collection to a Standard Collection

If you want to lock the results of a search collection so it no longer dynamically updates, convert it to a standard collection. To do this, click the tab of the collection you want to convert and choose View, Collections, Convert to Standard Collection from the menu.

Once you convert a search collection to a standard collection, this action cannot be undone. If you converted a collection in error, you need to create a new search collection.

Renaming Collections

Enter a name for a standard collection as part of the creation process, and the search collection assumes the name of the search by default. To rename either type of collection, double-click its name in the tab in the Collections pane; then type a new name and press Return (Enter).

You cannot rename the Search Results collection. This is a special type of collection that retains the results of the most recent project search.

Removing Collections

If a collection is of no further use to you, remove it from the Collections pane. Select the tab for the collection and click the Delete Collection (-) button in the Collections pane header. You cannot undo this action. In the case of search collections, you can re-create the project search and save the search to form a new collection. In the case of a standard collection, if you delete it in error, you must manually re-create it.

NOTE   There are two delete/remove buttons in the Collections pane, each with a specific purpose. The Delete Collection (–) button in the Collections pane header removes collections from the pane. The Remove Selected Documents (-) button in the header (on the Mac) within a standard collection removes documents from that collection.

Toggling the Collection View

If the multicolored spectacle of the Collections pane is distracting you while you work on a document, return to the Binder view. Click on the Binder tab and then select View, Collections, Hide Collections from the menu. Your collections still exist, but they remain out of sight until you choose to display them (View, Collections, Show Collections).

TIP If you hide collections while you are viewing a collection, the Binder only displays the contents of the collection. To return to the main binder, select View, Collections, Binder from the menu.

Setting Bookmarks (Mac Only)

When you read a physical book (yes, people still do that), you use bookmarks or dog-eared pages to note where you left off reading or a page to which you want to return at another time. Bookmarks in Scrivener are inline annotations formatted to do the same thing. Scrivener creates two types of bookmark annotations:

- **Bookmark Annotations**: Used to mark a location to which you want to return.
- **Bookmark Header Annotations**: Creates a hierarchy of bookmarks in which a bookmark header is inserted into a document and the bookmark navigation menu, shown in Figure 16.8. Other bookmarks appear indented beneath it until the next bookmark header appears in the document. This is a way to keep bookmarks organized in a document that is rife with them.

A WINDOWS VIEW: BOOKMARKING WITHOUT BOOKMARKS

Scrivener for Windows does not have bookmark functionality as such. Note, however, that even on the Mac these bookmarks are simply *annotations*. You can use the annotations tools in Scrivener for Windows to create your own bookmark system. Add an annotation wherever you want to add a bookmark, and enter an asterisk or a code such as BM into the text of the annotation. Locate bookmarks by conducting a Document Search for annotations containing asterisks or BM, as explained earlier in this chapter.

Adding Bookmarks

To add a bookmark on the Mac, position the insertion point in the paragraph to which you want to attach the bookmark and choose Edit, Insert, Bookmark Annotation from the menu or press Shift-Cmd-B. The bookmark annotation is inserted at the beginning of the paragraph, as shown in Figure 16.8.

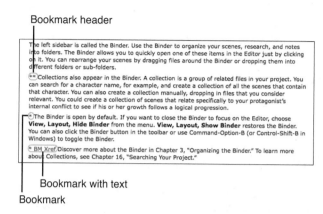

Bookmark header

Bookmark with text

Bookmark

FIGURE 16.8

Bookmark annotations appear at the beginning of a paragraph. One asterisk indicates a bookmark, and two asterisks indicate a bookmark header.

Using Bookmark Headers for Navigation

Once you have created bookmarks, you can view them in two locations, as follows:

- In the View, Text Bookmarks submenu
- In the Item Icon menu of the Editor header bar, as shown in Figure 16.9

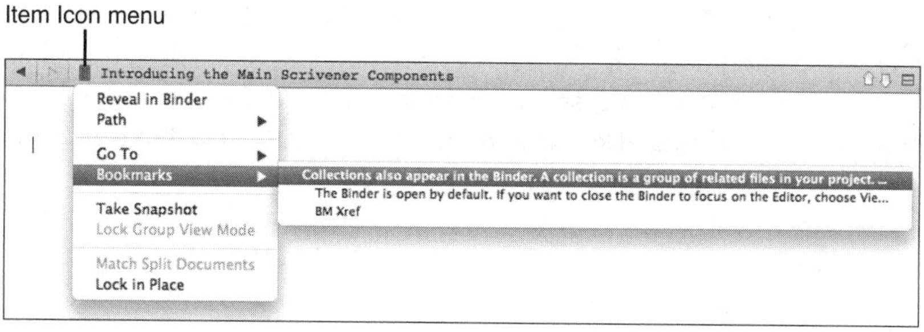

Item Icon menu

FIGURE 16.9

The Item Icon menu displays bookmarks, which you can use for navigation.

These menus only list bookmarks for documents currently loaded in the Editor. When you select a bookmark from one of these menus, you are taken to the location of the bookmark, and the paragraph to which it is linked is highlighted.

When navigating to a bookmark, Scrivener uses the first few words after the annotation to label the bookmark. You can override this feature by adding your own text to the annotation. Leave the asterisk(s) intact, but add your own label or words of text. As you can see in Figure 16.9, this text becomes the bookmark reference.

 NOTE When you are in Scrivenings mode, the bookmarks menu contains the bookmarks for all of the documents included in the Scrivenings.

Choosing Favorites (Mac Only)

As you work, you may find that you turn to certain documents repeatedly. On the Mac, you can set these documents as Favorites, which gives them priority seating on some of the navigation menus and their related entries on the context menus, such as the following:

- Edit, Append Selection to Document
- Edit, Scrivener Link
- View, Go To
- View, QuickReference
- Documents, Move, To

To add a Favorite to the menus, select the document in the Binder, right-click, and choose Add to Favorites from the context menu.

When I'm writing fiction, I add my character sketches to the Favorites menus. When I'm writing a tech book, such as the one you're reading now, I add a document listing keyboard shortcuts to the Favorites. In other words, I use this feature for documents I like close at hand no matter what I'm doing.

THE ABSOLUTE MINIMUM

The following are the highlights from this chapter:

- There are four types of searches in Scrivener: Project, Document, Formatting, and Synopsis.

- Project searches examine meta-data as well as the content of a document.

- Document and formatting searches locate matches within the document text.

- Collections store groups of files in your project that you want to examine or revise together.

- A collection is a flat list of files, so the hierarchy of the files is irrelevant.

- A collection can be manually organized or the result of a project search.

- Collections can be static or dynamic.

- Bookmarks help you return to a specific location in a document if you are a Mac user.

17

BACKING UP YOUR WORK

If there is one rule of writing, it's that as soon as you get lax about making backups, that's when your computer dies, your file gets corrupted, or you accidentally overwrite 20 pages of the best prose you've ever written with 2 pages you intended to delete. If any or all of these sound like something that has or could happen to you, then you probably don't need me to remind you to always make a backup!

In a perfect world, you make multiple backups, locally and offsite, to protect against the three major threats to your work:

- **Project corruption**: Back up frequently and automatically to a folder on your computer. Ideally, this folder automatically synchronizes with an Internet file storage service, such as Dropbox, which ensures you also have a copy offsite.

- **Computer failure**: Include your Scrivener project as part of your routine system backup to an external storage device using Time Machine or another backup utility.

- **Theft or catastrophic event**: Manually save a copy of your project onto a CD, DVD, or USB flash drive that you keep offsite in your car, home (if you work at an office), or office (vice versa), or with a trusted friend.

This chapter explores all of your backup options.

Setting Backup Preferences

Scrivener understands the importance of backups. Whenever you close your project, Scrivener automatically makes a backup to your hard drive. It compresses (into a Zip file) and stores the last five backups in your user folder.

This automatic, default backup is useful, but if your hard drive crashes or your computer gets lost or stolen, you've then lost both your saved project and all of the backups along with it. Fortunately, you can change the default to save to a folder that is automatically synchronized to a service on the Internet, such as Dropbox. Also, whereas Scrivener backs up when you close your project, you may want to create backups at other times, as well.

To customize the backup preferences, open the Preferences/Options window and select the Backup tab. In the Backup preferences, as shown in Figure 17.1, choose from the following options:

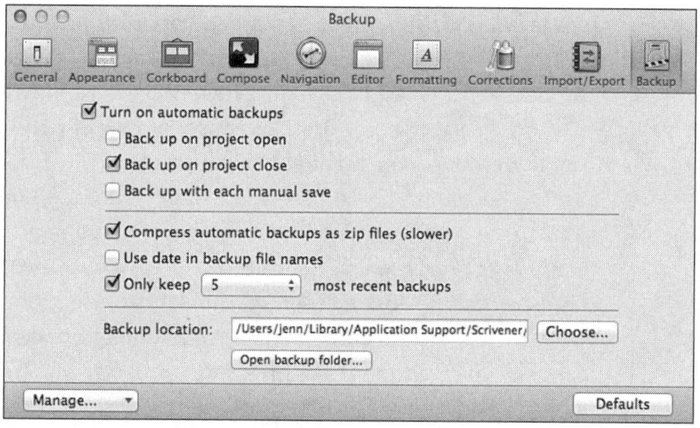

FIGURE 17.1

The Backup preferences/options configure Scrivener to automatically back up your projects to a local folder or ~~internal~~ storage device.

~~tic Backups~~: This option is selected by default. Automatic ~~~~at Scrivener is looking out for you even when you neglect ~~~~ backups.

~~~~ **Open**: This option saves a backup whenever you open ~~~~ositive side, this ensures you start each session knowing ~~~~ckup before you modify the project. On the negative ~~~~ longer to open your project as it performs the backup. ~~~~e even longer if Scrivener is set to automatically open projects as ~~~~e projects are backed up. Also, unless you save a backup upon closing Scrivener, you risk losing any of the changes you made during a session if something happens to your computer between sessions.

- **Back Up on Project Close**: This default setting saves a backup whenever you close a project or when you quit Scrivener. The positive side is that you can walk away from a writing session secure in the knowledge that your new material is backed up. To ensure that this happens, however, you must be certain to close the project or quit Scrivener entirely at the end of each session. If you leave Scrivener running with your project open, it does not get backed up.

- **Back Up with Each Manual Save**: If you manually save (File, Save or Cmd-S on the Mac and Ctrl+S in Windows) your project at regular intervals, this option automatically creates a backup version at the same time. The best aspect of this option is that you can keep your project open over long periods of time without sacrificing the ability to automatically back up. On the other hand, it takes time to perform a backup, so this can slow you down as you work. This option also relies upon you to manually save your project on a regular basis. If you neglect to do so, your work may be at risk.

CAUTION When you first transition from a word processor to Scrivener, you may be in the habit of saving your project compulsively. I used to save after every paragraph when I worked in Word. While this is a great practice in a word processor, you may undermine your manual backup solution if you retain this habit in Scrivener. If you only keep the five most recent backups, all of those backups may only be a few minutes apart, which means that changes you made the day before or even earlier the same day can be lost forever. If you want to use manual backups, you may want to save an unlimited number of backups and manually cull through them on a regular basis.

- **Compress Automatic Backups as Zip Files**: Selected by default, this option compresses backups into .zip files. Zip files take up less hard disk space and are also less likely to become corrupted, particularly when transferring Scrivener projects over the Internet. It takes more time to save a backup, however, because Scrivener needs to back up the project and create the Zip file.

- **Use Date in Backup File Names**: This option adds a date and time stamp to the filename of the backup, making it easier to determine exactly when the backup file was created. This is helpful if you want to restore a backup from a particular day or writing session.

- **Only Keep [Number] Most Recent Backups**: Scrivener keeps five backups by default. If you back up frequently, you might want to retain more backups so you don't inadvertently overwrite a backup from just a couple days prior. If storage space is a concern, you might want to keep fewer backups. Use the drop-down menu to choose 3, 5, 10, or 25 backups.

TIP To keep all backup files on the Mac, deselect the check box to the left of the Only Keep [Number] Most Recent Backups option. In Windows, you also have the option to Keep All Backup Files in the drop-down menu. If you choose this option, be sure to manually cull through the backup herd on a regular basis so you are not overrun with files. To do this, use Windows Explorer to navigate to your backup folder and delete backups you no longer need to preserve. You can also move them to a CD or DVD if you want them off your hard drive without losing access to them permanently.

- **Backup Location**: By default, Scrivener saves backups to `~/Library/Application Support/Scrivener/Backups` on the Mac and `C:\Users\YourUsername\AppData\Local\Scrivener\Scrivener\Backups` in Windows. If you're using Windows XP, the path is `C:\Documents and Settings\YourUsername\Local Settings\Application Data\Scrivener\Scrivener\Backups`.

To change this location, click the Choose button and select a new folder. If you have an external hard drive or USB flash drive connected to your computer, you can select a location on that drive to store your backups. You can also change the backup location to your Dropbox folder to store backups if you use that service, as explained in the next section. You can only choose one location for automatic backups, so consider how each option fits into your overall system backup plan.

 CAUTION   Scrivener displays a warning if it tries to back up to a location that becomes invalid, such as if you disconnect an external drive or if your online storage site becomes unavailable.

 NOTE   If you downloaded Scrivener 2.4 or lower from the Mac App Store, backups are stored in `~/Library/Containers/com.literatureandlatte.Scrivener/Data/Library/Application Support/Scrivener/Backups`, by default. If you downloaded Scrivener 2.4.1 or higher from the Mac App Store, you are prompted to choose a backup location the first time you launch Scrivener.

- **Open Backup Folder**: Click this button to open the backup folder in Finder or Windows Explorer.

 TIP   Although I provided the paths to the hidden directories for the default backup folders, the Open Backup Folder button is the easiest way to access this folder.

 CAUTION   Scrivener tracks automatic backups by filename. If you have two projects with the same filename in two different locations, they are still saved to the same backup folder, where those filenames will become confused. Scrivener will only keep the specified number of backups of the two projects combined, and you will not be able to tell which backup pertains to which project without opening it. For this reason, it is always best to give each project a unique name, even if you save your projects in different folders.

Backing Up to Dropbox

Dropbox is a free service that syncs a folder and any subfolders from your hard drive with storage in the cloud. If you set your Dropbox folder as your backup location, you get the benefit of saving a backup on your computer in the local Dropbox folder and having an automatic copy on an external server.

NOTE Go to www.dropbox.com for more information about this service. Dropbox offers a limited amount of storage for free, with options for increasing the limit by referring other customers or paying a monthly fee.

TIP These same steps apply to backing up to similar services, such as SkyDrive and Google Drive. If your cloud service does not require syncing only a specific folder, you can create a dedicated folder for Scrivener backups and then set it to sync via your cloud service.

To back up to your Dropbox folder:

1. Use the instructions on the Dropbox site to install Dropbox on your computer.

2. In Finder or Windows Explorer, create a new folder in your Dropbox folder for Scrivener Backups.

3. Choose Scrivener, Preferences (or Tools, Options in Windows) to open the Preferences/Options window.

4. Click the Backup tab.

5. In the Backup Location field, click the Choose button and navigate to the folder you created in your Dropbox folder.

TIP Also be sure to select the Compress Automatic Backups as Zip Files option to provide extra protection for the many files that comprise your project.

6. Click Open.

TIP You can also use Dropbox to store the project itself. For details on how to do that—and warnings on how to avoid corrupting your projects in the process—see Chapter 18, "Taking Scrivener Out and About." If you plan to use Dropbox to store your active project, I suggest keeping your backups elsewhere, such as a different cloud service or on an external drive. If Dropbox is down or your account becomes compromised, you don't want both the active project and all of its backups to be stored in one place.

Excluding a Project from Automatic Backups

If you have an exceptionally large project, the time it takes to automatically back up may exceed your patience. If you disable automatic backups, all your projects are affected, leaving even your smaller works at risk, so you need a different solution. You may also want to back up a particular project to a different location for security purposes. If you have created a dummy project for the purpose of designing a new project template, you might not want to back up the project at all.

For these or other reasons, you can exclude individual projects from the automatic backup settings. Take the following steps to do this:

1. Open the project you want to exclude.

2. Choose File, Back Up, Exclude from Automatic Backups from the menu. A check mark is added to the left of the menu item to indicate that it has been selected.

3. Repeat steps 1 and 2 for any other projects that you want to exclude.

Remember, if you are not automatically backing up a project, it remains at risk unless you perform a manual backup. If you change your mind, return to the File, Back Up, Exclude from Automatic Backups command to deselect it.

Performing Manual Backups

If you have excluded a project from automatic backups, you need to perform manual backups on a regular basis. If you want to save the backup to the same folder as the automatic backups for other projects, choose File, Back Up, Back Up Now from the menu.

To back up to a different folder or to a CD, DVD, or USB flash drive:

1. Open the project in Scrivener.

2. Choose File, Back Up, Back Up To from the menu.

3. In the Back Up To dialog box, shown in Figure 17.2, navigate to the location where you want to store the backup. In Windows, click the Browse button to choose a location.

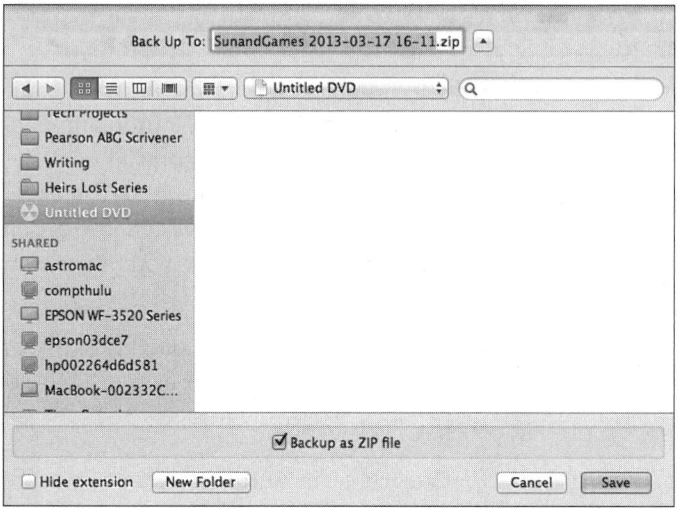

FIGURE 17.2

When you manually back up a project, you can select where the backup is stored.

4. Scrivener provides a filename with a date and time stamp. If you want to change the filename, enter a new name.

5. Click the Backup as ZIP File option to save space and make the backup more secure.

6. Click Save on the Mac or OK in Windows.

CDs, DVDs, and even USB flash drives are becoming increasingly quaint as people rely more on streaming and cloud services to transfer files, but saving your files onto physical media still has its uses. If you do not have access to the Internet, a disk backup can be essential. Because disks and flash drives are not always connected to your computer and tend to fill up quickly, it is best to perform manual backups to this media rather than using the automatic backup settings for this purpose.

On the Mac, if you chose to save to a CD or DVD, open the disk in Finder or the desktop and choose Burn; then follow the prompts, as shown in Figure 17.3. In Windows, follow the prompts shown in Figure 17.4.

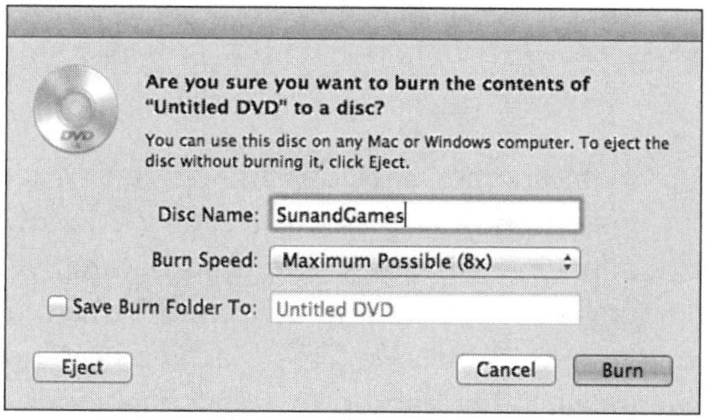

FIGURE 17.3

If you choose to back up to a CD or DVD on the Mac, you must take additional steps.

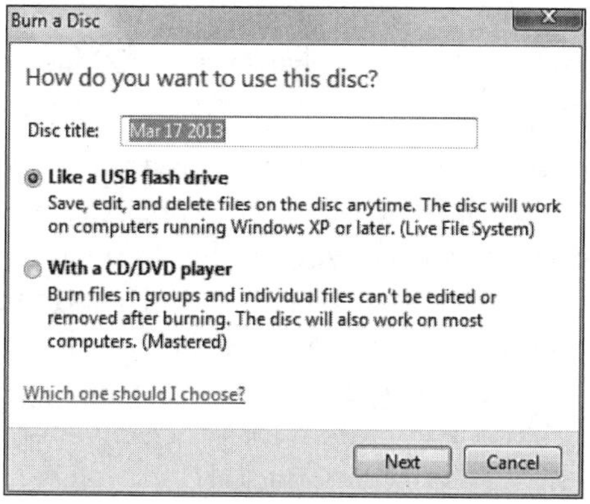

FIGURE 17.4

In Windows, you can choose to use your DVD as permanent storage or a more transient device.

NOTE Even though I automatically back up to a Dropbox folder, I also perform a manual backup onto a USB flash drive at least once a week. If the Dropbox site were to go down or I had a major computer malfunction, this physical storage device provides reassurance that all is not lost.

Backing Up to Time Machine or Windows Backup

Mac OS X (Leopard and higher) provides an automatic system backup feature called Time Machine. Windows 7 includes a similar Windows Backup feature, while Windows 8 offers File History. These tools back up your entire system on a regular—often hourly—basis, including Scrivener. Be careful, however, if you need to restore a Scrivener project from a Time Machine or Windows backup. If you are working in Scrivener while the backup routine is running, it is quite possible that the copy it makes of your project is incomplete.

As an example, suppose you are working on your project at 3:00 when Time Machine runs its backup routine. You continue writing for another 45 minutes and then go to bed. If your computer crashes while you're asleep and you need to restore from Time Machine, it only has the 3:00 files on it, so everything you added after that time is lost.

You can mitigate the potential damage by using a couple of techniques. First, you can manually run Time Machine or Windows Backup, so you might want to get into the habit of doing this when you are finished writing for the day, after you close Scrivener. In addition, Time Machine and Windows Backup are local backup systems, so if your equipment is stolen or damaged, the thief or catastrophe will likely take your external backup drive, as well. Therefore, a second technique is to always utilize another backup system for your Scrivener projects, as well, even if you use Time Machine or Windows Backup.

Restoring from a Backup

If the worst happens and you need to restore a project from a Scrivener-created backup, follow these steps:

1. In Scrivener, open the Preferences/Options dialog box and click on the Backup tab.

2. Click the Open Backup Folder button.

 NOTE If you had to reinstall Scrivener from scratch and the backup location is no longer set to your old folder, open Finder or Windows Explorer to navigate to your backup folder.

3. Locate the backup file you want to restore and copy it to another location. If the file is zipped, double-click to unzip the file. In Windows, right-click and select Extract All.

4. Double-click the project file to open it in Scrivener.

THE ABSOLUTE MINIMUM

Before you get busy creating your own backup strategy, here is what you learned in this chapter:

- Always have a backup plan for your projects.

- Scrivener automatically backs up every time you close the project. It saves five backups by default.

- You can change the backup preferences to back up to a different folder, save more backups, and back up when you open a project or manually save the project.

- Time Machine and Windows Backup/File History are good full-system backup options, but you should always use an additional backup system with your Scrivener projects to prevent corrupted or outdated files.

IN THIS CHAPTER

- Using Scrivener on multiple computers
- Using Dropbox to access your Scrivener project
- Syncing your project
- Using iPad apps with Scrivener files

18

TAKING SCRIVENER OUT AND ABOUT

Back in the old days, people were lucky to have one computer in the household. These days, every member of the family often has his or her own laptop, tablet, and smartphone (which does more than those desktop computers of old). You may begin a project on your office computer, add to it on your tablet during your evening commute on the train, and complete it at home.

With all this swapping of computers and platforms, it's important to understand how to transfer your Scrivener projects between them and how to keep projects in sync.

Using Scrivener on Multiple Computers

Scrivener is very portable. To open a project on another computer that is running Scrivener, you should first save the project as a Zip file. This ensures that all of the folders and files within the project are transferred as a group. It also prevents you from accidentally merging projects in Windows. To create a Zip file of your project, choose File, Back Up, Back Up To from the menu. Be sure to select the Backup as Zip File option in the Back Up To dialog box (the Backup Project To dialog box in Windows).Then choose one of the following:

- Save the project to a USB flash drive or other portable media to transfer it to the other computer. While you can work directly from the USB flash drive, it is faster to copy the file onto the other computer and work from there.

- Save the project to a cloud storage account that is accessible from the second computer.

- Save the project as a Zip file and email it to an account that is accessible from the second computer.

 CAUTION   Before transferring the file, be sure to save a backup copy just in case. Also be careful not to work on the same project from multiple computers at the same time. If you transfer the project from your home computer to your office, do not open the project on your home computer again until you have transferred the most recent version of the project back to the home computer.

Although there are differences between the Mac and Windows versions of Scrivener, they are fully compatible with each other. You can use the same project on both a Mac and in Windows, as long as you don't open it on both platforms at the same time. If a project contains a feature that is available in Scrivener for Mac but not Scrivener for Windows, such as custom meta-data, the Windows version simply overlooks it. This does not change your ability to use those features on the Mac, however.

 CAUTION   If you are sharing projects between a Mac and Windows, be sure the Mac is running version 2.0 or higher of Scrivener. Project files from earlier versions of Scrivener for Mac are not compatible with the Windows platform.

The Mac and Windows platforms save Scrivener projects differently. In Windows, your project appears as a folder, with all of the files and elements of your project within it. On the Mac, your project appears as a single file, but it is actually a folder, as well, simply one that takes advantage of the Mac's ability to package files together. Thus, when you transfer the `.scriv` file from the Mac to Windows, it appears as a folder. To open the project within Windows, open the folder and select the `.scrivx` file within it. When you transfer the `.scriv` folder back to the Mac, it once again appears as a single file, which can be double-clicked to open in Scrivener for Mac.

TIP When transferring a project between the two platforms, be sure to copy the entire `.scriv` folder from Windows. If you transfer a project from Windows to the Mac and see a yellow file icon bearing the letters XML and a filename with a `.scrivx` extension, shown in Figure 18.1, you will know you failed to copy the entire project.

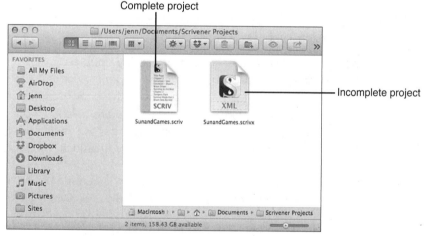

FIGURE 18.1

If you see a yellow XML icon after transferring a Scrivener project from Windows to the Mac, you've left critical portions of the project behind.

Using Dropbox to Access Your Scrivener Project

In Chapter 17, "Backing Up Your Work," you learned how to use Dropbox to store your automatic and manual backups in the cloud. You can also use Dropbox to save the working project file in order to access it from multiple computers.

To create a project in your Dropbox folder, follow the regular steps to select a project template and create a new project. When choosing a location for the file, select the Dropbox folder or a subfolder within it. You can also move a preexisting project into the Dropbox folder or subfolder.

Although Dropbox is a wonderful solution to working on your project cross-computer and cross-platform, there is the risk of corrupting the file or unintentionally creating multiple versions. Use the following best practices to avoid these problems:

- Only work on the project from one computer or device at a time. If you access the project from multiple devices at the same time, your project will become out of sync, and you will end up with multiple versions of the file, each containing different changes.

- Do not access the project when it is in the midst of being uploaded or downloaded from the Dropbox server. If the file displays a badge signifying it is syncing (usually a blue badge with two arrows circling), wait until the badge indicates the transfer is complete (usually a green check mark) before opening the project.

- Do not shut down your computer while Dropbox is syncing files. If the sync does not complete, your project will become corrupted.

- Get in the habit of always opening the project by double-clicking on it in the Dropbox folder instead of automatically opening it from within the Scrivener application. This forces you to look at the badge on the project icon so you will know if the file is busy. When you are finished working on the project, close it before exiting Scrivener in order to prevent yourself from automatically opening the project the next time you launch the application.

 TIP If all of your projects are stored on Dropbox, you can disable the Reopen Projects That Were Open on Quit option in the General tab of the Preferences window on the Mac. In Windows, the Open Recent Projects on Program Launch in Windows option in the General tab of the Options window is deselected by default.

- If you have a slow Internet connection, lengthen the interval at which Scrivener automatically saves your work. If you save every time you stop typing for 2 seconds, the project needs to update on the Dropbox server more frequently. Changing this interval in the General panel of the Preferences/Options dialog box means that the project is updated in larger chunks, but it doesn't need to access the Dropbox server as often.

TIP If you use Dropbox to share a project with coauthors or critique partners, use extra precautions. Unless you and your partners communicate effectively, you will not know when someone else is accessing the project, increasing the possibility of the project becoming out of sync.

One method for avoiding this problem is to create an icon for each member of the group. When you open the Scrivener project, upload your icon to the Dropbox folder. When you have completed your work and synced the file back to Dropbox, remove your icon from the folder. Once you establish this routine, you and your writing partners will know with a glance at the Dropbox folder if anyone is using the file before you open it.

Syncing Your Project (Mac Only)

When you transfer a project between computers that each have a copy of Scrivener, working on multiple computers and platforms is easy. But what if you cannot install Scrivener on your office computer? How do you continue working if your laptop goes in for repairs and you are forced to work on the local library computers? How do you share your project with a co-worker who does not use Scrivener? The solution to all these scenarios is to sync your project with an external folder.

When you sync with an external folder, the contents of your Draft folder (and other folders, if you want) are saved as `.rtf` or `.txt` files in a folder in Finder. You can then transfer these files to another computer or edit them in another application, save them back to the external folder, and synchronize the changes within Scrivener the next time you open the project. If you select a Dropbox folder as the external folder, the files are readily available from other computers or even your iPhone or iPad.

NOTE If you are a script writer, you can also sync files in Final Draft (`.fdx`) or Fountain screenplay syntax format.

CAUTION You cannot use the Sync with an External Folder tool to sync two versions of Scrivener. This feature is only for editing project files with other applications and synchronizing those files back into your project. Attempting to sync two Scrivener projects results in corrupted projects.

To set up synchronized folders:

1. Open the project in Scrivener.

2. Choose File, Sync, with External Folder from the menu.

3. In the Sync with External Folder dialog box, shown in Figure 18.2, click the Choose button.

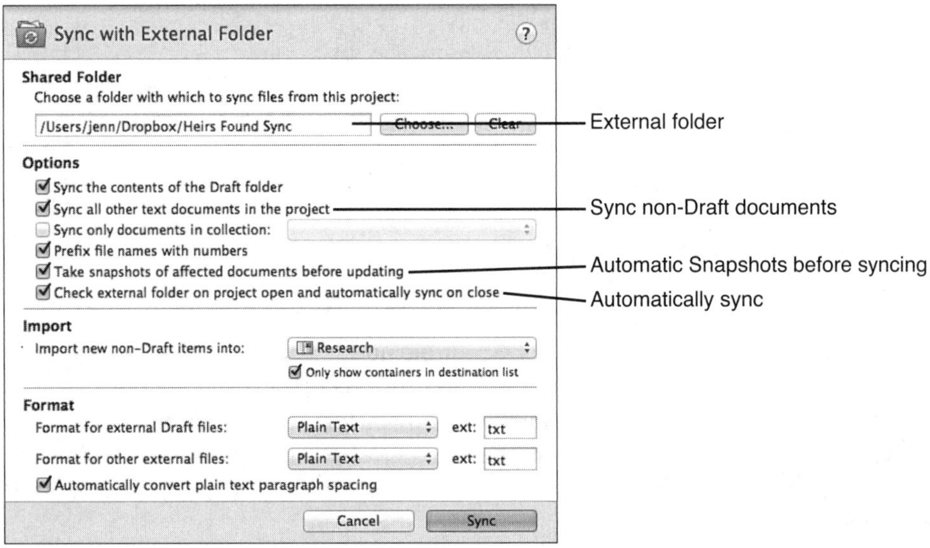

Sync with External Folder   (?)

Shared Folder
Choose a folder with which to sync files from this project:

/Users/jenn/Dropbox/Heirs Found Sync   [Choose...] [Clear] ——— External folder

Options
☑ Sync the contents of the Draft folder
☑ Sync all other text documents in the project ——————————— Sync non-Draft documents
☐ Sync only documents in collection: [⬍]
☑ Prefix file names with numbers
☑ Take snapshots of affected documents before updating ——————— Automatic Snapshots before syncing
☑ Check external folder on project open and automatically sync on close ——— Automatically sync

Import
Import new non-Draft items into: [🖼 Research   ⬍]
                                     ☑ Only show containers in destination list

Format
Format for external Draft files: [Plain Text   ⬍] ext: [txt]
Format for other external files: [Plain Text   ⬍] ext: [txt]
☑ Automatically convert plain text paragraph spacing

                              [Cancel] [**Sync**]

FIGURE 18.2

The Sync with External Folder dialog box, shown here set up to sync to a Dropbox folder, coordinates the transfer of synchronized files to and from your project.

4. In the Open dialog box, select an empty folder with which to sync your project file. Click the New Folder button to create a new folder. If you want to sync with Dropbox, select or create a folder within your Dropbox folder.

 CAUTION   You cannot save more than one project in a single external folder. Scrivener relies on a numbering system to determine which items to synchronize, and having multiple files meeting that criteria corrupts the project.

5. Click Open to select the folder and return to the Sync with External Folder dialog box.

6. Select from the following options:

   • **Sync the Contents of the Draft Folder**: Selected by default, this synchronizes all of the documents in your Draft folder.

- **Sync All Other Text Documents in the Project**: This option synchronizes any other text documents in the project. These documents are saved in a subfolder titled Notes within your external folder.

- **Sync Only Documents in Collection**: If this option is selected, only documents that are included in the collection specified in the drop-down menu are synchronized.

   NOTE This option works in conjunction with the two prior options. Only those files from the Draft or other text documents, depending on which options you selected, that also appear in the specified collection are synced.

- **Prefix File Names with Numbers**: Selected by default, Scrivener prefixes each filename with a number to note its position in the Binder hierarchy. This allows you to sort your files in order.

   TIP Keep this option selected unless you have a specific reason to deselect it. If you disable it, sorting the files causes them to appear in alphanumeric order based on the title of each file, making it more difficult for you to locate files. Disabling this feature does not change Scrivener's ability to maintain the files in their proper order in your project, however.

- **Take Snapshots of Affected Documents before Updating**: Selected by default, Scrivener automatically takes a Snapshot of each document that requires updating before performing the update. See Chapter 10, "Editing Your Manuscript," to learn more about Snapshots.

   TIP Although Scrivener makes this an optional setting, this is another one that should not be disabled unless you have a good reason for doing so. If you make changes to a document in your project at the same time a coauthor is editing the file in the external folder, this feature takes a Snapshot of the project document before updating with the external file. You can then use the Snapshot pane in the Inspector to compare the two versions of the document and edit the updated project document accordingly. Without this Snapshot, the changes you made in the project document would be lost.

- **Check External Folder on Project Open and Automatically Sync on Close**: Selected by default, this option checks the external folder whenever you open or close the project in Scrivener and synchronizes accordingly to keep the project updated.

- **Import New Non-Draft Items Into**: If you selected the Sync All Other Text Documents in the Project option, you can select a target container for any new items you create in the Notes subfolder of the external folder. This option is grayed out if you did not select to sync non-Draft items.

- **Format for External Draft Files**: This option sets the file type for files in the sync folder. If the files will be edited in Microsoft Word or another word processor, choose Rich Text. If you are going to edit files on your iPad or iPhone, as explained in the next section, choose Plain Text. For scripts, choose Final Draft or Fountain.

 NOTE Fountain is a text-based screenplay markup language. Visit http://www.fountain.io for more information.

- **Format for Other External Files**: If you select the Sync All Other Text Documents in the Project option, select a format for those documents.

- **Automatically Convert Plain Text Paragraph Spacing**: When this option is selected, Scrivener inserts an extra carriage return between paragraphs to make it easier to see paragraph separations. These carriage returns are automatically stripped when the file is updated back into the Scrivener project.

7. Click Sync. A progress bar displays as Scrivener exports your files. The message shown in Figure 18.3 tells you when the process is complete.

FIGURE 18.3

When Scrivener completes the synchronization process, a message indicates success.

NOTE You can also sync your project with Simplenote, a cross-platform text application. To do this, select File, Sync, with Simplenote and follow the prompts, assigning a unique keyword for each project. Simplenote's cloud system is proprietary, so your files are only available to apps that access that system. I prefer syncing my files through Dropbox because they are then available to a wider range of applications.

Using Files in the External Folder

Once the sync is complete, you can open the files in the external folder from other applications. If you sync to Dropbox, you can access the files from other computers and devices.

Scrivener exports the contents of the Draft folder into a subfolder titled Draft. If you selected to sync non-Draft items, they appear in the Notes subfolder, regardless of their parent folder in the Scrivener project. As you work with the project, a third folder titled Trashed Files may appear. This folder stores documents that had previously been synced but have been removed from the project or encountered a conflict with the project.

You can add new text files to either the Draft or Notes folders. These files are added to your project when you sync. Files created in the Draft folder are automatically added to the Draft folder in your project. Files created in the Notes folder are added to the folder you selected in the Sync with External Folder dialog box.

 NOTE You cannot add nontext files to a project via the external folder. Scrivener only syncs text files.

Unless you disabled the Check External Folder on Project Open and Automatically Sync on Close option, Scrivener automatically keeps your project in sync whenever you open and close it. If you or a co-worker has modified or added a file in the external folder while the project is open, you can manually sync by choosing File, Sync, with External Folder Now from the menu. To save time, Scrivener only synchronizes files that have changed in the project or in the external folder.

Working Wisely with Synced Folders

The sync feature works quite well, as long as you understand its capabilities and limitations:

- Scrivener uses the modification date of external files and project documents to determine which is the most current. The Take Snapshots of Affected Documents before Updating feature can help avoid conflicts, but it is still best to try to work in one application at a time.

- Do not rename files in the sync folder! Scrivener relies on the filenames to match up external files with project documents. Each file has a number appended to the end of the title to note its position in the Binder hierarchy. You can, of course, still rename items in the Binder.

- If you export files in Plain Text (.txt), any formatting in the document is lost. If you need to use bold, italic, or underlining, mark the text so you can search and replace later. For example, if you need to underline something, type it as _here is text_ so you can replace the underscores with proper underlines when you open the project document in Scrivener.

- If you export files in Rich Text Format (.rtf), you can add comments to the file in Word or another word processor. When you synchronize the file back into the project, those comments are preserved. This is an excellent way to solicit feedback on portions of your project from people who do not use Scrivener.

- Although Plain Text does not provide formatting options, it does allow you to work in more apps, particularly on the iPad or iPhone.

- If you need to duplicate a project, disable the Check External Folder on Project Open and Automatically Sync on Close option before doing so. If you duplicate a project while this feature is enabled, it attempts to synchronize to the same folder as the original project, which can corrupt both projects.

Using iPad Apps with Scrivener Files (Mac Only)

Although Scrivener is not yet available for iOS devices, you can still work on your project files from your iPad or iPhone. As you discovered in the previous section, Scrivener can sync to a Dropbox folder. If you install the Dropbox app on your iPhone or iPad, this folder will then be available on the device.

To add or edit files on your iOS device, you need to also install a text editor app. Popular apps include PlainText ($1.99), iA Writer ($4.99) , Elements ($4.99) , and Notebooks ($8.99) . Each app has its own method of accessing Dropbox and opening a file within the app.

NOTE Pages is a popular iPad word processing application, but it is not ideal for working with Scrivener projects. Pages syncs through iTunes or iCloud, not Dropbox. This limits the folder's availability to other applications and platforms.

Using iA Writer with Scrivener Files (Mac Only)

As an example, here are the steps to use iA Writer for a Scrivener project:

1. Use the step-by-step instructions earlier in this chapter to set up your Scrivener project to sync with an external folder in Dropbox.

2. On your iPad, open iA Writer, as shown in Figure 18.4.

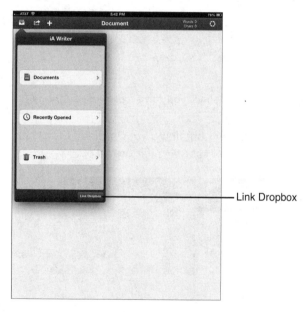

FIGURE 18.4

Before you can access your project files in iA Writer, you need to link your Dropbox account to the app.

3. Tap the File button.

4. Click the Link Dropbox button. The Dropbox app opens.

5. In the Dropbox app, click Allow to link your account to iA Writer. You are then returned to the iA Writer app.

6. Click the Dropbox option, shown in Figure 18.5.

Dropbox folder

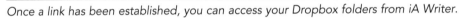

FIGURE 18.5

Once a link has been established, you can access your Dropbox folders from iA Writer.

7. Navigate to the folder containing your project; then click either the Draft or Notes folder to access your files (Figure 18.6) .

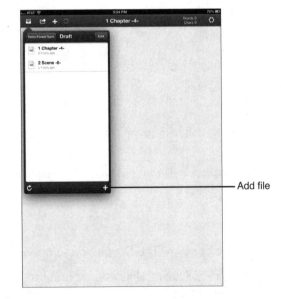

Add file

FIGURE 18.6

Your exported files appear in the Draft or Notes folder.

8. Select a file to open it in iA Writer.

When you have finished editing a file, it is automatically synced back to Dropbox, where it will then be synced with your Scrivener project the next time you open it.

If you want to add a file to the project, navigate into the Draft or Notes folder; then click the Add (+) button.

 TIP If you use your iPad for writing, consider connecting it to a Bluetooth keyboard. You will find you can type much faster, more comfortably, and more accurately. You are also then free to prop your iPad up on a stand or folded SmartCover to use it as more of a display. Just remember to position yourself close enough to touch the screen, as there is no mouse available (no matter how frequently you find yourself reaching for one).

A WINDOWS VIEW: GETTING AROUND THE LACK OF SYNC TOOLS

Scrivener for Windows users are anxiously awaiting the arrival of syncing capability on a future version of the app. In the meantime, you can work around this shortcoming with a bit of fancy footwork.

If you want to add new content, create a document in your word processor or text editor and save it in `.rtf` or `.txt` format. Transfer it to the computer running Scrivener. When you open your project, drag the file into your project.

Editing a Scrivener document is a more challenging process. You can export files from Scrivener and edit them in a different application, but you cannot automatically sync those changes to your project. Scrivener for Windows also cannot compare Snapshots. Instead, you need to manually cut and paste the changes into the project document or delete the original project document and drag the new version into the Binder. Note that either approach has risks, however, and if you have changed the Scrivener project in the meantime, you need to be very careful not to lose content.

The good news is that syncing is coming to the Windows platform. And the forthcoming iPad version of Scrivener will interface with both the Windows and Mac versions.

Using Index Card for iOS (Mac Only)

iPad users have another synchronization option. Index Card is an affordable ($4.99 for iPad, $1.99 for iPhone) iOS corkboard and outlining app. Inspired by Scrivener, it allows you to create and manipulate index cards on a virtual corkboard. Index cards contain a title, synopsis, and the main text of the item. Index Card also has a List view, similar to Scrivener's Outliner. Although you cannot change the order of Scrivener's Binder hierarchy using the Sync with External Folder feature, the Sync with Index Card for iOS feature was intended for exactly that.

Setting up the syncing process between Index Card and Scrivener takes several steps. This synchronization process relies on Dropbox, so you must have Dropbox installed on both your computer and your iPhone or iPad. You also need to install Index Card on your device before proceeding.

Index Card projects are flat lists rather than the multilevel hierarchical structure allowed by Scrivener. Thus, one of the limitations of Index Card is that you must first create a collection in Scrivener. That collection becomes the basis for syncing with Index Card. Take the following steps to do this:

1. Open your Dropbox folder in Finder and create a new folder titled IndexCard.

   If you have already saved the file from Index Card into your Dropbox folder, this folder might have already been created.

2. In Scrivener's Binder, select the documents you want to port to Index Card.

3. Select View, Collections, Show Collections from the menu to view the Collections pane.

4. Click the Add (+) button in the Header bar to create a new collection containing the selected documents.

5. Name the new collection and then press Return.

6. Choose File, Sync, with Index Card for iOS from the menu.

7. In the Sync with Index Card for the iPad dialog box, shown in Figure 18.7, choose the collection you created from the Collection drop-down menu.

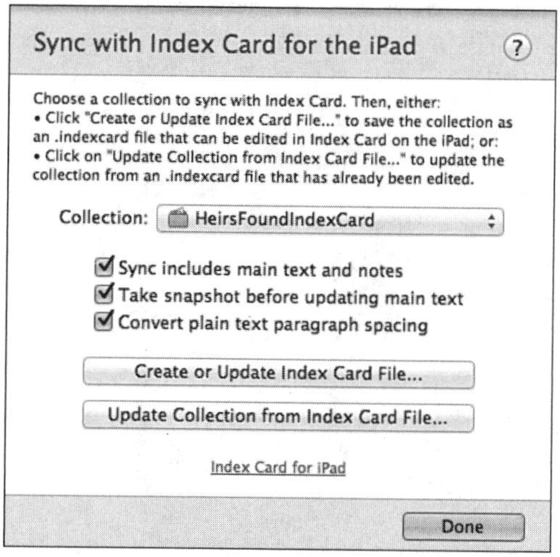

FIGURE 18.7

The Sync with Index Card for the iPad dialog box contains options for syncing your Scrivener project with the Index Card app.

8. Choose from the following options, all of which are selected by default:

    - **Sync Includes Main Text and Notes**: Scrivener stores the text of your document in the text field of the index card. If you have any document notes in the item, they are stored in the Notes field of the index card. If this option is not selected, Scrivener does not update the text of your project document even if you enter text on a card in Index Card.

    - **Take Snapshot before Updating Main Text**: Scrivener automatically takes a Snapshot of each item that has changed in the collection before updating the document text for that item.

    - **Convert Plain Text Paragraph Spacing**: This option adds an extra break between paragraphs to make it easier to view paragraphs.

9. Click Create or Update Index Card File. The Save As dialog box opens automatically in the IndexCard folder you created in your Dropbox folder.

10. In the Save As dialog box, enter a name for the .indexcard file.

After you complete step 10, Scrivener creates the .indexcard file. Now you can open it in the Index Card app on your iPhone or iPad by doing the following:

1. Open the Index Card app on your device.

2. Tap on the gear icon, shown in Figure 18.8, and select Dropbox Link from the Settings menu.

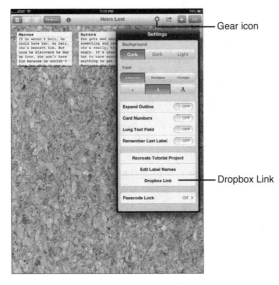

Gear icon

Dropbox Link

FIGURE 18.8

Before you can access your project in Index Card, you must link your Dropbox account to the app.

3. Click Allow to link your Dropbox account to the Index Card app.

4. Tap the Projects icon in Index Card to open the Projects menu, shown in Figure 18.9.

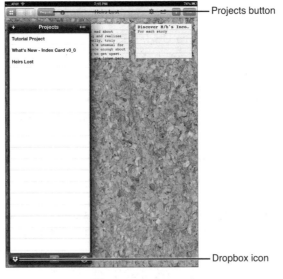

Projects button

Dropbox icon

FIGURE 18.9

The Projects menu lists all the projects in the app.

5. Tap the Dropbox icon at the bottom of the Projects menu, then select your project from the Copy from Dropbox menu. Your project is copied to the main Projects list and automatically opens in the Corkboard.

Once the project opens in the Index Card app, shown in Figure 18.10, you can edit cards, change the order of the cards, and add new cards. When you have finished your work, take the following steps to update the Dropbox folder and then sync with Scrivener:

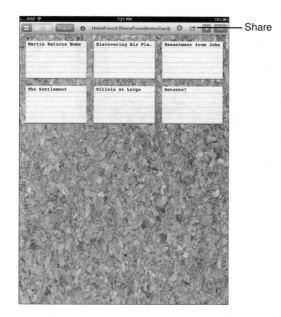

FIGURE 18.10

The Index Card app resembles the Corkboard in Scrivener.

1. Click on the Share icon at the top of the screen.

2. Click Copy to Dropbox from the pop-up menu.

3. In the Copy to Dropbox screen, shown in Figure 18.11, swipe the Export Notes switch to On in order to enable text changes to sync.

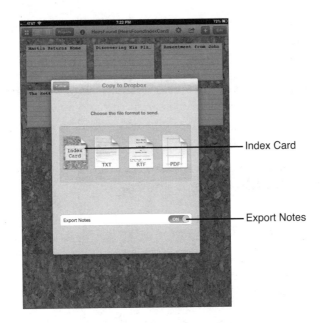

FIGURE 18.11

Use the Copy to Dropbox tool to save your changes to your Dropbox folder.

4. Tap the Index Card button to save the file to your Dropbox folder. Click Replace when prompted to overwrite the file or save using a different filename.

5. When the file transfer is complete, open your project in Scrivener.

6. Choose File, Sync, with Index Card for iOS from the menu.

7. In the Sync with Index Card for the iPad dialog box, click the Update Collection from Index Card file to update your project.

8. In the Open dialog box, select the file you edited and then click Open.

The collection in your Scrivener project reflects the changes you made in Index Card. Changes in the order of the documents appear in the collection, but not the Binder. If you want to update the Binder to sort in the order of the collection, press Cmd-A in the collection to select all the documents; then right-click on the selection to open the context menu and choose Move To from the menu. Choose the folder into which you want to move the documents. The Binder then reflects the new positions for the documents.

The next time you want to use Index Card, update your collection and then select File, Sync, with Index Card for iOS. Click the Create or Update Index Card File and overwrite the old .indexcard file with the new collection.

THE ABSOLUTE MINIMUM

The following are the highlights from this chapter:

- Scrivener projects are cross-platform. You can work on the same project on a Mac or in Windows.

- Dropbox makes it easy to share projects across platforms and devices, as long as you take precautions to prevent corrupting the file.

- On the Mac, sync with an external editor to be able to work on individual files in a third-party editor and return them to your project.

- Use the Sync with External Editor feature in conjunction with Dropbox to edit files on your iPad.

- Index Card for iPad and iPhone allows you to change the order of project documents and edit text on your iOS device, then sync back to your Scrivener project using Dropbox.

19

COMPILING YOUR COMPLETED WORK

After you've sweat blood and tears over your writing project, you are finally ready to produce a completed work. Before you can hold a printed thesis in your hand, submit a manuscript to your publisher, or upload an e-book to Amazon, however, you first need to compile all your separate project documents into a cohesive whole.

As fascinated as many new Scrivener users are about features such as project templates, they are terrified about tackling the Compile settings. This chapter attempts to break the process down into chunks and build up to a complete understanding, much the way Scrivener itself works.

Understanding the Compile Process

When you learned how to set up an external folder in Chapter 18, "Taking Scrivener Out and About," your project files remained the same, but you instructed Scrivener to export them into something new that could be used by other applications. In essence, the compile process is more of the same. Your project remains unchanged, but you instruct Scrivener to gather all of the files you select into a format that can be used in another way. For many types of projects, final editing and formatting are done in a word processor or screenplay application, so you can fine-tune the compiled document before printing or submitting the file. For others, you can print a hard copy directly from Scrivener.

To begin the compile process, choose File, Compile from the menu. You can also press Option-Cmd-E on the Mac or Ctrl+Shift+E in Windows. The first time you open the Compile dialog box, shown in Figure 19.1, it opens in a summary tab on the Mac or a condensed set of options in Windows. Once you have set all the compile options for your project, as you learn throughout this chapter, this Summary view is a good way to quickly recompile your project.

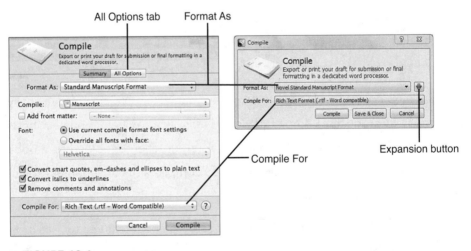

FIGURE 19.1

The Compile dialog box provides a Summary view to quickly compile your project.

At its most basic level, you compile a project following these steps:

1. Choose a compile format from the Format As drop-down menu.

2. Select an output format from the Compile For drop-down menu.

3. Click the Compile button.

This is only the beginning of your compile options, but that's a good place to start.

Choosing a Compile Format

The first decision you need to make is the format you require for your finished project. This is known as the *compile format*. The options available in the Format As drop-down menu depend upon which version of Scrivener you are using and the project template you chose for your project. Some types of projects may offer one or more variations, such as Non-Fiction Manuscript Format and Non-Fiction (with Subheads). The following lists the most common options for both platforms:

 NOTE The Format As drop-down menu list is a bit different for the Mac and Windows platforms, so some formats appear only on one platform or the other, and the menu options may be in a different order.

- **Original**: This format is the standard setting. It preserves your Draft folder without any additional formatting, making it a good place to start if you want to create your own custom Compile settings from scratch. On the Mac, this option appears at the top of the menu if you created your project from the Blank project template, but moves down the menu if you used a different template.

- **E-Book**: This option prepares to compile the project as an e-book, with containers treated as chapters and documents as scenes or sections. See Chapter 20, "Creating E-Books," for more information about e-book projects.

- **Enumerated Outline**: This format lists the titles of each document and a number to indicate its order in your project hierarchy. Subfolders and subdocuments are indented to indicate the structure of the project.

- **Non-Fiction Manuscript Format**: This format is good for academic and other nonfiction work. It treats folders and top-level file groups as chapters. Top-level files are titled, while those below the top level are untitled.

- **Paperback Novel**: This format is designed for creating a PDF file to submit to a print-on-demand (POD) service, such as CreateSpace. This preset is only available on the Mac.

- **Plain Text Screenplay (Celtx, Movie Magic)**: This screenplay format is intended to produce a plain text file that is compatible with screenplay applications such as Celtx and Movie Magic. This preset is only available on the Mac.

- **Proof Copy**: This format creates a double-spaced draft copy of your project so you can edit it or distribute it to co-workers for feedback. It adds a disclaimer after each chapter title and in the header that reads *Not for Distribution*. This format treats folders as chapters, and everything else includes the title of the item. This preset is only available on the Mac.

- **Script or Screenplay**: This screenplay format is intended to produce a file that is compatible with Final Draft version 8 or higher using the FDX format. This preset is only available on the Mac.

- **Standard Manuscript Format**: This format prepares your project for submission of a manuscript. It double-spaces your text, converts the font to Courier 12-point, and adds page numbers and scene separators.

- **Synopses and Titles**: This format is similar to the Enumerated Outline format, but synopses are added to each item. This format does not include hierarchical numbering. In Windows, the Outliner preset is similar to the Mac's Synopses and Titles preset.

- **Synopsis Outline**: This format is a good choice if you are writing a novel and trying to get a feel for how the scenes within each chapter flow or if you are writing an academic or nonfiction work and want to see how your supporting sections flow in order within a major heading. This option indents items to indicate their position within the project hierarchy. Files below the top level do not include their titles. This preset is only available on the Mac.

- **Custom**: This format contains your current Compile settings.

THE CREATIVE PROCESS: WINNING NATIONAL NOVEL WRITING MONTH

If you're using a Mac and created your project using the NaNoWriMo project template, the NaNoWriMo (Obfuscated) format preset appears in the Format As menu. This format obfuscates your manuscript by performing letter-to-letter substitutions of your text while retaining the same word count, and then outputs the file in plain text format so you can upload it to the NaNoWriMo site for verification. If you participate in NaNoWriMo but use a different project template to prepare your manuscript, click the Format As drop-down menu and select Manage Compile Format Presets. In the Manage Compile Format Presets dialog box, select NaNoWriMo (Obfuscated), and then click OK. You can then choose this option from the Format As menu. You can use the Manage Compile Format Presets options to select any of the other hidden presets, as well.

In Windows, import the NaNoWriMo (Obfuscated) compile preset using the Load Preset option and then import it into Scrivener.

To enter your obfuscated compilation into the word count validation tool on the NaNoWriMo site (http://www.nanowrimo.org), choose Plain Text (.txt) as your output format, then open the compilation file and copy and paste it into the validation tool. You must create an account and set up a novel on the NaNoWriMo site before you can validate.

Selecting an Output Format

Once you select a compile format, you need to choose an *output format*. Whereas the compile format specifies the type of product to compile, the output format specifies how that product is distributed. If you want a printed hard copy of your project, choose Print. If you want to disseminate or submit your project electronically or fine-tune it in another application, choose an appropriate file format.

 CAUTION   Do not let the terminology confuse you. Select your compile format from the Format As drop-down menu. Select your output format from the Compile For drop-down menu.

As with the compile formats, your output format options depend upon your Scrivener version, but most of the following options are available on both platforms:

- **Print**: This option compiles your project and sends it to your printer. It does not save the compiled project in a file.

   TIP   On the Mac, choose this format to quickly preview your compiled document with the current settings, then click the PDF button in the Print dialog box and select Open PDF in Preview to see how your document appears with the current Compile settings.

- **PDF**: This format saves the compiled project as a Portable Document Format (PDF). This format cannot be edited, but it is accessible from almost any computer platform or device. In Windows, choose this format if you want to quickly preview your compiled document with the current Compile settings.

- **Rich Text (.rtf—Word Compatible)**: This format preserves images, formatted lists, comments, footnotes, and tables in the compiled file. This is the best option if you plan to open the file in Word or another word processor because it is widely compatible and preserves your project's formatting integrity.

- **Rich Text with Attachments (.rtfd)**: This option is only available on the Mac. You should only select this option if you need to open the compiled document in an Apple-proprietary application such as Pages or TextEdit. It is not compatible with other word processors or on other computer platforms.

TIP If you use Pages, save in either Rich Text with Attachments or Microsoft Word (.docx) format. If you use headers, page breaks, or footnotes, you lose some formatting options, but you can edit the document in Pages to reformat it. Alternatively, save in Rich Text (.rtf—Word Compatible), open the file in another word processor, and then resave it as a Word .doc file. You can then open that file in Pages. If you are looking for a free word processor to use as the go-between, try OpenOffice.

- **Microsoft Word 97-2004 (.doc):** This format preserves the same settings as the Rich Text (.rtf—Word Compatible) option, but with the .doc extension. When you compile to this format on a Mac, you are prompted to install improved converters, which are capable of retaining most of your formatting.

CAUTION If you do not install the improved converters on the Mac platform, Scrivener uses Apple's Microsoft Word converters, which lose formatting such as bullets, footnotes, and comments.

- **Microsoft Word (.docx):** This is the current XML-based Word format. As with its predecessor, you are prompted to install improved converters to preserve your formatting. In Windows, this format is only available if you have Word 2007 or higher installed and have enabled the Use Microsoft Word or Open Office for Doc and Docx Conversions option in the Import/Export tab of the Options window.

TIP If you need to save your document in .doc or .docx format in order to submit your work electronically to a professor or editor, another approach is to compile your project into a Rich Text (.rtf) file in order to retain your formatting, then open the file in Word and save as a .doc or .docx file. I prefer this approach because it avoids formatting issues between Scrivener and Word since the document does not have to go through a conversion process. Many publishers now accept .doc/.docx submissions and use this format during the revision process.

- **OpenOffice (.odt):** This option saves the file in the native OpenOffice format. As with .doc and .docx, you are prompted to install the improved converters. If you encounter problems, use the Rich Text (.rtf) format, instead.

- **Plain Text (.txt):** This format removes all of your formatting, but creates a plain text file that can be accessed from almost any application on almost any platform or device.

- **Final Draft 8 (.fdx)**: This option is used to transfer scripts to Final Draft. It saves synopses as scene summaries on the Mac and preserves scene titles and custom script element formatting.

- **Final Draft 5-7 Converter (.fcf)**: This option is only available on the Mac and is intended to save a file that is compatible with earlier versions of Final Draft. You may lose formatting with this choice, as this format only supports basic screenplay formatting.

- **ePub eBook (.epub)**: This format creates an ePub file that is compatible with a wide range of e-readers.

 TIP If you save an e-book in ePub format, you can convert it to other formats using Calibre, a free, multiplatform e-book management application. Visit http://www.calibre-ebook.com for more information.

- **Kindle eBook (.mobi)**: This option requires Amazon KindleGen. It generates an e-book for reading on Amazon Kindle devices and apps.

- **iBooks Author Chapters (.docx)**: Use this format to save each section of your book as an individual .docx file, which can then be imported into iBooks Author to convert to .iba format. This format is only available on the Mac.

- **Web Page (.html)**: This format creates a single HTML file to publish on a website.

- **eXtensible Web Page (.xhtml)**: This option is only available in Windows. It is similar to the HTML option, but takes advantage of XHTML code.

- **Web Archive (.webarchive)**: This option is similar to HTML, but it saves the project into Apple's .webarchive format, with images bundled into a single file. This option is only available on the Mac, and can only be opened by Apple's Safari browser and some other Mac OS X apps.

- **PostScript (.ps)**: This format is only available in Windows. It creates a single file in a format commonly used in design and publishing apps.

- **MultiMarkdown (.md)**: Use this option or one of the other MultiMarkdown files to export a plain text MultiMarkdown file or a file formatted with MultiMarkdown support.

NOTE MultiMarkdown is a plain text markup language that allows you to separate the content and structure of your document from the formatting of the document. Coverage of MultiMarkdown is beyond the scope of this book, but you can find information about it on the Literature & Latte forum (http://www.literatureandlatte.com/forum) and Fletcher Penney's MultiMarkdown website (http://www.fletcherpenney.net/multimarkdown/).

 TIP This list of output formats may be intimidating, so let's cut to the chase with some best practices. If you want to print your compilation directly from Scrivener, choose Print. If you want to access the file from a word processor other than Pages, choose Rich Text (`.rtf`) format. If you are using Pages, output in Rich Text with Attachments (`.rtfd`) or Microsoft Word (`.docx`) format.

If you are a screenwriter or playwright using Final Draft, output in the Final Draft format that is compatible with your application. If you use Movie Magic Screenwriter or Celtx, save as plain text (`.txt`). If you use Montage, save in either Rich Text or plain text.

 NOTE If you are compiling an e-book, see Chapter 20 for details on formatting and compiling your project for the best results.

Compiling the Project Using Compile Presets

If you want to compile based solely on these basic criteria and presets, you can generally get good results. You give up control over fonts, chapter numbering, front matter, headers and footers, and other formatting options, but you will get an idea of what Scrivener can do without any further intervention.

In Windows, to complete the compile process, simply click the Compile button in the condensed Compile dialog box after choosing your compile and output options. In the Save As dialog box, enter a filename, choose where you want to save the file, and click Save.

On the Mac, to complete the compile process based only on the summary options:

1. Open the Compile dialog box, if it is not already open (File, Compile or Option-Cmd-E).

2. Select the compile format from the Format As drop-down menu.

3. Select the output format from the Compile As drop-down menu.

4. Choose a compile group from the Compile drop-down menu. You can choose to compile any of the following, as you can see from the example in Figure 19.2:

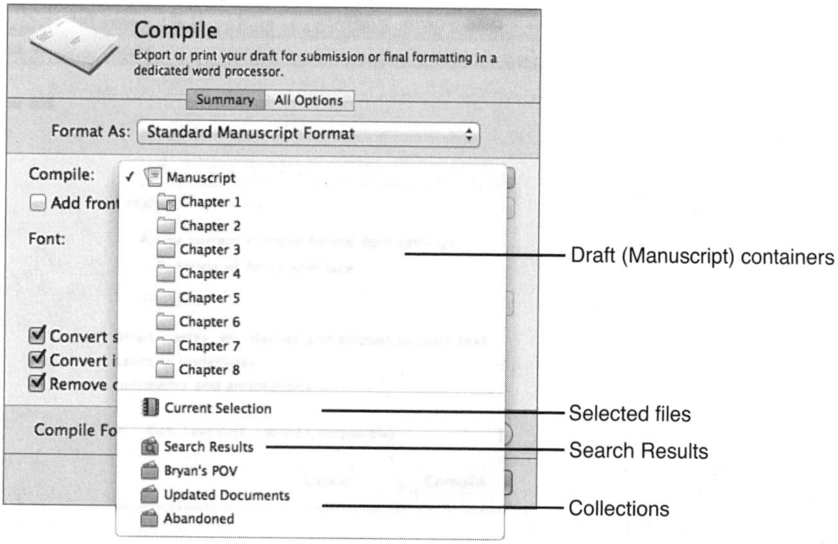

FIGURE 19.2

On the Mac, choose which items to compile from the Summary tab of the Compile dialog box.

- Your entire Draft folder
- Individual containers within the Draft folder
- Selected files in the Binder
- A collection or search results

5. You can opt to Add Front Matter by clicking the check box and then selecting a document from the drop-down menu.

6. In relevant formats, choose whether to use the current compile format font settings or to override any font settings and replace it with a font selected from the drop-down menu. This option is not available for plain text, scriptwriting, or e-book formats.

7. Select or deselect the options to Convert Smart Quotes, Em-Dashes, and Ellipses to Plain Text, Convert Italics to Underlines, and Remove Comments and Annotations.

8. Click Compile.

9. In the Export dialog box, enter a filename, choose where you want to save the file, and click Export. If you selected the Print option from the Compile For drop-down menu, the Print dialog box opens instead of the Export dialog box.

Using the Compile Window

Of course, while the compile process can be as simple as making a couple selections from drop-down menus and clicking a button, this is just the tip of the iceberg. There are many other settings and options that you can use to determine which items are included and the formatting of your compiled project. Once you select your Compile settings, they are saved with your project.

 NOTE Compile settings are also saved with project templates. If you want to apply a preformatted compile preset or a custom preset to projects based on a particular template, follow the instructions in this chapter to configure the Compile settings before saving the project template. For more information about project templates, refer to Chapter 14, "Creating and Using Project Templates."

On the Mac, click the All Options tab in the Compile dialog box. In Windows, click the Expansion button to the right of the Format As drop-down menu, as shown in Figure 19.1. The options available in the Compilation Options list on the left, as shown in Figures 19.3 and 19.4, depend on the output format you selected. The right pane contains the settings for the selected option tab.

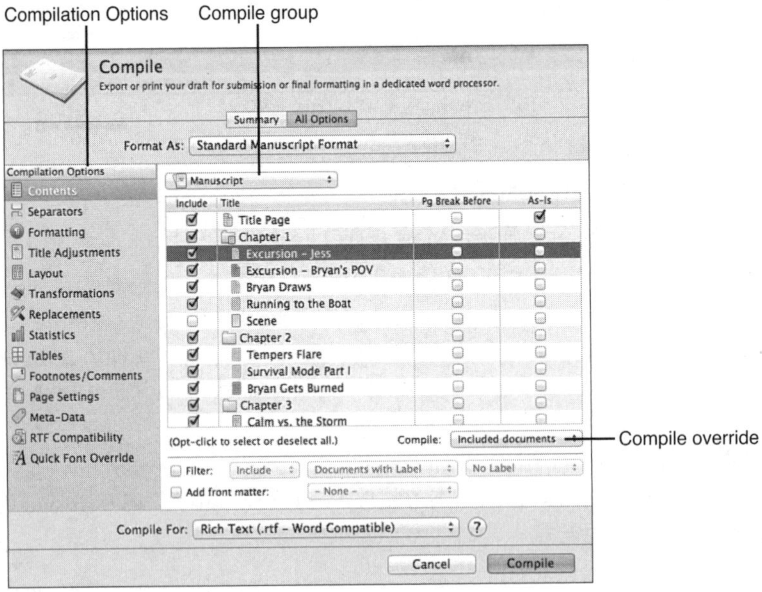

FIGURE 19.3

The All Options tab in the Compile dialog box on the Mac displays a list of compilation options and settings.

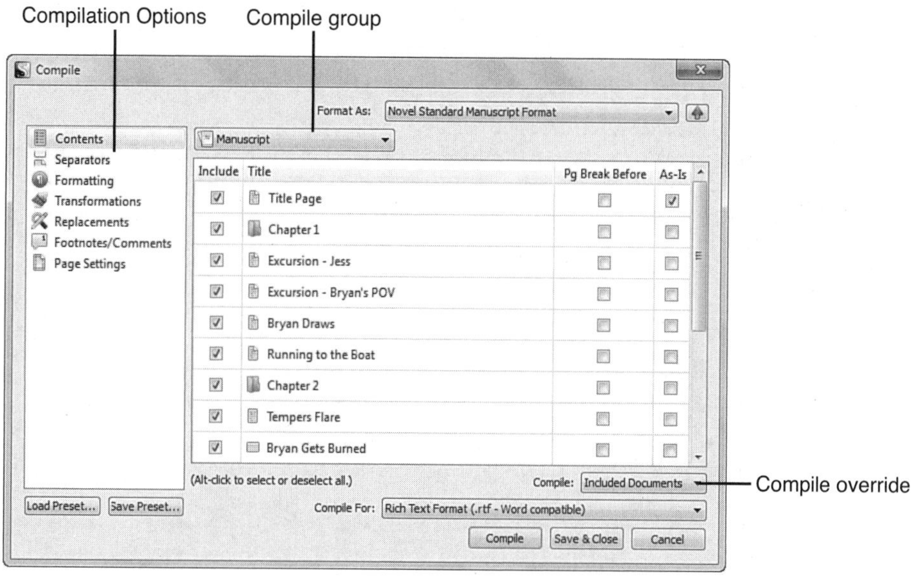

FIGURE 19.4

The expanded Compile dialog box in Windows allows you to customize your Compile settings.

> **NOTE** This chapter is not intended to be a comprehensive guide to all of the options in the Compile dialog box. To learn more about some of the advanced or less-common options, turn to some of the resources listed in the Introduction. I also blog about some of these features on my website at http://www.jenniferkettell.com.

Choosing the Contents to Compile

The Contents tab in the Compile dialog box, shown in Figures 19.3 and 19.4, displays the entire contents of your Draft folder by default. The compile group drop-down menu allows you to select from containers within the Draft folder, the current Binder selection (Mac only), the search results, or a collection. The Contents pane displays all of the files and folders in the compile group.

If you select only a portion of the Draft folder on the Mac, another menu appears to the right of the compile group field, as shown in Figure 19.5. The Compile Group Options drop-down contains the following two options, each of which can be independently enabled or disabled:

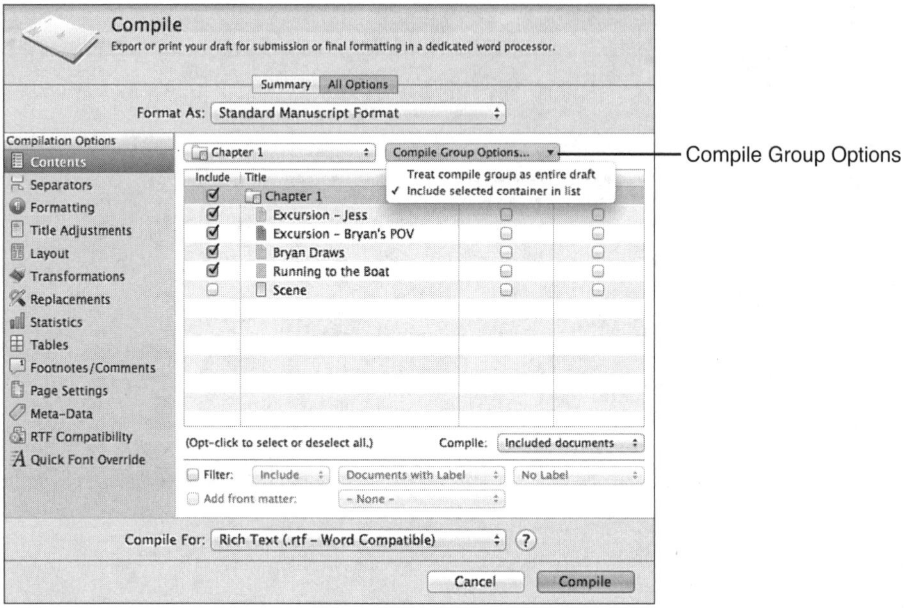

FIGURE 19.5

Select how to treat a selected subgroup of the Draft folder from the Compile Group Options drop-down menu.

- **Treat Compile Group as Entire Draft**: When this option is selected, the compile group is treated as if it were the entire project. Think of the compile group container as a designated Draft folder, with its subdocuments following in the project hierarchy. Chapter numbers begin at 1, and any other level-related compile formatting is assigned accordingly.

- **Include Selected Container in List**: This is the default option. When it is selected, the selected container is included in the compile group. If you disable this option, the compile group only includes the items beneath the selected container. If this option is selected by itself, the hierarchy of the project remains unchanged. If you select this option in conjunction with the Treat Compile Group as Entire Draft option, however, all of the items in the compile group shift up by a level, as items that were at Level 2 in the hierarchy are then considered to be Level 1 in the compile group.

The levels of the hierarchy are important in formatting the compiled output, as is explained in the "Formatting the Compilation" section later in this chapter.

Selecting Items in the Compile Group

The Include check box is linked to the Include in Compile option in the Inspector. To change these options, select or deselect items from the Contents pane by clicking the Include check box to the left of each item. To select or deselect all of the items in the pane, Option-click (Alt-click in Windows) the Include check box. As an example, if you want to compile only the first three chapters of your novel to submit a book proposal, choose your Draft (Manuscript) folder as the compile group, then select the first three chapters and deselect the remaining chapters.

 CAUTION If you select a container in the Contents pane, the items within the container are not included unless you select them, as well.

To the right of the item title are two additional check boxes:

- **Pg Break Before**: This option links to the Page Break Before option in the Inspector, and it inserts a page break before the checked document. Use this option primarily for title pages, a glossary, or a table of contents—documents that generally appear only once in a project.

 NOTE For chapter and section breaks, use the Separators tab in the Compile dialog box instead of the Page Break Before option.

- **As-Is**: This option is linked to the Compile As-Is option in the Inspector, and it instructs the Formatting pane of the Compile dialog box to ignore this document.

By default, items that are selected in the Include column are included in the compile. The Compile Override drop-down menu in the lower-right corner of the dialog box can alter these settings as follows:

- **Included Documents**: This is the default behavior and includes only selected documents in the compilation.

- **Excluded Documents**: This reverses the default behavior and includes only those documents that are not selected in the compilation. This option is helpful if you have added notes or other materials within the Draft folder that you do not want included in the default compile. This option allows you to compile those items separately.

- **All**: This ignores the Include in Draft selection and compiles all of the items in the compile group.

TIP A professor using Scrivener to generate course materials is an example of a good time to use the compile override options. Select your handouts and assignment sheets to Include in Compile in the Inspector when creating the items. Do not set your lecture notes with the Include in Compile option. Print the course materials for your students using the default Included Documents option. Then return to the Compile dialog box and select the Excluded Documents compile override to print just your lecture notes or the All compile override to print a complete set of course materials and lecture notes for yourself.

Filtering the Contents of a Compile Group (Mac Only)

On the Mac, you can filter the compile group to select files that match specific criteria. Using the professor's course material example, you can limit the compilation to files about a specific topic. For a novel, you can limit the compilation to files relating to a specific subplot, as shown in Figure 19.6.

CAUTION Filters require preplanning in the main Scrivener interface. If you plan to filter by label or status, you must create and assign label or status values to achieve the desired results. If you want to filter by a collection, you must create the collection prior to opening the Compile dialog box. Likewise, if you want to filter by a selection of items in the Binder, search results, or a collection, you need to preselect those items before opening the Compile dialog box.

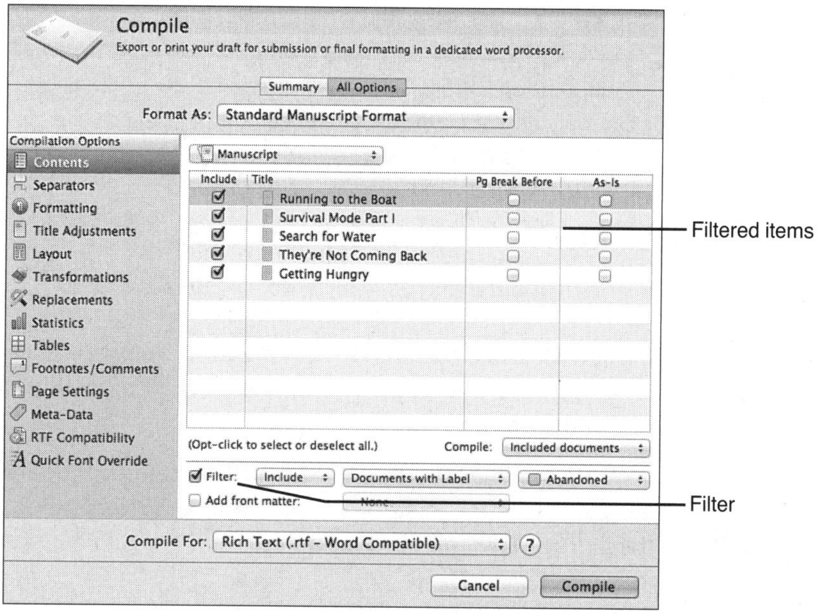

FIGURE 19.6

Use a filter to narrow down the items within a compile group.

To apply a filter:

1. Select the Filter check box.

2. In the first Filter drop-down menu, choose to Include or Exclude the filtered documents.

3. In the second drop-down menu, select the criteria for the filter from the following options:

   - **Documents with Label**: This is the default setting. Documents containing the label you select in the third drop-down menu are included or excluded from the compilation (based on your selection in step 2).

   - **Documents with Status**: Documents containing the status you select in the third drop-down menu are included or excluded from the compilation.

   - **Documents in Collection**: Documents within the collection you select in the third drop-down menu are included or excluded from the compilation.

NOTE Filtering a compile group by collection is different from selecting a collection as the compile group itself. When you select a collection as a compile group, text items in the collection from outside the Draft folder are included in the compile, and the compile group is a flat list without any hierarchy of documents. When you filter by a collection, however, only items in the collection that are also in the selected compile group are included or excluded by the filter. Also, the filtered documents retain their order in the hierarchy of the compile group.

- **Current Selection**: Documents that you select in the Binder, search results, or a collection prior to opening the Compile dialog box are included or excluded from the compilation.

4. Select a value from the third drop-down menu. The items on the menu vary depending on your selection in step 3. If you choose Current Selection in step 3, the third drop-down menu disappears.

Adding Front Matter (Mac Only)

Front matter items are documents such as the title page, author bio, and acknowledgments that may appear at the beginning of a book. You may require different front matter elements in different situations. If you self-publish, for example, you may want to include a static table of contents with page numbers in the PDF you send to a Print on Demand service, but a table of contents composed of links for the e-book file you load onto Amazon. Or you might want to include a set of review questions for copies of your work that you send to your critique group or beta readers, but a synopsis and title page for the copy you submit to an editor.

Some of the Scrivener for Mac project templates, such as the Novel template, include a Front Matter folder with subfolders and items for different publishing scenarios. You can customize these documents or create your own.

NOTE If your project does not include a Front Matter folder, you can create one. The folder does not need to be titled Front Matter, but this does help you remember its purpose as you work on your project and ensures that the folder appears at the top of the list when selecting from the Front Matter drop-down menu.

TIP You can only select one option from the Front Matter drop-down list, so if you need to add multiple documents, group them in a subfolder in your Front Matter folder prior to opening the Compile dialog box.

The Add Front Matter option on the Contents tab of the Compile dialog box lets you select these items from outside your Draft folder. You can then create presets for different types of compilations that automatically call up the proper front matter materials for each situation.

 NOTE Learn about how to create compile presets later in this chapter.

 CAUTION The Front Matter feature is disabled if you select a subgroup of the Draft folder as the compile group and disable the Treat Compile Group as Entire Draft compile group option. It is also disabled if your compile group is based on the current selection of documents.

To add front matter to your compilation:

1. Select the Add Front Matter check box.

2. In the Front Matter drop-down menu, shown in Figure 19.7, select the subfolder appropriate for the desired output format. The documents within the folder are added at the top of the items listed in the Contents pane.

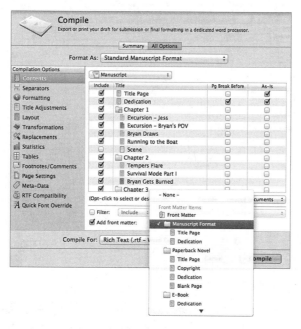

FIGURE 19.7

Adding front matter from a non-Draft folder makes it easy to customize your compilations for multiple formats.

3. Choose the Page Break Before and As-Is settings for each document that has been added to the Contents pane.

Formatting Separators Between Documents

Your project is composed of multiple files and folders. The Separators tab, shown in Figure 19.8, instructs Scrivener on how to transition between these items as it creates the compiled file. Separators automatically insert spaces, page breaks, or symbols between the items based on the options you select in this tab.

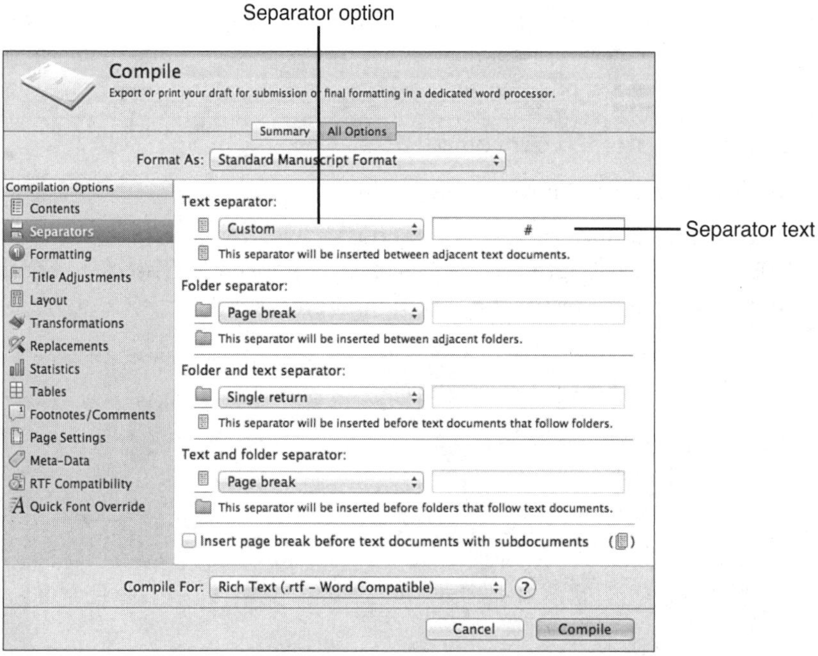

FIGURE 19.8

The Separators tab controls the transition between files and folders in the compile group.

 NOTE If you select the Page Break Before option in the Contents tab, it overrides the separators options for that item.

To understand the transition between items, think of a manuscript project. The manuscript is divided into parts, chapters, and scenes. The Draft folder contains subfolders for each part, and each part contains subfolders for each chapter. Those chapters, in turn, contain files for each scene.

NOTE   File groups are treated as files. This means that the transition between a file group parent and a child text file is governed by the Text Separator option.

There are four types of transitions between items:

- **Text Separator**: This option specifies the transition between two text files. In the previous example, the text separator specifies the type of separator used between scenes in the manuscript. Scenes are commonly separated by one or more pound symbols (#) or an empty line.

- **Folder Separator**: This option specifies the transition between two folders, such as a Part folder followed by a Chapter subfolder. These items are generally separated by a page break.

- **Folder and Text Separator**: This option specifies the transition between a folder and a text file (or file group). In the manuscript example, this determines the separator used between the chapter folder and the first scene in the chapter. These items are usually separated by a single return so as to make the transition invisible to the reader or an empty line to separate the chapter heading from the first line of the first scene in the chapter.

- **Text and Folder Separator**: This option specifies the transition between a text file and a folder, such as the last scene in a chapter and the beginning of a new chapter or part. This is generally done with a page break.

To set the separators, for each of the four types of transitions, select a separator option from the following:

- **Single Return**: Inserts a single return between items, making a seamless transition from one item to the next.

- **Empty Line**: Adds two returns between items, leaving an empty line between the items.

- **Page Break**: Inserts a page break between items.

- **Custom**: Inserts the characters or symbols you enter in the separator text box between items. This option automatically centers the custom characters and adds a single return before and after the characters so they appear on their own line.

TIP File groups are treated as files. This means that the transition between a file group parent and a child text file is governed by the Text Separator option. Scrivener for the Mac contains an additional option at the bottom of the Separators tab. Select Insert Page Break Before Text Documents with Subdocuments if you want Scrivener to insert a page break before all file groups. You can use this to approximate the same effect as choosing a page break for the folder separator and text and folder separator if you use file groups instead of folders in your project.

Formatting the Compilation

The Formatting tab of the Compile dialog box, shown in Figure 19.9, contains settings for the structure and appearance of your compiled document. This tab is divided into two sections: the Structure and Content table and the Formatting editor.

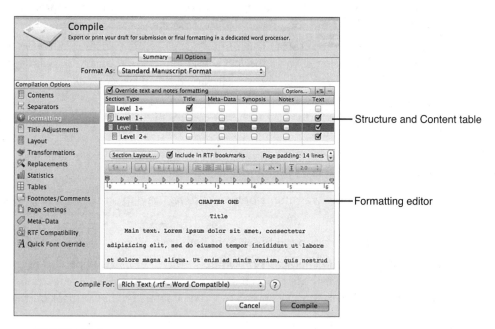

FIGURE 19.9

The Formatting tab controls the structure and appearance of the compilation.

The Formatting tab tends to cause the most confusion for Scrivener users. As with the rest of the compile process, taking this concept in parts helps lay the foundation so you can understand the whole process.

Understanding Level Hierarchy

The Structure and Content table uses the Binder structure to group items into a hierarchy and assign attributes to each level. Level 1 files and folders are at the top of the hierarchy. Level 2 files and folders are contained within Level 1 items. Level 3 files and folders are contained within Level 2 items, and so on.

For example, a novel may have parts (Level 1), chapters within those parts (Level 2), and scenes within each chapter (Level 3). A different novel may only have chapters (Level 1) and scenes (Level 2).

Interestingly, the best way to understand the level hierarchy is with a complex example rather than a simple one. Figure 19.10 shows the structure of this *Scrivener Absolute Beginner's Guide*, which has multiple levels.

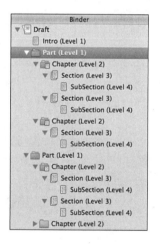

FIGURE 19.10

This is the hierarchical structure of the Scrivener Absolute Beginner's Guide.

Each level in a project hierarchy can contain a mix of folders, files, and file groups. In the example in Figure 19.10, the Introduction file is at the same level as the Part folders. Although their level is the same, the Structure and Content table allows you to set different options for each type of item at each level so that you can apply different formatting to them. The Introduction and the Part folders, for example, can be formatted differently while remaining at the same hierarchical level.

Establishing the Structure and Content Table

In the Structure and Content table, each Level item affects items at that level or below it, signified by the plus (+) sign following the level number. Thus, a Level 1+ folder specifies how all folders at the top level or below are formatted. To add a level to the structure:

1. Select the row with the type of item you want to add to the Structure and Content table. If you want to add another level of folders, for example, select the Level 1+ folder. If you want to add another level of text documents, select the Level 1+ text document.

2. Click the Add Another Formatting Level button.

Figure 19.11 shows the Structure and Content table for the hierarchy established in Figure 19.10.

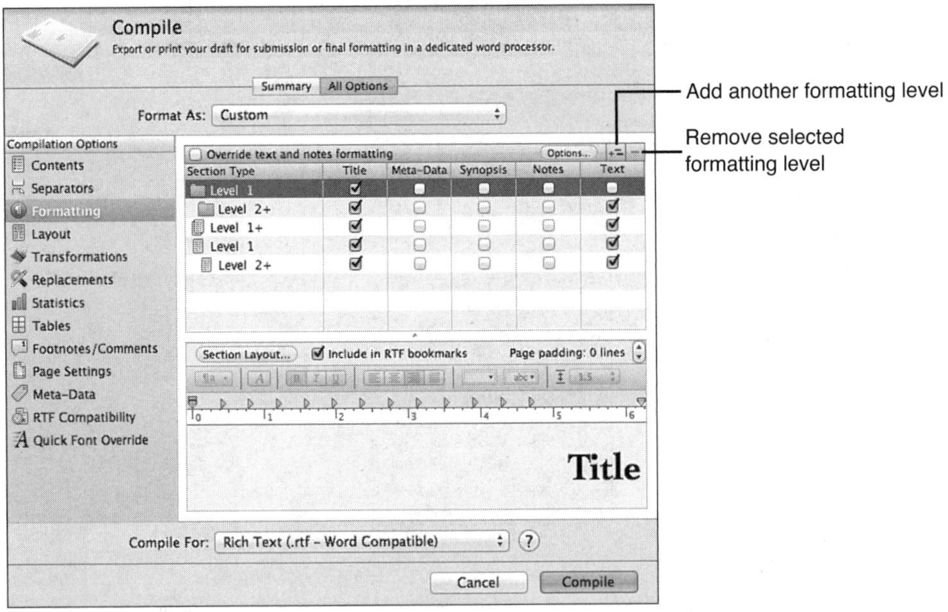

FIGURE 19.11

The Structure and Content table displays the level settings for the items in a project.

When you add a formatting level, the lowest level for each item type is followed by the plus (+) sign to indicate it is the lowest level of the formatting hierarchy and its formatting affects all items of that type below that level. A Level 1 text document only affects text documents at Level 1, whereas a Level 2+ text document affects text documents at Level 2 or lower, and so on.

The way to determine whether you need to add a level to the table or if it can be accommodated by a higher-level catchall is to think about how you want each level of your compilation formatted. This book, for example, has parts, chapters, sections, and subsections. Let's say you want the following layout for these items:

- Introduction, in a Level 1 file in the Binder, formatted with the Introduction title in a 24-point font, and the text in a 12-point font

- Parts, in Level 1 folders, formatted with just the part number and title on their own page in a 36-point font, right-justified

- Chapters, in Level 2 folders with text, formatted with the title in a 24-point font and text introducing the purpose of the chapter in a 14-point font

- Sections, in Level 3 file groups, formatted with the section heading in an 18-point font and text explaining a major concept in an 11-point font

- Subsections, in Level 4 files, formatted with the subsection heading in a 14-point font and text explaining a minor concept in an 11-point font

Although both Parts and Chapters appear in folders, the formatting is different for each, so you need two distinct levels of folders. The Introduction and Subsections are both files and both contain a heading and text, but the formatting of those components is different. There are three levels separating those two items in your hierarchy; however, because there are no text documents at those interim levels, you can create a Level 1 file to format the Introduction and a Level 2+ file to accommodate any other files at a lower hierarchy (of which there are only the Level 4 documents). There is only one level of file groups, so you can set the Level 1+ file group item knowing it only applies to the file groups you have at Level 3 in your hierarchy.

 TIP It may help to sketch out the hierarchy of your project on a sheet of paper or type it into a non-Draft document. For each item type at each level, list the formatting as demonstrated above. Add notes for how you want chapter or section headings to appear and which items should display the title of the scene or section; this will help you later in this chapter.

If your document is complex, such as this example, there are often multiple ways to configure the Structure and Content table to get the results you want. Don't let this table confuse you unnecessarily. If you create an overly complex Structure and Content table and realize you can get the same result in a simplified manner, select the level you want to delete, then click the Remove Selected Formatting Level button.

TIP To provide a much simpler example, if you have a manuscript with only folders for each chapter and text documents for each scene within a chapter, you only need to set a Level 1+ folder and a Level 1+ file.

Selecting Content for Structure Levels

Once you have laid out the structure of the compilation, you are ready to select the content for each level. The Structure and Content table contains the following five elements from which to select:

- **Title**: Displays the title of the item

NOTE Chapter numbering is handled in the Section Layout, explained below.

- **Meta-Data**: Displays the meta-data for the item—the created and modified dates for the item, the label and status values, assigned keywords, and custom meta-data
- **Synopsis**: Adds the synopsis for the item
- **Notes**: Adds the Document Notes from the Inspector
- **Text**: Includes the text of the item

The meta-data, synopsis, and notes elements allow you to structure a compiled outline or add this information to a draft of your project. If you are compiling a manuscript, nonfiction work, or another type of completed project, you most likely want to focus on the title and text elements.

In a typical manuscript, your chapters are formatted with a Level 1+ folder. If the chapters have titles, select the title element. Scenes are formatted with Level 1+ files with the text element selected.

Remember that folders can contain text. If you want to begin each chapter with a quotation, for example, type it in the chapter folder in the Editor before entering the Compile dialog box, and then select both the title and text elements in the Structure and Content table. The quotation appears below the title of the chapter in your compiled manuscript.

Formatting Content Elements

The final step in configuring the Formatting tab is to specify the formatting for each level in the Structure and Content table. The Formatting editor beneath the Structure and Content table allows you to change the appearance for each level of content. In Windows, this area is a preview pane.

As shown in Figure 19.12, the Formatting editor shows how the format of the selected elements appears in the compilation. If you selected the title element for a level, for example, a title element appears in the Formatting editor.

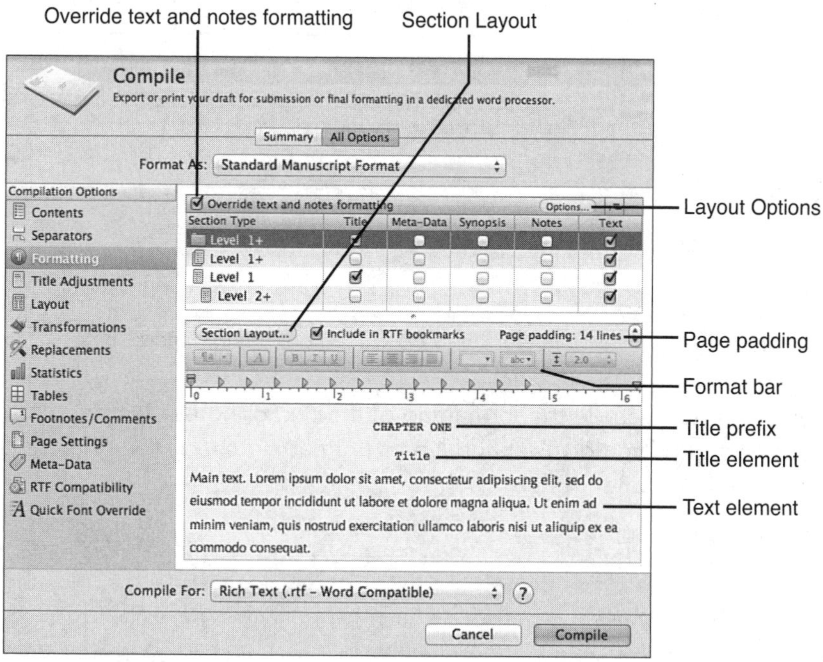

FIGURE 19.12

The Formatting editor controls the appearance of the content elements of your compilation.

The Format bar in the Formatting editor is similar to the Format bar and Ruler in the Editor. On the Mac, to change the appearance of each content element, click inside the element in the Formatting editor and then use the Format bar to modify it. There is no need to select the entire element because you are modifying the traits of the entire element, not a portion of it.

In Windows, click the Modify button to open the Formatting dialog box and modify elements, as shown in Figure 19.13. When you are finished, click OK to return to the Compile dialog box.

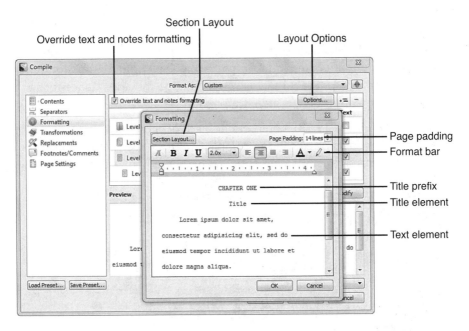

FIGURE 19.13

In Windows, click the Modify button to open the Formatting dialog box.

If you want to override the formatting of the text or notes elements, you must first select the Override Text and Notes Formatting check box at the top of the Structure and Content table.

 NOTE If you need a logical explanation of the need to override the text and notes formatting, consider that the other content elements are unformatted meta-data, including the title. Thus, the Formatting editor is adding formatting to elements that previously had none. The text and notes elements, however, were formatted in the Editor and Inspector, so you must make a conscious decision to override those settings.

If you were writing in 14-point Trebuchet MS in the Editor, you can change the font in your compilation to 12-point Times New Roman or Courier for submitting a completed manuscript to an editor. To do this, take the following steps:

1. Click the Override Text and Notes Formatting check box.

2. Select the relevant row in the Structure and Content table.

3. Click in the Text or Notes element of the Formatting editor. In Windows, you must click the Modify button first to open the Formatting editor.

4. Click the Font button on the Format bar to open the Fonts dialog box.

5. Select the new font and font size; then close the dialog box.

TIP In Windows, if you click the Override Text and Notes Formatting check box before you click the Modify button, you can format all of the elements in the Formatting dialog box at the same time instead of making repeated visits to this dialog box. To change the font, click on the Font button in the Format bar to open the Select Font dialog box.

NOTE If you selected As-Is for an item in the Contents tab or Compile As-Is in the Inspector, the item retains the settings from the Editor rather than modifications made in the Formatting editor.

Numbering Chapters with the Section Layout

The title prefix is configured differently from the other content elements. Several compile presets, including the Standard Manuscript Format, are preconfigured to include a title prefix and automatically number each chapter or part. You can also add this element manually.

The Section Layout button controls the content of headings, such as a chapter heading. It also controls how the first page of a section is composed following a page break. Click the Section Layout button to open the Section Layout dialog box, shown in Figure 19.14.

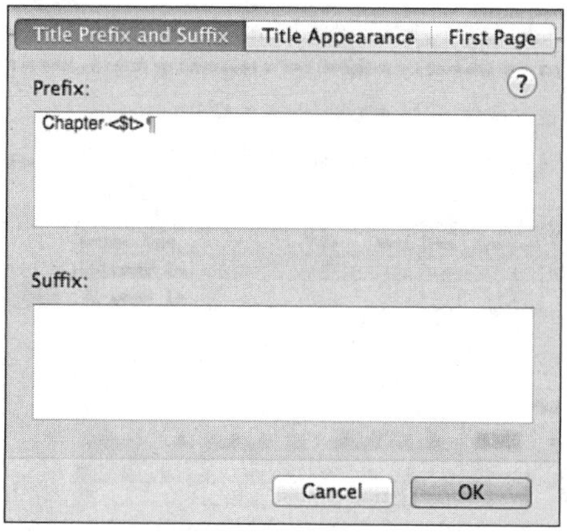

FIGURE 19.14

The Section Layout dialog box controls the content of headings.

The Section Layout dialog box contains three tabs on the Mac and two tabs in Windows:

- **Title Prefix and Suffix**: This tab lets you add text before or after the title element.

- **Title Appearance**: This tab is labeled Case in Windows. It controls the format of the title element (see Figure 19.15). On the Mac, you can change the appearance of the title element, the title prefix, and the title suffix to uppercase, lowercase, normal (title) case, or faked small caps. In Windows, you can change the appearance to uppercase and normal (title) case.

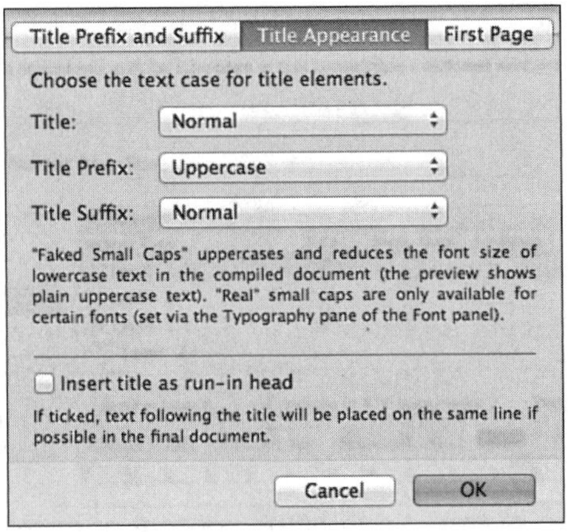

Title Prefix and Suffix	Title Appearance	First Page

Choose the text case for title elements.

Title:	Normal
Title Prefix:	Uppercase
Title Suffix:	Normal

"Faked Small Caps" uppercases and reduces the font size of lowercase text in the compiled document (the preview shows plain uppercase text). "Real" small caps are only available for certain fonts (set via the Typography pane of the Font panel).

☐ Insert title as run-in head

If ticked, text following the title will be placed on the same line if possible in the final document.

Cancel   OK

FIGURE 19.15

The Title Appearance tab controls the capitalization of the title prefix and element.

NOTE Faked Small Caps changes the title to uppercase but then decreases the font size of the letters other than the initial capitals to make the title appear to be in small caps. Alternatively, you can choose a legitimate small caps font.

- **First Page**: This tab does not appear in Windows. At the beginning of a chapter or section, you can set a certain number of words of the text to appear in uppercase as a stylistic choice (see Figure 19.16).

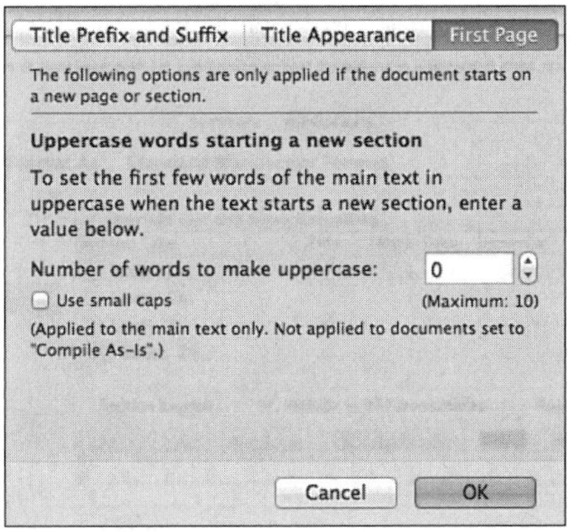

FIGURE 19.16

The First Page tab controls the appearance of the first few words of a document beginning on a new page or section of the compilation.

The key to setting the title prefix lies in the Title Prefix and Suffix tab. To add a numbered heading along with the title element:

1. Select the Title element in the Structure and Content table for the appropriate level.

2. Click the Section Layout button. In Windows, click Modify to open the Formatting dialog box; then click Section Layout.

3. In the Prefix pane, enter the word `Chapter` followed by one of the following placeholders:

   - `<$t>` to spell out the chapter numbers in title case (One, Two, etc.)

   - `<$W>` to spell out chapter numbers in uppercase (ONE, TWO, etc.)

   - `<$n>` to use Arabic numbers (1, 2, etc.)

4. Choose from the following options:

   - To add the title element to the same line as the title prefix, enter a colon (:) or a dash (—) immediately following the chapter element, followed by a space, such as `Chapter <$t>:` . The resulting chapter and title in the compiled document look like this: Chapter One: An Island Getaway.

   - To position the title element beneath the title prefix, enter the title prefix followed by a return.

5. Change the settings on the Title Appearance and First Page tabs, if necessary.

6. Click OK to close the dialog box.

If you want to add just the title prefix without including the title element, deselect the Title element in the Structure and Content table.

TIP The <$t>, <$W>, and <$n> codes are placeholder tags. If you need to number parts as well as chapters, use <$R> as a placeholder for uppercase Roman numerals to number the parts. Use this placeholder in the Section Layout for the level in your Structure and Content table that correlates with the parts of your project. To discover more placeholder tags, choose Help, Placeholder Tags from the menu on the Mac. In Windows, visit https://scrivener.tenderapp.com/help/kb/windows/placeholder-tags-list.

If you use the title prefix in the Section Layout dialog box, be sure you do not use chapter headings elsewhere in your project. If you see two chapter headings in your compiled document or chapter headings at the beginning of a scene, check these possibilities:

- You titled your folders Chapter 1, Chapter 2, etc., and selected the title element along with adding a prefix or suffix in the Section Layout.

- You entered text in your folders or files in the Editor reading Chapter 1, Chapter 2, etc.

- You have a title prefix or suffix assigned to the scene level in your hierarchy. Select each level of your project in the Structure and Content table in turn and then use the Section Layout to remove extraneous prefixes or suffixes.

Excluding Documents from the Section Layout

Certain sections of your project should not be included in the auto-numbering of chapters or parts. Front matter should be excluded, for example, as should the Introduction, Prologue, or Epilogue of the document, if you have any of these items. To exclude one or more of these items:

1. Click the Title Adjustments tab in the Compile dialog box.

2. In the Title Adjustments pane, shown in Figure 19.17, select the Do Not Add Title Prefix to Front Matter Documents and Do Not Add Title Suffix to Front Matter Documents options if your compile contents include front matter.

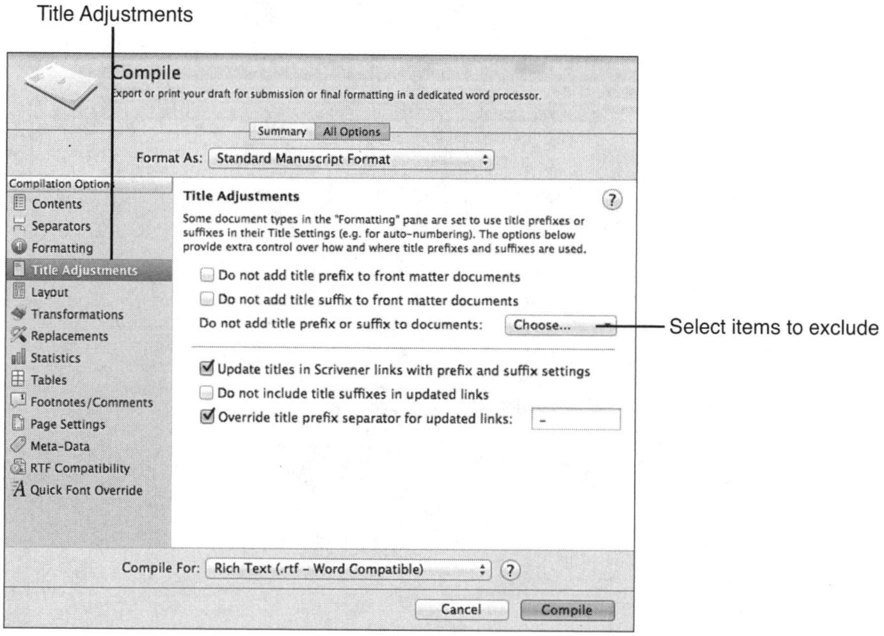

Title Adjustments

Compile

Export or print your draft for submission or final formatting in a dedicated word processor.

Summary | All Options

Format As: Standard Manuscript Format

Compilation Options
- Contents
- Separators
- Formatting
- **Title Adjustments**
- Layout
- Transformations
- Replacements
- Statistics
- Tables
- Footnotes/Comments
- Page Settings
- Meta-Data
- RTF Compatibility
- Quick Font Override

Title Adjustments

Some document types in the "Formatting" pane are set to use title prefixes or suffixes in their Title Settings (e.g. for auto-numbering). The options below provide extra control over how and where title prefixes and suffixes are used.

☐ Do not add title prefix to front matter documents
☐ Do not add title suffix to front matter documents
Do not add title prefix or suffix to documents: [Choose...] ────── Select items to exclude

☑ Update titles in Scrivener links with prefix and suffix settings
☐ Do not include title suffixes in updated links
☑ Override title prefix separator for updated links: [-]

Compile For: [Rich Text (.rtf – Word Compatible)] (?)

[Cancel] [**Compile**]

FIGURE 19.17

Exclude items from auto-numbering in the Title Adjustments tab of the Compile dialog box.

NOTE You are not required to use the auto-numbering options! You can title your items Chapter 1, Chapter 2, and so on, and use the title element instead of the Section Layout prefix. If your project has an Introduction, Prologue, or Epilogue, you may prefer to use this option to avoid mistakenly numbering these chapters.

3. Click the Choose drop-down menu to select an item to exclude it from the prefix and suffix settings.

4. Repeat step 3 to select additional items to exclude.

Changing Layout Options

The Options button in the Structure and Content table opens the Layout Options dialog box (Figure 19.18), which allows you to set certain formatting options for the entire project, as follows:

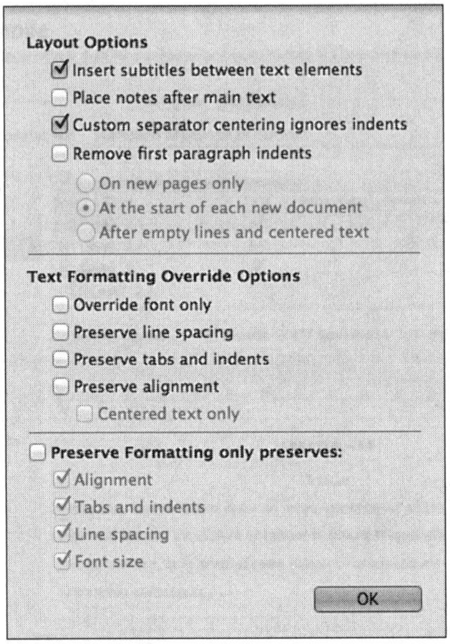

FIGURE 19.18

Layout Options affect the entire project.

- **Insert Subtitles Between Text Elements**: When you select synopsis or notes elements in the Structure and Content table, you can opt to insert a subtitle to set them apart from the text of the item.

- **Place Notes after Main Text**: By default, document notes appear above the text of the item when the notes element is selected. Check this option if you want to place notes below the item text.

- **Custom Separator Centering Ignores Indents (Mac Only)**: This option is selected by default and causes custom character separators to be centered on the page. If you prefer the separator to use the document indent settings, deselect this option.

- **Remove First Paragraph Indents (Mac Only)**: This option overrides the first-line paragraph indent settings for the first paragraph following a header or section break.

- **Text Formatting Override Options (Mac Only)**: This option ignores selected formatting you've done in the formatting. To select this option, you must select the Override Text and Notes Formatting check box.

- **Preserve Formatting Only Preserves (Mac Only)**: If you selected Format, Formatting, Preserve Formatting from the menu for any portions of your project while using the Editor, these settings set limits on which formatting options are affected.

Adding Page Padding

Common manuscript submission format dictates that new chapters begin a third of the way down a new page. Some teachers also require similar formatting for essays and research papers. To set page padding, click the toggle to the right of the Page Padding option at the top of the Formatting editor. In Windows, click Modify to open the Formatting dialog box; then enter the number of lines of padding or use the up and down arrows to adjust the number.

If you are printing your manuscript or paper in 12-point font, page padding of 14–16 lines is usually appropriate.

Making Adjustments to Your Compilation

Congratulations! The hardest part of configuring your compilation settings is over. The rest of the options involve tweaking elements of the compilation to produce exactly the finished product you want.

The Layout tab (Mac only), shown in Figure 19.19, contains options that are probably familiar to you if you've used a word processor. The specific options available depend on the output format you selected in the Compile For drop-down menu. Select Use Hyphenation to automatically hyphenate long words at the end of a line instead of putting the entire word on the next line. Select Avoid Widows and Orphans to avoid leaving a single line of a paragraph alone at the top or bottom of a page.

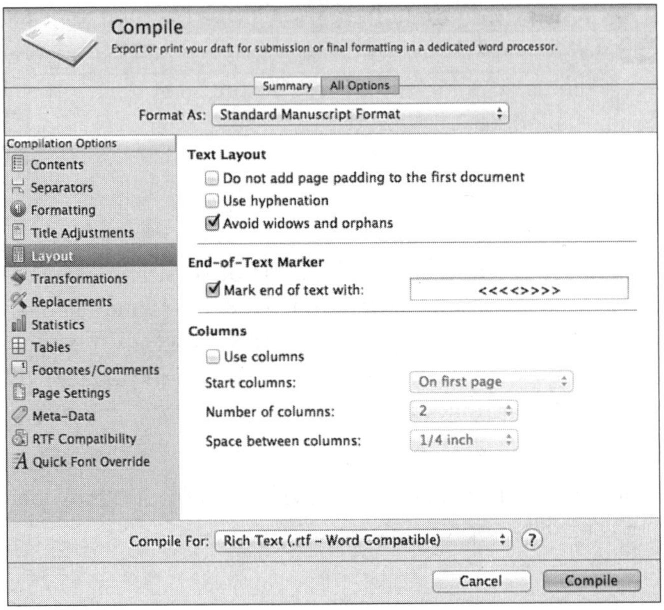

FIGURE 19.19

The Layout tab contains options that affect the layout of your text on the page.

If you added page padding in the Formatting tab, select Do Not Add Page Padding to the First Document in order to format this page differently from the rest of your compilation. The first page of a manuscript is generally a title page, and page padding interferes with the formatting of this page.

Laying Out Your Text in Columns

If you are compiling your project into Rich Text (`.rtf`) or PDF format using the Proofing option, you can lay out your text in columns. To do this:

1. Click on the Layout tab.

2. Select the Use Columns check box.

3. In the Start Columns drop-down, select from the following options:

    *   **On First Page**: Starts the columnar layout from the beginning of your compilation

    *   **After First Document**: Starts the columnar layout after the first document in the compile contents to allow for an introduction or similar document

- **After Front Matter**: Starts the columnar layout after all of the front matter items have been laid out

4. In the Number of Columns drop-down menu, select how many columns the page should be divided into.

5. In the Space Between Columns drop-down menu, suggest how much space should be left between columns to make the compilation more readable.

NOTE Laying out your text in columns does not change how the draft of your project appears onscreen. You will not see the compilation in columns until you compile the project and export the file to another application.

Adding an End-of-Text Marker

An end-of-text marker is commonly used at the end of magazine articles or books to signify the end. In a book, this can be a symbol or series of characters, including the words *The End*.

To add an end-of-text marker to your compilation, click Mark End of Text With and enter the characters you want in the text box. On the Mac, this option appears in the Layout tab. In Windows, this option appears in the Transformations tab.

Converting Special Characters

The Transformations tab, shown in Figure 19.20, converts special characters such as smart quotes to straight quotes. It also converts formatting such as italics to underlining. These conversions can improve compatibility with plain text and rich text editors.

NOTE The options in the Transformations tab vary by output format.

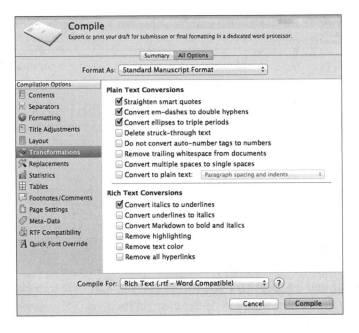

FIGURE 19.20

The Transformations tab enables you to convert formatted elements to comparable rich text and plain text elements.

The options to Straighten Smart Quotes, Convert Em-Dashes to Double Hyphens, and Convert Ellipses to Triple Periods are very straightforward. On the Mac, you can also choose from the following Plain Text Conversions:

- **Delete Struck-Through Text**: If you used Revision mode when editing your project, deleted text uses strike-through formatting so the text is not permanently removed. Select this option to delete struck-through text before compiling.

- **Do Not Convert Auto-Number Tags to Numbers**: This option disables any placeholder tags that automatically number elements of your project, such as chapter numbers. Other placeholder tags continue to function as normal.

- **Remove Trailing Whitespace from Documents**: This option removes extra spaces at the end of a line.

- **Convert Multiple Spaces to Single Spaces**: This option replaces two spaces after a period with a single space. If you learned how to type in the good ol' days, you may have learned to put two spaces between sentences. With the advent of proportional fonts, this is no longer standard practice, but Scrivener can clean up your old habit.

- **Convert to Plain Text**: This option replaces indents and paragraph spacing with actual spaces and carriage returns. If you select this option, select the conversions you want from the following drop-down menu choices:

    - **Paragraph Spacing**: Inserts carriage returns between paragraphs to approximate the space left by automatic paragraph spacing.

    - **Paragraph Spacing and Indents**: Inserts spaces to replace indents and carriage returns between paragraphs.

    - **All Whitespace**: Inserts spaces and carriage returns to preserve all whitespace, such as alignment, hanging indents, block quotes, and right-indents. This mode does not preserve full justification.

    - **All Whitespace (Add a One-Inch Margin)**: Inserts 10 spaces to the left of every line in addition to all of the conversions in the All Whitespace mode.

In addition to converting italics to underlines and vice versa, the following options are intended for Rich Text Conversions:

- **Convert Markdown to Bold and Italics**: Converts Markdown strong emphasis formatting to bold and emphasis formatting to italic.

- **Remove Highlighting**: Removes highlighter colors from your text before compiling.

- **Remove Text Color**: Removes all color from text. Although text continues to appear black onscreen for display purposes, the text does not have any color assigned. This option is available on both the Mac and in Windows.

- **Remove All Hyperlinks**: Removes all hyperlinks from the text and displays them as flat text. This is useful if you are outputting to Print as well as certain file formats.

The Transformations tab in Windows, shown in Figure 19.21, contains fewer options, but they are among the most common conversions.

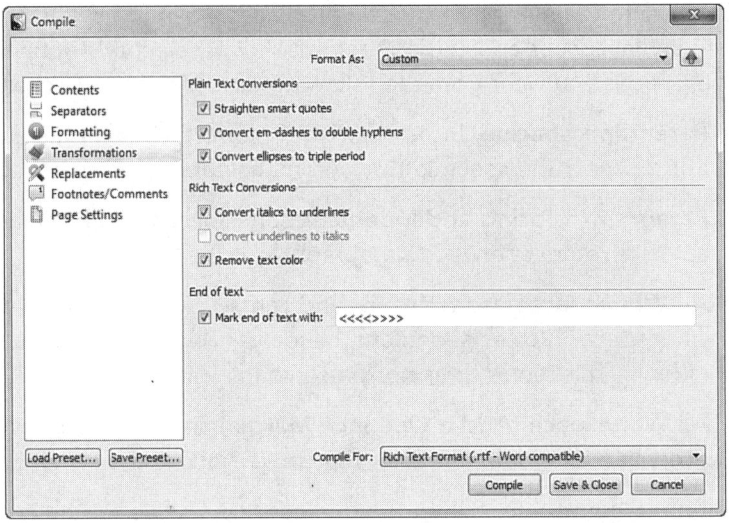

FIGURE 19.21

The Transformations tab in Windows lists the most common conversion options.

Replacing Words and Phrases

The Replacements tab, shown in Figure 19.22, can be used to replace abbreviations or other substitutions before compiling. In your project, for example, you may type CDC to save time, but you can set the Replacements options to replace it with *Centers for Disease Control*. The project itself remains unchanged; this replacement only appears in the compiled file.

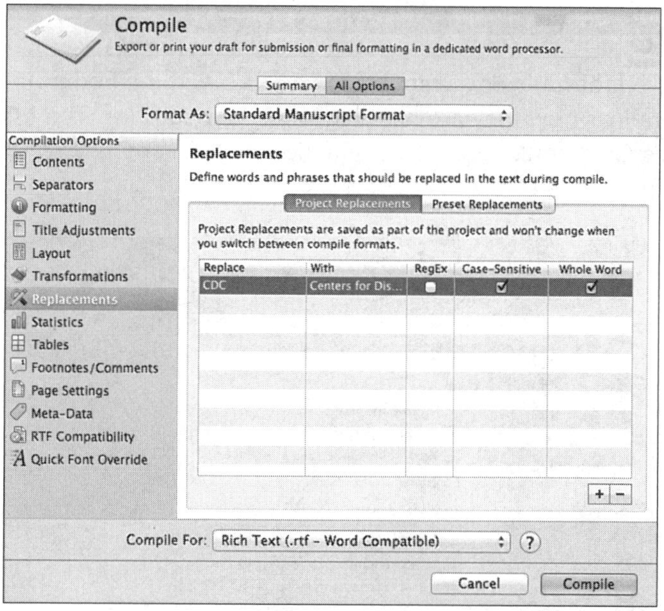

FIGURE 19.22

The Replacements tab performs find-and-replace processes before compiling without changing the underlying project.

There are two types of replacements: project replacements and preset replacements. Project replacements are stored with the project and are applied to any compile preset you use to compile the project. Preset replacements are stored with the compile preset settings for the project and are only applied when you use that compile preset with the project.

The Replacements table has four columns in Windows. The Mac version has five columns, with the addition of a RegEx column to indicate the substitution is using Regular Expressions to perform the replacement. The four columns both platforms have in common are as follows:

- **Replace**: This is the text you have entered into your project.

- **With**: This is the text you want to substitute into the compiled document.

- **Case-Sensitive**: This selection specifies that the Replace column must match exactly in order to be replaced.

- **Whole Word**: This selection specifies that the Replace column must stand alone rather than be part of another word. *Par* will not match *parlor*, for example, if this is selected.

Formatting Footnotes and Comments

If you have footnotes or comments in your project, the Footnotes/Comments tab determines how they are handled when you compile. The Mac version of the Footnotes/Comments tab is shown in Figure 19.23 and the Windows version in Figure 19.24.

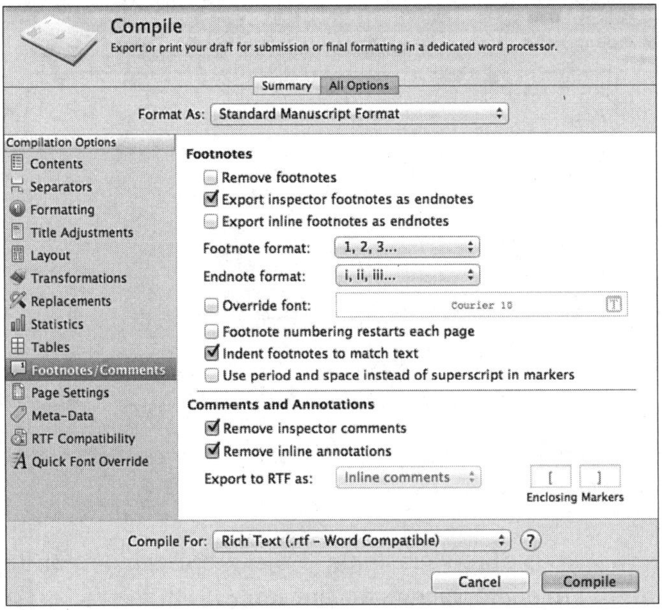

FIGURE 19.23

Convert or remove notations using the Footnotes/Comments tab.

If you select Rich Text (.rtf) as your output format, you can handle inline comments and footnotes and linked comments and footnotes each in a different manner. For example, you can retain inline footnotes as footnotes but export Inspector footnotes as endnotes. You can also embed inline annotations into your output but strip Inspector comments.

 NOTE Footnotes are covered in Chapter 22, "Using Scrivener for Nonfiction Writing." Comments are covered in Chapter 10, "Editing Your Manuscript."

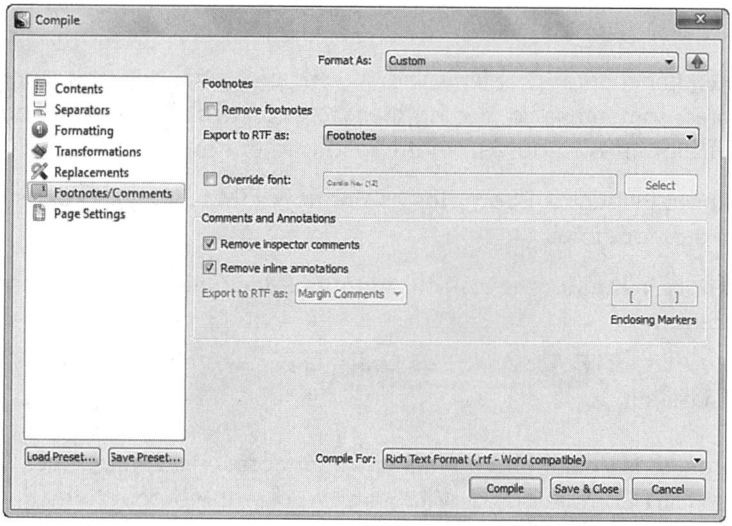

FIGURE 19.24

The Windows Footnotes/Comments tab has a different appearance but performs much the same actions as the Mac platform.

Removing Notations

Some applications stumble over footnotes, comments, and annotations when you attempt to open output files. In other cases, the output format itself does not support footnotes, so Scrivener attempts to convert them to endnotes, occasionally with poor results. If you encounter problems, remove the notations, as follows:

- To remove footnotes, select the Remove Footnotes check box in the Footnotes/Comments tab.

- To remove Inspector comments, select Remove Inspector Comments.

- To remove inline annotations, select Remove Inline Annotations.

> **TIP** When you remove notations in the Compile dialog box, the original notations remain untouched in your project. The formatting you select here only applies to the compilation output.

Converting Notations

When you encounter problems with a word processor app struggling with footnotes, sometimes converting them to endnotes alleviates the problem. To convert footnotes, choose from the following options:

- **Export Inspector Footnotes as Endnotes (Mac Only)**: Exports Inspector (linked) footnotes

- **Export Inline Footnotes as Endnotes (Mac Only)**: Exports inline (embedded) footnotes

- **Export to RTF As (Windows Only)**: Exports to either footnotes, endnotes, or comments

This process is similar for comments and annotations. If you select Rich Text (`.rtf`—Word Compatible) or Microsoft Word as the output format, you can open the compiled file in Word and see your comments in the margin notes. To convert comments and annotations into margin notes:

1. Deselect the Remove Inspector Comments and Remove Inline Annotations check boxes, as needed. You can decide to export only comments or only annotations, as well.

2. In the Export to RTF As drop-down menu, select Margin Comments.

If your word processor does not accept your margin comments, convert to inline comments, instead. Take the following steps:

1. Return to the Footnotes/Comments tab.

2. Deselect the Remove Inspector Comments and/or Remove Inline Annotations check boxes, if necessary.

3. In the Export to RTF As drop-down menu, select Inline Comments.

4. In the Enclosing Markers field, select an opening and closing marker.

Controlling Page Settings

If you are using Print, PDF, Rich Text, Microsoft Word, or Open Office as your output format, you can use the Page Settings tab to control margins and paper size in the output file. If you set Print, PDF, Rich Text (`.rtf`—Word Compatible), or Microsoft Word as the output format, you can also customize headers and footers in the output file.

On the Mac, select Use Project Page Setup Settings (Figure 19.25) if you want to use your project to determine the paper size and margins of your output file. View these settings in your project by choosing File, Page Setup from the menu. If you want to set different page settings, you must disable this option first.

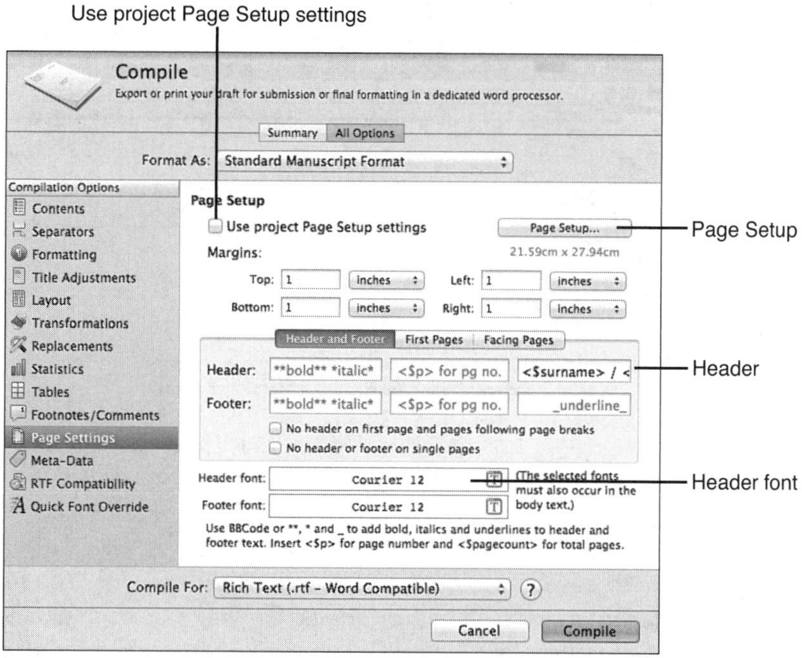

FIGURE 19.25

The Page Settings tab is used to specify margins, headers, and footers for your output file.

Setting Margins

To set the margins for the output file:

1. Click the Page Setup button to select the paper size and orientation of the paper from the Page Setup dialog box on the Mac. In Windows, click the Paper Size and Orientation drop-down menus to make these selections, as shown in Figure 19.26.

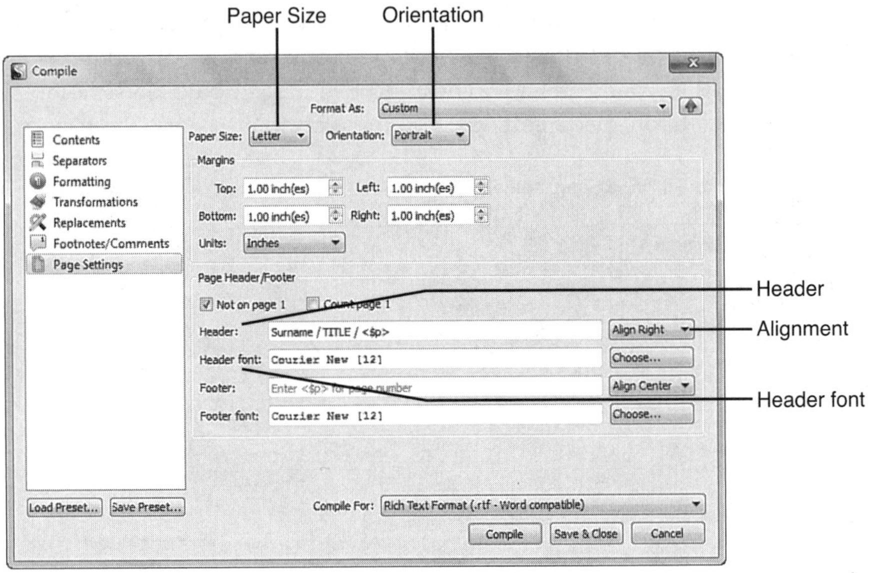

Paper Size   Orientation

FIGURE 19.26

The Page Settings tab in Windows allows you to select the paper size and orientation directly from the options.

2. Enter the width of the Top, Bottom, Left, and Right margins. You can measure the width in centimeters, inches, or points. On the Mac, each unit of measure is selected separately. In Windows, choose the Units setting for all of the margins at once.

Adding Headers and Footers

Headers and footers contain identifying information about the document. You can add page numbers, the project title, and your name to a document header to prepare a manuscript or academic paper for submission to an editor or professor.

 NOTE Headers and footers are available if you choose one of the following output formats: Print, PDF, Rich Text (.rtf—Word Compatible), or Microsoft Word. If you're on a Mac and enable the improved converters, headers and footers are also available for OpenOffice (.odt) format.

The Header and Footer settings, shown in Figures 19.25 and 19.26 previously, are different for the Mac and Windows.

On the Mac, the header and footer are each divided into three sections: left-aligned, centered, and right-aligned text. You can enter header elements in any or all of these sections. Select the font by clicking the Header font (or Footer font) text box to open the Fonts dialog box.

In Windows, enter the header in the Header text box, then choose one alignment for the entire header. To select the font for the header, click the Choose button to the right of the Header font option.

 TIP   Most manuscript headers are formatted as right-aligned and contain the following information: Surname/TITLE/Page Number. Most academic headers are formatted as right-aligned and contain only the author's surname and the page number.

Just as you used placeholder tags in the Section Layout of the Formatting tab to automatically number chapters, you can use placeholder tags to insert variable information into headers and footers. The placeholder tag for page numbers is <$p>. Thus, in Windows, the header for an academic paper would be formatted as the following: Kettell <$p>, with the Alignment drop-down menu set for Align Right.

On the Mac, you can also use placeholder tags for the author's surname (<$surname>) and the project title (<$projecttitle>). Thus, to create a manuscript header on the Mac, click in the right-aligned column of the Header field and enter the following: `<$surname>/<$PROJECTTITLE>/<$p>`.

On the Mac, the project title and surname placeholders acquire their information from the Project Properties tab of the Meta-Data Settings dialog box in the project. To access this information, choose Project, Meta-Data Settings, Project Properties from the menu. You must exit the Compile dialog box first.

 TIP   Before exiting the Compile dialog box, save your settings. To do this on the Mac, press the Option key. The Compile button changes to a Save button. In Windows, press the Save & Close button.

Using a Different First Page Header/Footer

The first page of a manuscript or academic paper usually contains title and contact information, so you generally want your header and footer to begin after the first page. In Windows, you can select the Not on Page 1 check box to remove the header and footer from the first page of the compilation. If you still want the page numbering to begin with page 1 on the first page of the document, even though it no longer displays a header, select the Count Page 1 check box.

On the Mac, you can either remove the header (or footer) or create a replacement. To create a different first page header on the Mac:

1. On the Page Settings tab, click the First Pages tab above the Header and Footer section.

2. On the First Pages tab, shown in Figure 19.27, select the Different First Page Header/Footer check box.

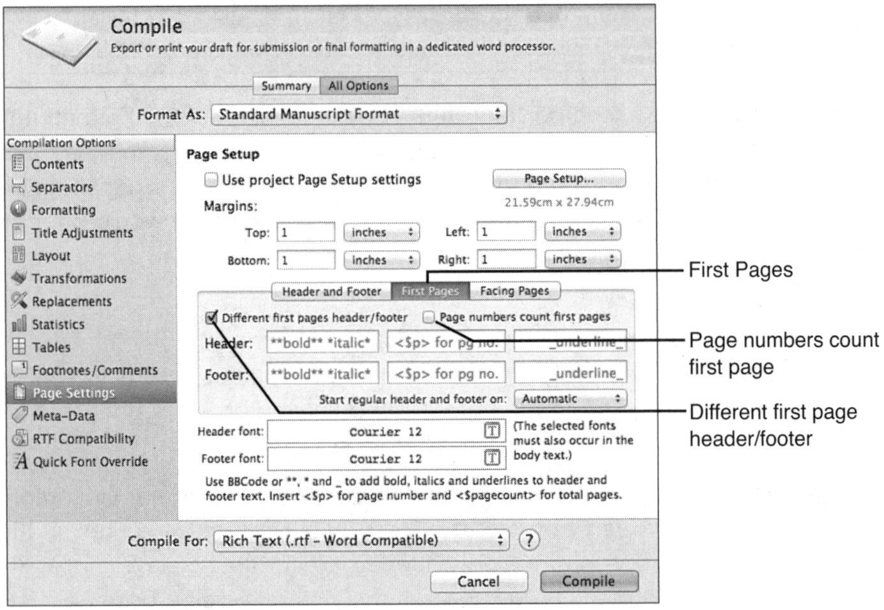

FIGURE 19.27

Use the First Pages tab to create a different header or footer for the first page of the compilation.

3. Enter a different header or footer in the Header or Footer fields. Leave these fields blank if you want to remove the header or footer from the first page. The gray text that appears in the box does not affect the settings; it is merely there to guide you.

4. If you want to begin numbering the pages of the document beginning with the first page, even if it does not contain a header, select the Page Numbers Count First Pages check box.

Adjusting Word Count on the Title Page (Mac Only)

Some project templates, such as the Novel template, include a title page in the front matter. This title page contains a placeholder tag for the word count. If you want to change the way this word count is calculated in your compiled manuscript, click the Statistics tab, shown in Figure 19.28.

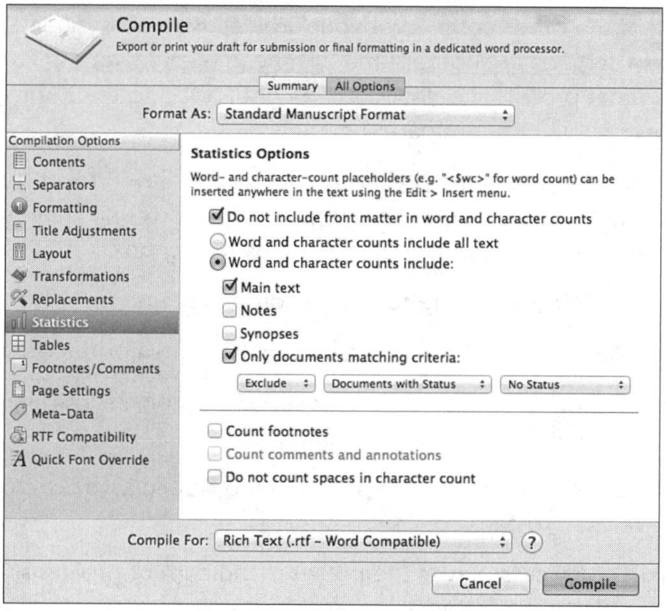

FIGURE 19.28

Adjust the calculation of the word count for your manuscript in the Statistics tab.

The Statistics Options allow you to opt whether or not to include front matter or content elements in the calculation of the word count. You can also opt to include footnotes and other notations.

Saving Compile Settings

Scrivener saves your settings when you compile so that you can recompile your project at another time. If you click Cancel to exit the Compile dialog box before you have compiled, however, your updated settings are lost. If you're on a Mac and want to save your Compile settings without compiling the project, hold down the Option key. The Cancel and Compile buttons change to Reset and Save options. The Reset button reverts to the default settings if you have never compiled the project before or to the last saved settings if you previously compiled. The Save button saves your current settings and closes the Compile dialog box. In Windows, click the Save & Close button to save your Compile settings without compiling the project.

Creating Compile Presets

After all of the effort you put into creating a Structure and Content table and setting all of the other options for your project, wouldn't you like to be able to reuse those settings at another time or maybe even in your next project? Create a compile format preset, and your settings get added to the Format As drop-down menu along with all the preloaded presets.

In Windows, save a compile preset by clicking the Save Preset button below the Compilation Options pane in the Compile dialog box and then enter a name for the new preset in the Save Compile Settings dialog box.

On the Mac, do the following to save a compile preset:

1. Select Manage Compile Format Presets from the Format As drop-down menu.

2. In the Manage Compile Format Presets dialog box, shown in Figure 19.29, choose one of the following options:

   • **Global Presets**: Saves the preset in the Application Support folder to make it available to all projects

   • **Project Presets**: Saves the preset in the current project so it is only available to that project

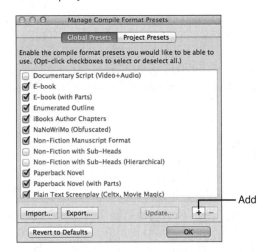

FIGURE 19.29

Add, remove, select, and deselect compile presets in the Manage Compile Format Presets dialog box.

3. Click the Add (+) button.

4. Give the preset a name in the Enter a Name for This Compile Format dialog box, and then click OK.

5. Click OK to exit the Manage Compile Format Presets dialog box.

You can see your new preset in the Format As drop-down menu.

Deleting Compile Presets

If you no longer need an old or outdated preset and want to delete it, take the following steps on the Mac:

1. Open the Compile dialog box, if it is not already open.

2. Click the Format As drop-down and select Manage Compile Format Presets from the menu.

3. In the Manage Compile Format Presets dialog box, click the preset you want to delete. You cannot delete built-in presets.

4. Click the Delete (–) button.

5. Click OK in the warning that pops up about the deletion.

6. Click OK to return to the Compile dialog box.

In Windows, do the following to delete a compile preset:

1. In the Compile dialog box, click Load Preset.

2. Select the preset in the Load Compile Settings dialog box. You cannot delete built-in presets.

3. Click Delete.

4. Click OK to return to the Compile dialog box.

Compiling Your Project

After you've tweaked, poked, and prodded your Compile settings, it's finally time to compile your project. To compile:

1. Double-check that the compile format (Format As), output format (Compile For), compile group, and other settings are as you want.

2. Click Compile.

3. In the Export dialog box (Save As in Windows), choose a filename and location, and then click Export (Save in Windows).

If you selected the Print output format, the Print dialog box opens in step 3. Click Print.

Once you've exported your compilation, always check it in an appropriate application to ensure you didn't lose any formatting unexpectedly.

Congratulations! You are now a Compile Master.

THE ABSOLUTE MINIMUM

In this chapter, you learned how to pull all the separate elements of your project together into a finished product. The following are the highlights:

- To compile your Draft folder, select a compile format to specify the formatting and purpose of the document and select an output format to specify the file format of the compiled work. You can also print directly from Scrivener.

- You can specify exactly which items should be included or excluded from the compiled work.

- Make changes to hierarchical levels of your compilation from the Formatting tab of the Compile dialog box.

- Scrivener can automatically number chapters and parts.

- On the Mac, store front matter in a non-Draft folder so you can quickly add the appropriate front matter to different compile presets for various output formats.

- You can convert footnotes to endnotes or strip them entirely from the output file without changing the footnotes in your project.

- You can save Compile settings to use them at a later time. You can also save Compile settings in a project template.

IN THIS CHAPTER

- Preparing your front matter
- Compiling an e-book
- Adding front matter to the Contents tab (Mac only)
- Adding a cover
- Generating an e-book table of contents
- Reviewing HTML settings (Mac only)
- Adding document properties to e-books
- Using KindleGen for Kindle MOBI files
- Compiling an e-book for iBooks (Mac only)
- Previewing your e-book file

20

CREATING E-BOOKS

The publishing world is changing rapidly, as is the technology that allows a reader to access thousands of books from a device smaller than the average paperback. If you are one of the many venturing into the world of online publishing, this chapter explains the details of how to create an e-book from your Scrivener project.

The overall compile process for an e-book is the same as what you learned in Chapter 19, "Compiling Your Completed Work." There are certain details that are specific to compiling an e-book, however. Unlike compiling a Rich Text Format (.rtf) file in order to open and fine-tune your compilation in another application, an e-book is a final product intended for a wide audience. It requires cover art, copyright and ISBN information, and a table of contents. Your e-book is a public face for your work, so you want it to be perfect.

TIP If you need to fine-tune a compiled e-book, compile it in `.epub` format and then use Sigil, an ePub editor. You can find it at http://code.google.com/p/sigil. If necessary, you can then open the edited `.epub` file in Kindle Previewer to automatically convert it to `.mobi` format.

Preparing Your Front Matter

Before you begin the compilation process for your e-book, you need to make sure your project as a whole is prepared. The table of contents for your book stems from the structure of your project, so be sure you have your chapters organized as you want them to appear in the e-book. The most common approach is to organize your chapters as folders or file groups, with scenes (or sections, in the case of nonfiction) as text items within each chapter. You can, however, organize your project as a flat series of text items. Just be consistent.

If you are on a Mac and your project template created a non-Draft folder for Front Matter, that is your next stop. Figure 20.1 shows the Front Matter folder for a project. If your project does not contain such a folder, I highly recommend you create one. Using a separate folder for your front matter keeps it separate from the rest of your project. Consider some scenarios that may require you to format your project differently:

FIGURE 20.1

The E-Book subfolder of the Front Matter folder contains a cover and a title page, as well as other supplemental pages.

- You want to sell your book in different e-book formats.

- You want to sell your book through different e-book distributors, each of which has different submission requirements.

- You want to use a service like Lulu or CreateSpace for print-on-demand (POD).

- You want to submit the manuscript to a publisher to sell your print rights.
- You want to post an excerpt on your website with copyright and other info.

Those situations may each require different cover art, ISBN numbers, copyright page, or other elements. If you store these pages in the Draft folder, you need to manually revise them or swap them out for each different compile scenario. If you use a Front Matter folder, however, you can prepopulate a subfolder for each scenario with exactly the materials required for that format. This will speed up your compile process later.

A WINDOWS VIEW: HANDLING FRONT MATTER

Scrivener for Windows cannot make use of a non-Draft Front Matter folder in the same way as the Mac platform. That is not to say that a Front Matter folder is of no use in Windows. If you create your own Front Matter folder, you can add subfolders for each publishing scenario and prepare your title page, add copyright and ISBN information, and import your cover art for each format in advance. When it is time to compile, swap the appropriate front matter pages into your Draft folder. You cannot move your cover art into your Draft folder, but you can select it from the drop-down menu in the Cover tab of the Compile dialog box.

When you need to compile in a different format, swap out the front matter files and repeat the compile process. Preparing and organizing everything in advance makes this much faster.

Adding Cover Art to Your Project

Success in the e-book world is all about discoverability and marketing. If the public doesn't notice your book, they won't buy it. If they notice your book but don't think it looks like a professional work, they not only won't buy it but may be less inclined to purchase future books from you as well. One critical element to both discoverability and marketing is cover art.

It is beyond the scope of this book to instruct you in how to create or obtain cover art, but here are some basic specifications and tips. You may need to create multiple sizes of the art for different distribution channels, as noted below. Also keep in mind that your cover is viewed as a thumbnail on the bookshelf or description of most e-readers, and too much detail can make the thumbnail look muddled.

To ensure the widest compatibility with the fewest number of images, you should format your cover art with the following specifications:

- **Image size**: 1400×2100 pixels for most publishers; 1267×1900 for Barnes & Noble

- **Image resolution**: 72DPI

- **File size**: <2MB

- **Image type**: `.jpeg`, `.jpg`, or `.png`

You should also create a 300DPI resolution image for POD or use on printed promotional materials.

Import your cover art into the Front Matter folder of your project before you compile. See Chapter 8, "Organizing Your Research," to learn how to import nontext materials into non-Draft folders.

Formatting Other Front Matter

Prepare your other front matter before entering the Compile dialog box. Enter your ISBN information on the Copyright page, as shown in Figure 20.2. Your e-book distributor, such as Smashwords, may have specific instructions for a title page and copyright format, so follow its requirements. Add Dedication and Acknowledgment pages or an About the Author page.

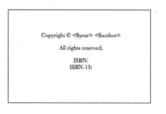

FIGURE 20.2

The Copyright page includes room for your e-book's ISBN number.

You can use placeholder tags for some of the information in your front matter materials. In Windows, the <$projecttitle> tag gets replaced during the compile process, so you can use this in place of the title on a title page.

On the Mac, you can use placeholders to access project meta-data entered into the Project Properties tab of the Meta-Data Settings dialog box (Project, Meta-Data Settings on the menu). You can also use the <$year> placeholder tag for the year on the copyright page.

THE CREATIVE PROCESS: A WORD ABOUT ISBNS

ISBN stands for International Standard Book Number. It is a 10- or 13-digit number used to uniquely identify a book for distribution and sales purposes. If you are going to self-publish your e-book, you need to obtain an ISBN for the work. ISBNs are issued by a registration agency in each country. In the United States, RR Bowker (http://www.myidentifiers.com) is the agency of record. It charges $125 for a single ISBN and $250 for a pack of 10 ISBNs.

You may think 10 ISBNs is a lot. What if you don't publish 10 books? Those 10 ISBNs can go faster than you think. The ISBN identifies not only the title of your book but also the edition and format. If you distribute different editions of your work, such as e-book and POD, you need unique ISBNs for each edition. You should also have a different ISBN for each format in which you distribute your e-book. In other words, if you sell your book in Kindle format on the Amazon site and .epub format on the Barnes & Noble site, you should have a unique ISBN for each. If you substantially change the work at a later time—add extra content or an epilogue, for example—you should also assign a new ISBN, as that is considered a new edition.

From a Scrivener standpoint, this is yet another reason to keep your front matter separate from your Draft folder. You can create a subfolder for each format in the Front Matter folder containing the proper ISBN to quickly compile each unique e-book.

Compiling an E-Book

The compile process itself follows the same routine as for any other project. See Chapter 19 to learn more about this process. For an e-book, follow these steps:

1. Open the Compile dialog box using one of the following:

   - Click the Compile button on the toolbar.

   - Choose File, Compile from the menu.

   - Press Option-Cmd-E on the Mac or Ctrl+Shift+E in Windows.

2. Click the All Options tab in the Compile dialog box if it is not already selected. In Windows, click the expansion button if the dialog box is not already expanded.

3. In the Format As drop-down menu, choose E-Book (Figure 20.3).

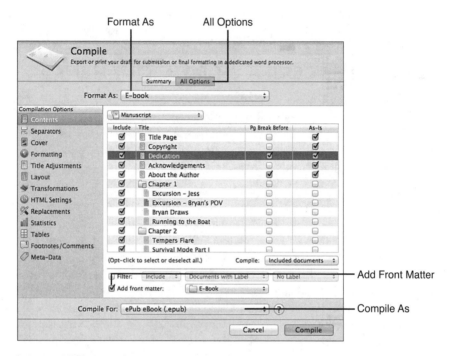

FIGURE 20.3

The Compile dialog box displays Compilation Options specific to formatting e-books when you select an e-book format from the Compile As drop-down menu.

4. In the Compile For drop-down menu, choose one of the following:

- **ePub eBook (.epub):** Select this format for the Barnes & Noble Nook, Sony Reader, and most other e-readers, with the exception of the Amazon Kindle. You can also read .epub format on your computer or on iOS or Android devices using an app.

- **Kindle eBook (.mobi):** Select this format for the Amazon Kindle series of devices. You can also read Kindle e-books on your computer or on iOS or Android devices using the Kindle app for that platform.

5. Use the Compilation Option tabs to format your e-book, as explained in the remainder of this chapter and Chapter 19.

6. Click the Compile button.

7. In the Export (Save As in Windows) dialog box, enter a name for the e-book file and click Export (Save in Windows).

Adding Front Matter to the Contents Tab (Mac Only)

If you are on a Mac and you utilize the Front Matter folder, select the Add Front Matter check box at the bottom of the Contents tab and choose the appropriate subfolder from the drop-down menu. The Front Matter pages appear in the compile group, with the As-Is check box selected by default. If you want a page break before any of your front matter, select the Page Break Before check box for that item.

 NOTE   The Front Matter folder only adds text documents to the Contents. Add your cover on the Cover tab, as explained in the next section.

If you are using Windows or you elect to not use a Front Matter folder, be sure your front matter is included in the compile group pane.

Proceed to the Formatting tab to configure your structure and content table and set up your Layout Options and Section Layout, as explained in Chapter 19.

Adding a Cover

When you select an e-book format as your output (Compile For) format, some extra tabs appear in the Compilation Options. One of these is Cover. To add the cover to your e-book:

1. In the Cover tab, shown in Figure 20.4, click the Cover Image drop-down menu. The drop-down menu lists any images you added directly to the Binder.

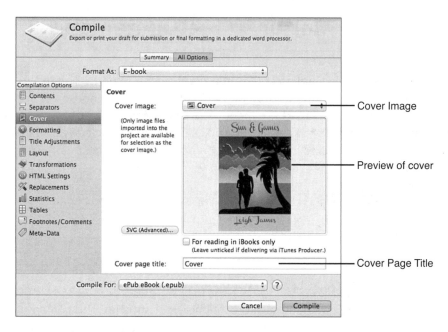

FIGURE 20.4

Add a cover for your e-book in the Cover tab of the Compile dialog box.

NOTE On the Mac, you cannot use an image you added to a synopsis or embedded within a text document. If you want to choose one of these images, you need to import it directly into your project as a standalone item. In Windows, images you add to a synopsis appear in the Cover Image drop-down menu, but it is still easier to locate an image imported directly into the project as a standalone item.

2. Choose your cover image. A preview of the image appears below the drop-down menu.

3. In the Cover Page Title field, enter how the cover page should appear in the book's table of contents. I suggest using the default option, Cover.

CAUTION Do not enter the title of your book in this field. The title is only used on the table of contents page to help readers navigate your book. It is not used to identify the book as a whole.

Generating an E-Book Table of Contents

E-books have a table of contents that allows readers to quickly navigate to a specific chapter or subsection of the book. On the Kindle, the table of contents serves as the foundation for the navigation dots on the progress bar as you read. Each top-level section is represented by a navigation dot.

On the Mac, the Layout tab, shown in Figure 20.5, has options to allow Scrivener to automatically generate a table of contents so you do not have to manually create one. The options for generating a table of contents are as follows:

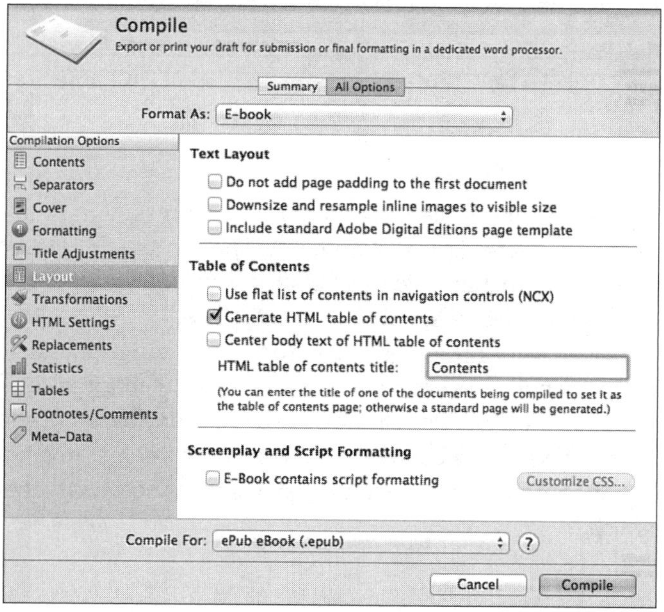

FIGURE 20.5

The Layout tab contains options to generate a table of contents in your e-book.

- **Use Flat List of Contents in Navigation Controls (NCX)**: The table of contents generated by Scrivener is nested by default. Subsections are indented and listed below their parent sections. Because the Kindle only uses top-level items on the progress bar, if you want the navigation dots on the Kindle to reflect subsections of your e-book, you must flatten the list of contents so each item is at the same level in the table of contents.

NOTE   If you prefer the nested table of contents and are willing to sacrifice some of the detail on the Kindle progress bar, do not select this option.

- **Generate HTML Table of Contents**: Most e-readers provide a software-based table of contents to navigate to key elements in the current e-book. If you want to generate a separate table of contents into the text of the book, select this option.

- **Center Body Text of HTML Table of Contents**: If you opt to generate an HTML table of contents, this option centers it on the page. If you deselect this option, the table of contents is left-aligned.

- **HTML Table of Contents Title**: You can also create your own table of contents using Scrivener (internal) links. If you have done this, specify the title of that document here so it is picked up by the e-reader's navigation tools.

 NOTE Scrivener links are explained in Chapter 23, "Discovering New Uses for Scrivener."

Scrivener generates the table of contents based on section breaks in your Compile settings. Section breaks are established in the Separators tab, as shown in Figure 20.6. The Text and Folder Separator option is set to create a section break by default. This is referred to as a page break in Windows, but functions as a section break. If your project is organized in the common manner with chapters in folders and scenes or sections in files within each chapter, this option means that if a scene/section (file) is followed by a chapter (folder), a section break is inserted. In the text of the book, the new chapter begins on a new page, whereas in the table of contents, the section break instructs Scrivener to add the folder title to the list.

 TIP If you format your project with file groups rather than folders, click the Insert Section Break Before Text Documents with Subfolders option in the Separators tab.

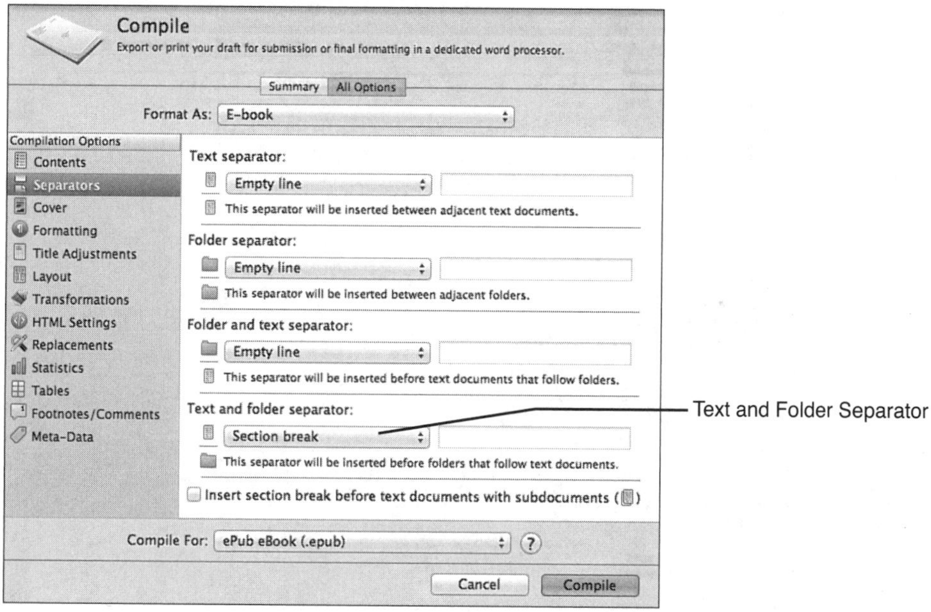

Compile

Export or print your draft for submission or final formatting in a dedicated word processor.

Summary | All Options

Format As: [E-book   ⬍]

Compilation Options

- Contents
- **Separators**
- Cover
- Formatting
- Title Adjustments
- Layout
- Transformations
- HTML Settings
- Replacements
- Statistics
- Tables
- Footnotes/Comments
- Meta-Data

Text separator:

[Empty line   ⬍] [   ]
This separator will be inserted between adjacent text documents.

Folder separator:

[Empty line   ⬍] [   ]
This separator will be inserted between adjacent folders.

Folder and text separator:

[Empty line   ⬍] [   ]
This separator will be inserted before text documents that follow folders.

Text and folder separator:

[Section break   ⬍] [   ] ———— Text and Folder Separator
This separator will be inserted before folders that follow text documents.

☐ Insert section break before text documents with subdocuments (▯)

Compile For: [ePub eBook (.epub)   ⬍] (?)

[Cancel] [**Compile**]

FIGURE 20.6

The Text and Folder Separator option creates a section break by default.

Scrivener also generates a section break if an item is marked with the Page Break Before tag in the Inspector and the Contents tab of the Compile dialog box. Use this to your advantage when adding front matter to the Contents tab so those pages appear in the table of contents.

 NOTE   In Windows, the table of contents is generated automatically based on the settings in the Contents and Separators tabs. There are no options to modify how the table of contents is generated.

Reviewing HTML Settings (Mac Only)

If you're on a Mac, the HTML Settings tab, shown in Figure 20.7, appears in the Compilation Options when you elect to compile in .epub or .mobi e-book format. Use the settings here to convert Scrivener (internal) links to HTML links in your e-book. If the link refers to an item that is not included in the compile group, it is removed from the compilation.

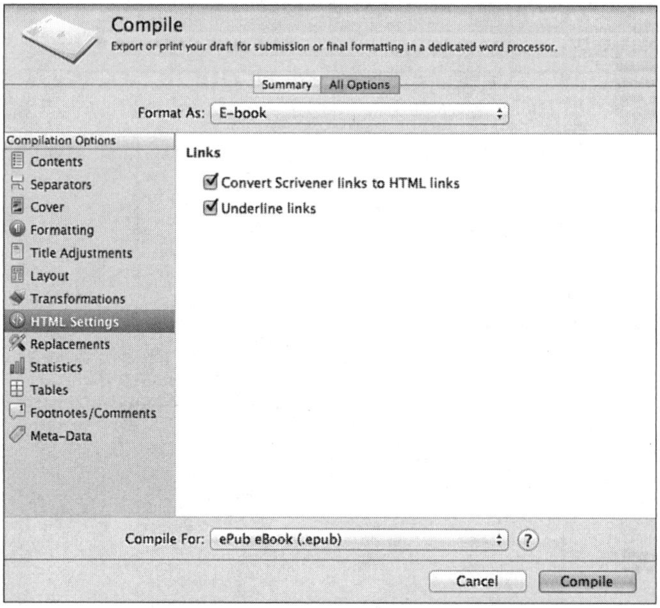

FIGURE 20.7

The HTML Settings tab is used to convert Scrivener (internal) links to HTML links for use in e-books.

> **NOTE**   If you have footnotes in your project, they are converted to endnotes in your compiled e-book, as you can see in the Footnotes/Comments tab. These notes also use internal links to cross-reference from the footnote marker to the text in the endnotes.

Links are not underlined by default. If you want your links to be underlined when converted to e-book format, select the Underline Links check box. Otherwise, links will not be underlined in your e-book.

Adding Document Properties to E-Books

The meta-data associated with an e-book is used to generate the description of the book online and in the e-reader. Enter the properties of your e-book in the Meta-Data tab, shown in Figure 20.8.

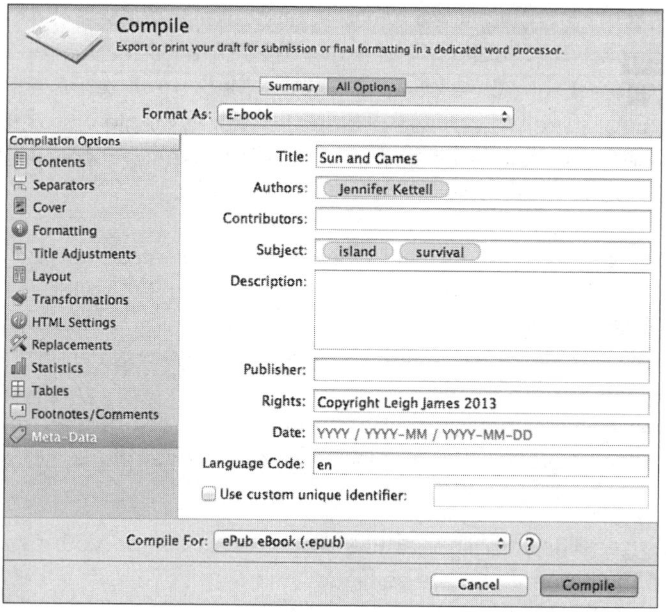

FIGURE 20.8

The Meta-Data tab prompts you for the properties of your e-book.

At a minimum, fill out the Title, Author, Date, and Description fields, but ideally you should fill out all of the fields. Although some e-readers cannot make use of the full meta-data properties, others can. The Meta-Data tab contains the following fields:

NOTE Calibre is a free, open source, multiplatform e-book management application. Many readers use Calibre to manage their e-book libraries, search for new books, access e-book distributors, and convert e-books to different formats. To aid in many of these processes, Calibre makes full use of an e-book's meta-data. You can download Calibre from http://calibre-ebook.com.

- **Title**: The title of your book, as you want it to appear on distribution sites and in e-readers.

- **Authors**: The name of each author, as it should appear in e-book store listings and in e-readers. Separate author names with a semicolon in .epub format or with a comma in Kindle .mobi format.

- **Contributors**: The name(s) of contributors to the work. Use the Contributors field if you compiled and edited the work of others (with permission, of course) instead of directly authoring the work.

- **Subject**: The keywords by which your book can be searched in Calibre and other apps. The Subject field is not used by all e-readers or stores. Separate each subject term by a comma. On the Mac, these terms are converted to tags. Subject terms can use phrases as well as single words, but keep in mind that the more detailed it becomes, the less likely people will stumble upon your e-book when they're searching for books.

 TIP Do not add subjects that are unrelated to your e-book. As tempting as it may be to add *twilight* to your subject terms, if your e-book is about being stranded on a deserted island, readers will punish you with 1-star reviews when they are misled.

- **Description**: A brief blurb about your book. Think of it as marketing copy, the e-book version of a dust jacket or back cover blurb, not a complete plot summary.

- **Publisher**: The publisher of the e-book. This can be your own name or your company name if you are self-publishing.

- **Rights**: The copyright information. Because the copyright symbol (the c in a circle) does not always render properly in all e-readers, spell out the word *Copyright*.

- **Date**: The publication date for the book. The grayed-out placeholder information shows the format for this information.

- **Language Code**: The two-letter ISO standard language code. In Windows, click on the Language drop-down menu and select the language; Scrivener generates the proper code. On the Mac, you must manually enter the code. The complete list of Codes for the Representation of Names of Languages can be found at http://www.loc.gov/standards/iso639-2/php/code_list.php. The code for English is *en*.

- **Use Custom Unique Identifier**: A unique code to distinguish your e-book from other books. Select the Use Custom Unique Identifier check box and enter the ISBN, if you have one. If you do not enter an ISBN, Scrivener creates its own identifier based on the author, title, and date fields.

 TIP If you are compiling a Kindle `.mobi` e-book to sell through the Kindle Store, you can use the ASIN code assigned to the book in place of an ISBN number. This code is unique to Amazon, however, so I recommend using ISBNs to track your books.

Using KindleGen for Kindle MOBI Files

The Amazon Kindle dominates the e-reader market. Not only can you read a Kindle-formatted e-book on a dedicated Kindle e-reader, but you can also read it on almost any computer platform, mobile device, or tablet using a Kindle app. The only downside to a Kindle is that it uses its own proprietary file. If you want to tap this e-reader market, you need to compile a separate e-book for the Kindle format.

Before you can format a Kindle e-book, you must download the KindleGen app from Amazon. Go to http://www.amazon.com/kindlepublishing to download the KindleGen file for your Mac or Windows platform. Unzip the file and store the KindleGen folder in a safe place on your computer.

When you select Kindle eBook (.mobi) from the Compile For drop-down menu, a KindleGen tab is added to the Compilation Options. In this tab, click the Choose button and navigate to the folder you decompressed. Select the executable file in the KindleGen folder and click Open. The Choose button becomes a Change button, as shown in Figure 20.9.

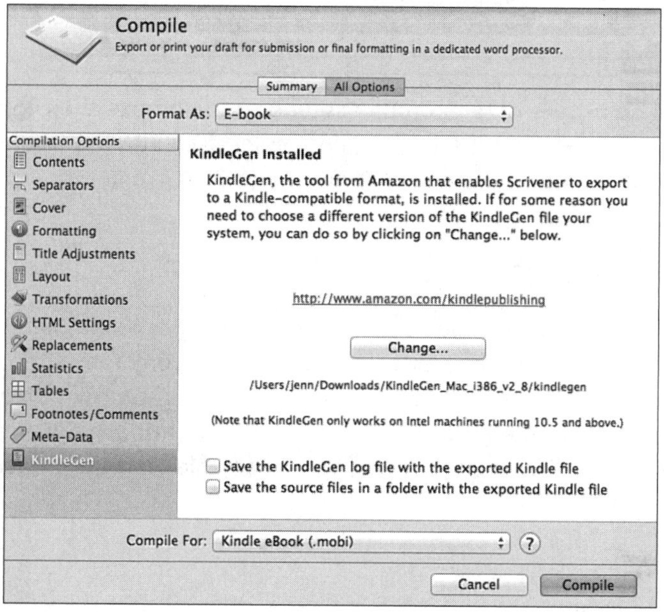

FIGURE 20.9

The KindleGen tab only appears if you select Kindle eBook (.mobi) as your output format.

As long as this file remains in the same location on your computer, this tab remains set. You can then proceed to set the other tabs in the Compile dialog box and compile your project as described earlier in this chapter and in Chapter 19.

Compiling an E-Book for iBooks (Mac Only)

If you want to create an e-book for use in iBooks on the iPhone or iPad, you must take additional steps. The iBooks format is proprietary, and Apple does not authorize third-party applications such as Scrivener to create an iBooks Author format file directly. Instead, you must save your project as a series of individual files for each chapter or section of the book and then import them all into the iBooks Author app on your Mac.

To begin this process, choose iBooks Author Chapters (.docx) as your output format from the Compile For drop-down menu. This format automatically breaks up your compile group into separate .docx files where there is a section break in the compilation. As with generating a table of contents, section breaks are based on the options in the Separators tab and the Page Break Before settings in the Inspector. In the Text and Folder Separator drop-down menu in the Separators tab, select Chapter Break. This option replaces the Section Break option the other e-book formats use.

After you adjust the other Compile settings and compile the project, open iBooks Author and drag the entire folder of compiled files into the app. Use iBooks Author to complete the process of preparing your project for iBooks.

Previewing Your E-Book File

Before uploading your e-book to Amazon, Barnes & Noble, and other e-book stores, you should ensure that your e-book is properly formatted. View .epub files in an e-reader such as Adobe Digital Editions. To preview your Kindle e-book, download the Kindle Previewer app from http://www.amazon.com/kindlepublishing. When reviewing your e-book file, inspect the following items for problems:

- Cover art
- Front matter
- Chapter names and numbering
- Table of contents formatting
- Section breaks

- Scene separators
- Endnote formatting, if your project contained footnotes that were converted to endnotes

THE ABSOLUTE MINIMUM

The following are the highlights from this chapter:

- You can save your project into three e-book formats—`.epub`, `.mobi`, and, on the Mac, into `.docx` format for import into iBooks Author.

- Create cover art and import it into the project before you compile; then use the Cover tab in the Compilation Options to add it to the e-book.

- The Meta-Data tab adds important descriptive information about your e-book.

- You must download KindleGen to your computer before compiling a Kindle `.mobi` file.

- iBooks must be saved in separate chapter files, which you can then import into iBooks Author to complete the process of creating an iBooks file.

- Always preview your e-book before submitting it to your distribution channels.

Index

Q - R

S

X - Y - Z